Reasons First

In the last five decades, ethical theory has been preoccupied by a turn to reasons. The vocabulary of reasons has become a common currency not only in ethics, but in epistemology, action theory, and many related areas. It is now common, for example, to see central theses such as evidentialism in epistemology and egalitarianism in political philosophy formulated in terms of reasons. And some have even claimed that the vocabulary of reasons is so useful precisely because reasons have analytical and explanatory priority over other normative concepts—that reasons in that sense come first.

Reasons First systematically explores both the benefits and burdens of the hypothesis that reasons do indeed come first in normative theory, against the conjecture that theorizing in both ethics and epistemology can only be hampered by neglect of the other. Bringing two decades of work on reasons in both ethics and epistemology to bear, Mark Schroeder argues that some of the most important challenges to the idea that reasons could come first are themselves the source of some of the most obstinate puzzles in epistemology: about how perceptual experience could provide evidence about the world, and about what can make evidence sufficient to justify belief. Schroeder shows that, along with moral worth, one of the very best cases for the fundamental explanatory power of reasons in normative theory actually comes from knowledge.

Mark Schroeder is Professor of Philosophy at the University of Southern California. His research ranges widely in ethics, epistemology, and related areas, and his work has appeared in over two dozen journals. He is the author of *Slaves of the Passions* (OUP, 2007), *Being For: Evaluating the Semantic Program of Expressivism* (OUP, 2008), *Noncognitivism in Ethics* (Routledge, 2010), *Explaining the Reasons We Share* (OUP, 2014), and *Expressing Our Attitudes* (OUP, 2015).

T0347007

Reasons First

MARK SCHROEDER

OXFORD
UNIVERSITY PRESS

OXFORD
UNIVERSITY PRESS

Great Clarendon Street, Oxford, OX2 6DP,
United Kingdom

Oxford University Press is a department of the University of Oxford.
It furthers the University's objective of excellence in research, scholarship,
and education by publishing worldwide. Oxford is a registered trade mark of
Oxford University Press in the UK and in certain other countries

© Mark Schroeder 2021

The moral rights of the author have been asserted

First published 2021
First published in paperback 2023

Published in the United States of America by Oxford University Press
198 Madison Avenue, New York, NY 10016, United States of America

British Library Cataloguing in Publication Data
Data available

Library of Congress Cataloging in Publication Data
Data available

ISBN 978-0-19-886822-4 (Hbk.)
ISBN 978-0-19-890064-1 (Pbk.)

DOI: 10.1093/oso/9780198868224.001.0001

Preface

Over the last half century, philosophical work in ethics and related areas has come to be increasingly preoccupied with reasons. Reasons have become a sort of common currency in which controversial normative theses like egalitarianism in political philosophy and evidentialism in epistemology can be formulated. And disputes about many other topics can be and have been traced to more fundamental disputes about reasons, leading important arguments for both normative and meta-normative theses to be formulated in their vernacular. Some philosophers have taken the centrality of 'reason' talk so seriously that they have proposed, either semi-stipulatively or intended as a matter of substance, that all philosophically interesting normativity is the normativity of reasons. It is common to see the clarification, for example, that a philosopher is interested in what someone 'ought, in the sense of most reason, to do', or that she is interested in the 'normativity of reasons'.

It is the business of this book to explore the centrality of reasons in normative inquiry, and in particular to defend a version of the strong idea that in some important sense, reasons can and should come first—or at the least, relatively early. Appealing to reasons, I will argue throughout, has the potential to give us powerful explanations of the complicated and generalization-defying yet somehow predictable behavior of other normative concepts such as obligation, value, rationality, and knowledge. The power of these explanations derives from the way in which reasons *compete* against one another, in a way that is helpfully illustrated by the metaphor of *balance*. And many of the most important differences between ethics and epistemology arise, in a way that is exhibited by the jacket illustration, by the number of competing options.

Yet at the same time, we will see that there are specific—and not inconsiderable—obstacles to the idea that reasons even could come first. Surmounting these obstacles will require taking on very specific commitments. Since I hold that the attractions are worth the costs, it is my view that this is evidence that these very specific commitments are true. But if my task in the book is successful, it will help us to see just a bit better how the pieces need to fit together, even for those who are unwilling to follow me the whole way.

The conviction that structures the outline and choice of topics of this book is that both the advantages of and obstacles to the hypothesis that reasons come first are particularly well illustrated by their impact in epistemology. As a result, the book is structured around a small group of what I take to be central and traditional problems in epistemology, as well as around the more general idea that epistemology can benefit from a perspective that is inclusive enough to see epistemology as just one normative discipline among others.

Given my own previous publishing history—somewhat more in ethics than epistemology—one might be tempted to read this book as an exercise in philosophical imperialism. In the pejorative sense, philosophical work is imperialistic when theses or ideas that are motivated wholly within some domain are applied *mutatis mutandis* by analogy in some other domain. In contrast, as I hope this volume illustrates, my view is that both ethics and epistemology can and should be deeply shaped by an informed understanding of the common features of their subject matters. Though the reader will be the judge, my hope is to be broadening our perspective, rather than simply importing one narrow perspective across subdisciplinary boundaries. I don't claim to be the first to think in this way; and since I began thinking about epistemology and ethics in parallel over twenty years ago, one of my great pleasures has been to stand witness to an incredible growth of fellow travelers. My aim in this volume is simply to add to the cumulative case for the fruitfulness of this perspective.

I make no claims whatsoever to comprehensiveness in my coverage of any central topic in epistemology—nor indeed, in my coverage of any topic at all—but only to whatever partial illumination can be provided by showing how to see them in the light of the central claims about reasons to be evaluated in the course of the book. My hope is that this light is in at least some cases a fresh one, and where not fresh, that it at least casts clearer shadows than my earlier passes at similar material.

* * * * *

Although the ideas in this book have come together slowly over a very long time and I believe that they are important and worth thinking carefully about, I am unfortunately in a position neither to express the naive confidence of youth nor the intransigence of age. I have both sufficient experience to know that I will turn out to be wrong not merely about a few things I say in what follows, but about many, and enough years in front of me to know in advance that I will probably come to admit it (for at least some of those cases). I offer it in the spirit of a contribution to that great ongoing conversation in which it has been such an unexpected privilege to be able to participate, and in the hopes that where I am wrong, I may be wrong in ways that are a fraction as instructive as those of the philosophers I most admire.[1]

Becoming a father—the portion of my life that has coincided almost exactly with the formal process of writing this book—has pressed upon me the unfathomable luck of the circumstances of my upbringing, education, and intellectual

---

[1] Not to mention the hope that where I am stridently wrong, my stridency is half as effective at provoking a corrective response as the strident wrongness of the philosophers from whom I have learned the most.

influences as never before. I would never be where I am today if not for my own father's insistence on thinking critically about received views, or for my mother's patience in listening as I tried out thoughts and arguments as a teenager, following her around the house and talking a mile a minute. I was extraordinarily blessed to discover philosophy in such a rich environment as Carleton College, surrounded by other students bound for graduate study in philosophy and taught in a seminar-style environment that gave me so many early opportunities to think collaboratively about the topic at hand, and so many chances to be safely wrong.

In early January of 1999, Gary Iseminger began my first epistemology course by bringing copies of Edmund Gettier's 1963 article, "Is Justified True Belief Knowledge?" for us to read and discuss during class. Later that spring, Keith Lehrer visited Carleton as the Cowling Visiting Professor and taught a ten-week seminar on the theory of knowledge. The Gricean implicature of Lehrer's frequent references to the freshmen in his other course as his 'undergraduates' was instrumental in giving me the confidence that would help to sustain me through real graduate school. This book is as much a delayed combined term paper for those two courses as anything else. It is also the intended product of my 2002 generals exam at Princeton University, on the topic of "Reasons for Action and for Belief". It is the book that I predicted to my friend Brett Sherman in spring 2004 would shortly follow my dissertation. And it was supported by a generous fellowship from the National Endowment for the Humanities in the 2014–15 academic year. So it has been a long time coming, and shaped as much by being slowly written as by anything else.

Because I have been working on the topics of this book for many years, most of it draws on, expands on, or in some cases simply summarizes ideas previously introduced or developed at greater length in other published work. Chapters 3, 4, and 5, for example, develop and advance themes from "Having Reasons", "What Does it Take to 'Have' a Reason?", "Knowledge is Not the Most General Factive Stative Attitude", "Perceptual Reasons and Defeat", "The Unity of Reasons", and "Getting Perspective on Objective Reasons". Chapters 6 through 8 draw on, abstract from, and in some ways try to advance themes from "Stakes, Withholding, and the Subject-Sensitivity of Knowledge", "The Ubiquity of State-Given Reasons", "State-Given Reasons: Prevalent if not Ubiquitous", "What Makes Reasons Sufficient?", "When Beliefs Wrong", "Sins of Thought", "Rational Stability under Pragmatic Encroachment", "Doxastic Wrongs" (with Rima Basu), and (with Jake Ross) "Belief, Credence, and Pragmatic Encroachment". And Chapters 9 through 11 draw on "Knowledge is Belief for Sufficient (Objective and Subjective) Reason", "Is Knowledge Normative?", "In Defense of the Kantian Account", "Holism, Weight, and Undercutting", "Believing Well", and "The Fundamental Reason for Reasons Fundamentalism". Although no material from any of these papers is directly replicated here, I thank each of their publishers for giving me the opportunity to take an important step in working out some of the ideas developed in this book.

As a result of coming together over so many years, work on the topics in the book has benefited from discussion over the years with many different audiences. Among them are audiences for talks at Ben Gurion University, Boston University, California State University at Northridge, the Central Division Meeting of the American Philosophical Association, the *Episteme* Conference in the Galápagos, Humboldt University, the Institute for Philosophy in London, Kent University, Lingnan University, Lund University, the NYU-Abu Dhabi workshop on Normativity and Reasoning in New York, Northwestern University (twice), Oxford University, the PeRFECt conference at the University of Pennsylvania, Sarah McGrath's graduate seminar at Princeton University, the Pontificia Universidad Católica del Perú (twice), Rice University, Shandong University, Sheffield University, Southampton University, the Southern California Epistemology Workshop, Stanford University (twice), the Theistic Ethics Workshop at the College of William and Mary, the University of Arizona, the University of Birmingham, the University of North Carolina at Chapel Hill, the USC Dissertation Seminar, the USC Philosophy Club, the USC/UCLA graduate conference, the University of Texas (twice), and York University.

I've been blessed to have discussed ideas related to this book with Maria Alvarez, Yuval Avnur, Alisabeth Ayers, Rima Basu, Hagit Benbaji, Selim Berker, Sven Bernecker, Bruce Brower, Stewart Cohen, Kenny Easwaran, Jeremy Fantl, Jan Gertken, Eleanor Gordon-Smith, John Hawthorne, Tim Henning, Ulrike Heuer, Jeff Horty, Benjamin Kiesewitter, Aleks Knoks, Jennifer Lackey, Barry Lam, Marc Lange, Ben Lennertz, Janet Levin, Lauren Leydon-Hardy, Alida Liberman, Clayton Littlejohn, Errol Lord, Matthew McGrath, Sarah McGrath, Susanne Mantel, Sarah Moss, Mark Murphy, Shyam Nair, Ram Neta, Kate Nolfi, Calvin Normore, David Owens, Hille Paakunainen, Abelard Podgorski, Kathryn Pogin, Lewis Powell, Jim Pryor, Baron Reed, Gideon Rosen, Jake Ross, Jeff Russell, Karl Schafer, Kevin Scharp, Susanna Schellenberg, Tim Schroeder, Nate Sharadin, Gila Sher, Nico Silins, Declan Smithies, Justin Snedegar, Scott Soames, Jason Stanley, Kurt Sylvan, Jim Van Cleve, Ryan Walsh, Jonathan Way, Brian Weatherson, Timothy Williamson, and Masahiro Yamada, among many others I am inexcusably leaving out.

Portions or all of the manuscript have benefited from comments from Nathan Howard, Benjamin Kiesewetter, Ben Lennertz, Shyam Nair, Indrek Reiland, and especially from Daniel Whiting, Matthew McGrath, Daniel Star, and two other generous and detailed but anonymous reviewers. Reader C, you told it to me straight, with a teaspoon of sugar to help the medicine go down. I hope the book has benefited from it—you know who you are.

In early 2011, I made the rash decision to commit to teaching much of this material in my graduate seminar in the spring of 2012—essentially everything except the material in Chapters 5, 9, and 10. Despite not being nearly as ready for the seminar as I had hoped, I learned an immense amount through exposure of my ideas to the participants in that seminar, particularly to Greg Antill, Stephen Bero, Justin Dallmann, Michael Hatcher, Janet Levin, Shyam Nair, Abelard Podgorski, Justin Snedegar, Aaron Veek, and Ryan Walsh, in addition to Greg Ackerman, Ara Astourian, Rima Basu, Erik Encarnacion, Keith Hall, Nick Laskowski, Ben Lennertz, Jen Liderth, Matt Lutz, Michael Milona, Indrek Reiland, Lauren Schaeffer, Kenneth Silver, and Julian Stone-Kronberg, along with other visitors to the seminar over the course of the semester.

A large portion of my time over the last few years has been spent in the company of the exceptional group of up-and-coming philosophers who I've been lucky enough to supervise as PhD students. As a result, this is my first large-scale work that is deeply indebted to my own students. I'm particularly grateful to Rima Basu, Stephen Bero, Joshua Crabill, Justin Dallmann, Michael Hatcher, Nathan Howard, Ben Lennertz, Alida Liberman, Michael Milona, Shyam Nair, Caleb Perl, Abelard Podgorski, Indrek Reiland, Sam Shpall, Justin Snedegar, Ryan Walsh, and Shane Ward, for stimulating conversations, forceful criticisms, and ideas I've shamelessly borrowed for my own. Rima Basu deserves singling out, in particular, because she is responsible for inspiring and influencing my views developed in what has become a full chapter of this book, devoted to the question of whether and how beliefs can wrong, and parts of that chapter draw on our collaborative work.

I have also been blessed with an extraordinary group of professional colleagues at USC, who have stretched me and sustained me, both by engaging directly about one another's work, and through our common work on PhD student dissertation committees. Janet Levin attended the entirety of the graduate seminar in which I taught this material in spring 2012 and it was discussions with Janet that helped me find and latch onto the apparent factive attitude view defended in Chapter 5. John Hawthorne and I co-taught a graduate seminar on reasons in fall 2016 which accelerated my ruminations on what I now call the Fundamental Argument for Reasons First. And I have served on more common dissertation committees with Steve Finlay than I think either of us can count. His skepticism about reasons and his conviction in the value of philosophical system-building have fueled this project, each in their own way, and I am lucky to count him as a friend.

Ralph Wedgwood has long been one of my closest intellectual fellow travelers, always interested in the same questions, but in ways that constantly lead us to different conclusions. I am sorry that my answer to his challenges to Reasons First, now published in *Ethics* as "Getting Perspective on Objective Reasons", became too large and involved to fit into this volume. And finally, my intellectual debts to Jake Ross will be apparent in Part III, which draws on and develops many conversations that we had over meals in our first two years together at USC, only some of which appear in our joint paper, "Belief, Credence, and Pragmatic Encroachment on Knowledge". Jake is not responsible for my errors, but I hope that he will not think that I have fallen too far astray, despite my overfondness for reasons.

Over the last decade I have had the immense privilege to mold a life together with Maria Nelson. Without her support and encouragement, none of this would be possible. Despite being the least philosophical person I know—indeed, because of it—she is responsible for some of the core ideas of the book, particularly about the nature and role of binary belief, as described in Chapter 8.

And finally, the book is dedicated with love to Caroline Maria Schroeder and William Nelson Schroeder—the steps in my groove. May they live with reason and each find their own balance.

Contents

List of Figures   xiii

PART I. THE ISSUES

1. Introduction   3
2. Reasons are Competitors   23

PART II. RATIONALITY AND TRUTH

3. Basic Perceptual Reasons   51
4. Subjective Reasons and Truth   77
5. The Apparent Factive Attitude View   101

PART III. HOW EVIDENCE RATIONALIZES BELIEF

6. Balance in Epistemology   127
7. Epistemic Reasons as Right-Kind Reasons   146
8. Pragmatic Intellectualism   168
9. Doxastic Wrongs   183

PART IV. KNOWLEDGE AND MORAL WORTH

10. Acting and Believing Well   201
11. The Kantian Account of Knowledge   224
12. Reasons First?   244

References   257
Index   271

List of Figures

3.1.	Twentieth-century epistemology	59
3.2.	The disjunctivist alternative	63
3.3.	The forced choice	74
6.1.	The two-stage model	136
9.1.	Moral–epistemic harmony	193
10.1.	Well first	209
10.2.	Right first	215
10.3.	Reasons first	219
11.1.	Reasons first package	225
11.2.	Cleanup package	225

PART I

THE ISSUES

In the beginning was Reason [λόγος].
John 1:1.

1

Introduction

1.1 Introducing Reasons First

Abby has a big decision to make. She is about to graduate from college, and must decide between a job at a startup in Silicon Valley and pursuing graduate school in philosophy. Both paths have an uncertain future, but the startup offers triple the pay and the prospect of future financial rewards. On the other hand, teaching philosophy has been her dream since she first read Descartes. She loves the teamwork she's experienced at the startup, and is worried about the fact that dissertations and most articles in philosophy are single-authored. But she doesn't feel like the company's minor variant on mobile photo-sharing technology is meaningful in the same way as the philosophical questions about truth, knowledge, and justice that animate her. Still, she knows from experience that she can make a real contribution to the startup, and wonders how she could make such a real contribution to questions that have puzzled many of the world's greatest thinkers for millennia. Of course, perhaps that is the wrong perspective. After all, the best prospect for making money at a startup these days is to be bought up by Google, Facebook, or Apple as a way to stifle competition, and if that happens, all she'll have to show for her efforts will be a pile of money. Then again, that's more money than anyone seems to make doing philosophy.

Abby knows that moral philosophers have had advice to offer about decisions like hers. She's tried applying Kant's Categorical Imperative to her decision, but the more she thinks about it, the more convinced she is that it's irrelevant. For starters, both careers seem to pass the test of the Categorical Imperative, but even if they did not, the Categorical Imperative seems to miss most of the important aspects of her decision. She can't see how the salary or the prospect of teamwork could have anything to do with the Categorical Imperative, for example, but both strike her as very important for helping her figure out what she ought to do. She's also tried applying utilitarianism to her decision, but that hasn't helped, either; she's unsure which career will make even her happier, let alone anyone else. And even if she was sure which would lead to the greatest balance of net collective happiness that still only feels like one more consideration that matters, along with the prospects for advancement, flexibility of work hours, and retirement benefits.

As Abby thinks through each of the relevant aspects of the options that she is considering, they phenomenologically strike her as counting in favor of one or

Reasons First. Mark Schroeder, Oxford University Press (2021). © Mark Schroeder.
DOI: 10.1093/oso/9780198868224.003.0001

another of the two options. This is why she finds it so natural to use expressions like 'but' and 'on the other hand' as she shifts between considering features that feel like they point or weigh in different directions. This phenomenology—the phenomenology of different considerations pointing or weighing in different directions in a choice situation—is the phenomenology of *reasons*.

According to a simple and natural hypothesis of growing popularity in contemporary ethical theory, the reason why it is so natural for Abby to experience the phenomenology of different reasons pulling in different directions, when she thinks hard about what she ought to do, is just that what *makes it the case* that she ought to do one thing, rather than another, is simply that it is what is best-supported by her reasons. On this picture, when Abby considers the factors that pull her in different directions, she is not simply paying attention to one source of evidence among others bearing on what she ought to do; rather, she is gaining the kind of insight to help her understand *why* she ought to do it.

According to this view, reasons explain what you ought to do not merely in the sense that no matter what you ought to do, the explanation of why you ought to do it counts as a 'reason' for you to do it, but in the sense that facts about what your reasons are and the direction in which they point are prior to and explanatory of what you ought to do. Something counts as being what you ought to do *in virtue* of the fact that it is what the balance of your reasons favors, and that is *what it is* for it to be what you ought to do. With respect to the question of what you ought to do, this view is that reasons have—or put more carefully, the *reason* relation has—both *analytic* and *explanatory priority*.[1]

According to many contemporary moral philosophers, the priority of reasons extends not only to what we ought to do, but to many or all of the other concepts distinctive of ethics or practical philosophy—concepts like *good, better, admirable, just, wicked, outrageous, jerk, unfair, justified, correct*, and many others. Just as what Abby ought to do can be thought of as a matter of what her reasons best support, these philosophers claim that each of these other concepts needs to be understood and explained in terms of reasons. These philosophers give reasons priority over a much wider range of important ethical, evaluative, or more broadly, normative, categories and concepts.[2]

---

[1] The reason relation could, of course, have explanatory priority without analytic priority. This question will return in Chapters 2 and 12.

[2] Philosophers often distinguish between concepts, which are constituents or properties of thoughts, and properties and relations, which are corresponding features of reality. Talk about properties and relations has the unfortunate feature that there is no single word that quite satisfactorily covers both monadic properties and polyadic relations. So sometimes in my informal remarks, as here in the main text, I will employ the conceit of using terms like 'concept' or 'categories' loosely. But throughout I will be interested in features of reality, rather than in our thoughts. When I make claims about analytic priority, these are intended as claims about features of reality, rather than about our thoughts. I leave it open whether any of the features of analytic priority that I discuss are matched by corresponding features of our thoughts.

Obviously, not every moral philosopher who finds it congenial to appeal to reasons in her work thinks that reasons have this kind of explanatory centrality, but those who do may take the explanatory centrality of reasons to help explain why it is so often helpful, in moral philosophy, to formulate difficult and controversial theses in the vernacular of reasons. For example, Jonathan Adler (2002, 9) describes the thesis of *evidentialism* in epistemology as the view that "to (fully) believe that *p* one needs adequate reasons". Similarly, according to Derek Parfit (1997, 209), one important form of *egalitarianism* is the view that "we always have a reason to prevent or reduce inequality, if we can". Nor are Adler and Parfit alone; it has become routine to formulate interesting theses in epistemology and in moral and political philosophy in the vernacular of reasons.

In this book, I will be interested in the strongest version of the idea that reasons are explanatorily central in ethics. According to this version of the idea, reasons are prior to and explanatory of not only what we ought to do, and prior to and explanatory of *many* ethical or evaluative properties and relations, but prior to and explanatory of *every* normative property and relation. According to this version of the thesis, reasons aren't just useful for formulating theses in neutral terms, and they don't just come prior to some interesting or important range of other concepts, but they come first *simpliciter*, at least among normative concepts. Among normative properties and relations, reasons are the *most fundamental.* I will call this the thesis of *Reasons First.*

The word 'normative' has sometimes been used in moral philosophy to contrast with 'evaluative', so that 'normative' encompasses 'wrong', 'must', 'ought', and 'just', but not 'good' or 'swell'.[3] Others contrast the 'genuine' normativity of reasons with the 'pseudo'-normativity of *rules*.[4] I do not intend to restrict my use of the word 'normative' in either of these ways. The scope of the thesis of Reasons First is intended to apply to every property or relation that is 'normative' in the sense that contrasts with 'positive', and picks out the widest possible range of topics with respect to which the standard concerns of metaethics apply. Except in some particular cases, I will not take a stand on exactly which properties and relations are included in this class—for example, I will not take a stand on whether 'nice' expresses a property that we happen to approve of people for having, or somehow builds in something evaluative.[5] I require only that whichever properties

[3] Tappolet (2013).   [4] Parfit (2011, 144–5).
[5] On another view, kindness is a normative property. Perhaps it is the property of being *appropriately* empathetically responsive. Or perhaps, less plausibly, it is the property of being empathetically responsive *and that's being good.* This view is less plausible because it carries the controversial commitment that thick concepts like *kind* can be decomposed into separate descriptive and normative components. See Hurka and Elstein (2009) for exploration of how thick concepts can be analyzed in terms of thinner normative concepts without being decomposable in this way; Gibbard (2003, ch. 8) for a sophisticated expressivist treatment and Väyrynen (2013) for more extended discussion of plausible models for thick language.

and relations you take to be relevantly similar to paradigms like 'ought', 'good', and 'correct', you understand the scope of Reasons First accordingly.

Just as it is important to clarify what I mean by 'normative', it is also important to clarify what I mean by 'reason', in order to make the thesis of Reasons First precise. Philosophers routinely distinguish between many different kinds of claim that can be made using the word 'reason'. I will have much more to say about how I will be understanding what reasons, in the relevant sense, are, in Chapter 2. For now it will suffice to say that it is some *normative* sense of 'reason' in which reasons come first. It does not suffice to defend Reasons First, for example, to argue that every normative property or relation needs to be understood in terms of explanation, and hence in terms of the answers to 'why' questions, or put differently, reasons why something is the case. Such a view would make so-called 'explanatory' reasons out to be more fundamental than any normative property or relation, but it would not by itself amount to the claim that reasons come first *among* normative properties and relations.

The thesis of Reasons First falls into a family of priority theses. In different eras, moral philosophers have been wont to proclaim that the subject matter of ethics is simply the subject matter of the good, or alternatively that it is simply the subject matter of what ought to be.[6] Each of these proclamations typically comes—particularly clearly in the case of Moore—with commitment to a conception of which normative property or relation comes first. Reasons First shares with each of these views the idea that some normative property or relation is central, but offers a distinctive answer to what that is.

Over the last half century, something very much like the thesis I am calling Reasons First has become orthodox within moral philosophy to quite a striking degree. Though it is far from uniformly accepted, especially in the strong form that I have stated it here, it is at least recognizable as a familiar or even default option, against which it is helpful for other views to distinguish themselves. This book is, to a first approximation, about whether this development constitutes progress.

1.2 Epistemology as a Normative Discipline

Though the remarks of many philosophers suggest that the thesis of Reasons First has become fairly orthodox within moral philosophy, moral philosophy is not the only branch of normative inquiry. Epistemology is also a normative discipline, in

---

[6] Compare Moore (1903, 55): "This, then, is our question: What is good? And What is bad? And to the discussion of this question (or these questions) I give the name of Ethics, since that science must, at all events, include it." See also the discussion in Hurka (2015) of the competing views that rightness or fittingness is the basic normative property.

the broad sense of 'normative' that is at issue in the thesis of Reasons First.[7] Epistemology is concerned with such questions as under what circumstances it is rational to believe that the bank will be open tomorrow, and why. And when is it reasonable to be more confident that a Republican will be elected than that a Democrat will? Epistemology also asks questions about how much evidence you need, before you should make up your mind, and whether you should become less confident in your views, when you discover that there are equally intelligent people who have come to different conclusions on the basis of the same evidence. So epistemology is, at least in part, a normative discipline.

Now, even if epistemology is, as I claim, a normative discipline, the claim that reasons come first among normative properties and relations is *not* the same as the thesis that reasons come first among all of the concepts explored in epistemology. It may well be—indeed, much of the moral of Part II of this book may be taken fairly as suggesting—that a fair bit of important work in epistemology is or can be construed as being concerned with the distinctive mental or psychological features of reasons or the conditions of 'possessing' reasons[8] for belief. So there may, in that sense, be much of explanatory theorizing in epistemology that is prior to reasons. Similarly, the claim that reasons come first among all normative properties and relations does not entail that nothing studied in *moral philosophy* is prior to reasons—only that whatever is so prior is not itself normative. Nevertheless for the sake of simplicity, I will often use the phrase "reasons come first within epistemology" to refer to the idea that reasons come first among the normative properties and relations deployed in epistemology—just as I will for the analogous claim for ethics.

For example, questions about what you 'rationally should' believe are, of course, only one sort of question in epistemology. Epistemologists have also been very much concerned, particularly over the last fifty years or more, in the concept of *justification*. Justification is also, I believe, clearly a normative concept, in the sense in which 'normative' contrasts with 'positive'. So epistemology is also a normative discipline, insofar as it is concerned with justification.

According to a traditional conception, of course, epistemology is the theory of *knowledge*. And it might intelligibly be asked whether knowledge itself is normative. While it is reasonably plausible that knowledge is *important*, that is not quite the same as knowledge itself being a normative relation. Many properties and relations that are not themselves, as I will put it, normatively *contentful* are nevertheless normatively *relevant*. For example, facts about happiness, pain, and death may have immediate consequences for what we have reasons to do—and

---

[7] "On this way of conceiving of the discipline, the most fundamental question in epistemology is 'What should I believe?' [. . .] One virtue of viewing epistemology in the manner I have been proposing is that it brings to the fore the *normative* character of the discipline" Berker (2013, 338–9).

[8] More on reason 'possession' later.

hence be highly normatively relevant—without themselves *being* normative.[9] Earlier I noted that there may be some properties, such as that of being *nice*, such that it is unclear whether they are normatively contentful, or merely obviously normatively relevant. If knowledge is like happiness, pain, and death in being obviously normatively relevant without being normatively contentful, then it could be that the core of epistemology is non-normative.

An important and central tradition within epistemology, however, holds that part of *what it is* to know is for some normative condition to obtain. According to Ayer, for example, to know that P is, in part, to *have a right* to be sure that it is true that P.[10,11] Different members of this tradition make different claims about which normative condition is part of the nature of knowledge. Some say that it is justification or rationality; others that it is entitlement or warrant. Whatever it is, all of these views share a conception on which some normative condition is part of the nature of knowledge. I will take for granted throughout this book that if part of something's nature is normative, then that thing itself counts as normative, in the relevant sense. So these are all views, I take it, on which even knowledge is normative.

If knowledge is *not* normative, then the thesis of Reasons First, as I understand it, may be easily reconciled with the ultimate priority of knowledge within epistemology. This reconciliation is made possible by appeal to the idea that knowledge plays an explanatory role with respect to reasons. But I will ultimately be arguing in this book not only that knowledge is normative, as maintained by the traditional views just mentioned, but that knowledge is actually one of the *very best cases* for the analytic and explanatory priority of reasons.

---

[9] Death, I take it, is a biological property. This is consistent with the claim that the boundaries of death are vague, or that we have come to think of it differently over time, due to our interests and the availability of better medical technology, or that there are important distinctions to be made among closely related concepts of death that would never have been distinguishable before the advent of modern life-support technology such as artificial respirators. Compare Engelhardt (1975), Walton (1979).

[10] Ayer (1956, 34).

[11] A small pedantic note. Throughout this book, I will use capital letters ('P', 'Q', etc.) as schematic letters to be read as replaceable by sentences, and such claims should be understood as expressing a willingness to make similar claims, for other ways of filling in the schematic letter. This sometimes makes it awkward to quantify the full import of the claims that I wish to make, and for that reason I have sometimes avoided this manner of speaking in the past, but I believe that this is the lesser of two evils. In accord with the common philosophical view that belief and desire are propositional attitudes, many philosophers use 'p' as a variable, and write not of 'believing that P', but of 'believing p'. Where necessary in discussing the views of others, I will use lower-case italicized letters ('p', 'q', etc.) in this way, but I prefer not to do so. Even though I agree that belief and desire relate agents to propositions, and even though the English verbs 'believes' and 'desires' can grammatically take nouns, when they do take nouns as their objects, they do not consistently express a relation to propositions. So the common tactic in philosophical prose of writing 'believe p', where p is a variable ranging over propositions, requires a special, philosophically regimented, use of 'believe' (this is even more obvious with 'desire'). I believe it is more advisable to couch our discussion in non-technical, theory-independent language, and the technical appearance of letters throughout the text can easily be eliminated by reading in your favorite substitution instance for 'P'.

Regardless of what we say about knowledge, however, the breadth of normative concepts of interest within epistemology is great. Over the last several decades, epistemologists have emphasized the importance of the concepts of *rights*, *duties*, *responsibilities*, and *virtue*, along with more familiar categories like *rationality* and *justification*. What distinguishes epistemology from ethics is therefore not *which* normative concepts it applies, for the most part, but what they are applied *to*—its distinctive subject matter. In epistemology, many of the questions that we ask—including about what is rational, justified, or supported by reasons—are of the same kind as similar questions that we sometimes ask in other branches of normative inquiry. They employ what appear to be the same normative concepts, but apply them to a distinct domain—the assessment of cognitive attitudes like belief, doubt, and credence. And even when we employ concepts in epistemology that are not obviously of the same kind of concern in other branches of normative inquiry—such as when we make claims about knowledge—it seems that we are taking on commitments about what is rational, as well.

Because belief, doubt, and credence are in many ways different from action, intention, and the emotions, it should be no wonder if there turn out to be especially important truths or challenges in epistemology which couldn't have been predicted by merely considering the other domains of normative inquiry. And because the questions of epistemology are methodologically important for much of philosophical inquiry, we shouldn't be surprised if they are sometimes tackled in isolation from analogous questions in other branches of normative inquiry. But because epistemology employs—indeed, is riddled with—many of the same normative concepts as other branches of normative inquiry, we should also not be surprised if pursuing distinctively epistemological questions without keeping this in perspective might sometimes lead to problems.

The *Core Hypothesis* of this book is that the comparison to other branches of normative inquiry does sometimes make a difference—indeed, an important difference—for even very core topics of traditional epistemology. I may sometimes put the Core Hypothesis in a somewhat loaded way by characterizing it as the hypothesis that views about core topics of traditional epistemology have sometimes been *distorted* by lack of the perspective that we can gain by considering the commitments we incur in answering them in light of similar questions about normative inquiry outside of epistemology.

One way in which epistemologists might take on problematic commitments because of a narrow perspective is as part of an analytic project. If both belief and action can be rational, but the epistemologist purports to provide an analysis of the relevant way in which belief can be rational, and this analysis does not have the right sort of structure to extend to action, then it would seem that the analysis is obviously too narrow. A better analysis should help us understand how both belief and action can be assessed as rational, but also why, given the differences between action and belief, the rationality of action turns out to be different from the rationality of belief.

Let me illustrate this observation with two examples. According to *subjective Bayesians*, a state of confidence—a so-called *credence*—is rational just in case it probabilistically coheres with one's other states of confidence. If we ignore the fact that rationality applies to things other than credences, accepting the thesis of subjective Bayesianism might lead us to think that it could be an adequate account of *what it is* for a credence to be rational, and not just *what it takes* for a credence to be rational. But this would be a mistake. Since actions, intentions, and emotions can also be rational or irrational, but actions, intentions, and emotions cannot probabilistically cohere, either with each other or with credences, this cannot be what it is for *them* to be rational. So if subjective Bayesianism is correct as an account of what it *takes* for a credence to be rational, that must flow from a more general account of what it is for something to be rational, together with important facts about the nature of credences.

To take just one more example, one of the important developments in the history of responses to the Gettier problem was the development of so-called 'conclusive reasons' theories of knowledge.[12] According to such theories, knowing that P requires having conclusive reasons to believe that P. And having conclusive reasons to believe that P is to be in possession of some reason—that R—to believe that P, such that it would not have been the case that R unless it were the case that P. This definition of 'conclusive reasons' may have great intuitive merit if the only thing that we are concerned about having conclusive reasons for its belief. But we may also have conclusive reasons to act or intend, or to have some emotion. The conditions under which we have conclusive reasons for such things are clearly going to be different. So an adequate account of *what it takes* to have conclusive reasons to believe that P should see this as derived from a more general account of *what it is* to have conclusive reasons to do something, together with distinguishing facts about belief, in particular.

These are just two examples, but they illustrate the way in which *analyses* or what I will call *constitutive* accounts of *what it is* for some condition to obtain are best informed by paying attention to the general case. It is worth noting that there are some times when a philosopher *presents* herself as giving an analysis that would be revealed to be too narrow by this reasoning, but it does not matter for her purposes whether it is truly an analysis or only a correct characterization of the conditions under which, say, one has conclusive reasons for a belief. I have no principled dispute with such philosophers. In some cases, philosophers actually have independent arguments that any adequate constitutive account should

---

[12]   The canonical source of this view is Dretske (1971). But I would argue that similar points go for a wide range of other externalist views in epistemology, including the influential reliabilist treatment of justification in Goldman (1979).

predict their view as a special case. For example, the subjective Bayesian can appeal to a variety of well-known independent arguments for the 'only if' direction of her view. Given the independent evidence for this part of her view, it is more likely that her view will constrain what a general account of rationality can be like, than that the general account of rationality will lead us to the conclusion that credences do not need to probabilistically cohere in order to be rational.

But sometimes the independent evidence for some view in epistemology is substantially weaker. For example, in the case of the conclusive reasons analysis of knowledge, there is no rich literature developing multiple independent strands of argument, each of which yields the conclusion that it is a conclusive reason to believe that P, that R, just in case it would not be the case that R, unless it were the case that P. On the contrary, part of the support for the idea that this is *when* R is a conclusive reason seems to come from the fact that it is hard to find another way of defining conclusive reasons in terms of simple non-normative terms involving counterfactuals, truth, and the like. If this is sometimes the case in epistemology, then the implications of taking a broader perspective may turn out to be profound. My goal will be to illustrate this lesson in more detail over the course of the book.

Our leading case study for the importance of the continuity between epistemology and other normative disciplines will be the thesis of Reasons First. As I've already noted, the thesis of Reasons First has become strikingly orthodox within moral philosophy. And I've argued that given the intended scope of the thesis, it applies to many of the central concepts of epistemology, including at least rationality and justification. I will eventually be arguing, in Chapter 11, that it applies to knowledge as well. It then seems to follow that many moral philosophers are committed to the thesis that reasons come first, even among the normative concepts deployed in epistemology. But the idea of Reasons First has not, it seems to me, enjoyed similar popularity in epistemology to that it has enjoyed in ethics. Consequently, one of the most important themes throughout this book will be that of whether the case of epistemology provides fruitful work for, or evidence against, the idea of Reasons First.

1.3 Reasons and Evidence

To see why we might think that reasons play some important explanatory role in epistemology, it's best to start with some important observations about the explanatory role of *evidence*. I will assume without argument that the concept of evidence plays an important and central explanatory role within epistemology— that it matters greatly for what you know and what it is rational for you to believe, what your evidence is. I will not, in contrast, be making any substantive assumptions about the nature or structure of evidence anywhere in this book. I will not, for example, be assuming that raising the probability that P is either necessary or sufficient for being evidence that P, and I will assume that it is possible to have great differences in the amounts of evidence supporting propositions of the same probability. I take it, rather, that any theoretical account of evidence should be answerable to the roles that we expect evidence to play in epistemology, and so I will work throughout with an intuitive notion of evidence.

It is important, however, to distinguish between what we might call *objective* and *subjective* evidence. Suppose that Christine is smiling. That is evidence that she is happy. But if no one is aware that she is smiling, then this is not evidence that anyone *has*. Facts that are evidence, even though no one is aware of them, are what I will call *objective* evidence. They are what we seek, when we seek evidence that bears on some question. When we *have* evidence that bears on the question, because we see that Christine is smiling, that is what I will call *subjective* evidence. It is subjective evidence that matters for what it is rational for us to believe. If Christine is smiling, but I have no idea that she is, that does not contribute in any way to whether it is rational for me to believe that she is happy. But if I believe that Christine is smiling, that does help to make it rational for me to believe that she is happy.

If I see that Christine is smiling, but her friend told me that she is unhappy, then I have evidence both for and against the conclusion that she is happy. In that case, my evidence is in competition, and what it makes most sense for me to believe will depend, at least in part, on which evidence is more compelling. So evidence *competes*. In this competition, it is important to distinguish between two ways in which evidence can be defeated. If I have better evidence that Christine is happy than that she is not, then we may say that my evidence that Christine is not happy has been *countervailed* or *outweighed*—it is overruled by more compelling evidence on the other side. But sometimes evidence is defeated not because there is better evidence on the other side, but because it is *undercut*. For example, suppose that I find out that Christine's friend hasn't spoken to Christine since yesterday. That isn't evidence that Christine is happy, but it does render her testimony that Christine is unhappy much less compelling.

Finally, for some purposes it matters not only what evidence there is for some conclusion, and what evidence I *have* for that conclusion, but on which evidence I *base* my belief in that conclusion. For example, suppose that I see that Christine is smiling and hear her gushing to me about what a wonderful day today has been, but remain irrationally distrustful, and only believe that she is happy because I am told so by a friend I trust who talked to her last week. Although I believe what is supported by my evidence, in this case I do not base my belief on all of the evidence, but only on a part of it, and the least helpful part, at that. The basis for my belief matters. When I base my belief on selective evidence, my belief can be irrational, even though I believe something that is well-supported by my evidence. So we can *base* our beliefs on evidence, and it matters which evidence we base them on.

We've just seen that evidence admits of a distinction between objective and subjective, that evidence competes, that it can be both countervailed and undercut, and that our beliefs can be based on it. All of these observations apply to reasons as well—both reasons for belief, and reasons for action. The same examples suffice for reasons for belief. If Christine is smiling, that is reason to believe that she is happy. But if no one is aware that she is smiling, it is not a reason that anyone *has*. This is the objective/subjective distinction for reasons for belief. Similarly, if there is dancing at the party, that is a reason to go there (for people who like to dance). But only people who are aware that there is dancing at the party have this reason, and the dancing at the party only makes it rational to go there for people who are aware of it.

We've already seen that reasons compete against one another, weighing on one side or another of some question, and so in this respect, too, evidence is like reasons. Similarly, reasons can be both countervailed and undercut. The fact that Christine is smiling is a reason to believe that she is happy, but the fact that she is watching her mother die is a better reason to believe that she is not happy. Similarly, if she is acting, the fact that she is smiling is not such a good reason to believe that she is happy after all—it is undercut. Similar points go for reasons for action. The fact that you know that your friend is in the basement is a reason not to tell the people at the door that she has left town, but contra Kant, this is outweighed (countervailed) by the fact that the people at the door are a lynch mob. Similarly, the fact that you are playing the game Diplomacy may render the fact that some assertion would be a lie a less weighty reason than it otherwise would be—and thus undercut it.

Finally, actions or beliefs can be *based* on reasons, and it matters for many purposes on which reasons they are based. When you realize that Christine is smiling, you may conclude from this that she is happy, and thus base your belief on this reason. Differently put, we may say that the reason for which you believe that she is happy is that she is smiling. And similarly for action. Though you may have several reasons to take out life insurance, you may act on some of them but not others. And which reasons you act on can make a difference for how well-justified your action is. Julia Markovits (2010) has even argued persuasively that it makes the crucial difference for the moral worth of actions.[13]

So just like evidence, reasons admit of an objective/subjective distinction, compete with one another, can be either countervailed or undercut, and admit of basing.[14] Given these four striking similarities between evidence and reasons,

---

[13] Compare also Arpaly and Schroeder (2014).

[14] In fact, the parallels between talk about evidence and talk about reasons go even deeper. For example, as we will discuss in Section 4.2, ascriptions of both subjective evidence and subjective reasons are sensitive to whether the ascriber thinks that the subject's beliefs are *true*, and according to many, whether they are *knowledge*. For example, if you think that William knows that Christine is smiling, then you may say that one piece of evidence he has that she is happy, or one reason he has to believe

there are two very natural explanatory hypotheses. The first, defended in a series of papers by Stephen Kearns and Daniel Star, is the hypothesis of *Reasons as Evidence*. According to this hypothesis, there is so much in common between reasons and evidence because to be a reason is just to be evidence for something.[15] In particular, according to Kearns and Star, to be a reason for someone to φ is just to be evidence that she ought to φ.[16] So to be a reason for someone to believe that P is just to be evidence that she ought to believe that P.

Reasons as Evidence   For R to be a reason for X to φ is for R to be evidence that X ought to φ.[17]

Reasons as Evidence is, I think, an unpromising view, for a number of reasons. Among these the most glib but also I think the most important is that it gets the explanatory direction wrong. This is because as I'll argue in Chapter 2, reasons explain what you ought to do. But what you ought to do is not, in general, explained by the evidence of what you ought to do. Moreover, it predicts too many reasons. For example, if most of the people in the room ought to φ and you are in the room, that is evidence that you ought to φ. But it is not, intuitively, a reason for you to do it. Similarly, one way in which you can have evidence that you (subjectively) ought to believe that P is to believe that you lack evidence that ~P.[18]

---

this, is that she is smiling. But if you think that she is not really smiling, then even if you know that William rationally believes that she is, you would not say either of these things. We'll return to this issue in Chapter 4.

[15] See especially Kearns and Star (2008, 2009). The parallels between reasons and evidence are not Kearns and Star's primary motivation for their thesis, but they do note that both evidence and reasons have weight and that both admit of an objective/subjective distinction, and take this to be auxiliary support for their view. Note that in most places, Kearns and Star only explicitly defend Reasons as Evidence as a *necessary biconditional*, and not as an analysis of reasons. I will ignore this qualification both on the grounds that a biconditional cannot do the same explanatory work (as they admit (2008, 219), and on the grounds that my objections are to the biconditional, in any case.

[16] Pedantic note. It is common in moral philosophy to use 'φ' as a schematic letter to stand in for a verb phrase. In previous work, I have eschewed this way of talking in favor of the expression 'do A', where 'A' ranges over names for actions, so that this argument place can be quantified into. In keeping with the principle of only using language that makes pre-theoretical sense, however, throughout this book I will reserve capital letters for schematic letters for sentences, and the Greek letters 'φ' and 'ψ' as schematic letters for verb phrases of any kind, including those of the form, 'believes that P'.

[17] Kearns and Star's view is in one very significant way much stronger than what is required in order to defend the view that we see the parallels that we do between evidence and reasons because reasons are a special case of evidence. But it is by far, I think, the most natural such view. This is because any such view must fill in an account of what something must be evidence *for*, in order to be a reason to φ, and Kearns and Star's answer is the simplest and most general. I believe that most of the objections that I give in the main text to their view generalize.

[18] Final pedantic note. '~P' should be read as to be replaced by the appropriate syntactically well-formed negation of whichever sentence is read in for 'P'. This cheat will make many things much easier to say.

But a lack of evidence that ~P need not automatically be a reason to believe that P (there may be no evidence that P, either).[19]

Kearns and Star are not unaware of the fact that it is easy to identify evidence that you ought to φ that is not, intuitively, any reason for you to φ. Their favorite example, slightly more congenial to their case, involves testimony. A newspaper says that people are starving in Africa. This is evidence that people are starving in Africa, and hence it is evidence that you ought to donate to Oxfam. Again, the worry is that though the fact that people really are starving in Africa is a reason to donate, the fact that the newspaper says so is not. Following a line of reasoning employed by two of their arguments for Reasons as Evidence, Kearns and Star reject this claim. They insist that the fact about the newspaper really is a reason to donate to Oxfam, on the grounds that it would be appealed to in good reasoning supporting the action of donating to Oxfam.

The problem with this response, I want to suggest, is that it conflates reasoning that supports a belief with practical reasoning on the basis of that belief.[20] A natural way of testing for the importance of this distinction is to imagine Stephen asking Daniel why he donated money to Oxfam. Daniel says, "because the paper reported that people are starving there." Stephen replies, "it's a good thing those starving people have you watching out for them." Daniel replies, "what starving people? I don't believe the report; I just didn't have any good reasons not to donate, so the newspaper report was a good enough reason for me." This is bizarre, and I think that it is suggestive that the newspaper report does not support donating to Oxfam directly at all. What it does do, is to support the belief that people really are starving in Africa, and *that* supports donating.[21] The same test vindicates our other examples: for example, suppose that Stephen is in a room with mostly women age forty and up, so he believes that most of the people in the room ought to get a mammogram. So he goes to get a mammogram, even though he doesn't believe that he ought to get one, because he has nothing better to do with his time, so that reason is good enough.

So the thesis of Reasons as Evidence suffers from clear counterexamples, and resisting those counterexamples requires conflations whose consequences can be tested. But there are further problems with this thesis. Here is a third: all of the examples that I offered of evidence were examples that sound equally good as observations about reasons to believe. This is no coincidence; any evidence that P is naturally described as a reason to believe that P, and it is hard to think of what

---

[19] The first of these two kinds of example comes from Dancy (2004); the latter is borrowed from John Brunero (2009), who also credits Dancy. Appealing to another, less forceful, Dancian example, Fletcher (2013) argues that Kearns and Star's own account of evidence entails that given the thesis of 'ought' implies 'can', the fact that you can do A is evidence that you ought.

[20] Compare McNaughton and Rawling (2010).

[21] It also supports the conclusion that people are *probably* starving in Africa, which could also be a reason to donate, though I will not explore that in this volume—compare Schroeder (2018a)—and this complicates the dialectic.

could be a reason to believe that P without being evidence that P. In fact, Kearns and Star *seem* to think it is so obvious that their account is extensionally right about reasons for belief that they do not even bother discussing it—and it is a bit hard to see why they would think this, without taking for granted *some* connection between reasons and evidence in the case of belief.

But Kearns and Star's view does *not* identify reasons to believe that P with evidence that P. They instead identify reasons to believe that P with evidence that the agent *ought* to believe that P. And this means that they can only capture the generalization that the reasons to believe that P are all and only the evidence that P if they assume that the evidence that P is all and only the evidence that the agent ought to believe that P. But this generalization is, I think, false.[22] Facts about what an agent believes, or about her rational priors, can be evidence that she ought to believe that P without being themselves evidence of P. Indeed, even if you ought to believe that P just in case P, it does not follow that evidence that P is all and only evidence that you ought to believe that P, because this equivalence is itself something which there could be evidence for or against.[23]

Kearns and Star's formulation of Reasons as Evidence is not the *only* possible way that reasons might be analyzable in terms of evidence, but it is natural given the diversity of things that there can be reasons for (actions, beliefs, and other attitudes), and I believe that it is representative. Hence, I believe that the failures of the hypothesis of Reasons as Evidence lend support to the alternative explanation that evidence matters in epistemology because evidence that P is reason to believe that P. I will call this the hypothesis of *Evidence as Reasons*. Evidence as Reasons offers, I think, by far the most promising explanation of why reasons and evidence exhibit so many similar properties. So: if evidence matters in epistemology because evidence is reason to believe, then if evidence plays an explanatory role in epistemology, that explanatory role will be played by reasons.

Evidence as Reasons   Evidence matters in epistemology because if something is evidence that P, it is a reason to believe that P.[24]

---

[22] Kearns and Star explicitly leave open that it may be false, touting as a virtue of their view that it leaves open the possibility of pragmatic reasons for belief (2008, 217); but my point here is that it is false even if there are no pragmatic reasons for belief.

[23] Kearns and Star advance their thesis of Reasons as Evidence in parallel for both objective and subjective reasons. If objective reasons to believe that P are evidence that you objectively ought to believe that P, and you objectively ought to believe that P just in case P, then it is plausible that the evidence that you objectively ought to believe that P will be the same as the evidence that P. But it is not remotely plausible that you subjectively ought to believe that P just in case P. So the equivalence is hopeless for subjective reasons.

[24] One natural objection to Evidence as Reasons as formulated here is that the fact that a ticket is one of only 100 in a fair lottery that has not yet been held is evidence that it will not win, but is not a reason to believe that it will lose (intuitively, because from this it follows that you *should not* form a belief either way about whether it will lose). As I've noted, I do not assume that everything that raises the prior probability that P must count as evidence that P, and so I am neutral about whether this is indeed evidence that the ticket will lose. The other half of the reasoning required to motivate the counterexample may also fail—if,

This leaves us with a conditional argument that reasons play an important explanatory role in epistemology. If we add to this a background assumption about the distinctive *kind* of explanation provided by reasons—for example, that since it is non-causal, it belongs to the kind of *constitutive* brand of explanation by which the fact that the figure has three sides explains why it is a triangle—then we can get stronger conclusions about the kind of role played by reasons in epistemology.[25] This might help support the thesis that reasons have analytical as well as explanatory priority over justification and knowledge, given that justification and knowledge are explained, at least in part, in terms of evidence.

1.4 Two Obstacles

So far I've explained the thesis of reasons first, argued that since epistemology is a normative discipline, this thesis must be true of the central normative concepts deployed in epistemology, if it is true at all, and provided one source of indirect evidence that reasons do, in fact, play a central explanatory role in epistemology—because evidence plays such a central explanatory role, and evidence matters in epistemology only because evidence is reason to believe. All of this looks good for the prospects of *Reasons First*. Unfortunately, however, there are at least two very direct and distinctively epistemological obstacles to seeing how reasons could come first, in the relevant sense.

The first of these obstacles is what I will call the *problem of unjustified belief*, and it derives, as its name suggests, from the case of unjustified beliefs.[26] It is a problem about how to successfully characterize the kinds of reasons that can be used to explain knowledge, justification, and rational belief, without needing to appeal, in turn, to knowledge, justification, or rational belief. The problem is therefore a direct challenge to the idea that reasons come first within epistemology, because it

---

for example, although this is a reason to believe that the ticket will lose, it also guarantees the existence of a stronger reason against believing this. But if you are persuaded by such examples, then I will retreat to the formulation that *when* evidence matters in epistemology, it matters by being a reason—and in particular, when it matters for the epistemology of outright belief, it matters by being a reason for belief. This weaker thesis is neutral about whether *all* evidence that P is reason to believe that P.

[25] For more on constitutive explanations, see "Cudworth and Normative Explanations", reprinted in Schroeder (2014).

[26] Brief note on the terms 'justified' and 'rational'. Gettier introduced the term 'justified' to refer to the component in the analysis of knowledge that is shared by Ayer's (1956) appeal to the "right to be sure" and Chisholm's (1966) appeal to "adequate evidence". The analysis of justification then took on its own life. Like many internalists, I suspect that the most interesting notion of justification collapses into assessment of beliefs with respect to their rationality, and so for the most part I take these terms to be interchangeable for my purposes in this book. I realize that this is contentious, and that many theorists insist on an externalist account of justification while allowing for a more internalist account of rationality. But the issues that interest me are really those that concern knowledge and the rationality of belief, so I am happy to have this whole book read as silent with respect to justification—despite my use of this name for this problem.

challenges how reasons even *could* come first—for in order to successfully explain knowledge, justification, or rational belief, they would need to be in turn explained by one of them.[27] The second challenge, which I'll turn to shortly after getting the problem of unjustified beliefs fully on the table, suggests that reasons are too impoverished to explain any of knowledge, justification, or rational belief, without appeal to prior facts about how much reason it takes in order for a belief to be justified or rational.

The problem of unjustified belief is just what it says—a problem about how to rule out unjustified beliefs providing reasons. In normal cases, what someone believes can have an effect on what else it is rational for her to believe. When you observe Christine and recognize that she is smiling, that gives you reason to believe that she is happy, and can make it rational for you to believe that she is happy, in the absence of defeating considerations. But if your belief that Christine is smiling is unjustified, then things are not normal, and your belief does not help to make it rational for you to believe that Christine is happy. For example, if instead of seeing for yourself that Christine is smiling, you simply have an unsupported hunch that she might be, and come to believe that she is smiling by imagining it vividly, that does not make it rational for you to believe that she is happy, even in the absence of defeating considerations. Similarly, though evidence is required for knowledge, and you can acquire evidence that Christine is happy by coming to believe that she is smiling, if your belief that she is smiling is itself unjustified, then it doesn't count toward the evidence that you need in order to ground knowledge.

It follows from these observations that whatever sort of contribution beliefs make to knowledge or to the rationality of downstream beliefs by constituting subjective reasons for belief, no such contribution is made in cases in which a belief is unjustified or irrational. The usual and most natural response to this,[28] is to build into the notion of a subjective reason that it must satisfy some condition that rules out being unjustified. For example, according to Richard Feldman (1988), in order to be part of one's reasons, a belief must be justified. And according to Williamson (2007), in order to be part of one's reasons, a belief must be knowledge.

But if we need to appeal to a justification or knowledge condition in our analysis of subjective reasons, then subjective reasons cannot be prior to and explanatory of both justification and knowledge. They cannot be *analytically* prior to both, because either knowledge or justification is part of their analysis. And they cannot be *explanatorily* prior, because it is only in virtue of some fact about

---

[27]   Recall that I have not yet argued that knowledge is itself normative. I will argue this in Chapter 11. The problem of unjustified belief is only a problem for the thesis of Reasons First on the assumption that reasons must be prior to and explanatory of knowledge.

[28]   Notice that I do not say that it is the only possible response—I will be advocating an alternative in Chapters 3 and 4. The problem comes into view once we accept it as the *natural* or *correct* response.

justification or knowledge that they get to be subjective reasons, in the first place. Yet if we are to understand either knowledge or rational belief in terms of reasons at all, surely subjective reasons—the ones that are within our ken—need to be some part of the story. So the problem of unjustified beliefs presents a very general obstacle to understanding how reasons could be prior to and explanatory of both justification and knowledge, and hence to how reasons could possibly come first—unless, of course, it turns out that knowledge is not normative.[29]

Notice that the problem of unjustified beliefs is not exactly distinctively epistemological. It is possible to get a weaker version of this problem going by merely considering reasons for action. In general, what you believe affects what it is rational for you to do, but plausibly not when your beliefs are irrational. So similar reasoning can lead to the conclusion that subjective reasons for action must be grounded in beliefs that are themselves rational—and so subjective reasons cannot be prior to rationality, full-stop. But so long as we restrict ourselves to thinking of this as a problem about using reasons to understand the rationality of action, it is not particularly forceful. It is much more plausible, for example, to claim that irrational beliefs can make *actions* rational, than to claim that irrational beliefs can make downstream beliefs rational. It is also easy to come to the view that the rationality of belief and the rationality of action are different—perhaps rationality of belief is prior to subjective reasons for action, but subjective reasons for action are prior to the rationality of action. If so, there is no trouble for understanding the rationality of action in terms of reasons.

On the contrary, once we extend the scope of our ambition for the thesis of Reasons First, to explain knowledge and the rationality of belief in terms of reasons, the problem of unjustified belief becomes much sharper. This means, I think, that this problem is the right kind of thing to explain why epistemology, in particular, may have been a domain in which it has been *reasonable* not to find the thesis of Reasons First to be so attractive.

The second obstacle to the thesis of Reasons First within epistemology is what I call the *problem of sufficiency*. The problem of sufficiency derives from the fact that whereas *actions* are rational when they are favored by reasons that are at least as good as the reasons against them, belief is never rational when the evidence is tied. When the evidence is tied, the only rational course is not to form any belief either way. So whereas with action it may be plausible that we can simply weigh the reasons on each side, with respect to belief—since only evidence can be epistemic reason—it is hopeless simply to compare the reasons on each side. Instead, we must have some *independent* characterization of how good the evidence must be in order to be *sufficient*.

---

[29] For a somewhat different take on the central problem in the area of what I am calling the problem of unjustified belief, see Sosa and Sylvan (2018).

This problem is especially pressing, given that it seems like the reasons that matter for the rationality of belief are all and only the evidence that bears on its content. After all, not everything that might be cited as an advantage of having some belief is relevant for what it is rational to believe, or whether you know. If, for example, someone offers you money to believe that P, that does not, in general, make it more rational for you to believe that P, except in special cases where the proposition that P is the proposition that someone has offered you money, or the like. So, not just anything is the right kind of consideration to count towards the rationality of belief.

Hence, according to some philosophers, this shows that though monetary offers may be the kind of thing that can be reasons in favor of action, they are not the kind of thing that can be reasons in favor of belief.[30] According to others, it shows only that some reasons in favor of belief—call them *non-epistemic* reasons—do not contribute to making beliefs rational.[31] What these two views disagree about, is whether such non-epistemic reasons are really reasons at all. What they *agree* about, is that in order to count in favor of the rationality of belief, considerations need to be *epistemic* reasons for belief—a condition that is not satisfied by monetary offers.

So far, calling reasons that bear on the rationality of belief 'epistemic' tells us little about what it takes to be an epistemic reason. But we do know one thing: monetary offers are not, in general, epistemic reasons for belief. In contrast, the clear examples of epistemic reasons for belief are all considerations that seem to make the *content* of the belief more likely to be *true*. That is, clear examples of epistemic reasons for belief are all *evidence* for the content of the belief. So it is no wonder that it is widely held that not only, as claimed by *Evidence as Reasons*, that evidence *is* epistemic reason for belief, but also that *only* evidence can be epistemic reason for or against belief.

So this brings our problem to a head. If characterizing the rationality of belief in terms of reasons means characterizing the rationality of belief in terms of evidence, then what are we saying, when we say how good evidence must be, in order to be sufficient? We are saying, surely, that it is sufficient *for rationality*, or *for justification*, or the like. But what we wanted to do was to be able to explain in virtue of what it is rational for someone to believe something, by adverting to her reasons. But if doing so requires adverting to a prior fact about rationality—namely, how much reason it takes to be sufficient for rationality—then we will have at most the explanatory priority of reasons over particular cases of rational belief, but not analytic priority of reasons over rationality.

---

[30] Pink (1996), Parfit (2001), Kelly (2002), Hieronymi (2005), Shah (2006), Skorupski (2010), Way (2012).
[31] Schroeder (2010).

As with the problem of unjustified belief, it is clear that this difficulty is especially important from the perspective of epistemology. When it comes to actions, it is not at all obvious that what makes reasons sufficient for rationality is not just a matter of whether they are at least as good as any competing reasons. But given that only *epistemic* reasons matter in epistemology, and epistemic reasons are assumed to only include evidence, the perspective that we can understand the sufficiency of reasons independently of appeal to prior facts about justification, rationality, or knowledge is hard to maintain. So this is a special difficulty for Reasons First that arises within epistemology, and hence it is natural to think that it is part of a good explanation for why it truly is reasonable to find the thesis of Reasons First less compelling from the perspective of epistemology than from the perspective of ethics. But this problem is more general. Whereas the problem of unjustified belief gets its force from the assumption that knowledge is normative, the problem of sufficiency is independent of how we rule on the normativity of knowledge.

1.5 Looking Forward

In the last section I argued that the problem of unjustified belief and the problem of sufficiency are both serious obstacles to the thesis that reasons come first within epistemology. The problem of sufficiency is a problem for the thesis of Reasons First proper—that reasons are prior to all other normative properties and relations, and the problem of unjustified belief is an obstacle to Reasons First proper, conditional on the assumption, which I will argue for in Chapter 11, that knowledge is itself normative. Because these two problems are distinctive to epistemology, moreover, they help to explain why it is likely no mere sociological phenomenon that the thesis of Reasons First has such differential popularity in ethics and in epistemology. This sets the stage, finally, for the main argumentative tasks of this book.

In the remainder of this book, I will be arguing for four main ideas. The first is that there are *independent* reasons, within epistemology, to find an alternative solution to the problem of unjustified belief—one that is consistent with the thesis of Reasons First. My reasoning for this conclusion will be that the reasoning underlying the problem of unjustified belief plays an unacceptable role in constraining the options for understanding how perception could be a source of evidence. So by rejecting this reasoning, we can open up space for better views about basic perceptual justification. This will be the argumentative task of Part II of the book, in Chapters 3 through 5.

The second idea for which I will be arguing is that there are also important independent reasons, within epistemology, to find an alternative solution to the problem of sufficiency—one that is consistent with the thesis of Reasons First. My reasoning for this conclusion will be that it is independently hard to understand many of the features of how evidence helps to explain justified or rational belief, but that once we accept the thesis of evidence as reasons, we can allow that there are epistemic reasons *against* belief that are not evidence. Showing not only what problems this would solve and how, but making logical room for this possibility and then making good on an argument that it is actually true will be the project of Part III of the book, in Chapters 6 through 9.

So together, these two ideas, if they are right, show not only that the obstacles to Reasons First *can* be surmounted within epistemology, but that doing so benefits our understanding of problems that are wholly within epistemology. The third main idea for which I will be arguing is that these benefits actually go deeper: once we have these benefits on board, we are going to be in a much better position to understand how knowledge could be analyzable. Chapters 10 and 11, which make up the bulk of Part IV of the book, will be devoted to the task of motivating and articulating an analysis of knowledge in terms of reasons.

Finally, the biggest idea for which I will be arguing throughout this book is that we can get leverage on many of these problems by taking a broader perspective. In this chapter, I've already started to explain why we might expect this to be the case. But the virtues of this strategy can only be borne out by its fruits.

So that is the plan. But first, before we can get started on any of these ideas, we need to clear a little bit more ground. In Chapter 2 I will have much more to say about how I am thinking about reasons, for purposes of this book, and also about why anyone might think that they might be explanatorily and analytically prior to other normative properties and relations.

2

Reasons are Competitors

2.1 Why Reasons?

In Chapter 1, I introduced the idea of Reasons First, as the thesis that reasons are the basic normative concept, in virtue of which all others count as normative. I also argued that the central concepts of epistemology are normative in the sense appealed to by this thesis, so if Reasons First is true, reasons must be prior to and explanatory of knowledge and justification.[1] And then I gave an indirect argument that reasons are in fact prior to and explanatory of both knowledge and justification, by arguing for the thesis of Evidence as Reasons, which says that insofar as evidence matters for epistemology, it is by being reason to believe. It follows from the thesis of Evidence as Reasons that if evidence is prior to and explanatory of knowledge and justification, then so are reasons. We saw, however, that there are important puzzles about how reasons could be prior to and explanatory of both justification and knowledge, and that set the stage for the project of this book.

The argument of Chapter 1 was indirect, in that it assumed without argument that evidence plays a fundamental explanatory role within epistemology, in the explanation of both knowledge and justified belief. I personally find that assumption to be *ex ante* extremely plausible, and so I find the indirect argument to be illuminating. But it will help to have a more direct argument. In this chapter I will provide more direct evidence for an explanatory role for reasons. To do so, I will first back up, to look at why reasons seem important in the first place, at their distinguishing features, and at how those distinguishing features support the thesis of Reasons First. As we will see, the most important distinguishing feature of reasons is that they are *competitors*. This feature is at the heart of what makes it plausible that reasons are prior to and explanatory of what we ought to do, and Reasons First is motivated by the idea that this same reasoning extends to other central normative concepts, including *good*. The same considerations apply, I will go on to argue in Chapter 11, to the concept of *knowledge*.

When I first introduced reasons in Chapter 1, I did so by illustrating what I called the *phenomenology* of reasons—the experience of different considerations as pulling in different directions, with respect to an important decision, or as weighing on different sides of a scale. In Abby's decision, the prospect for

[1] All of the same qualifications apply to the last two sentences as in Chapter 1, of course.

Reasons First. Mark Schroeder, Oxford University Press (2021). © Mark Schroeder.
DOI: 10.1093/oso/9780198868224.003.0002

teamwork pulls toward taking a job with the startup, while meaningfulness of work pulls in the opposite direction—toward pursuing graduate study in philosophy. This feature of reasons—that they compete with one another—is, I believe, the dominant reason why reasons have come to play such an important role in moral philosophy over the past seventy or more years. It is what I will call the *classical* motivation for Reasons First.

To appreciate not just the importance of competition, but the pressure toward seeing reasons as normatively basic, it suffices to rehearse one of the most important developments in normative ethical theory over the last 150 years. Normative ethical theory, in its most ambitious form, seeks out generalizations about what moral agents like us ought to do in the widest possible range of circumstances. On one conception, the goal of such theory is an account of *what it is* for something to be what you ought to do. On another conception, the goal of moral theory is a list of basic obligations—things that everyone ought to do, no matter what—from which all other obligations can be derived.[2] On either conception, achieving the goal requires being able to formulate highly general principles that state sufficient conditions for something to be what someone ought to do— and enough of these to cover the full range of things that people ought to do, in the full range of situations that people can find themselves in.

The problem with this is that such conditions are terribly hard to come by, and the most plausible candidates are too narrow to cover the moral terrain. Take, for example, the case of lying, which was proposed by many as intrinsically odious, something that everyone always ought not to do, no matter what their circumstances. Samuel Clarke (1738) wrote in his sermon 108, "On the Nature of Lying", for example, that "the duty enjoined by these words, *speak every one truth with his neighbor*, has ever been acknowledged by men of all conditions, to be our necessary and indispensable duty". Kant was taken to task by Benjamin Constant for a similar view. But life is complex, and examples with some complexity call the principle into question. If there is a murderer at the door,[3] asking for the whereabouts of your friend, who shelters within, is it really your duty to tell him the truth? In *The Methods of Ethics*, Sidgwick (1907) worried about other, more complex cases, such as where meaning is shifting over time—white lies to 'invalids', telling fiction to children, and asserting truths from which falsehoods are naturally inferred. When we restrict our generalization to leave out these complexities, it fails to encompass all of the situations in which deception is genuinely wrong, and so we are forced to add additional conditions. And no matter how we restrict it, it is difficult not to make it vacuous in the face of examples in which everything else is in place to make the lie wrong, but telling the truth simply has overwhelmingly drastic but totally predictable consequences, or

---

[2] Compare the introduction to Schroeder (2014).
[3] The case famously raised by Constant (1797) to which Kant (1798) responds.

comes into conflict with other, more pressing, duties, such as the duty to keep a promise to a friend.

It could be that the question of what we ought to do is simply a patchwork of thousands of incredibly complex principles that build in, in advance, every possible exception in any philosopher's imagination. If this were so, there would be no fundamental and explanatory moral theory of any interesting level of generality. If it were so, it would be a bit unclear whether we ever truly know about any of these very specific principles, or whether we are ever guided by them. But it could be. Or it could be that there are no ethical principles at all, as particularists like Jonathan Dancy claim.[4] Still, in *The Right and the Good*, Ross (1930) offered a better, more natural, way to think about why it is that we can put pressure on generalizations about particular plausible duties, such as the duty not to lie, by putting them in tension with other apparent duties, such as the duty to keep promises or not to cause great harm to innocent people. It is because these duties *really are* in tension, in such cases, and to determine what we ought to do overall, we must pay attention to which duties are more *important*.

On Ross's view, what we ought to do is determined by what he called our *prima facie* duties. Our *prima facie* duties, he postulated, are like moral forces, and what we ought to do is like the net moral force acting on us. Like physical forces, these moral forces can sometimes come into conflict with one another, and when they do, what we ought to do is always a matter of the result of the *competition* among these duties. Indeed, even when our duties do *not* come into conflict, what we ought to do is a matter of the competition among our duties; it just turns out that in this case that competition is vacuous. It is because some duties rarely come into conflict or usually win their conflicts when they do, that it can seem plausible that they support generalizations about what we ought to do, but once we see how they come into conflict, we should resist this pressure.

Ross's main idea therefore opens up the possibility of making robust generalizations about what any agent ought to do, in every possible circumstance. What every agent ought to do is whatever is the product of the competition among her reasons—whatever she has *most reason* to do. This structural generalization about what everyone ought to do offers striking promise not just as necessary and sufficient conditions for what everyone ought to do, but as an account of *what it is* to be what someone ought to do. On this view, no further explanation is needed as to *why* each agent ought to do whatever is supported by the balance of her reasons, because that is just what it is to be what she ought to do.

Moreover, this view is compatible with a startling range of more concrete views about what agents ought to do in possible situations, so long as those are accompanied by corresponding views about what reasons apply in those situations—and it

---

[4] See in particular Dancy (2004).

is highly natural to attribute such assumptions about reasons to the very people who hold the corresponding views about what agents ought to do. For example, some people believe in absolute prohibitions—things like torturing infants—that it is wrong to do, no matter what.[5] It is plausible to attribute to the adherents of this view, the view that there are some reasons that are so forceful that they *cannot* lose out in competition with other reasons, and that one of the reasons not to torture infants is among them.

This Rossian view about the nature of what we ought to do also makes sense of why it seems that in realistic situations, many things matter for determining what we ought to do. According to this view, when Abby is deliberating about whether to take the job with the startup or go to graduate school in philosophy, she feels pulled in different directions because there are genuinely competing considerations that pull in those different directions. So the phenomenology of reasons that she experiences as she deliberates about whether to take the job *matches* the structure of the features of the world that make it the case that she ought, or ought not, to take the job. When she feels pulled in these different ways, she is *getting something right*.[6]

And it's a consequence of this matching relationship between the structure of human deliberation and the structure, according to the Rossian view, of what makes it the case that you ought to do one thing rather than another, that we get an explanation of at least one important reason why it has seemed to many philosophers that there is something valuable about deliberating for yourself about what you ought to do, as opposed to relying on the testimony of others.[7] There is something valuable about deliberating for yourself, because in deliberating for yourself, you are paying attention to the very features that make an action what you ought to do, and not just to indirect evidence. And this means that deliberating for yourself, when it is successful, gives you not just knowledge, but understanding. Since everyone is able to deliberate, moral understanding is available, at least in principle, to everyone.[8]

In the decades after Ross, moral philosophers came to use the words 'prima facie duty' only when talking specifically about Ross's own view, and to reject many of his other commitments. But Ross's main idea—that what we ought to do is the result of a competition between moral 'forces' pulling in different directions—is one of the main developments in twentieth-century ethical theory.

---

[5] Compare Nozick (1974) on side-constraints.

[6] She is 'getting it', morally, in the terms of Howard (ms).

[7] I don't say that there is something bad about relying on others' testimony; in cases in which you know that someone else is better informed about the non-moral features of the situation—for example, that they know whether there is a lady or a tiger behind the door on the left—it is best all things considered to rely on their testimony. But there does seem to be a problem with relying exclusively on others' testimony, and there seems to be something valuable about not doing so in particular cases, when there is an alternative.

[8] Compare McGrath (2011) and especially Hills (2009). Sliwa (2012) prominently defends a role for moral testimony. We will return to this topic in Chapter 10.

It gives us an explanation of why earlier attempts to formulate highly general moral theories were on the wrong track, and subject to exceptions in complicated cases that introduce combinations of morally relevant factors. Such theories may have latched onto one among other morally important features, but were missing the full picture. It was also discovered that we already appear to have us a word for these competing factors, at least in English: *reasons*.

Reasons are important, therefore, because they come into competition with one another, allowing us to explain what we ought to do in terms of the results of this competition. But more: observe that it is a consequence of this claim that reasons, or at least, facts about what is a reason for what, are *prior* to, and explanatory of, what we ought to do. They earn their keep by allowing us to give better and more general explanations of what we ought to do in terms of them, and if the version of the Rossian idea that I have proposed is correct, these explanations are *constitutive*—to be the result of the competition between one's reasons for action is just *what it is* to be what one ought to do. So reasons do not simply play *some* role in explaining what we ought to do, in this picture; they play a *constitutive* role. So they are prior to *ought* not only in the order of explanation, but in the order of analysis.[9] If Ross is right, then reasons have a kind of *local* fundamentality or *relative* priority.

The thesis of Reasons First is the thesis that reasons have both explanatory and analytic priority over each other normative concept. It is a direct extension of the thesis that reasons have explanatory and analytic priority over what we ought to do into a global, absolute, thesis. There *are* some direct motivations for Reasons First. But the most forceful motivations, and the ones considered in this book, are all of this kind—they start with the local priority of reasons over some other concepts, and then extend similar reasoning outward. In Section 2.5, I will have more to say about how the very same dialectic about what we ought to do extends to other central normative concepts. But first, I need to say something in Section 2.2 about why Ross's solution to Sidgwick's worries is preferable to Sidgwick's own, and to further qualify, in Sections 2.3 and 2.4, what I will mean by 'reasons' throughout this book.

2.2 Reasons and Value

As I noted above, Book III of Sidgwick's *Methods of Ethics* (1709) gives a particularly incisive treatment of the problems of formulating highly general principles

---

[9] Here in the main text I am focused on presenting the attractions of reason-based explanations in their most compelling light, but I do not mean to imply that significant issues do not remain in distinguishing between a wide variety of deontic concepts, including not just what someone ought to do, but what is permitted, required, or supererogatory. A wide variety of strategies have been proposed to apply to such cases and I will not have occasion to pursue the relevant issues further in this volume—for some discussion, see Snedegar (2016).

about what anyone ought to do. The structure common to many of the compli-cated cases that Sidgwick considers, I suggested, is that they introduce competing reasons, and that trying to directly formulate principles about what one ought to do that do not derive the answer as the consequence of the competition of different reasons is like trying to formulate general laws about what a particle will do that do not derive the answer as the consequence of the addition of separate forces.

Sidgwick was not aware of this diagnosis of the force of his examples; he held, on the contrary, that they supported the competing diagnosis that *utilitarianism* gives us a better treatment of what is going on in these cases. Sidgwick's (1709) reasoning—and the reason why Ross's diagnosis did not occur to him—derived from his basic, somewhat idiosyncratic, conception of his project in *The Methods of Ethics*. Sidgwick observed that if utilitarianism or egoism is correct, then ultimately the only way to determine what you ought to do in any situation will be empirical—you must determine the long-run consequences of your decision, and that is an empirical question. So he held that if intuitionism is to be a relevantly different *method* of ethics, we must be careful to understand it in such a way as to preserve the idea that moral reasoning can be suitably a priori. Even if we can discover our basic duties a priori, Sidgwick held, if downstream bad consequences of doing our duty could make it turn out that we ought to do otherwise, then we haven't isolated a suitably independent method of ethics, on which moral reasoning can be genuinely non-empirical. So Ross's view, on which the duty to tell the truth can compete with the duties to do good and to avoid doing harm, does not preserve the features that Sidgwick took as central when trying to formulate intuitionism as a distinct method of ethics.

The background presuppositions set up by the way in which Sidgwick formu-lated his primary question about methods led him to see utilitarianism as the best account of why there sometimes appear to be tradeoffs in complicated examples. Utilitarianism was a familiar ethical framework, and specifically one of those that he set out to investigate. And it was familiar since at least Bentham that the utilitarian answer to what to do in any given situation must take account of *tradeoffs*—it must be the result of a calculus that takes into account both pleasures and pains, and which does so *comparatively*, by comparing them to the pleasures and pains foregone through opportunity cost. So when considering cases like the murderer at the door, it seemed natural to Sidgwick to see these as cases in which the ordinary good consequences of telling the truth must count against the unusual bad con-sequences in this particular case.

The problem with this diagnosis is that utilitarianism as Sidgwick conceived of it is too narrow for its diagnosis of the tradeoffs involved in complicated moral examples to be general. Just as the plausibility that you ought always to tell the truth breaks down when we consider examples where telling the truth will result in a death that you are in a position to avoid, the plausibility that you ought always to do what will result in the most overall happiness breaks down when we consider examples where you can gain just a small amount of net happiness by breaking a promise or by killing rather than allowing someone else to kill. Sidgwick (1907) had a great deal to say about cases like these in Book IV of the *Methods*—there is, in fact, a full industry consisting of different ways of dealing with them in utilitarian terms. But a simpler and more plausible diagnosis is that they are illustrations of the fact that Sidgwick's diagnosis of tradeoffs is insufficiently general. Just as the benefits of various actions can be traded off against one another, the benefits of an action can be traded off against *other* kinds of reasons not to do it, that do not derive from the effects on happiness at all. The Rossian diagnosis offers a symmetric treatment of the tradeoffs that trouble utilitarians and deontologists, alike—and that is the heart of its appeal.

So, utilitarianism does not offer the most plausible diagnosis of the tradeoffs visible in complicated moral examples. But utilitarianism is just a special case of a broader form of moral theory, *consequentialism*, according to which one ought always to do what will have the results that are best. A consequentialist who rejects utilitarianism can offer a diagnosis of the tradeoffs involved in complicated examples, by appealing to different features that make outcomes *good* or *bad*. And so long as she makes the right claims about which features of outcomes are good or bad, she can claim to match the explanatory breadth of the Rossian diagnosis. Wherever the Rossian appeals to conflicting reasons, the consequentialist will appeal to conflicting *values*. The things the Rossian claims that you have reasons to do, the consequentialist will counter by claiming are things it is good *that* you do. So the consequentialist and the Rossian offer competing accounts of moral tradeoffs. According to the Rossian, these are the result of competition among reasons, but according to the consequentialist, they are a matter of competing values, or competing effects on value.

Of these two accounts, however, the account offered by the Rossian is a better fit. This is because reasons are *act-oriented*, rather than being *outcome-oriented*. Reasons are reasons *to* or *not to*; they are considerations that count for or against something we can do (in the broadest grammatical sense of 'do', construed so as to include believing, feeling, and intending). When we make claims like "the fact that it would be a lie is a reason for Xander not to tell Beth it is over", we are asserting that a certain *reason* relation holds between Xander, the fact that it would be a lie, and telling Beth that it is over. Things that we can do, in this sense, are a kind of property of agents. Non-finite clauses like "to tell Beth that it is over" and gerundive clauses like "telling Beth that it is over" are naturally interpreted as expressing *properties* that agents can have—the property that all agents share who are telling Beth that it is over.

'Good' and 'better', in contrast, as appealed to by consequentialism, are predicated of propositions, rather than properties. We speak of it being good that Jack is happy, it being better for Jack to be happy than for him to be sad, and of it being better if he stays happy than if he doesn't. The words 'that', 'for', and 'if' are *complementizers*; they syntactically combine with sentences to form *complementizer clauses*, which are the syntactic arguments of attitude verbs like 'believes', as well as adjectives like 'true' and 'good'. Insofar as we think of propositions as the objects of the attitudes and the bearers of truth and falsity, therefore, we should be thinking of them as what is expressed by complementizer clauses.[10] Hence, we should take 'good', as used by consequentialists, to designate a property of propositions, and 'better' to designate a relation (perhaps *inter alia*) among propositions.[11]

This difference between 'reason' and 'good' means that proponents of the Rossian diagnosis and consequentializers must appeal to different generalizations, when accounting for the same phenomena. For example, if an agent faces a forced choice between killing an innocent person and allowing that person to die, it is intuitive that she should let her die, rather than intervening and killing her herself, even if all other consequences are the same.[12] In order to capture this claim, the proponent of the Rossian diagnosis will say that there are moral reasons—shared by everyone—to prevent death, but there are also *additional* moral reasons—again shared by everyone—against killing. So long as we can understand what the difference is between preventing a death and not killing, we can make sense of the view that there are stronger reasons in favor of the latter than in favor of the former.

To deal with the same case, the consequentializer must say that for each person, it is worse if that person kills than if she merely lets die, other things being equal, because in addition to whatever is bad about deaths, there is something extra that is bad about killings. But now compare a case in which an agent faces a forced choice between killing and allowing another person to kill the same person. The proponent of the Rossian strategy who goes in for the doing/allowing distinction already has an explanation of why allowing the other person to kill is the preferable alternative, for the only reasons that she has postulated so far are the reason to prevent death and the reason not to kill, and the novel feature of this new case does not affect what is going on. But the consequentializer is forced to posit a new source of value. Just as she had to posit that there is something extra that is bad about killings, in order to accommodate the original case in which the badness of death contributed equally to evaluating both options, in this case she must posit that there is something extra that is bad about killings that prevent killings, in order to discriminate between the two options, whose effects are otherwise identical.

---

[10]   See my "Two Roles for Propositions: Cause for Divorce?" reprinted as ch. 3 of Schroeder (2015a).

[11]   Compare especially Shanklin (2011) and Finlay (2014). Some will quibble that 'good' modifies *states of affairs* rather than propositions. But although I think that this is not right, it is orthogonal to the point that I am making here. So in the main text I will continue to refer to propositions or, more neutrally, 'outcomes', without worrying about this.

[12]   Contrast Scheffler (1982).

There is nothing that prevents the consequentializer from saying this. In fact, there is an important and underappreciated result due to Graham Oddie and Peter Milne (1991) which shows that the consequentializer will *always* be able to pull this sort of trick, provided that she makes the right claims about what is better than what. But the full set of *claims* about what is better than what, that are required includes many that are implausible. Whereas her first suggestion is plausible—that in addition to the badness of death, there is something further that is bad about killings—her second suggestion, that in addition, there is something extra that is bad about killings that prevent killings, is not.[13]

Worse, even if the assumption that there is something extra that is bad about killings that prevent killings were plausible, it would be the wrong kind of explanation. The case in which you can prevent a killing by killing and the case in which you can prevent a death by killing are of a kind. It is preferable not to kill, in each case, for the very same reason. The consequentialist gets this wrong. Her explanation makes it look like a coincidence that not killing is preferable in each case—one that only follows because of a second, and independent, source of value. And this looks especially bad, because there are many, many other similar pairs of cases, all of which pattern in exactly the same way.

For example, an agent might face a choice between destroying someone's property or allowing it to be destroyed—for example, by an avalanche. Intuitively, it is preferable for her to allow it to be destroyed, and the consequentialist can say that there is something extra that is bad about acts of destroying property that is not bad about property getting destroyed. But the agent might instead face a choice between destroying someone's property or allowing a third party to destroy it, instead. Again, it is intuitively preferable for her to allow the destruction—whether the destruction is deliberate or natural should not matter. But now the consequentialist must appeal to a separate disvalue of destroying property that also prevents someone else from destroying it.

If the consequentialist somehow had an explanation of why we should expect that every time there is a disvalue to some outcome, and a further disvalue to acts of producing that outcome, there is yet a further disvalue to acts that produce the outcome in a way that prevents someone else from producing it, then she could resist the charge that this is a coincidence. This is not in itself a totally outlandish idea. As Tom Hurka (2001) has argued at length, it is plausible that there may be a number of recursive principles about intrinsic value—principles which tell us that given that it is better for one sort of thing to occur, it is better (or in some cases worse) for another, related, sort of thing to occur. Hurka does not himself consider recursive principles like the one that would be needed in this case, but we might

---

[13] For a different kind of worry about the unrestricted application of Oddie and Milne's result, see Nair (2014); for general discussion, see Carlson (1995).

take inspiration from Ralph Wedgwood (2009), who does endorse a similar kind of principle about what makes *acts* good.

Now, Wedgwood is not himself a consequentialist, so his principles are not intended as recursive principles about what makes one *outcome* better than another. But they do have the right sort of structure. His basic idea is that if an outcome makes an act good (or bad), then the more *agentially involved* the agent is, in the production of that outcome, the *more* good (or bad) it makes the act. So the idea is that since someone who allows a death is less agentially involved in the death than if she kills them directly, killings are worse than lettings-die. But though it is intuitively clear how there might be more agential involvement in a doing than in an allowing, there is no clear and independent sense of 'agential involvement' on which there is more agential involvement in a doing that prevents another doing, than in the doing that would have been prevented. This isn't a problem for Wedgwood, because he intends his principles only to explain the goodness of acts, not the goodness of outcomes. But it does mean that his approach can't really be borrowed to help the consequentialist. Since it is hard to see how to constructively guarantee that the right pattern of value claims must be true, therefore, I conclude that in addition to being implausible, the specific claims about value that the consequentialist needs in order to account for cases like these are also ad hoc and ptolemaesque.

So the fact that reasons are act-oriented while value is outcome-oriented—that reasons support properties, while 'good' is ascribed to propositions—makes competition between reasons a better diagnosis of the tradeoffs visible in complicated moral cases than competition among values. In order to defend something closer to the spirit of consequentialism, therefore, some have observed that the problem on which I have been focusing derives from the assumption that 'better' expresses a single ordering, on which each agent ought to do what would result in the consequences that would be best on that ordering. If, somehow, there were different orderings for each agent, then we wouldn't have gotten this problem. We could *mimic* the Rossian's appeal to properties, by appeal to separate orderings on propositions for each agent. Whereas the Rossian says that the reason not to kill is stronger than the reason to prevent death, the *agent-relative teleologist* says that for each person, it is worse-relative-to that person for her to kill than for her to fail to prevent death, other things being equal.[14]

Whether this move makes sense depends on what these agent-relative orderings of outcomes are, and whether they have anything to do with what is good and bad, on any independent sense of those terms. Fortunately, we *do* clearly have a use of 'good' and 'bad' on which they are relativized to agents, or at least, to subjects of some kind. To get a grip on it, compare the sentences, "it is better for

---

[14] Compare Sen (1983), Dreier (1993), Smith (2003), Louise (2004), and Portmore (2005) for classic sources.

him to be happy, than for him to be sad" and "it is better for him to be happy than to be sad".[15] In the former sentence, 'for' is syntactically a complementizer. Two propositions are being compared: that he is happy, and that he is sad. In the second sentence, in contrast, 'for' is syntactically a preposition. Again, two things are being compared—him being happy, and him being sad—but now they are being compared in a way that is explicitly relativized to him. When philosophers talk about what is *good for* someone, it is this latter use that they have in mind. When we talk about what is better *for* someone, we are still ranking propositions, but we are ranking them in different ways for different individuals. What is good for you may not be good for me, and conversely.

If the agent-relative teleologist is to cast her view in terms of *good for*, then what she needs to do is to claim that each person ought always to do what will have the outcome that is best for them.[16] This view has a traditional name in moral philosophy; it is called *egoism*. Egoism is an implausible way of accounting for our cases; it is not plausible that anyone's death is intrinsically bad for every other person, or that it is always intrinsically worse for one to be a killer than to be someone who let a death happen. So in general, proponents of agent-relative teleology are forced to say that the rankings in which they are interested are not expressed by claims like "it is better for Jack to be happy than to be sad", any more than they are expressed by claims like "it is better for Jack to be happy, than for Jack to be said". There is much, much more to be said about this topic, but it turns out that the best existing accounts of what they *could* mean by these rankings all appeal to reasons, and so reasons end up being more fundamentally explanatory, after all.[17]

Moreover, there is a deeper problem about appealing to agent-relative value in order to determine what agents ought to do in terms of an ordering of outcomes, rather than a ranking of acts. And that is because in order to avoid the conclusion that very different moral considerations govern the acts of different agents, the agent-relative teleologist must claim that at least with respect to all important moral considerations, there are strong *parallels* between what is good-relative-to each agent, and how good it is. For example, it must turn out that it is bad-relative-to every agent that she allows someone to die, and several times worse-relative-to her that she kills. But these parallels between what is good-relative-to each agent cry out for explanation. The best explanation is that they drop out of the fact that

[15]   Compare Finlay (2014).

[16]   See Schroeder (2007) for discussion. Note that Hurka (2003, 2015) disagrees; he believes that agent-relative value *is* the ordinary concept expressed by natural language talk about what is good for someone. Hurka's grounds for this claim are that the analyzes of *good for* that were offered by Sidgwick, Ewing, and others resemble the analyzes favored by contemporaries for agent-relative value.

[17]   See especially Smith (2003), Portmore (2011), and Suikkanen (2011). All of these views, of course, still count in some sense as 'consequentialist' in the sense that they explain what someone ought to do in terms of the value of consequences rather than directly in terms of reasons, but they are not alternatives to the ultimate explanation of what they ought to do in terms of reasons.

what we are really ranking are *properties*.[18] We can *say* that it is good-relative to an agent that she has some property, but that goes hand-in-hand with the claim that it is good-relative-to another agent that she has the same property precisely because both fall out as trivial consequences of the fact that the first property is more highly ranked than the second. So again, we are led back to the conclusion that what we are fundamentally ranking and comparing against one another, when we are considering what an agent ought to do, are properties of agents.

In this section I've been arguing that Ross's diagnosis of the tradeoffs involved in complicated moral cases is to be preferred to Sidgwick's—even if we strip Sidgwick's utilitarianism down to its barest consequentialist bones. Both diagnoses allow us to see complicated cases as involving genuine tradeoffs, but the consequentialist, outcome-oriented, conception of those tradeoffs conceptualized them in the wrong, propositionally oriented, way, and this forces her to draw too strong a connection between the tradeoffs that one agent faces, and those faced by another. So insofar as there is something compelling about capturing the force of the tradeoffs as the result of a kind of competition, I conclude that must be a competition among *reasons*.

2.3 Acting for Reasons

In Section 2.1 I claimed that reasons are important because they admit of competition, and in Section 2.2, I argued that reasons are act-oriented, rather than outcome-oriented, which I took to mean that they count in favor of possible *properties* of agents—things that agents can do, in a very broad sense of 'do'. It is because reasons are act-oriented competitors that reasons have such attractive explanatory power to ground deep generalizations about what we ought to do. To these two features of reasons—that they are act-oriented, and that they compete—I will add one more. In at least normal cases, reasons can be *acted on*. At least sometimes, we do things *for* reasons—and it matters which reasons we do them for.

What does it mean to say that we do things for reasons? It means *at least* this: sometimes, we do not just act, but we act *for reasons*. Moral philosophers have a special term for talk about the reasons for which we act—*motivating* reasons.[19] But following Michael Smith (1994), many philosophers who introduce the term 'motivating reasons' use it to distinguish and contrast motivating reasons from reasons in the sense of considerations that count in favor of outcomes or compete with one another in determining what someone ought to do—so-called 'normative' reasons. So when I say that reasons compete and also can be acted on, I could easily be misunderstood as meaning that there is no distinction between

---

[18] Compare Dreier (2011), Milona and Schroeder (2019).
[19] See especially Smith (1994) and Dancy (2000).

motivating reasons and normative reasons. But I do not mean this. When I say that reasons can be acted on, I mean *more* than that we sometimes act for reasons. I mean that when we act for reasons (in the sense of motivating reasons), we at least sometimes count as acting *on the basis of* the very considerations that count in favor of things we can do, and thereby compete in the determination of what we ought to do. And in at least all normal cases,[20] when there is an act-oriented consideration that figures in the competition determining what someone ought to do, it is the sort of thing that could, at least in principle, be the basis on which she acts.

But it is important to be clear on what it amounts to, to say that a consideration that counts in favor is the basis on which you act. In *Practical Reality*, Jonathan Dancy argued for the importance of being able to act for normative reasons. He concluded that there cannot be any ontological distinction between normative reasons and motivating reasons. On this view, what makes you count as acting for a normative reason is—at least in part—that the motivating reason for which you act is *identical* to that normative reason for you to act.[21] Moreover, he held that we could infer a lot about the ontology of motivating reasons, given that they are both things that count in favor and also things on which we can act—he held that it follows from this that they must be states of affairs.[22] Similarly, in *Slaves of the Passions*, I also held that since we can act on normative reasons, at least sometimes our normative reasons must be literally identical to our motivating reasons. Like Dancy, I took this to have consequences for the ontology of motivating reasons, which I argued can be identified with *propositions*. And Nathan Howard (2019, forthcoming) takes this reasoning in reverse, arguing that we can get evidence about the ontology of *normative* reasons from the fact that our normative reasons can also be identical to our motivating reasons.

---

[20] Excepting cases of elusive reasons like that of the surprise party (Schroeder (2007, ch. 2)).

[21] Sylvan and Lord (unpublished) discuss important reasons why the "at least in part" qualification is important.

[22] Dancy has an argument that reasons must be states of affairs, rather than propositions, but it is fallacious in the same way as the argument that desire cannot be a propositional attitude, because you don't want propositions (compare Brewer (2006, 2009), Thagard (2006)). In the case of desire, 'desire' and 'want' can be followed by a determiner phrase, a complementizer phrase, or a non-finite clause, and the thesis that desire is a propositional attitude is the thesis that the others are to be understood in terms of complementizer-desire ascriptions. So to describe this as the view that what you want is a proposition is to recast it in terms of a determiner phrase (DP) desire ascription. And according to the theory, to want DP is always to want to bear some specific, contextually relevant relation to DP. So in particular, to want a proposition is to want *to have* a proposition or *to hold* a proposition. So *even according to the view that desire is a propositional attitude*, it is not accurate to say that what you really want, are propositions. Similarly, "X's reason is" can be followed by either a determiner phrase or a complementizer phrase. The view that reasons are propositions is the view that such DP reason ascriptions must be interpreted as complementizer-phrase reason ascriptions. So "his reason is the proposition that P" has to be interpreted as "his reason is *that he believes that P*" or "his reason is *that it is true that P*". So even according to the view that reasons are propositions, it is not accurate to say that someone's reason is a proposition.

I do not deny this earlier view, but nothing that I say in this book will depend on it. What is important for my purposes is not the ontology either of normative reasons or of motivating reasons, but simply the fact that at least sometimes, there is a *close enough relationship* between one's motivating reason—the reason for which one acts—and an act-oriented competitor, that one can count as acting *on the basis* of that act-oriented competitor. This close relationship could consist in or involve identity of normative and motivating reasons, or it could be some weaker relationship. What is important is that we must be able to make sense of it, because it often *matters* whether the reasons for which one acts are related to the considerations that count in favor of acting in the right way.

In the opening passages of the *Groundwork for the Metaphysics of Morals* (2002), Kant gives the most famous illustration of why it matters whether the reasons for which we act correspond in the right way to the features that make an act right. A shopkeeper is morally required not to cheat his customers, and Kant imagines a prudent shopkeeper who never does cheat his customers—and so who always acts rightly. But the shopkeeper Kant describes avoids cheating his customers only because he worries about the bad long-term effects that it would have on his business. If not for that fear, he would readily cheat his customers for an extra buck. Kant's shopkeeper does what he ought to do, but he does not act well. The difference between Kant's shopkeeper and someone who does act well lies in their *motive*—Kant's shopkeeper does the right thing but only for coincidental reasons. Someone who acts well acts for the *right* reasons.[23]

The relationship between what grounds the normative status of an action and the basis on which someone acts is also important for assessment of the *rationality* of actions. Just as Kant imagines a shopkeeper who does the right thing but for the wrong reasons, we can easily imagine someone who acts in the way that it is rational for her to act, but for reasons that are only coincidentally related to what makes it rational. For example, in the version of Poker known as Texas Hold 'Em, it is not generally rational to match aggressive early bets if one has been dealt mismatched low cards of different suits. Karl is playing Texas Hold 'Em, and has been dealt the three of spades and the six of hearts, and other players around the table are raising the stakes. Karl makes all of his decisions about whether to bet or fold on the basis of whether the number of other players who have taken sips of their drinks since the round began is even or odd, and on this basis, he folds. He does the rational thing, but he does not act rationally. And this is because the reason for which he acts and the features that ground the rationality of his action are not connected in the right way.

---

[23]   See especially Markovits (2010) for a lucid and rich treatment of this issue. Also Hills (2009) and Arpaly and Schroeder (2014) for some of its important upshots. We will return to this topic in depth in Chapter 10.

In epistemology, the corresponding contrast is called the distinction between *propositional* and *doxastic* justification.[24] A belief can be propositionally justified without being doxastically justified, if the agent has a justification to believe it, and believes it, but for reasons other than those that make it a justified thing to believe. The terms 'propositional' and 'doxastic' are unfortunately insufficiently general to cover the case of actions that are rational things to do and of cases in which someone acts rationally, unfortunately, since actions don't have propositional objects and are not doxastic states. But these are just names, within epistemology, for a distinction that is much broader than epistemology. And it is important for this distinction what the *basis* of one's action or belief is.

So far in this section, I've been noting that there is sometimes the right sort of correspondence between the motivating reasons for which one acts and the considerations that compete in the determination of what one ought to do—and arguing that this correspondence plays an important role in whether agents act well, whether they act rationally, and whether their beliefs are doxastically justified. So it is *important* whether the reason for which someone believes is related in the right way to reasons in the normative sense in which we are interested—act-oriented considerations that compete in the determination of what someone ought to do. Two further observations are important to make, before moving on.

The first important observation is that nothing follows from the foregoing considerations about whether it is *always* possible to act for a normative reason—even in principle. At most, what I have been arguing is that sometimes when we act, the reasons for which we act correspond closely enough to the normative reasons for us to act, that we count as acting on the basis of those normative reasons. And in fact, I think that in normal cases, it is at least in principle possible to act on the basis of a normative reason. Some philosophers believe that it must *always* be possible to act on the basis of a reason—of the two roles which reasons play, of competing in the determination of what we ought to do, and of being considerations on the basis of which we can act, they privilege the latter, basis, role.[25]

But I think that this is a mistake. As I argued in *Slaves of the Passions*, there are some reasons on which it is impossible to act, because they are elusive—they disappear once the subject knows enough in order to be able to act on them, or if the subject does actually try to act on them. The case of the surprise party is like this. Nate loves successful surprise parties—especially those thrown in his honor—but hates unsuccessful surprise parties, especially when thrown for him. The fact that there is a hitherto-unexpected surprise party awaiting him in the next room is a reason for him to go into the next room—it counts in favor of his

---

[24] Compare Firth (1978), Swain (1979, 25), Conee (1980), Alston (1985, 190), Pollock and Cruz (1999, 35), and Feldman (2002, 46); and for a contrasting view about the relationship between propositional and doxastic justification, Turri (2010b).
[25] See, in particular, Setiya (2014), Way (2017), Gregory (2016), Silverstein (2016, 2017), and Asarnow (2017).

going into the next room, and competes against contrary considerations such as that he only has an hour until an important deadline. But it is not a reason that he can act on, because it goes away once he knows about it.[26]

Whether or not you are comfortable using the word 'reason' to describe the consideration that counts in favor of Nate going into the next room, this case shows that features that help to make it the case that Nate ought to go into the next room and features on the basis of which he could go into the next room must come apart. If we follow Setiya, Way, Silverstein, and others in treating 'reason' as going with the latter role, then some of the competing factors that help to determine what we ought to do are not reasons. But there still need to be such factors, because there is still a fact of the matter about whether Nate ought to go into the next room, and it depends, *inter alia*, on whether there is a hitherto unsuspected surprise party awaiting him.

Skeptics about surprise party cases might push back. The most germane way of doing so is to deny that whether Nate ought to go into the next room depends after all on whether there is a hitherto unexpected surprise part awaiting him. To say that it does is to say that 'ought' is *objective* or what is sometimes called 'fact-relative'. But some philosophers argue that in order to be practical, what someone ought to do must depend only on her own mental states or only on her own evidence or perhaps only on what she is in a position to know. Kiesewetter (2016), for example, defends the view that Nate ought to do something only if it is permissible for Nate to believe that he ought to do it—a general principle that leads to denying not only that the surprise party is a reason for Nate in any ordinary sense, but also that it helps to determine what Nate ought to do.

Although this is I think the most interesting and forceful way of pushing back against the surprise party cases, I also think that it is based on a mistake about the practical import of claims about what we ought to do. It may well be that it is rational for Nate to do something only if it is rationally permissible for him to believe that he ought to do it. But what Nate should or ought to do and what it is rational for him to do are simply two different things. It makes perfect sense for Nate to miss out on the surprise party, find out about it later, and exclaim, "shoot—I should have checked out the living room", despite conceding that it would not have been rational for him to have done so. So if Nate's evidence or information matters when he asks himself the question "what ought I to do?" or "what ought I to have done?", it is the information that he has as the asker of this question, not the information that he has as its subject.[27] I conclude that we can't explain competition-allowing act-oriented factors in terms of considerations that can be acted on.

---

[26] Contrast Sinclair (2016).
[27] For further discussion of this contrast, see Schroeder (2018a) and especially Schroeder (ms).

But we *can* explain considerations that can be acted on in terms of competition-allowing act-oriented factors. In general, the default is that all reasons can be acted on, and the exceptions can all be explained as in the surprise party case—the only reason why it is not possible to act on them is that they are too fragile—they do not survive being acted on. In general, cases in which we find that there is a counterfactual condition that holds over a very wide range of cases but fails in very special, carefully engineered, cases, are familiar from the phenomenon known as the *conditional fallacy*.[28] The correct lesson, in typical cases of the conditional fallacy, is that there is a categorical feature that grounds the counterfactual, but which is counterfactually fragile in some carefully constructed cases. In this case, that categorical feature is that there is a normative reason for Nate to go into the next room. In general, normative reasons ground the possibility of action, but this one simply happens to be counterfactually fragile—knowing what it takes to act on it makes the reason go away.

Since no view on which it must be possible to act on reasons can explain the full range of cases in which reasons count in favor and compete in the determination of what someone ought to do, but the view on which reasons primarily count in favor and compete can explain why reasons fail to be actionable in the cases in which they are not actionable, I infer that it is the role of reasons in the competitive determination of what agents ought to do that is central, and their role in action that is derivative. But I have no objection to those who think that talk about reasons in ordinary language is restricted to considerations that are actionable or which can play a role in good reasoning—proponents of such views may interpret me as using the word 'reason' in a specialized sense, for something for which they must have some other name.

This leaves us with one more important observation to make before moving on. And it is that once we grant the importance of acting for normative reasons, we lay the basis for a new argument that reasons are prior to, as well as explanatory of, what we ought to do. This point is important, because one way in which someone might superficially grant that reasons are explanatory of what we ought to do, is by holding, as does John Broome (2004), that reasons just *are* the things that explain what we ought to do. On Broome's view, reasons do explain what we ought to do, but they are not analytically prior. So they do not come first. Another way of putting this point that does not depend on my identifying *Reasons First* with a claim about analytic priority is that on this view, *reasons* explain what we ought to do, but *facts about what is a reason* do not.

But the importance of acting for normative reasons forces us to draw a distinction among factors that explain what we ought to do. Acting for a normative reason requires being sensitive to it in some way. But acting well does not

---

[28] Shope (1978).

require being sensitive to *everything* that explains what you ought to do. For example, it may be that you ought to smile at Ken because it would make him happy, and that what explains why it would make him happy is some fact about his neurophysiology. So the fact about Ken's neurophysiology explains why you ought to smile at him. But you do not have to be sensitive to facts about Ken's neurophysiology in order to act well—even though you *do* have to be sensitive to what would make him happy. So not just anything that figures in an explanation of what you ought to do is relevant for whether you are acting on the right reasons.

The view that reasons are analytically, as well as explanatorily, prior to *ought* can easily explain why this is so. On this view, reasons are not just anything that explain what you ought to do; instead, they count as explaining what you ought to do by virtue of the fact that what you ought to do simply *consists in* the outcome of the competition among reasons. So this view allows for a relationship between reasons and explanations of what you ought to do without being pushed toward collapsing a distinction between reasons and explanations of reasons. It makes sense of why it is that not everything that explains why something is a reason is itself a reason.[29] In contrast to the *classical* motivation for Reasons First that derives from the Rossian strategy, we might call this the *fundamental* motivation for Reasons First, and I'll have much more to say about it, and about why we should reject Broome's contrary picture, in Chapters 10 and 11.

2.4 A Further Grip on Reasons?

So far, in this chapter, I have been arguing that the best theories of what we ought to do will see it as the result of a competition among different factors, where those factors are act-oriented, or associated with the support of *properties* that agents might have, rather than outcome-oriented, and where, at least in normal cases, these factors can correspond closely enough to the motivating reasons for which someone acts to count as being the *basis* on which she acts. These three marks— competition, act-orientation, and acting for—are what I will take to be the distinguishing marks of reasons. They are the features that allow reasons to play their potentially powerful role in explanatory moral theory (and, I will argue, in epistemology),[30] and together they exhaust the characteristic features of reasons that I will take for granted in this book.

---

[29] This is what in *Slaves of the Passions* (2007, ch. 2) I called the "No Background Conditions" view.

[30] Daniel Fogal (2016) argues that the mass noun use of 'reason' is prior to and explanatory of count noun uses. I have been throughout using 'reason' in its count noun use. But so long as we can make sense of what it is to act for some reason and not for other reason (used as a mass noun), I don't think that my characterization in this chapter rules Fogal's mass relation out. But the choice between mass and count candidates for the fundamental reason relation can still affect other issues raised in this book—particularly in Part II. I'll continue to use 'reason' as a count noun but will return to this in Chapter 3.

In particular, I will not be assuming any particular ontology of reasons—for example, whether reasons are considerations,[31] facts or states of affairs,[32] propositions,[33] predicates,[34] mental states,[35] proposition-objective pairs,[36] or otherwise. Nor will I assume that objective and subjective reasons have the same ontology. All that I will need is the assumption that whatever reasons are, they can be attributed or characterized by citing an appropriately associated proposition. For example, if one reason to study epistemology is its parallels with ethics, then we can cite this by saying that one reason to study epistemology is *that epistemology has parallels with ethics*. And if your obsessive-compulsive disorder is a reason to trust the thoroughness of your copyediting, then we can cite this by saying that one reason to trust the thoroughness of your copyediting is *that you have OCD*.

Similarly, although I will be interested throughout in uses of 'reason' as a count noun, and will in general formulate my discussion in this way, I intend to be neutral in principle regarding Daniel Fogal's (2016) provocative arguments that 'reason' when used as a mass noun (as in 'there is reason to') expresses a relation that is prior to and explanatory of 'reason' in its count noun use. I will try to comment where possible complications arise later, particularly in Chapter 3.

Notice also that I have picked out reasons by their role, rather than by reference to the meaning of the word 'reason'. This is important. It does matter, for my purposes in this book, that we can talk about what I have in mind by reasons, by using the word 'reason', and that this is not a matter of pure stipulation. I would be more than happy to stipulate a word for the act-oriented factors that compete with one another in the determination of what we ought to do and can be acted on, but if I were to do so, I could not ever rely on the intuitive force of claims about these factors. Indeed, if my term were a matter of stipulation, it would be misleading to use a word that has familiar uses with respect to similar topics, because that would encourage the sense that I have something non-stipulative in mind. And I must admit that I *will* sometimes be relying on the intuitive force of some claims that I make about reasons. I will be assuming, therefore, that we *can* make claims about the act-oriented factors that compete in the determination of what we ought to do and can be acted on using the word 'reason'.

It does *not* matter for my purposes, however, what the exact relationship is between the claims that I wish to make and the semantics and pragmatics of the word, 'reason'. It could be, at least in principle, that there is a special, distinct, linguistic meaning of the word 'reason' on which its semantic value is precisely the fundamental normative relation in which I am interested. But I do not need this to be so. I only need it to be the case that reasonable and informed speakers like us can succeed at making claims about the relation in which I am interested by using the word 'reason', together with clues about context and pragmatic factors.

---

[31] Scanlon (1998).   [32] Dancy (2000).   [33] Schroeder (2007).   [34] Nagel (1970).
[35] Davidson (1963).   [36] Howard (forthcoming).

For example, Justin Snedegar (2013) discusses a view he calls 'shallow contrastivism', according to which 'reason' semantically expresses a relation, one of whose relata is a set of alternatives.[37] The fact that R is a reason to do A out of C, according to this view, just in case the fact that R counts in favor of A more than it counts in favor of any other alternative in C. This view is a kind of *contrastivism*, because it claims that 'reason' claims are all relative to a set of alternatives. But it counts as *shallow*, in Snedegar's terms, because it defines this contrastivist relation in terms of a non-contrastive notion of *counting in favor*. If shallow contrastivism is right, then the reason relation and the counting in favor of relation are distinct, and so Scanlon's (1998) identification of being a reason with counting in favor is a mistake. Still, it is an intelligible mistake. To see it, you have to focus on the assessment of claims about what someone has a reason to do out of sets of alternatives that are less than exhaustive, and Scanlon was not interested in such claims.

If shallow contrastivism is true, then all of the relevant competition between act-oriented factors happens because of the way in which considerations *count in favor* of actions, and so they might more accurately be called *favorers*, than *reasons*, if we are to be pedantic. But still, if shallow contrastivism is true, there is no puzzle about how we could have managed to talk about the favoring relation by using the word 'reason', even though semantically speaking, the word 'reason' picks out a relation that is contrastive and the favoring relation is non-contrastive. This is because according to shallow contrastivism, the relation strictly semantically expressed by 'reason' is defined in terms of the favoring relation. So whenever we make claims about 'reasons', we *are*, in turn, making claims about favoring. I will not be taking any stand on whether shallow contrastivism is true or false, though Snedegar offers a very interesting argument that it is true. If it is true, then by 'reason' throughout, I mean *favorer*. It will not matter for my purposes whether the fundamental reason relation is directly expressed by the word 'reason', or only something that we successfully manage, in context, to talk about using the word 'reason'.

Indeed, even setting aside substantive views like shallow contrastivism, there is a variety of reasons to doubt that there is a privileged meaning of 'reason' that semantically picks out exactly what I have in mind. Most importantly, we saw already in Chapter 1 that reasons admit of an objective/subjective distinction. It is highly controversial how objective and subjective reasons are related to one another—we will actually devote a full chapter to this question in Chapter 4. But it is clear that when we use the word 'reason' in each of these cases, we are interested in making different claims—at least one of which can be true, without the other.

Philosophers would once have said that this shows that there are at least two *senses* of 'reason'—meaning by this that there are two readings of sentences

---

[37] Snedegar actually endorses a stronger form of contrastivism, particularly in Snedegar (2014, 2017).

involving the word 'reason' that we must take methodological care to distinguish when we are talking about reasons. But this way of talking is misleading.[38] When we talk about whether Alex is ready, we need to take care to distinguish whether we are talking about whether she is ready to roll, or whether she is ready to rumble. If we are interested in both of these, the sentence "Alex is ready" admits of multiple readings—multiple claims which we could be understood to be making by it. If this is all that we mean by saying that 'ready' has multiple 'senses', then 'ready' has multiple senses.

But this is a misleading way of speaking, because these two readings of 'ready' arise from a single underlying linguistic meaning, together with different interpretations of something that is ellipsed or supplied as a contextual parameter: what Alex is ready to do. That is why "there is something that Alex is ready to do" follows univocally from each of these readings of "Alex is ready". The mere fact that 'reason' talk admits of both objective and subjective readings does not tell us whether this comes from genuine semantic ambiguity or from a missing contextual parameter.[39] I do not know which of these views is correct, and I will not take a stand on it. But if the subjective and objective readings of 'reason' talk result from context filling in some parameter, then strictly speaking the semantic value of 'reason' must be *neither* the objective nor subjective 'reason' relation, but rather some more fundamental relation which, by filling in different parameters, results in the subjective or objective reason relation.

In addition to objective and subjective claims about 'reasons', philosophers often distinguish two other important 'senses' of 'reason'—that is, two other importantly different kinds of claims that we often make using the word 'reason' as a count noun, even setting aside its use as a verb and as a name for the faculty of rational cognition. The first of these important topics—which has again already come up—is that of *motivating* reasons. If you ask why Elise did something, and I tell you that she did it in order to impress her friend, or that she did it because she believed that it would impress her friend, I have told you something about her reasons, but the claims that I have made are not exactly the same as any claims that I might make about her objective or subjective reasons. Objective and subjective reason claims can both be true even if someone does not do what they have a reason to do, but motivating reason claims cannot. Conversely, motivating reason claims can be true even if someone is mistaken about the relevant facts,[40] but only truths can be objective reasons.

Finally, philosophers often distinguish *explanatory* reason claims from each of the others. For example, if you say that the reason why primates evolved trichromatic vision was that it made it easier to distinguish yellow and orange-colored

---

[38] See Henning (2014).   [39] Compare Henning (2014), Weaver and Scharp (2019).
[40] In Chapter 4 we will see that this claim is controversial, but I will defend it there.

fruit in a green forested environment,[41] then you are making an explanatory reason claim. It is easy to see how explanatory reason claims are distinct from objective and subjective reason claims, but it is also important to distinguish them from motivating reason claims, since motivating reason claims also appear to be interested in explaining something that happened. To see why they must still be distinguished, note that it is possible to make explanatory reason claims about why someone did something that are not motivating reason claims. For example, if it satisfies you when I tell you that the reason why Garrett released his travel logs was that he was manipulated into doing so by Francis, then you are interested in explanatory reasons; but if you care about his motivating reasons, then this explanation will not satisfy you. You will need to hear, instead, that he did so in order to clear his name. So an explanatory reason claim can be true without the corresponding motivating reason claim being true. It is not clear, however, that they can come apart in the other direction, and so it is natural to suppose that motivating reason claims are a special case of explanatory reason claims—either where we have a special kind of explanation in mind, or are trying to explain not just why an event occurred, but why it counted as an action.

So even as a count noun, 'reason' is used in at least four different ways—ways which allow us to make claims whose truth-conditions cross-cut one another in the ways I've indicated above. This could be a matter of context-dependence, if there is some way of understanding the univocal semantic value of 'reason' on which the rest of these differences can be derived from differences in a contextual parameter. Or it could be a matter of polysemy; with related meanings clustering around a single word. Or it could be a combination, with one linguistic meaning underlying objective and subjective reason talk, and another underlying motivating and explanatory reason talk, and the two of them clustered together because of similarity or a relationship between their meanings.

What matters for us is that we *do* talk about these importantly different things using the word 'reason', and that at each point, it will be important to keep in mind which we are endeavoring to communicate about. Explanatory reasons are not act-oriented factors that compete in the determination of what we ought to do; they are not reasons in the sense that is important for moral philosophy or the theory of the normative. Later in this book, motivating reasons will turn out to be important for understanding some central normative concepts, including knowledge, and so I will have more to say about them. But motivating reasons are not act-oriented factors that compete in the determination of what we ought to do, either. So the role which suits reasons to be so central in moral philosophy, and as I am about to argue for normative inquiry more generally, applies, at most, to objective and subjective reasons. Indeed, according to nothing that I have said so

---

[41] See for example Regan et al. (2001).

far, does it discriminate between them in any way. So the thesis of *Reasons First*, as I will understand it for purposes of this book, does not tell us which, if either, of these two relations comes first.[42] It is, rather, the thesis that together, they have explanatory and analytic priority over all other normative concepts.

2.5 Extending the Thesis: Apt, Good, Admirable

So far in this chapter, I have explained how two of the central features of reasons— that they *compete*, and that they are *act-oriented*—contribute to the classical explanation of why the explanatory and analytic priority of reasons to facts about what we ought to do is so theoretically well-motivated in moral philosophy. And I have argued that reasons have one more important feature that we must keep in mind—that in normal cases, they can be the basis on which we act—which lies at the heart of a further, *fundamental*, motivation for Reasons First. These theoretical motivations to put reasons at the center of normative ethical theorizing about what we ought to do, do not turn on judgments about the word 'reason' or on any background assumptions about the semantic value of 'reason'. So they do not show anything so strong as that the relation semantically expressed by 'reason' is central in ethics. But to the extent that we do naturally and successfully use the word 'reason' to make claims that compete against one another, weighing reasons on each side, and to the extent that when we make such claims we are counting considerations in favor of actions, we are making claims about something that competes, is act-oriented, and for which we can act. That is why it is appropriate to call this a thesis about reasons, and that is the basis on which I will do so.

But as we will now see, the very same sorts of considerations that make it look like facts about what we ought to do are best explained by the interaction of competing act-oriented considerations for which we can act apply just as well to other normative properties and relations too. So if appealing to reasons in order to explain what we ought to do is a good idea at all, it is likely to be a good idea across the board—including in epistemology.

Let's take value first. By 'value', I mean what we are talking about when we say that something is good, good for someone, or a good thing of its kind, as well as, more generally, claims to the effect that it is 'of value' or 'valuable', and the like. There is a venerable tradition in moral philosophy of associating the claim that something is valuable, and the claim that it is good.[43] There is much merit in this

---

[42] Note that this contrasts with the view that I took in *Slaves of the Passions* (Schroeder 2007), where I held that objective reasons are analytically prior to subjective reasons. For the record, I am now inclined to the view that neither is prior to the other, but they share a common core. But nothing in this book will turn on this claim. Whether objective or subjective reasons come first or instead they share a common core is an issue for proponents of the thesis of reasons first to hash out among themselves.

[43] Compare Mill (1861) on 'good' and 'desirable'.

association; if it would be good for Jack to assist Jill, then there is value in Jack's assisting Jill, and so it would be valuable for Jack to assist Jill. Conversely, if it would be valuable for Jack to assist Jill, then his assisting her must be a good thing, and it must be good for him to do it.

But 'valuable' belongs to a large class of expressions that combine verbs for attitudes or actions with normative suffixes. Other members of this class include 'laudable', 'admirable', 'praiseworthy', and 'contemptible'. It is most natural to analyze the properties picked out by this class of normative adjectives as composed in the way that we should expect, given the composition of these terms—as picking out some attitude or action, and saying that that attitude or action is *apt* or *merited* by the thing in question.[44] For example, to say that Elsa is admirable is to say that she merits admiration, or that it is apt to admire her. Similarly, to say that Hans is contemptible is to say that he merits contempt, or that it is apt to have contempt for him. By similar reasoning, to say that it would be valuable for Jack to assist Jill is to say that the prospect of Jack's assisting Jill merits valuing, or that it is apt to value it. If 'good' patterns with 'valuable', therefore, we should understand being good as meriting being valued. This is what is held by *fitting attitudes* theories of value.[45]

Some have claimed that *apt* or *fitting* is the basic normative concept.[46] But it is just as difficult to formulate exceptionless sufficient conditions for aptness, as for what we ought to do. Someone may be intelligent, charming, and witty, for example, without it being apt to admire them, for they could also be selfish and cruel. Someone else may be admirable *despite* being selfish and cruel, but if it is in virtue of their charm, they must be *more* charming to make up for their selfishness, in order to merit admiration. So it is most natural to see the aptness of admiration as the result of the interaction of competing considerations, which count in favor or against admiring someone.[47] Similar remarks go for the aptness of contempt, of fear, or of blame. So it is most promising to see aptness in general as the result of the interaction of competing factors.[48]

Moreover, the factors which must balance in order to determine whether admiration or fear is apt must be act-oriented, rather than outcome-oriented. If Wolfgang's keyboard skills count in favor of admiring him, they do so by counting in favor of a property—*admiring Wolfgang*—not propositions, such as that Liz admires Wolfgang, or that Karl admires Wolfgang. This explains why convincing someone else to admire Wolfgang is just not as good a way of responding to these

---

[44] Contrast Sosa's (2011) use of 'apt', which is quite different than this one—see discussion in Chapter 10.

[45] See Schroeder (2010).

[46] Compare Brentano (1889), Ewing (1948), McHugh and Way (2016).

[47] Notably contra Maguire (2018), whose arguments are helpfully rebutted in Faraci (2020).

[48] Rabinowicz and Rønnow-Rasmussen (2004) explore issues that come up once we try to explain fittingness in terms of reasons.

considerations as admiring Wolfgang yourself. So, aptness is determined by the competition of act-oriented factors—*reasons*.

And we can admire *for* these reasons. You can admire Wolfgang for his keyboard skills, and if his keyboard skills are what make him admirable, then you may not just be admiring someone who it is apt to admire, but admiring *well*. If you admire him instead because his grandfather was a bookbinder or because his great-grandfather was a mason,[49] then even though you are admiring someone it is apt to admire, your admiration itself is not well-grounded. So not only can we admire for the features that make people admirable, but it matters whether or not we do.

I conclude that the same considerations that support taking reasons to be prior to and explanatory of what we ought to do support taking reasons to be prior to and explanatory of which attitudes are apt—including admiration, desire, fear, and valuing. So if what outcome is good is a matter of what outcome it is apt to value, reasons are prior to and explanatory of what is good, as well. Reasoning like this generalizes, I tentatively suggest, to provide at least some support for the conclusion that reasons come first among the normative, full-stop.

---

[49] Johann Georg Mozart, the father of Leopold Mozart, was a bookbinder, and *his* father, Franz, was a master mason.

PART II

RATIONALITY AND TRUTH

Friction spinning is an 'open-end' or 'core-type' form of spinning (or both), in which the yarn formation takes place with the aid of frictional force in the spinning zone. Friction-spun yarns are characterized by a distinct wrapper surface.

Ishtiaque, Salhotra, and Gowda (2003)

3

Basic Perceptual Reasons

3.1 Taking Stock

Recall that the project of the book is to explore what we might learn from the continuities between epistemology and other normative disciplines, with special focus on the thesis of *Reasons First*, which has had more appeal in moral philosophy than in epistemology. To establish our Core Hypothesis, we must show that our understanding of substantive issues within epistemology has been substantially shaped (distorted, as I will continue to say) by a neglect to pay close attention to the parallels between epistemology and moral philosophy. And to vindicate Reasons First, we will have to show that the less distorted perspective that paying close attention to the parallels between epistemology and moral philosophy enables leads to a picture that is consistent with Reasons First.

More specifically, I argued in Chapter 1 that there are at least two prominent reasons *why* the thesis of Reasons First has been less prominent or widely accepted in epistemology, deriving from problems it faces that are distinctive to, or at least especially hard in the context of, epistemology. The plan for the book is to argue that each of these problems for Reasons First is related to an independent and more general problem in epistemology. Solving each problem in a way that is consistent with Reasons First, I will be arguing, opens up appealingly simple but dramatically different options within epistemology for understanding the way in which perceptual experiences justify beliefs and the way in which evidence bears on the rationality of belief—options which, I claim, have been essentially invisible. Adopting the perspective on which epistemology is continuous with other areas of normative inquiry, I will be arguing, has the benefit of helping us to see these previously invisible options, so that they can be evaluated and accepted or rejected on their own merits, rather than because they are invisible, thus vindicating our Core Hypothesis. The previously invisible option, I will argue, will also vindicate Reasons First.

The two distinctively epistemological problems for Reasons First, recall, were the problem of unjustified belief and the problem of sufficiency. My task in Part II of the book, in this and Chapters 4 and 5, is to pursue the dialectic that I have just described for the case of the problem of unjustified belief, and in Part III I will turn to the analogous task for the problem of sufficiency. So the tasks for the chapters in this part of the book are to articulate a general problem in epistemology; to spell out a view that offers an attractive answer to this problem but has seemingly been

Reasons First. Mark Schroeder, Oxford University Press (2021). © Mark Schroeder.
DOI: 10.1093/oso/9780198868224.003.0003

invisible; to diagnose the seeming invisibility of this view as at least partly attributable to the dialectic surrounding the problem of unjustified belief; and to offer a way forward that allows us a different solution to the problem of unjustified belief—one that is consistent with the thesis of Reasons First.

My strategy will be to break these tasks down as follows. This chapter will lay out the general problem for epistemology with which I will be concerned, which is a problem about how perception can provide us with a privileged source of evidence about the external world. I will be arguing, following but expanding on important observations by both John McDowell and Timothy Williamson, that the available options for how to understand how perceptual experiences can provide evidence for our beliefs are all unsatisfactory in familiar ways (Sections 3.2, 3.3, 3.4). Having established what I think is so deeply unsatisfactory about the available options, I will show how the available options turn on a false forced choice—for there is an alternative, generally invisible, option that has all of the advantages of each of two of its competitors, but without any of their distinctive costs. And then I will show that what forces this choice is the idea that reasons must be appropriately associated with *truths*—in a slogan, that *only truths can rationalize*. So if we can get over the idea that reasons must be associated with truths in this way, the theoretical options for understanding how perceptual experiences justify become much more attractive (Section 3.5).

In Chapter 4, I will take up the question of whether reasons—in particular, subjective reasons—must be associated with truths. After clarifying the important theoretical role for subjective reasons given the thesis of Reasons First, I will turn to the reasons why philosophers have assumed that they must be (Sections 4.1, 4.2). The best of these, I will argue, derives from the problem of unjustified belief (Section 4.3). To address it, we need a way of explaining the phenomena that underlie the problem of unjustified belief without building justification or something stronger into what it takes to have a subjective reason. And this, as it turns out, is also what we need to solve the problem of unjustified belief in a way that is consistent with Reasons First. Borrowing ideas from Jeff Horty, I will outline a simple model for how subjective reasons combine that allows unjustified beliefs as inputs without incurring the problem of unjustified belief (Sections 4.4, 4.5).

If the arguments of Chapters 3 and 4 are on the right track, then it is intelligible to think that subjective reasons need not be or involve cognitive access to truths (Chapter 4), and hence possible to occupy an attractive and otherwise unavailable space in accounting for basic perceptual reasons (Chapter 3). On such a view, basic perceptual reasons are *world-implicating* but *non-factive*. But not every non-factive, world-implicating account of basic perceptual reasons is viable. In Chapter 5 I will explain why not, and defend the commitments of my preferred treatment of basic perceptual reasons, the *apparent factive attitude* view.

Throughout this chapter I will distinguish between different claims about *what* evidence or reason you have about the external world, in virtue of your perceptual experiences. All of the claims that I make will be couched in the propositional idiom. I will consider the hypothesis, for example, that when you have a visual experience as of P, one piece of evidence about the world that you acquire is that you see that P. It is important, of course, that not all theorists accept that reasons (or evidence) strictly speaking *are* propositions. According to some theorists, reasons (either objective or subjective) consist in mental states, and attributing your reason by saying that your evidence includes that you see that P is just loose talk for saying that your evidence is the concrete state of *your seeing that P*.

But as I hinted in Chapter 2, I will try to respect this view by offering a translation scheme into my way of speaking, rather than by fumbling over trying to formulate everything in a way that is neutral. It will be important throughout this section and throughout this book how motivating reasons, subjective reasons, and objective reasons are related to one another. So when we are interested in the rationalization of belief, we are interested not only in the condition under which you have a subjective reason to believe, but also in the related question of under what condition there would be the right sort of objective reason—objective evidence—for you to count as believing for that objective reason in virtue of believing for your subjective reason.

But speaking in terms of the ontology of mental states as reasons makes it too easy to occlude this distinction if we are not careful. If we simplify (as I will) and assume that evidence/reasons are propositions, then a proposition can be your subjective reason only if you bear some kind of psychological relation to it— *having* it, in a semi-technical sense. And similarly, a proposition can be objective evidence/reason for you only if it is true. These are obviously distinct conditions. And this is a distinction that we have to respect, in order to distinguish between Bernie's believing that his glass contains gin and tonic—the condition under which it is rational for him to drink—and his glass really containing gin and tonic—the condition under which there is an objective reason for him to take a drink. Any view about the ontology of reasons that does not collapse this distinction can safely translate everything that I say about the identity of subjective reasons or evidence in this chapter as a claim about the condition under which the objective reason would exist, that the agent could believe for, by believing for this subjective reason. And similarly, everything that I say about the condition of *having* a subjective reason can be even more straightforwardly translated as a claim about the condition under which they have that subjective reason.

3.2 How Can Perceptual Experience Equip Us with Evidence?

Much of what we know of the world in which we live is grounded in perceptual experience. Indeed, perceptual experience alone is the proper tribunal for empirical judgment. When a priori reflection leads us to suspect that the universe is arranged as concentric rigid spheres but experience reveals an expanding universe of elliptical orbits of varying eccentricity, we put our trust in experience, and rightly so. Experience therefore seems, at least pre-philosophically, to be a privileged source of both knowledge and rational belief about the external world. Indeed, I could just as well have said that experience is a privileged source of knowledge and rational belief about the *empirical* world, which means simply, the world that is revealed to us in experience. The puzzle in which I will be interested, in this and Chapters 4 and 5, is how perceptual experience could be a privileged source of *evidence* about the external world.

It is natural to hope that perceptual experience can be such a privileged source of evidence. If there is any privileged relationship between evidence and rational belief, or between evidence and knowledge, then it is hard to see how perceptual experience could be a privileged source of knowledge or rational belief, unless perceptual experience somehow equips us with evidence about the external world. Even if there is no *general* requirement that beliefs must be based on evidence, it would be strange indeed if the beliefs most directly based on experience could not be!

Indeed, this thought is so central to epistemology, I will conjecture and argue in what follows that it is possible to see many of the central views and options in epistemology more generally as motivated as responses to the puzzle of how perceptual experience could be a source of evidence. Similarly, I will argue, it is plausible to see views which *deny* that basic perceptual beliefs must be based on any evidence as motivated by the feeling that these alternative views are simply unpalatable. If this conjecture is even close to accurate, then the puzzle about how perceptual experience could provide evidence about the external world is an important puzzle indeed.

The easiest way to get into the puzzle about how perceptual experience could equip us with evidence about the external world is to start with a common and often undisputed claim about the nature of perceptual evidence. Classical skeptical arguments typically start by describing skeptical scenarios in which all or some significant range of our beliefs about the external world are false—but which are alleged to be entirely consistent with our evidence.[1] For example, it may be proposed that there is a possible world in which you are being deceived by an evil demon who manipulates you into having exactly the same subjective phenomenal state that you are having right now, and that this possibility is entirely consistent with your evidence. Or it may be proposed that there is a possible world in which you are plugged into the Matrix of film lore,[2] and a computer program is manipulating you into having exactly the same subjective phenomenal state that you are actually in—and that this possibility is entirely consistent with your evidence. If these possibilities are entirely consistent with your evidence, then it would seem that

---

[1] Compare discussion in Williamson (2000).   [2] Pryor (2005a).

your evidence cannot rule them out, and hence, since they are empirical possibilities, that there is no way that you can know them not to obtain.

It is worth digressing somewhat to be careful, here, to distinguish between the
idea that skeptical hypotheses are consistent with your evidence and the idea that
they are consistent with your *having* that evidence. What skeptical arguments
require to get started is the idea that absolutely everything could be as your
evidence takes it to be—that you have no evidence *against* them. They are in
this sense claimed to be consistent not only with your *having* some evidence, but
with the evidence that you have.[3]

The idea that there are skeptical scenarios for the external world that are
entirely consistent with our evidence—and the fact that anyone might grant this
idea to the skeptic, in order to get her argument started—reveals an important
tacit assumption about the nature of basic perceptual evidence—that the evidence
provided by perceptual experiences includes only propositions about your own,
internally individuated, subjective psychological state. Let us call this the *phenomenal* conception of evidence. If the phenomenal conception of evidence is true,
then there is a large *gap* between basic perceptual evidence and conclusions about
the external world—a gap that is exploited by skeptical arguments. Much of
twentieth-century work in epistemology took the phenomenal conception of
evidence or some equivalent for granted, and was concerned with exploring
ways to cross or narrow this gap.[4]

I have just said that according to the phenomenal conception, basic perceptual
evidence consists only in propositions about one's own, internally individuated,
subjective psychological state.[5] I will have more to say later in order to explain why
someone might believe this to be true. But first, I want to show how the gap
between perceptual evidence and conclusions about the external world that is a
consequence of the phenomenal conception plays a central role in driving many of
the other most important central views in traditional epistemology.

Given the gap between perceptual evidence and conclusions about the external
world, it is natural to think that it can be rational to form beliefs about the external
world on the basis of perceptual evidence only given some *background* beliefs or
assumptions about how our perceptual evidence *correlates* with facts about the
external world.[6] This is the view that perceptual evidence can provide only

---

[3] Refer back to Section 3.1 for how to translate this back into your preferred idiom, if you do not
think that reasons or evidence are propositional.

[4] Some of the highlights include Russell (1914), Carnap (1928), Lewis (1946), and Chisholm (1966).

[5] I am not assuming that evidence, or that reasons, consist in propositions. But both reasons and
evidence are typically ascribable by reference to that-clauses. So I will assume in what follows that when
you have evidence for some conclusion, there should be some answer in terms of a that-clause that
answers what your evidence is. Compare the discussion in Pryor (2007).

[6] After all, the logical relationship between phenomenal evidence and conclusions about the external
world is exactly the *same* as its relationship to conclusions about the intentions of the evil demon, or the
arrangement of 1s and 0s in the matrix.

mediated justification for external world belief, and the background beliefs that are needed for this justification are known as the *mediating* beliefs.

The contrary, non-skeptical view that rejects the need for mediated justification is known as *dogmatism*.[7] According to dogmatism, there is a direct rationalizing link between perceptual experience and external world belief. Dogmatists who accept the phenomenal conception of evidence hold that this direct rationalizing link holds *despite* the fact that the logical relations between basic perceptual evidence and true external world beliefs are on a par with the logical relations between basic perceptual evidence and skeptical scenarios.

Each of mediationism and dogmatism comes with a distinctive set of traditional consequences or challenges. If basic perceptual justification is mediated by a background belief, we face the question of the justificatory status of that background belief. Views on which it must itself be grounded in experience are committed to *coherentism*, because the only way for experience to justify mediating beliefs, according to this view, is by way of further mediating beliefs. Indeed, adding mediationism to the phenomenal conception of evidence is the principal traditional motivation for coherentism, as exhibited by, for example, the views of both Keith Lehrer (1974) and the early Laurence Bonjour; Bonjour (1985) gives one of the most forceful and elegant statements of the view.

On the other hand, if we hold that the background belief does not itself require evidence from experience, then it follows that it has a kind of a priori status. This leads us to various kinds of *rationalist* views. On some such views, such as that of the later Laurence Bonjour (1996), the mediating beliefs that enable perceptual experiences to justify external world beliefs receive a special kind of synthetic a priori justification. According to others, such as Crispin Wright (2004, 2009), the mediating beliefs are rational because we are *entitled* to them, without the need for further justificatory support. And according to others, such as Harman and Sherman (2004, 2011) they are *assumptions* that play a role in our reasoning without needing to be justified as beliefs. Each of these views amounts to a strong kind of epistemological *rationalism*, because each not only grants a kind of a priori status to some beliefs or assumptions, but holds that experience itself can be an arbiter of belief only against a background of beliefs or assumptions with this a priori status.

So if we add the *mediated* view to the phenomenal conception of evidence, then we face a choice between coherentism and rationalism. It may be that either of these views is correct (or even both—the justification of the mediating belief could be a priori, but a priori justification itself could have a coherentist structure). I will not be arguing here that they are not. But each of these views has the character that adherents are led to it by philosophical *argument*, as the view that is forced by the

---

[7] Burge (1993), Pryor (2000).

options available. And each leaves only a diminished role for perceptual experience as the rational arbiter of belief.

Moreover, each only pushes back the puzzle of how some epistemically privileged class of beliefs could be supported by *evidence*. According to both views, the epistemic privilege of basic perceptually grounded beliefs about the external world depends on the epistemic privilege of the *mediating* beliefs. But whether these mediating beliefs have a justification that is a priori, based in coherence, or is simply a matter of entitlement, we are still left with a picture that *posits* the rationality of belief or assumption without grounding it in *evidence*. Yet what we were looking for was a way of making sense of the commonsense idea that ordinary perceptual beliefs have a privileged basis in evidence about the external world. So it is intelligible to feel like each of these views misses out on something. This is certainly how *I* feel about such views. These are the kinds of consequences that I could talk myself into embracing, if I was convinced that all of the alternatives were equally problematic—I could see them as surprising *discoveries*. But they are definitely not independently plausible predictions of these views; and in order to be talked into them by a comparison to the alternatives, we need to see why the alternatives are really so bad.

The alternative to holding that perceptual justification must be mediated by a background belief is to hold that it is *direct*. This is what is held by the *dogmatist*. And as will emerge in what follows, I take myself to be a dogmatist. But dogmatism can be particularly puzzling—especially when paired with the phenomenal conception of evidence.[8] Why should it be that forming ordinary external world beliefs on the basis of perceptual experience is rationally privileged, given that forming the corresponding matrix beliefs is just as well supported by the evidence?

The dogmatist who accepts or even simply does not disavow the phenomenal conception of evidence is put in a particularly awkward position by this combination of views. There must be *some* explanation of why ordinary external world beliefs are rationalized by perceptual experience but the corresponding matrix beliefs are not, because this doesn't look like the kind of thing that could be brute. But if there is such an explanation, it must appeal to features *other* than the evidence available to the subject at the time. It must appeal to the fact that the ordinary world beliefs are *more likely to be true*, or that the perceptual experiences are *caused* by the external world, rather than by the matrix simulation, or the like. But according to the dogmatist, the subject does not need to be aware of these facts, or to assume them, or even to have access to them, in order for her

---

[8] Note that dogmatism itself is consistent with rejecting the phenomenal conception of evidence. Indeed, the view that I will ultimately defend in Chapter 5 is a version of dogmatism. The difference between the view that I will ultimately defend and the sort of flat-footed dogmatism that accepts the phenomenal conception of evidence is that my favored view gives a more satisfying *explanation* of *why* perceptual states rationalize belief, by making good on the claim that they are a privileged way of having *evidence* about the world that does not require a privileged set of priors.

perceptual experience to justify ordinary external world belief. So whatever kind of explanation is given by these factors seems to have to be one that is *non-evidential* and *external* to the subject's awareness.[9]

David Armstrong (1973) forcefully argues, on this basis, that if justification or knowledge is to be empirically grounded in experience at all (and hence rationalism and coherentism are to be avoided), then that *forces* the conclusion—that is, everyone must agree—that the justificatory story about *why* basic perceptual beliefs are justified by experience must be fundamentally externalist in nature— it must appeal to facts about reliability or causation that are the currency of *pure externalist* theories of knowledge.

And Armstrong is right—if phenomenal evidence justifies conclusions about the external world but does not justify conclusions about the intentions of the evil demon, or about the arrangements of ones and zeros in the matrix, then there is a justificatory asymmetry that must be explained.[10] But this, Armstrong argues, is the *Externalist's In*—a kind of partners-in-crime proof that all good empiricists— that is, those who do not accept the worse options of rationalism or coherentism— are committed to pure externalist explanations of at least basic perceptual justification. Once we acknowledge that basic perceptual justification is fundamentally externalist in character, Armstrong argues, then the internalist has fundamentally given up the game, and we might as well give a *uniform* account of justification and the rationality of belief that does not need to mention evidence or reasons at all.[11] There are many reasons to find externalist ideas attractive in epistemology, of course, and nothing that I say in this book will rule out a large role for them. But Armstrong's is I think by far the most powerful reason to reject the expectation wholesale that an adequate account must rationalize, as well.

---

[9] This isn't quite fair—Michael Huemer's (2006) "Phenomenal Conservatism" offers a kind of explanation that does not turn on any external factor. The account that I'll offer is Chapter 5 is in some ways quite close to Huemer's, except that by sticking to an explanation in evidentialist terms, it aims to capture more forcefully why this is the right sort of explanation to ground knowledge.

[10] Silins (2007) defends dogmatism from White (2006) by allowing, as I have argued here the dogmatist must, that some distinction in priors must be justified, without requiring that perceptual justification is *based* on that further justification, as with mediationist views. Silins's defense of dogmatism plays in to Armstrong's point.

[11] Goldman (1967, 1988), Dretske (1981), and Nozick (1981) are some of the other leading examples, in addition to Armstrong, of what such *pure* externalist theories of knowledge and justification can look like. Lyons (2009) is a forceful and clear example of applying pure externalist ideas to basic beliefs while retaining an important and distinctive role for inferential justification. Here is Hilary Kornblith on Armstrong's point: "Simple perceptual beliefs raise a host of complex issues for those who put reasons at the center of their epistemological theories. If we examine the etiology of perceptual beliefs, then in the typical case, although beliefs about sensory experience do not come into play, sensory experience itself is surely found in the causal chain that leads to belief. [...] The reasons eliminationist proposes a simple solution. We should stop talking about reasons here [...]" (Kornblith 2015, 229–30).

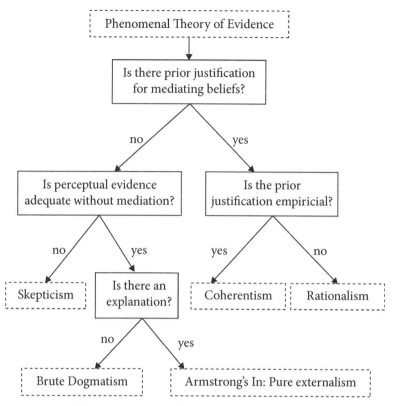

Figure 3.1 Twentieth-century epistemology

John Greco describes the pure externalist attitude toward evidence this way:

. . . once we adopt externalism about knowledge-relevant normative status—once we are reliabilists, or causal theorists, or safety theorists about such status —it is hard to see why evidence itself should be so important. At most, it would seem, evidence is required for knowledge because it is required for reliability, or safety, or some other modally strong relation to the world. But why think even that is the case?[12]

So the combination of dogmatism with the phenomenal conception of evidence leaves us with a minor and unstable role for evidence in basic perceptual justification. The phenomenal conception of justification places a sharp and

---

[12] Greco (2010, 65).

unsatisfactory restriction on the role for evidence in the justification of basic perceptual beliefs, which opens up the door for the most compelling motivation for pure externalist theories. And these theories, in turn, offer only a diminished role for evidence in general, either in the explanation of knowledge or the explanation of justification.

For all that I have said here, it may well be that the correct view of epistemic justification consists in dogmatism, paired with the phenomenal conception of evidence. And it may well be that the truth is some form of pure externalism that offers no or only a diminished role for evidence in the explanation of knowledge and rational belief. Pure forms of externalism avoid the problem of explaining how basic perceptual beliefs could be well-grounded in adequate evidence only by giving up on its premise. But I believe that we can take what these views get right, and *add* to them by making better room for the role of evidence in the rationalization of belief.

3.3 Perceptual Reasons as World-Implicating

We saw in Section 3.2 that the familiar choices that dominated most of twentieth-century epistemology—skepticism, coherentism, rationalism, and pure externalism—can be seen as framed by the phenomenal conception of basic perceptual evidence. The phenomenal conception of evidence leaves a gap between our evidence and the world, so either that gap fails to be bridged, it is bridged a priori or through some kind of coherence, or the bridge is one whose conditions can only be detected third-personally, as the pure externalist claims.

The alternative is to reject the phenomenal conception of evidence, and claim that perceptual evidence can entail things about the world outside of our heads. I call this the idea that basic perceptual evidence can be *world-implicating*. Since the consequences of the phenomenal conception of evidence all derive from the fact that on that view, any possibility about the external world is completely consistent with the totality of your perceptual evidence, the way to avoid those consequences is to deny precisely this.

We may illustrate the idea that perceptual reasons can be world-implicating by considering two examples of this view.[13] According to the first of these views, which I will call the *factive content* view, when you see that the grass is green, you come to have the proposition *that the grass is green* as evidence that the grass is green. But the proposition that the grass is green *entails* that the grass is green. So this is the *very best* sort of evidence that one could have that the grass is green. So it

---

[13] It should be obvious that these are not the only two possible examples of such a view. I choose them only because they are conveniently representative for my purposes, and because they concretely illustrate the dialectical force of disjunctivism. In Chapter 6 we will return to the space of options, here.

is no wonder, on this view, that we naively think that perception is a privileged way of acquiring evidence about the external world—for it is *true*, on this view, that perception is such a privileged way of acquiring evidence.

factive content view	Where ψ is a factive perceptual relation...
possession condition	You ψ that P.
your evidence is	That P.

Moreover, since our evidence is clearly so good, on this view, there is no need to justify mediating bridge premises, or to give externalist, reliabilist, or causal explanations. Such explanations would clearly be redundant, given that the perceptual evidence entails the conclusion that it is supposed to justify.[14] And similarly, there is no skeptical 'in', because skeptical scenarios are not consistent with our evidence. Timothy Williamson (2000) accepts a version of the factive content view. He claims that your evidence is what you know—which is the thesis known as 'E=K' – and he claims that seeing entails knowing—which he puts as the thesis that knowledge is the most general factive, stative attitude. Together, these two theses entail the factive content view of basic perceptual evidence, and Williamson emphasizes the advantages of this view in avoiding the consequences of the phenomenal conception of evidence—particularly for evading skepticism.[15]

An alternative way to hold that basic perceptual evidence is world-implicating is to hold what I call the *factive attitude* view, endorsed by Alan Millar and Duncan Pritchard (2012) and which Comesaña and McGrath (2015) attribute to McDowell.[16] According to the factive attitude view, when you see that the grass is green, you come to have the proposition *that you see that the grass is green* as evidence that the grass is green. Since seeing that P entails that P, this is also a view

---

[14] Note that it does not follow that there is no role for explanations of the reliability of perception— for it could be that no perceptual state comes to have a content about the external world unless it is related to the external world in a sufficiently reliable way. So the benefit of this view is not that it allows perceptual states to justify belief in the absence of any background of reliability, but rather than it explains *why* reliability might play a role in rationalizing belief. (Compare Burge (1997, 2010), Brewer (2002).) Moreover, the relationship between reliability and content is not straightforward. Much of contemporary science of perception is grounded in treatment of perceptual *illusions*, which are *not* reliable signs of what they represent, but can in general be characterized as generalizations on or interactions among processes that are reliable in some domain.

[15] Williamson (2007) explicitly generalizes this view to the thesis that your *reasons* are what you know, a view also defended explicitly by Hyman (1999), Hawthorne and Stanley (2009), and Hawthorne and Magidor (2018). Both the thesis of *Reasons as Evidence* and the thesis of *Evidence as Reasons* support the view that the condition for having a subjective reason and the condition for having subjective evidence will be the same.

[16] For Millar, see for example Pritchard et al. (2010, 139). The passages from McDowell which Comesaña and McGrath have in mind come from McDowell (1994, 2006, 2008). See also McDowell (1995). I was also tempted to attribute the factive attitude view to McDowell when I wrote Schroeder (2008), but it is not at all clear to me that this is really what McDowell thinks. Much of the language that he uses in each of these three works is consistent with the view that I will ultimately defend in Chapter 5.

on which your basic perceptual evidence is world-implicating. So it is also a view on which skeptical scenarios are not consistent with the totality of our evidence, on which there is no need for a mediating bridge premise, and on which no further externalist explanation needs to be given for why this perceptual evidence justifies belief, because clearly, no evidence could be better.[17]

factive attitude view	Where ψ is a factive perceptual relation...
possession condition	You ψ that P.
your evidence is	That you ψ that P.

Even if Comesaña and McGrath are wrong to attribute the factive attitude view to McDowell, it is certainly consonant with many of his commitments. It offers a way to avoid the 'Scylla' of coherentism and the 'Charybdis' of pure externalism,[18] by explaining how perceptual beliefs can be grounded in the world in a way that rationalizes, rather than merely explains. It is a natural way of making good on McDowell's claim to sidestep the oscillation between unsatisfactory alternatives left to us by the phenomenal conception of basic perceptual evidence. And I will ultimately argue, in Chapter 5, that it is a little bit closer to the truth than Williamson's factive content view. So it will be a helpful point of comparison throughout what follows, even if it departs from or goes beyond what McDowell would actually accept.

The factive content view and the factive attitude view, it turns out, share a *pair* of commitments. Both agree that the basic evidence that you have in virtue of having perceptual experiences is *world-implicating*, in the sense that it entails conclusions about the world outside of your experiences, rather than leaving a gap between your evidence and the world. But they *also* agree that you only have this evidence when you are in what is known as the *good* case—that is, when you actually have a veridical perceptual experience. In particular, in the case of vision, having a non-veridical perceptual experience as of the grass being green does *not* give you this evidence—only *seeing that* the grass is green gives you this evidence. The factive content view carries this commitment because it says that you have the proposition that the grass is green as your evidence only if you see that the grass is green. And the factive attitude view has this commitment because it says that you have the proposition that you see that the grass is green as your evidence only if it is true.

Because the factive content view and the factive attitude view distinguish between the good case and the bad case in this way, they count as *disjunctivist* views about perceptual justification. In general, what disjunctivist views of perceptual justification have in common, is that they are committed to offering

---

[17] Again, some externalist explanation may still be given of why your perceptual state counts as having the content that the grass is green. But this explanation will be different in character than an externalist attempt to explain directly why this particular state rationalizes belief.

[18] Compare the language in McDowell (1994).

different stories about how perceptual experiences rationalize beliefs in so-called 'good' and 'bad' cases—depending on whether the perceptual experience is veridical or non-veridical.[19] But on the face of it, this is a striking conclusion to be led

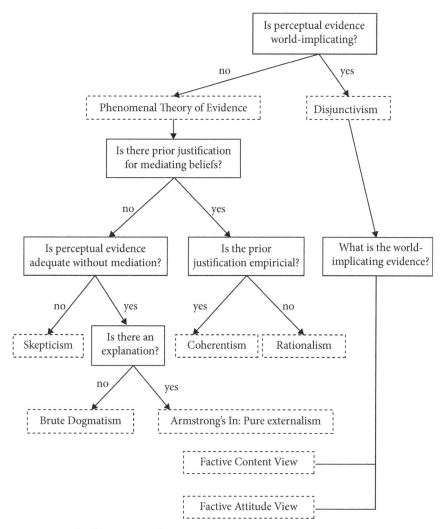

Figure 3.2 The disjunctivist alternative

---

[19] Note that Pritchard (2012) defends a view he calls 'epistemological disjunctivism' that is merely a special case of epistemological disjunctivism, as I have defined it. It is also natural to define corresponding versions of epistemological disjunctivism for cases of justification by testimony or by memory, but I will continue to restrict my attention to the case of perceptual justification, which is the case that has traditionally gotten the most attention and done the most to shape the traditional options in epistemology.

into, in trying to understand how perceptual experiences provide evidence that rationalizes beliefs—one that is not obviously more palatable than the competing views of coherentism, rationalism, and pure externalism that the world-implicating views of evidence help us to avoid. In fact, it is arguably worse.

In order to focus most clearly on what I think is problematic about the disjunctivist branch of our perceptual epistemology flowchart, however, it is time to come clean more explicitly about what is and is not at stake in this chapter. Throughout this book I have been referring both to justification and to the rationality of belief—sometimes alternatingly. Moving back and forth between these two terms makes sense if, like me, you suspect that talk about justification in epistemology is best construed as talk about what it is rational to believe. But here it is worth separating them more clearly—at least nominally—because some philosophers advocate disjunctivist accounts of justification *without* adopting disjunctivism about rationality. Once justification is pulled apart from rationality in this way, however, I lose my sense of what is at stake over it. What is really deeply puzzling, I believe, is disjunctivism about how perceptual beliefs are *rationalized*.

To see this, consider any ordinary case in which you have an ordinary, veridical, perceptual experience, and form the corresponding belief. Call this case C_1. Both McDowell's and Williamson's accounts of basic perceptual belief apply in case C_1, and both say that it is rational[20] for you to have this belief, because you have the best kind of evidence for it. But now suppose that things had been just slightly different in a way that was indistinguishable to you, so that you had an indis-criminable perceptual experience, but it failed to be veridical, because it was instead a kind of perceptual illusion. Call this case C_2. Both McDowell's and Williamson's accounts of basic perceptual belief fail to apply in this case. They both claim that you have *different* reasons to believe in cases C_1 and C_2, and in particular, that in case C_2, you lack the reason that plays such a privileged role in explaining what makes your belief in C_1 rational. From this it seems to follow that your belief in C_2 is *not* rational, even though your belief in C_1 *is*—or at least that this can happen in some similar pairs of cases.

But cases C_1 and C_2 differ in a way that is incredibly minimal. Not only are they the same in their internal, subjectively accessible features, they also shared exactly the same history up until just before the formation of this very belief—over which both you and your counterfactual counterpart have been in exactly the same environment, employed ways of forming beliefs with exactly the same reliability, and been causally hooked up to the world in exactly the same ways. It is very hard to deny, as the factive content and factive attitude views seem pushed to do, that beliefs in such minimal pairs of cases cannot differ in their rationality, merely

---

[20] Holding fixed, of course, that we interpret these options as views about rationality, and not just about justification.

because one perception is veridical and one is not. To say this is not to say that the rationality of belief supervenes on subjective factors or cannot be affected by reliability or the existence of causal links to the world.[21] It is just to say that the bare truth of a single-case perceptual experience cannot be the difference-maker in the rationality of belief. Any view that denies this is hard to credit.

Pure externalist theories like process reliabilism and causal theories, insofar as they can be aptly interpreted as attempting to say something about the rationality of belief at all, have traditionally been taken by many to be implausible because they make the rationality of belief turn on factors like facts about causation and reliability that may be inaccessible to the subject. But the disjunctive treatment of the rationality of basic perceptual beliefs that is endorsed by both the factive content view and the factive attitude view suffers from a particularly egregious form of this problem,[22] because it allows the rationality of belief to hinge on single-case differences in the veridicality of a single perceptual experience. In deference to McDowell, we might aptly call this *Charybdis' Revenge*, since McDowell sought to evade the tentacles of the Charybdis of pure externalism, but the resulting view still suffers from one of the central obstacles for pure externalist theories.

3.4 Tightening the Screws

The received view in much of the epistemology of perception has been that we must pick our poison. If we evade the problems of the phenomenal view of evidence by holding that basic perceptual evidence is world-implicating, then we must accept different accounts of the rationality of belief in cases of veridical and non-veridical perception. And if we want a uniform account of the way that perceptual experiences rationalize beliefs, then we must have a phenomenal conception of evidence, and choose among the options in the familiar dialectic accordingly. In Section 3.5 and throughout Chapters 4 and 5, I will argue that this is a false forced choice—it is perfectly possible to get all of the distinctive redeeming features of a world-implicating account of basic perceptual evidence without any disjunctivist commitments. The fact that this possibility has been insufficiently appreciated in epistemology, I will be arguing, is because of a background assumption that too many people have been taking completely for

---

[21] As, for example, is claimed by very strong forms of epistemological internalism, such as that advocated by Bonjour (1985).

[22] Note that some *other* forms of epistemological disjunctivism, such as that defended by Pritchard (2012), cannot be characterized in this way, because they deny the claim about inaccessibility. However, I think the general intuitive point that the failure to treat cases like C_1 and C_2 alike resembles what traditional internalists have found problematic about pure externalist theories survives the failures of attempts to gloss this claim it more precisely, and I think this gloss is apt for the factive content and factive attitude views.

granted—one that is closely related, I will argue in Chapter 4, to the problem of unjustified beliefs. But before we get there, in this section I want to pay a little bit closer attention to what I think is unsatisfactory about the form of disjunctivism to which the factive content view and the factive attitude view both commit us—and to whether our difficulties turn illicitly on the propositional ontology for reasons.

The first thing that it is important to clarify is that the feature of the factive content and factive attitude views that I think is problematic concerns their treatments of the *rationality* of belief, not their treatment of *knowledge*. It should not be controversial that seeing that the grass is green puts you in a better position to *know* that the grass is green than merely having a non-veridical perceptual experience as of grass's being green. And so both the factive content view and the factive attitude view, I believe, give natural and plausible treatments of when perceptual experiences are apt to ground knowledge. This is a feature that I think any attempt to improve on these accounts should aim to maintain, and I will show how to do so in Chapter 5.

What is problematic about these views, therefore, is not that they treat knowledge differently in the good and bad cases, but that this leads them to *also* treat the *rationality* of belief differently in the good and bad cases.[23] What we set out to look for, in this chapter, was why perceptual experiences provide us with a particularly privileged sort of evidence about the external world, of the kind that can make beliefs grounded in perceptual observation particularly *rational*. The consequence of these views that concerns me is therefore that they offer different views of the *subjective* reasons available in the good case and the bad case—the reasons that bear on what it is rational to believe.

And this observation leads us to an important loophole in my argument, as I have presented it in the last section. Strictly speaking, the factive content and factive attitude views entail that there is one important reason that you have in C_1, the actual good case, but not in C_2, the counterfactual bad case. But it is not *directly* intuitively compelling that this is not the case—judgments about reasons like this are not terribly reliable.[24] What is directly intuitively compelling is that whatever it is rational for you to believe in C_1, it is rational for you to believe in C_2. And so, one possibility is that though you have more reasons for your belief in C_1 than you do in C_2, your reasons in C_2 are still good *enough*. In order to avoid the possibility of *some* pairs like C_1 and C_2 that differ in the rationality of belief only

---

[23] Schellenberg (2013, 2014) is very good on this point, arguing that we must distinguish between two sorts of evidence—factive evidence that we have only in the good case, and another kind of evidence that is shared between the good case and the bad case, and which is responsible for accounting for the rationality of belief. I accept all of this, but resist Schellenberg's characterization of the evidence that is shared as phenomenal.
[24] Compare the discussion of the negative reason existential fallacy in Schroeder (2007, 2011).

because they exhibit a one-off difference in the veridicality of a single perceptual experience, it would have to turn out that the extra reason that you have in the good case can *never* make a difference to the rationality of your belief. This idea is worth taking seriously, and we need to set it aside, in order to be confident that the factive content and factive attitudes views' different treatments of the reasons in the good case and the bad case really do force the results that I have argued are problematic.

A first important observation to make in response to this idea is that without further elaboration, it defeats the point of the world-implicating account of basic perceptual evidence. The point of holding that basic perceptual evidence is world-implicating, after all, was that it gives us a picture on which perception is a *better* source of evidence than it is, on the phenomenal view, on which basic perceptual evidence is not world-implicating. But the evidence that is available in the bad case is only phenomenal evidence. So if we thought that phenomenal evidence was just as good as world-implicating evidence, then we would not need to supplement perceptual experiences with mediating background beliefs, or to hold that perceptual evidence is actually world-implicating, in order to respond to the skeptic. So the defender of the asymmetric treatment of the reasons in the good and bad cases should not say that phenomenal evidence is *always* as good as world-implicating evidence, on pain of undermining the advantages of treating basic perceptual evidence as world-implicating, to begin with. At best, she can say that it is *sometimes* as good. But *when*?

It turns out that there is a clever argument for the claim that when *you* are in case C_1, your phenomenal evidence for the belief that you form is just as good as your world-implicating perceptual evidence. It turns on the idea that the evidence provided by your phenomenal evidence—the reasons that you share with your counterpart in C_2—is mediated by a background belief that *if* your phenomenal experience is such-and-such, then the world is so-and-so. But to say that *your* phenomenal evidence is just as good as your world-implicating evidence because this background belief is justified is not to say that *anyone's* phenomenal evidence is just as good, because it may not be that the background belief is justified for just anyone. On the contrary, this view goes, the reason that it is justified for *you* is that you have such extensive experience with world-implicating evidence, which, moreover, you share with your counterpart in C_2.

So the idea is that so long as you are have a history of being in good cases in a sufficiently large proportion of cases, you can bootstrap a justification for the conditional belief that puts your purely phenomenal evidence (and hence the evidence of your C_2 counterpart) in good standing. Call the proponent of this loophole the *good-case bootstrapper*. According to the good-case bootstrapper, there are *some* minimal pairs C_3 and C_4 which differ only in the veridicality of a single perceptual experience and as a result, differ in what it is rational for the subject to believe. But for normal adult humans in the actual world, there are no nearby such cases because in order to get such cases we must imagine agents in unreliable environments, whose perceptual experiences are often unveridical.[25]

The possibility of good-case bootstrapping shows that the theorist who holds that the reasons in the good case and the bad case differ is not forced to conclude that the rationality of belief differs in cases C_1 and C_2. It is not enough, of course, to evade the conclusion that the rationality of belief may differ in pairs of cases that are subjectively indistinguishable but also differ in their histories. And so the good-case boostrapper still runs afoul of a stronger set of internalist-leaning intuitive judgments. We can still set it aside by appealing to judgments about slightly less minimal pairs of cases, or by judgments about minimal pairs in counterfactual, unreliable environments. I have some sympathy with the intuitive judgments about such cases, but they are not as clearly compelling as the intuitive judgments about cases C_1 and C_2. So the possibility of good-case bootstrapping is worth taking very seriously.

But I have wanted to rest my case against McDowell and Williamson on the weakest possible kind of internalist-leaning intuitive judgment. And we can still do that, by paying attention not to the question of what it is prospectively rational *for* you to believe in cases C_1 and C_2, but what you are doxastically rational *in* believing. As I've suggested in Chapter 2 in drawing this distinction, what you are rational *in* believing depends on what the reasons are *for which* you believe it. But presumably, in the good case, the reasons for which you believe are your fact-implicating evidence. And since the question of what the reasons are for which you believe is at least partly a psychological question, it is hard to see how the bare fact of the single-case non-veridicality of a single perceptual experience could make it the case that you count as believing for phenomenal reasons.

I don't take this to be conclusive; there is room to maneuver over what sort of psychological condition basing a belief on certain reasons imposes, and hence to try to evade this conclusion. For example, Errol Lord (2018), even though he is not a good-case boostrapper in my sense, spends substantial effort on this problem, which he dubs the 'new new evil demon problem'. Lord defends an account of the basing relation whose goal is to be liberal enough that you can always count as acting or believing for backup reasons that would also support your action or belief even if your primary reasons turn out to be false. On Lord's view, whether you believe for a reason depends only on whether you are dispositionally sensitive to whether it is a reason—and not on whether it actually plays any causal role in forming or sustaining your actual belief.[26]

---

[25] Thanks to Greg Antill for helping me to appreciate the importance of this possibility.

[26] "**Normative-Sustaining:** A φ's for a normative reason r if A is disposed to revise her φ-ing if r ceases to be a normative reason to φ" Lord (2018, 138). This is the first of two clauses that Lord takes to each be sufficient and disjunctively necessary for φ-ing for a normative reason (he goes on in the next chapter to offer a different treatment of φ-ing for motivating reasons that are not themselves good normative reasons).

Because Lord holds that acting or believing for a reason only requires that you be dispositionally sensitive to it, it makes it possible that you could believe both on the basis of phenomenological evidence—say, that it seems to you that P—and on the basis of factive worldly evidence—say, that P—at one and the same time. This will be true so long as your belief is in fact dispositionally sensitive to both. But Lord's account is too demanding to do the work that the good-case bootstrapper needs.

It is too demanding because you can believe for a reason without being disposed to revise your belief if it ceases to be a normative reason. For example, among the ways that the consideration on which you base your belief could fail to be a normative reason is that it is subject to objective defeating conditions of which you are unaware.[27] For example, you could have been unwittingly wearing rose-colored glasses, making your apparent perceptual evidence of color no reason at all to believe that there is something red in front of you. But you do not have to be dispositionally sensitive to whether you are unwittingly wearing rose-colored glasses in order to believe on the basis of perceptual evidence that you are seeing something red. So Lord's condition is too demanding in order to make good on the idea that we actually believe for redundant reasons.

So this is an important and difficult challenge. To confront it, it is not enough that it should be *possible* to believe for backup reasons in addition to our primary perceptual reasons—it must also turn out that we *always* do. And so unless this challenge can be satisfactorily met, we can set aside the good-case bootstrapper without needing to rely on stronger internalist intuitions at all.

So what, then about the possibility that I have illicitly drawn on the propositionalist ontology for reasons in laying out my arguments in this chapter? As I indicated in Section 3.1, I think I have not. Appealing to a non-propositional ontology for either subjective or objective reasons can't change the fundamental issues about what worldly condition must obtain in order for the objective reason to exist that someone would act on, by acting on their subjective reason. If Bernie believes falsely that his glass contains gin and tonic, the fact that the world as he believes it to be is the way that would give him an objective reason to take a sip is not orthogonal to the fact that believing this gives him a subjective reason to take a sip—it helps to explain *why* this is the case. All that I have been asking for, in this chapter, is how the analogous story goes in the case of basic perceptual beliefs. And that story is one that we should be able to tell on any reasonable choice for the ontology of reasons—it is just a little bit more fluid to tell it in the way that I have been doing.

Another important worry worth addressing is that in Chapter 2 I professed the goal of remaining neutral about Fogal's (2016) thesis that *mass* noun uses of

---

[27] Cases like these will be introduced and play an important role in Chapter 5.

'reason' pick out a relation that is more normatively fundamental. But this, of course, leaves open the possibility that there is reason to do something but *nothing* is a reason to do it. On the version of Fogal's view to which I am the most attracted, however, the basic mass noun use of 'reason' does not vary between agents or circumstances.[28] But perceptual evidence is, of course, highly contingent and which perceptual evidence is available varies between circumstances and agents. So basic perceptual beliefs is not a good candidate for something for which there is reason to believe, but nothing such that *it* is the reason to believe.

Nor, I think, does this idea hold up well when translated into the idiom of evidence.[29] So it seems to me that appeal to the possibility of reason to believe without any particular answer to what the reason is to believe will be much more promising for dealing with the epistemology of the a priori than for the rational-ization of basic perceptual beliefs. I conclude that appeal to the mass noun uses of 'reason' and 'evidence' is not a promising way of evading my question as to what the evidence is that we acquire for basic perceptual beliefs in virtue of having perceptual experiences about the world.

Finally, before moving on, I should address the reasons that Timothy Williamson has given for doubting any kind of internalist intuitions. Williamson conjectures that internalist judgments about rationality are grounded in the assumption that it must always be possible to know what it is rational for you to believe. But Williamson notes that what it is rational for you to believe surely depends on facts about your psychology, and his anti-luminosity argument shows that it is not always possible to know the facts about your own psychology. So, Williamson concludes, facts about what it is rational for you to believe cannot be luminous, either, and so internalism is built on an untenable foundation.

Note, however, that nowhere in this chapter have I assumed any strong form of internalism. I have nowhere claimed that internal duplicates must be equally rational, that rationality must supervene on internal states, or that it must always be possible to know or rationally believe the truth about what it is rational for you to believe.[30] All that I have claimed is that the rationality of belief never turns on single-case differences in the veridicality of a single perceptual experience. It is possible, I suppose, that the only reason for accepting this judgment is an abstract argument about the luminosity of rationality, but it is doubtful, because this judgment is more compelling, I claim, than the assumption that it must always be possible to know what it is rational for you to believe. Indeed, I myself believe for broadly Williamsonian reasons that it is *not* always possible to know what it is rational for you to believe.[31]

---

[28]   As I argue in "The Price of Supervenience", in Schroeder (2014).
[29]   "There is a great deal of evidence that there is something red in front of you, but nothing is evidence for it."
[30]   Compare Cohen (1984).   [31]   Compare Schroeder (ms).

So I am happy to grant that Williamson is right to diagnose borderline cases of mental states as cases in which what it is rational to believe and what it is rational to believe that it is rational to believe come apart.[32] I just maintain that although the distinction between what it is rational to believe and what it is rational to believe that it is rational to believe is an important tool to keep in our philosophical and diagnostic toolbox; applying it to the distinction between cases C_1 and C_2 is like seeing a nail just because we have a hammer. There is an important difference between a pair of cases in which we have perceptual experiences with contents just on either side of the borderline between red and orange, I believe, and a pair of cases one of which is veridical and one of which is a subtle illusion. Much more plausible, I believe, is the diagnosis that rationality is not the kind of thing that can depend on single-case differences in veridicality.

In this and in Section 3.3, I have been arguing against the disjunctive treatment of the evidence available in so-called 'good' and 'bad' perceptual cases that is a commitment of familiar world-implicating accounts of basic perceptual evidence such as the factive content view and the factive attitude view. But as with my discussions of skepticism, coherentism, rationalism, and pure externalism in Section 3.2 it doesn't ultimately matter, for my purposes here, whether I have said enough (and I haven't) to establish that this view is not ultimately correct. What is important for my purposes, is to make intelligible a set of reasons why we might see these available options as unsatisfying. What I am really interested in, is the fact that it has been so commonly taken for granted that we must *choose* between attaining the virtues of world-implicating accounts of evidence like Williamson's and McDowell's, and avoiding their disjunctivist commitments. For what I will argue in the remainder of this chapter is that the options that we have been considering so far have been shaped by an important but tacit assumption about the nature of subjective reasons, and correlatively of subjective evidence. By rejecting this tacit assumption, we can see our way to a view that attains all of the chief virtues of McDowell's and Williamson's views, without becoming committed to what I have been arguing are their views' distinctive costs. The resulting view would be the best of both worlds.

3.5 A False Forced Choice—Factivity and Subjective Reasons

As we saw in Section 3.2, both the factive content view and the factive attitude view avoid the gap between our perceptual evidence and conclusions about the external world by holding that basic perceptual evidence is *world-implicating*. But both are led immediately to conclude that this means that there is a difference in your

---

[32] Indeed, I claim that this is quite important in "How to Be an Expressivist about Truth", reprinted in Schroeder (2015a).

reasons between the good case and the bad case—even when the good case and the bad case differ only in a single-case matter of the veridicality of a single perceptual experience, as in cases C_1 and C_2. And this is what leads them to the conclusion that there can be differences in the rationality of belief in pairs of cases like C_1 and C_2. But this conclusion, I argued, is deeply implausible. So it is natural to wonder: is this a false choice? Is there any way to seize the benefits of holding that basic perceptual reasons are world-implicating without being forced to postulate a difference between the subject's reasons in the good case and the bad case?

The main idea of this part of the book is that this is indeed a false forced choice. There are perfectly intelligible views on which basic perceptual reasons are world-implicating, but there is no difference in your subjective reasons between the good case and the bad case. To get this view, we need only to allow that having a subjective reason needn't involve standing in a cognitive relation to a *truth*. We need to allow, that is, that subjective reasons can be *false*. What makes this view perfectly possible is that as I noted earlier, the factive content view and the factive attitude view actually share a *pair* of commitments—one about the nature of basic perceptual reasons, and one about the relationship that you must bear to those reasons, in order for them to rationalize *your* beliefs. The commitment that I have been arguing leads to the advantages of these views is their view that perceptual *reasons* are world-implicating.[33] The commitment that leads to their costs, in contrast, is their view that the *relation* that you must bear to these reasons, in order to rationalize your beliefs, is world-implicating. Since the advantages come from one commitment and the costs come from the other, it is straightforward to get the advantages without the costs. You just have to accept one commitment without accepting the other.

Compare, first, the factive content view. According to this view, recall, your basic perceptual evidence, when you have visual evidence that there is something square in front of you, is the *content* of your visual experience: that there is something square in front of you. This is what makes it world-implicating. But the factive content view holds that you do not *have* this perceptual evidence—it does not rationalize *your* beliefs—unless you bear a factive attitude to the world: unless you *see that* there is something square in front of you. And of course, because *seeing that* is a factive attitude, you do not see that there is something square in front of you unless there really is something square in front of you. So this is what leads Williamson to conclude that you can only have this reason in the good case.

But there is a straightforward non-factive analogue of the factive content view, which we might call the *non-factive content view*, which offers the same identification of your basic perceptual reason but allows that you count as having this

---

[33] Note that Pritchard (2012) has a contrasting view about why his favored version of epistemological disjunctivism (which confusingly, he also attributes to McDowell) provides an answer to skepticism. Pritchard's answer to the skeptic does turn, I believe, on the *having* relation that you must bear to your perceptual reasons, and not just on the content of those reasons.

evidence as a *subjective* reason for belief, so long as you bear a *non-factive* perceptual experience relation to it.[34]

non-factive content view	Where ζ is a *non*-factive perceptual relation...
possession condition	You ζ that P.
your evidence is	That P.

On this view, when you have a visual experience as of something square in front of you, you come to have the proposition that there is something square in front of you as one of your subjective reasons to believe that there is something square in front of you, regardless of whether this perceptual experience is veridical or not. Since the perceptual relation required in order to have this reason is one that you can have in both the good case and the bad case, cases C_1 and C_2 do not differ in your subjective reasons, and hence do not differ in what it is rational for you to believe. Of course, in the bad case, C_2, your subjective reason is not true, and so it cannot ground knowledge—that is something that the disjunctivists' distinction between the good and bad cases gets right. But with respect to *rational* belief, as I have been arguing, there should not be such a distinction.

Similarly, there is an analogue of the factive attitude view that avoids distinguishing between the good and bad cases. The factive attitude view, recall, says that your basic perceptual reason to believe that there is something square in front of you on the basis of visual experience is that you see that there is something square in front of you. This reason is world-implicating because *seeing that* is a factive attitude, and so that is what closes the gap between your perceptual evidence and the world. But the factive attitude view also assumes that this cannot be your reason unless it is *true*—unless you really do see that there is something square in front of you. But that means that there is a non-factive analogue of the factive attitude view—what we might call the *apparent factive attitude view*—which offers the same identification of your basic perceptual reason, but allows that this can be your subjective reason even if it is not true, on the grounds that in general, subjective reasons do not need to involve any cognitive relation to a truth.

apparent factive attitude view	Where ψ is a factive perceptual relation...
possession condition	It appears to you that you ψ that P.[35]
your evidence is	That you ψ that P.

[34] Compare Schroeder (2008, 2011a), Smithies (2018). Schroeder (2011a) and Smithies (2018) each offer accounts of what the relation ζ must be, but for our purposes I will simply note that it is a placeholder that must be accounted for and defended in any full defense of the non-factive content view.

[35] The first-personal element of the apparent factive attitude view is non-essential; it could be that what appears to be the case is just that *there is* a ψ-ing that P, or that some particular state is a ψ-ing that P. As we'll see in Chapter 6, my preferred version of the apparent factive attitude view takes such a form. But I find it simpler in the abstract to describe the view in first-personal terms, and so I will continue to do so.

On this view, though the objective evidence available to you differs between the good case and the bad case, your subjective reasons are exactly the same. In both C_1 and C_2, it appears to you that you see that there is something square in front of you, so you have the same, world-implicating, reason in both cases.

What these analogues of the factive content and factive attitude views demonstrate is that the question of whether basic perceptual reasons are world-implicating and the question of whether they can be had in the bad case cross-cut one another. What is needed in order to close the gap between basic perceptual evidence and the world is just the view that basic perceptual reasons are world-implicating. This just means that the reason itself—or the proposition associated with it, on non-propositional ontologies of reasons—entails something about the external world. The factive content view and the factive attitude view both *assume*

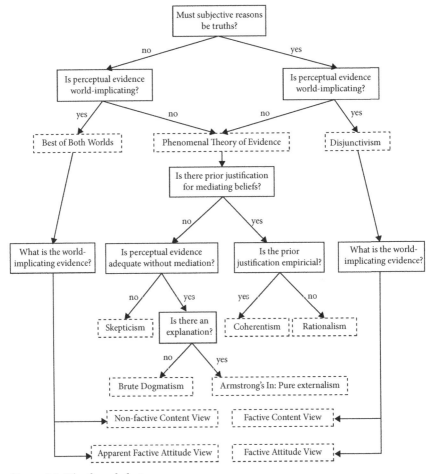

Figure 3.3 The forced choice

that you cannot have such a subjective reason unless it is *true*. But if subjective reasons need not involve any cognitive relation to a truth, then basic perceptual reasons could be world-implicating but non-factive. And if they are, then we could get all of the virtues of McDowell and Williamson's treatments of skepticism, coherentism, and rationalism, without the cost of distinguishing between the rationality of belief in minimal pairs like C_1 and C_2.

This suggests that the assumption that subjective reasons must involve a cognitive relation to a truth is doing quite powerful work in the dialectic about basic perceptual justification. It poses a powerful dilemma. Either this truth is world-implicating, or it is not. If it is world-implicating, then no one has this subjective reason in bad cases, and hence it can't play a role in rationalizing belief in the bad case. This leads to the conclusion that beliefs are less rational in the bad case—even if the only difference between the good case and the bad case is a one-off difference in the veridicality of a single perceptual experience. On the other hand, if the truth required to have a subjective reason is not world-implicating, then the subjective reason can be shared between the good case and the bad case, and so belief in cases like C_1 and C_2 can be equally rational. But that leaves a large gap between perceptual evidence and conclusions about the world—a gap occupied by skeptical scenarios, and which can seem to require mediating background beliefs in order to be bridged—beliefs whose justification must either be on rationalist grounds, or must take us back into a coherentist-style loop. The alternative is to deny that basic perceptual beliefs need to be grounded in evidence at all, but that is what opens up Armstrong's Externalist In—the question as to why the justification of *any* beliefs requires evidence.

The basic dilemma that drives this complex dialectic about basic perceptual justification can therefore rightly be thought of as set in the first place by the driving assumption that having a subjective reason requires standing in a cognitive relation to a truth. With some qualifications, I will gloss this as the assumption that subjective reasons are *factive*, or that subjective reasons *are* truths.[36] This makes the assumption that subjective reasons must be factive arguably the central framing background assumption that sets the agenda for the epistemology of basic perceptual beliefs—for better or for worse—and hence for much of epistemology in general. But this is a very general assumption about *reasons*. So it is exactly the sort of thing that we should expect a more general perspective on reasons, which pays attention to reasons for action as well as reasons for belief, to allow us to evaluate more carefully. This makes it a particularly fruitful testing ground for this book's *Core Hypothesis*: that the comparison to other branches of normative

---

[36] In particular, though I myself prefer the view on which both objective reasons and subjective reasons are propositions, here I mean to remain neutral about their ontology. For those who think that subjective reasons are propositions, the claim that they are factive is the claim that they *are* truths. For defenders of psychologism, who think that strictly speaking subjective reasons are states of mind, factivity is the claim that this state of mind must have a true content.

inquiry does sometimes make a difference—indeed, an important difference—for even very core topics of traditional epistemology.

In Chapter 1 I suggested that views about core topics of traditional epistemology may sometimes have been *distorted* by lack of the perspective that we can gain by considering the commitments we incur in answering them in light of similar questions about normative inquiry outside of epistemology, and the assumption that subjective reasons must be factive will be my first major proof of this hypothesis. I will be arguing that—especially in light of consideration of the role of subjective reasons in rationalizing action as well as belief—it is more reasonable to hold that subjective reasons *need not* be factive, and hence that there is a very serious and neglected possibility, in epistemology, of realizing the virtues of McDowell's and Williamson's world-implicating treatments of basic perceptual reasons without taking on what I have argued are their costs. It may not be—for anything that I will say here—that this is the *right* view to take about basic perceptual justification, but it has very attractive virtues that have been systematically overlooked simply because it has been taken for granted that subjective reasons must be factive.[37]

So in Chapter 4, I will turn to consider arguments to the effect that subjective reasons have to involve a cognitive relation to a truth. I will argue, in contrast, that subjective reasons need not involve any cognitive relation to a truth, and explain why we should think that the chief arguments to the contrary are unconvincing. However, there is one motivation for thinking that subjective reasons must be factive that I take very seriously, and it is rooted in the problem of unjustified belief, which as we saw in Chapter 1 is one of the chief obstacles to the thesis of Reasons First that is distinctive to epistemology. So the problem of unjustified belief, I will be arguing, actually plays a central role in making forceful the central framing dilemma of explaining how basic perceptual beliefs could be grounded in evidence. Hence, in order to fully escape this dilemma, we will need to find an alternative solution to the problem of unjustified belief—one that is friendly to the thesis of Reasons First.

---

[37] Some of the main voices of resistance to this dominant assumption are Schroeder (2008, 2011) and Comesaña and McGrath (2014, 2015).

4

Subjective Reasons and Truth

4.1 Why Think Subjective Reasons Must Be Factive?

In Chapter 3, I argued that there is a powerful and attractive idea about basic perceptual justification that has appeared to come with a serious cost, but that this appearance is driven by the assumption that subjective reasons must be factive. If subjective reasons need not be factive, then the dilemma about basic perceptual justification is a false forced choice, and we can attain the virtues of McDowell's and Williamson's treatments of basic perceptual reasons without what I have argued is their most striking and obvious cost. In this section we turn to the question of whether it is indeed true that subjective reasons must be factive. I will first describe a natural and attractive picture on which subjective reasons need not be factive, and argue that this view is correct. Then I will consider and dismiss a number of possible reasons why someone might come to think that subjective reasons must be factive. In Section 4.3 I will introduce a different reason why someone might be driven to the conclusion that subjective reasons must be factive which I take more seriously, and which is driven by the problem of unjustified belief. And finally, I'll show in Sections 4.4 and 4.5 how I propose to evade this difficulty.

My picture of subjective reasons is simple. Subjective reasons are act-oriented factors that compete in the determination of what it is rational for someone to do or to believe, and on the basis of which it is possible to believe. Since what it is rational for someone to do or to believe does not turn on facts external to the subject's perspective, the facts about which subjective reasons a subject has do not turn on whether she stands in cognitive or perceptual relations to any truths. Sometimes, what a subject believes or perceives to be the case makes a difference to—goes into the competition for determining—what it is rational for him/her to believe. In such cases, we can and do naturally describe the contents of the subject's beliefs or perceptual states as his/her reasons. Whether we describe them in this way may turn on whether we believe that these contents are true. But whether it is relevant to include these factors in the competition for determining what it is rational for him/her to do or to believe does not turn on whether these contents are true.

Compare, for example, a classic case from Bernard Williams (1981). Bernie is at a cocktail party, and is handed a glass by his trusted bartender, who says, "here is your gin and tonic, Bernie". He believes that he is holding a gin and tonic. But

Reasons First. Mark Schroeder, Oxford University Press (2021). © Mark Schroeder.
DOI: 10.1093/oso/9780198868224.003.0004

unbeknownst to him, the glass contains gasoline. The fact that it is gasoline counts against taking a sip, but doesn't make it more rational for him to not take a sip, because he is unaware of it. Similarly, the fact that he believes that it is a gin and tonic tends to make it more rational for him to take a sip, but it doesn't help to make taking a sip a good idea, because it is not true. Objective reasons support correct courses of action—the ones that are a good idea to take. Subjective reasons support rational courses of action—the ones that make sense from the agent's subjective perspective. Since actions can be correct without being rational and rational without being correct, we should therefore not be surprised if there can be subjective reasons without objective reasons, just like there can be objective reasons without subjective reasons. And Bernie's case, I suggest, shows us that these relations simply cross-cut one another.

So why might someone think that subjective reasons *do* involve cognitive relations to truths? Much less, why might someone find this so obvious that it does not deserve to be questioned even when it leads directly to such difficult forced choices as we observe in Chapter 3? This assumption is so deeply taken for granted in some parts of epistemology that it is hard to find something that even looks like an argument for it. Here, for example, is what Williamson has to say about it:

> For one's evidence fully to support a falsehood, the evidence must contain falsehoods, in which case some truths are *inconsistent* with one's evidence: hardly an attractive view.[1]

It is hard to call this an argument—the thesis that one's evidence contains falsehoods is *equivalent* to the thesis that some truths are inconsistent with one's evidence, so it is straightforwardly question-begging, and all that Williamson tells us about why we should not believe this, is that it is "hardly an attractive view", which he doesn't even assert directly, but puts in an appositional clause, which is a rhetorical device for implicating that what is being said is uncontroversial. So if we want to find the reasons why philosophers have taken this thesis for granted, we will have to dig deeper.

One reason why someone might think that subjective reasons involve cognitive relations to truths derives from the idea that subjective reasons are just a special case of objective reasons. This thought is encouraged by the way that we originally distinguished between subjective and objective reasons, and correlatively, the way in which we distinguished between subjective and objective evidence. And it fits

---

[1] Williamson (2013, 92). Of course, Williamson does have arguments that evidence must be true, insofar as he offers arguments that E=K, and knowledge is factive. But what the quote here illustrates is that Williamson sees what is philosophically at issue is just what the possession condition on evidence is—and not its factivity, which he sees as something that is so obvious as not to be worth controverting.

with Williamson's broader commitments, as well—he *does* think that subjective evidence is a special case of objective evidence. Your subjective evidence, according to Williamson's E=K thesis, is just objective evidence that you know.

Recall that when we originally made that distinction, in Chapter 1, we started with the observation that the fact that Christine is smiling is evidence that she is happy, but it might not be evidence that you have, because you might not be aware of it. Talk like this encourages using language like "evidence there is" to contrast with "evidence you have", in order to draw the contrast between objective and subjective evidence, and similarly, to use language like "reasons there are" to contrast with "reasons you have", in order to draw the contrast between objective and subjective reasons—a practice that I have followed in Chapter 3.[2] This kind of talk encourages the perception that subjective reasons are just a special case of objective reasons—ones to which the agent bears the right kind of cognitive relation—*having* it. Since objective reasons need to be truths, it follows, on this reasoning, that to have a subjective reason, you must stand in a cognitive relation to a truth.[3]

The problem with this reasoning is that although 'there is' and 'has' talk *can* be used, in the right sort of context and given the right sorts of contextual clues, to communicate the contrast between objective and subjective reasons, there is no privileged relationship either between "there is a reason" talk and objective reasons or between "has a reason" talk and subjective reasons. Either can be used to pick out either the objective or the subjective reason relation. This is a consequence of the fact that 'reason' can be used to talk about both objective and subjective reasons and that 'has' talk is pleonastic.

To see this, it helps to distinguish the following cases. Ronnie and Freddie like to dance, but Bradley does not. Ronnie and Bradley know that there will be dancing at the party, but Freddie does not. So there is a reason for Ronnie and Freddie to go to the party that is not a reason for Bradley to go—namely, that there will be dancing at the party. This is not a reason for Bradley to go, because it doesn't count in an act-oriented way toward making it the case that Bradley ought to go, but it does count toward making it the case that each of Ronnie and Freddie ought to go. When we make such claims, we are talking about objective reasons. This is illustrated by the fact that I stipulated that Freddie does not know about the dancing.

Yet just as I can say that the fact that there is dancing at the party is a reason for Ronnie to go, but not for Bradley, I can say that it is one of Ronnie's reasons, but not one of Bradley's, and similarly, that it is a reason that Ronnie has but Bradley does not. Moreover, there is no mystery as to why I can talk in this way, because in

---

[2] Compare Scanlon (2003), and Williamson's (2000, 2013) analogous claim that something can't be *your* evidence unless it *is* evidence.

[3] This is the thesis that I called the Factoring Account in Schroeder (2008). The following remarks summarize the upshot of the arguments of that article. The Factoring Account is endorsed explicitly by, among others, Williamson (2007), Lord (2010), and Hawthorne and Magidor (2018).

general, the possessive construction and 'has' talk are pleonastic. There is no privileged relation picked out by these constructions; rather, they can be used to pick out any salient relation. If there are four dogs, each bred by one of four people, each trained by a different one of the four, each now owned by yet a different one of the four, and each now being held by the last one of the four, then we can use expressions like 'Albert's dog' to refer, alternatively, to the dog Albert bred, the one he trained, the one he owns, or the one that he is holding, and 'has' talk patterns similarly.[4] Since this is a general fact about the possessive construction and about 'has' talk, it is no surprise that 'has' talk can be used to talk about objective reasons.

Of course, we can also use 'has' talk to contrast Ronnie with Freddie. We can say that there is a reason for Ronnie that isn't available to Freddie, or that isn't a reason Freddie has to go to the party. But it doesn't follow that we are contrasting an objective reason with a subjective reason. On the contrary, this claim makes perfect sense as a claim about contrasting *subjective* reasons. In our scenario, Ronnie has a subjective reason that Freddie doesn't, i.e., it is one of Ronnie's reasons but not one of Freddie's. So it is a reason for Ronnie but not for Freddie. All of these are perfectly possible ways of contrasting Ronnie with Freddie. So, there is no special link between 'there is' talk and objective reasons. I conclude that talk like this gives us no special reason to think that there are not perfectly cross-cutting objective and subjective reason relations—where the objective relation places a constraint on the mind-independent facts,[5] and the subjective relation places a constraint on the agent's psychology.

One way that this can be very hard to see is if we assume that everyone's objective reasons are the same. If we assume that everyone shares the same objective reasons, then we will not think that there is an interesting distinction between objective reasons that are reasons for Ronnie and objective reasons that are reasons for Bradley. So we will not think that "objective reason for" is a good candidate for a salient relation to be picked out by 'has' talk or by the possessive construction. This is the sort of thing that could lead someone to think that 'has' talk specially picks out subjective reasons, and hence to assume that it is a kind of talk about possessing objective reasons, rather than simply talk about an independent, cross-cutting, relation. Strikingly, Timothy Williamson *does* assume that objective evidence is everywhere the same. He believes that there is such a thing as the *epistemic probability function*, so differences in agents' subjective evidence can only derive

---

[4] Compare Villanueva (2012, ch. 2) on prenominal possessives. This is why, for example, Grice's (2001) attempt to single out motivating reasons using the possessive construction is particularly unhelpful.

[5] As always, it is worth reminding ourselves that among the mind-independent facts that matter for what we ought objectively to do are facts about our psychologies. Compare: "if you think everyone is after you, you ought to change your locks regularly" vs. "if you think everyone is after you, you ought to see a psychiatrist".

from differences in what the agents know.[6] Consideration of reasons for action, reasons which do clearly vary between agents, as in Ronnie and Bradley's case, is a helpful antidote to this.[7]

But the observation that the objective reason relation is a poor candidate to be the salient relation picked out by 'has' talk, if we assume that objective reasons are everywhere the same, also has an important corollary. In conversations where it is clear that we are discussing two agents whose objective reasons we know to be the same, the objective reason relation will also be a worse candidate to be the salient relation picked out by 'has', which serves to contrast the agents in question. So in such conversations, the subjective reason relation is more likely to be the preferred candidate for the referent of 'has'. And that is why it is so easy to use 'has' talk to pick out the subjective reason relation, given the right sorts of contextual clues. And none of this requires supposing that subjective reasons are just objective reasons to which you bear the right 'having' relation.

4.2 Report-Based Arguments

A second, different kind of reason for thinking that subjective reasons must involve bearing a cognitive relation to a truth turns on observations about reports of subjective reasons. I'll call this class of motivations *report*-based arguments. Report-based arguments can be run in different ways, depending on whether they apply directly to reports of subjective reasons, or apply instead to motivating-reason explanations of action or belief. I'll take each in turn, but my answer to both classes of argument will be the same: judgments about reports only tell us something interesting about how we *talk* about reasons, not about what must be true in order for there to be act-oriented factors that figure in the competition that determines what it is rational or correct for someone to believe or to do. And arguably, they do not even establish the claim that they need about how we *talk* about reasons.

The first class of report-based arguments is not as forceful as the second, but it is more direct, and it will be instructive to consider it, in order to see what goes wrong with both classes of argument. To get the first class of report-based arguments up and running, start by observing that in at least very many paradigmatic cases, there is a close relationship between objective and subjective reasons. Very roughly, when the fact that P is an objective reason for an agent to φ, that agent also has a corresponding subjective reason to φ, provided that she bears the

---

[6] Williamson (2000, ch. 10).

[7] Even in epistemology, of course, it is also plausible, though more controversial, that what is evidence for different agents may not be the same—even holding fixed that we are talking about objective evidence. This idea naturally corresponds to the idea that there are multiple possible rational *priors*.

right cognitive relation to the proposition that P—knowledge uncontroversially suffices for this relation, but on some views other, weaker, relations also suffice. Conversely, when an agent has a subjective reason to φ in virtue of believing that P, then if it is true that P, the fact that P is typically[8] also an objective reason for her to φ.

It turns out that there are many different views about the metaphysics of the agent's subjective reason, in such cases.[9] On some views, her subjective reason is her belief. (One virtue of this view is that it generalizes well to cases in which there is an act-oriented factor that helps to determine what it is rational for the subject to do but is not a belief.) On other views, her subjective reason is the *content* of her belief. (This view has the virtue that it can say something privileged about the relationship between the agent's subjective reason and her objective reason.) But regardless of what we say about the metaphysics, in ordinary language we will say things such as that "one reason she has to φ is that P".

The problem arises because we do not say this unless we think that it is really true that P.[10] If subjective reasons are the contents of beliefs, but we can only say that an agent's subjective reason is that P if it is true that P, then one conclusion to draw is that the agent does not have this subjective reason unless her belief is true. So: no subjective reason without a cognitive relation to a truth.

The problem with this argument, I believe, is that it shows us more about how we can use the expression "her reason is that P" to report subjective reasons, than it does about what factors must be like in order to count in an act-oriented way in the determination of what it is rational for the agent to do. It could very well be that it is inapt to report subjective reasons in this way, but they are there, all the same. And there is independent evidence for this. Suppose that you are unaware that Bernie's glass contains gasoline, and share Bernie's belief that it contains gin and tonic. I ask you whether Bernie has a subjective reason to take a sip, and you say, "yes—one reason he has to take a sip is that it is his favorite drink". Then I point out that it isn't really gin and tonic in the glass; it's gasoline. Now I ask you again what subjective reason Bernie has to take a sip, and you say, "that he believes it is his favorite drink". Here you report Bernie's reason differently based on what *you* believe about whether his glass contained gin and tonic. But it doesn't seem to me that you have changed your mind about what subjective reason he has to take a

---

[8] Qualifications to this generalization are needed in both directions for familiar conditional fallacy reasons. For example, someone who believes that there are no objective reasons might thereby have a subjective reason to believe that the fact that Christine is smiling is not an objective reason to believe that she is happy, but this is not the kind of thing to have a corresponding objective reason—if it is true, then there *are* no objective reasons. Compare Shope (1978). Also, depending on how we individuate reasons, other complications arise. For further discussion, see Vogelstein (2012), Whiting (2014), Sylvan (2015), Wodak (2019), and Schroeder (2018a).

[9] For example, see Wiland (2003), Turri (2009), Mitova (2015), and Alvarez (2018).

[10] As already discussed in Chapter 1, n. 14.

sip. If I pressed you on it, you shouldn't admit that you were wrong about what his reason is, but only about whether his glass contained gin and tonic.

One way in which language could be inapt, in this case, is that strictly speaking, what Bernie's subjective reason is, is in both cases his belief state, regardless of whether it is true; but for some reason we prefer to identify this state by its content, in the case in which that content is true.[11] I don't really know why we would have this preference for indirectly attributing subjective reasons in this way, so this is not my preferred view. But it is a common view about the ontology of subjective reasons shared by many philosophers that aptly explains why our ways of reporting subjective reasons would be misleading in this way.

An alternative, I think better explanation for how language could be misleading in this way is that subjective reason attributions carry an extra layer of communicated content that communicates the truth of the reason complement. This extra layer could be an implicature, either conversational or conventional.[12] Or, as I think more likely, it could be a presupposition.[13] In general, presuppositions *project* out of constructions like negation and disjunction. "It was Tom who called" presupposes that someone called, and so does "it wasn't Tom who called". So "it wasn't Tom who called" presupposes that someone called, without entailing it. Similarly, "her reason to φ is that P" is only admissible for a speaker who assumes that P, but so is "her reason to φ is not that P". Another feature of presuppositions is that they are typically *filtered* by conditionals.[14] In general, if 'P' carries the presupposition that Q, then 'if Q, P' does not. Similarly, though "her reason to φ is that P" is admissible only for speakers who assume that P, "if P, then her reason φ is that P" is fine even for speakers who do not assume that P.

Another mark of presuppositions is their interaction with attitude verbs like 'knows', 'hopes', and 'wonders'. If 'P' carries the primary content that Q and the

---

[11] This view is usually known as *psychologism*—see Turri (2009) for a defense.

[12] Compare Hazlett (2010, 2012) for skepticism about factive entailments in the case of other paradigmatic factive verbs, including "knows". Hazlett defends the conversational implicature view. Daniel Whiting has also suggested to me that the factivity of subjective reason reports is conversationally cancelable, and that would be fine for my purposes here, but I think it would be much more surprising that it has been so often confused with an entailment if that were so.

[13] Comesaña and McGrath (2014), who are fellow-travelers with me in seeking to make room for the idea that basic perceptual reasons can be non-factive (see also their 2015), also defend the view that subjective reason claims, along with emotive factives like "is happy that" and "is upset that", presuppose but do not entail their complements. However, note that Comesaña and McGrath grant their opponent that many other presuppositions, including clefts like "it was Sally who rang the bell" also entail their presuppositions. This is wrong, I think, for the reasons articulated clearly in Perl (2020), based on data about how presuppositional constructions interact with attitude reports. But a clearer model, I think, is the case of gendered pronouns. If I say, "he gave her a note", what I say presupposes, but does not entail, that she is female (speakers who misuse gendered pronouns because of a stroke or because they take the wrong view about gender identity do not fail to say anything true). Similarly, "he hoped that she got his note" can be true if he took for granted that a given person is female and hoped that person to have gotten his note, but not if he took for granted that a certain person got his note and hoped that person to be female.

[14] Karttunen (1973).

presupposition that R, then "she knows that P" communicates that the subject knows that Q and that the subject assumes or accepts that R, but does not require that the subject *knows* that R. For example, "she knows that it wasn't Jack who did it" can be true even if she does not know that someone else did it—so long as she knows that Jack didn't. Similarly, "she hopes that P" communicates that the subject hopes that Q and that the subject accepts that R, but not that the subject hopes that R, or that the subject hopes that Q and R. For example, "she hopes that it wasn't Jack who did it" means that she hopes that Jack didn't do it, and communicates that she assumes that someone did, but cannot be used to communicate that she assumes that Jack did not do it but hopes that someone did.[15]

Subjective reason reports also pattern with presuppositions in this way. Even after you find out that Bernie's glass is full of gasoline, you can still, rightly, insist that you knew *what* Bernie's reason is. This is just what we would expect if knowledge that Bernie's glass contains gin and tonic is not required for you to know that Bernie's reason was that his glass contained gin and tonic. Similarly, you can hope that Bernie's reason is that his glass contains gin and tonic without hoping that his glass contains gin and tonic, so long as you assume that his glass really does contain gin and tonic. You might hope this, for example, if you believe that his glass contains gin and tonic, hope that he drinks, and hence hope that this is a reason for him to drink. But you can't count as hoping that Bernie's reason is that his glass contains gin and tonic simply because you assume what Bernie's motive is and hope that his glass really does contain gin and tonic.[16] So what I actually suspect is that non-factive subjective reason ascriptions get into trouble not because there are no act-oriented factors that figure in the determination of what it is rational for the subject to do, in such cases, but rather simply because "her reason is that P" carries the presupposition that P.[17]

The second class of report-based arguments for the factivity of subjective reasons is more indirect. Instead of focusing directly on reports of subjective reasons, these arguments focus directly on motivating reasons explanations of action or belief. The thesis—held by many—that *motivating* reason claims are factive can then be used to draw a *link* to subjective reasons. The link to subjective reasons is based on two

---

[15] Compare Perl (2020).

[16] According to Perl (2020), attitude reports with presuppositional complements *implicate*, but do not *entail*, that the matrix subject accepts the presupposition; but the tests that I am focusing on in the main text do not turn on this question.

[17] The presuppositional account also helps to explain what seems to be helpful about Dancy's employment of so-called *appositional* ascriptions of reasons, where he says things like "Bernie's reason to take a sip is, as he believes, that his glass contains gin and tonic". The insertion of "as he believes" serves not only to note that Bernie believes this, but to distance the speaker from the assumption that this is true. So we should expect some pragmatic reasons, given the use of such constructions, not to attribute to the speaker commitment to the proposition that is ordinarily presupposed—namely, that P. The fact that presuppositions are not easily canceled helps to explain why many do not find this a wholly satisfactory way of talking about non-factive subjective reasons, but the fact that it helps at all is explained by the fact that the factivity is a presupposition rather than an entailment.

premises: first, that if an agent has a subjective reason to act or believe in some way, then it is possible for her to act or believe *for* that reason; and second, that if an agent acts or believes for some reason, then that can be reported by saying that "she acted [/believed] because P", for some way of filling in 'P'. Given these two assumptions, the idea is to argue that motivating reasons explanations of the form "she acted [/believed] because P" can only advert to truths, or more strongly, that they require the subject to know that P (which of course entails that P). Since these explanations can only advert to truths, reasoning contrapositively by our second assumption leads to the conclusion that an agent can act for a reason only if there is a truth for which she acts, and hence again reasoning contrapositively, this time by our first assumption, that the agent can have a subjective reason only if she stands in a cognitive relation to a truth.[18]

Arguments based on ascriptions of motivating reasons must come to grips with the fact that motivating reasons can be reported using many different locutions. I can say that the reason for which someone acted was that P. Or that her reason for acting was that P. Or that she acted because P. And many authors assume that what goes for one of these locutions must go for the others. So since 'because P' obviously entails that P, from this assumption it follows that each of these locutions has a factive entailment. But if what we mean by motivating reasons is not tied to any particular locution, but rather to the communicated content that these have in common, when understood in context, then there is no reason to suppose that they must all be equivalent. Even if "she acted because P" entails that P, "the reason for which she acted was that P" may not.

Moreover, we should agree with the proponent of this argument that it is admissible for us to issue reports like "she opened the door because someone knocked" only if we believe someone really knocked. And I think it is safe to grant that if someone has a subjective reason for action or belief, then it is possible for her to act or believe for that reason. But the problem arises in trying to read off of this fact about the admissibility of *reports* of the reasons why someone acted, anything about the identity of the reasons for which someone acts or believes. As before, suppose that you believe that Bernie's glass is full of his favorite drink, gin and tonic. Together, we watch him take a sip, and then look away. I ask you why he took a sip, and you say, "because it was his favorite drink". Then we turn to see Bernie sputtering and spitting out his drink, and we learn that it was gasoline. You amend, "because he *thought* it was his favorite drink". Have you changed your mind about the reason for which Bernie acted, or only about whether his glass

---

[18] Arguments in this family have been offered by Unger (1975), Hyman (1999), Hornsby (2008), Hawthorne and Stanley (2009), and many others. Many of these authors claim, following Unger, not only that an agent's motivating reason must be a *truth*, but that she must *know* it. The explanation I give in the main text of why it would seem that the agent's reason must be a truth does not carry over to explain why it would seem like it must be known, but Hughes (2014) and Locke (2015) give convincing reasons to think that the arguments that motivating reasons must be known rest on a mistake.

contained his favorite drink? I contend both that you have changed your mind only about the latter and that you knew all along what his reason was.

Again, we could take different views about why reports are misleading, in this way. We can even take different views about different locutions used to attribute motivating reasons. One possible view is that motivating reasons are always belief states, irrespective of whether those beliefs are true. On this view, there may be some reason why we cite the contents of these beliefs, rather than the beliefs themselves, if they are true (and perhaps only if they are knowledge). This is compatible with the main lesson that I want to argue for in this chapter, but I don't know what this reason would be, so it is not my preferred account of what is going on. Instead, what I suspect is going on is that strictly speaking, motivating reasons are the contents of beliefs, but that constructions like "the reason why he acted was that P" and "he acted because P" *presuppose* that P, at least when their conversational import is to attribute motivating reasons.

This is supported by the observation that "the reason why he acted wasn't that P" also appears to be inadmissible for speakers who believe that it is false that P, and by the observation that even a speaker who is unsure what is in Bernie's glass can felicitously say, "if his glass contained gin and tonic, then the reason why he acted was that it was his favorite drink". And finally, although you can hope that Jack and Jill both come to the party without hoping that Jill comes—so long as you hope that Jack comes and take for granted that Jill will—you cannot hope that the reason why Bernie took a sip is that his glass contained gin and tonic simply because you hope that his glass did indeed contain gin and tonic, and take for granted the rest. These are all, again, among the characteristic earmarks of presuppositions.

So I conclude that report-based arguments all tell us a great deal about how we *talk* about reasons, but that they tell us very little about the act-oriented factors that compete in the determination of what it is rational for someone to do. In fact, not only do they not tell us that subjective reasons in this sense must be factive, they positively suggest that subjective reasons need *not* be factive. And this is because the presuppositional account of the factivity of subjective reason and motivating reason attributions supports the view that the *primary*—non-presupposed— content of subjective and motivating reason attributions do *not* entail that subjective or motivating reasons must be true. So if anything, the fact that the *primary* contents of subjective and motivating reason attributions do not require truth strongly suggests that subjective reasons and motivating reasons themselves—the things we are reporting when we make these attributions—do not require truth.

4.3 The Problem of Unjustified Belief

As promised, in this chapter and the last chapter I have introduced a general problem from epistemology, and I have traced this problem to a thesis about reasons—the thesis that having a subjective reason requires standing in a cognitive relation to a truth. I have argued—partly by appeal to the general case of reasons for action—that there are independent reasons—outside of the fact that it would avoid this puzzle in epistemology—to be doubtful of this thesis, and that the most obvious reasons to think that it is true trade on subtle mistakes. This completes the first leg of my argument for the fruitfulness of this book's *Core Hypothesis*, by showing how more careful attentiveness to the parallels between reasons for action and reasons for belief can shed light on important issues in epistemology.

But there is an argument that having subjective reasons requires standing in a cognitive relation to a truth that I take very seriously, and that I do not think trades on any subtle mistakes. It is intimately connected to the problem of unjustified beliefs. Seeing what this argument is and how it works will complete my argument that solving the problem of unjustified beliefs in a way that is friendly to the thesis of Reasons First has an important payoff for the epistemology of basic perceptual beliefs.

Recall from Chapter 1 that the problem of unjustified beliefs stems from the fact that sometimes, agents have subjective reasons in virtue of their beliefs. But beliefs that are themselves unjustified do not add to the rationality of beliefs that follow from them. The problem for Reasons First is that the obvious ways to avoid this problem are to suppose that either justification or knowledge is required in order to have a subjective reason.[19] This makes either knowledge or justification both explanatorily and analytically prior to subjective reasons. So it follows from either of these views that subjective reasons cannot be explanatorily and analytically prior to both justification and knowledge. But both justification and knowledge are, as I have promised to argue in Part IV, normative, and so *Reasons First* can be true only if reasons are both explanatorily and analytically prior to each. But plausibly, in order for *reasons* to be both explanatorily and analytically prior to either justification or knowledge, it must be *subjective* reasons that are prior, since it is subjective reasons that are relevant to rationality, and knowledge entails rationality of belief. So it follows that unless knowledge is not, after all, essentially normative, Reasons First rules out the obvious response to the problem of unjustified beliefs. That is how the problem of unjustified beliefs poses a problem for Reasons First.

But the problem of unjustified beliefs also grounds an intriguing argument that subjective reasons must be factive. It goes like this: in order to solve the problem of unjustified beliefs, we need to build either justification or something stronger, like knowledge, into the nature of subjective reasons. (Note that this is the same first

---

[19] Compare Feldman (1988, 227): "If I believe, for no good reason, that P and I infer (correctly) from this that Q, I don't think we want to say that I 'have' P as evidence for Q. Only things that I believe (or could believe) rationally, or perhaps, with justification, count as part of the evidence that I have. It seems to me that this is a good reason to include an epistemic acceptability constraint on evidence possessed..."

step that led to the trouble for *Reasons First*.) So we need to assume either that it is part of the nature of subjective reasons that no one can count as having a subjective reason in virtue of being in some mental state, unless that state is justified, or the analogous assumption for knowledge.

But note that though beliefs can be justified or unjustified, perceptual states themselves, at least in normal cases, cannot. So if we build justification into the nature of subjective reasons, we will rule out the possibility that perceptual experiences could rationalize basic perceptual beliefs. (It is possible, of course, that perceptual states do *not* ground reasons for beliefs, but much of the force of the dialectic discussed in Sections 3.2 and 3.3 assumes that there are at least some important attractions of avoiding this conclusion, so we should grant the force of this as an objection.) In contrast, seeing that there is something square in front of you is a perceptual state, but according to Williamson, at least, it is also knowledge.[20] So it is at least intelligible, and arguably natural, to think that knowledge is a restriction on subjective reasons that applies unequivocally to both perceptual reasons and inferential reasons. Hence, the argument goes, in order to solve the problem of unjustified beliefs, we should build knowledge into the condition required in order to have a subjective reason. But since knowledge is factive, it follows that having a subjective reason requires standing in a cognitive relation to a truth.[21]

In what follows, I want to respond to this argument in two different ways. First, in the remainder of this section, I will argue that the problem of unjustified belief cannot successfully be solved in this way, because it is *not* true that seeing that P is a way of knowing that P. And then, in Section 4.4, I will show that the problem of unjustified belief can instead be solved in another way that is consistent both with Reasons First and with the idea that having a subjective reason need not involve standing in any relation to a truth.

The preceding argument tries to show that subjective reasons must be truths *by* arguing that they must be knowledge, and it tries to motivate the claim that they must be knowledge as a solution to the problem of unjustified beliefs. This solution trades on the assumption that perceptual experiences can be knowledge—an assumption that follows from Williamson's (2000) claim that knowledge is the most general factive, stative attitude. But I will now give two arguments that seeing that P does *not* entail knowing that P.[22]

---

[20] Compare also French (2012, 2013), Hyman (2014).

[21] This argument is the focus of Schroeder (2011a). Compare Byrne (2014).

[22] Fricker (2009), Cozzo (2011), and Hyman (2014) each give different sorts of reasons for dissenting from Williamson's thesis that knowledge is the most general factive stative attitude, each of which is consistent with the claim that seeing that P entails knowing that P. Pritchard (2012) argues directly that seeing that P does not entail knowing that P; his argument is very similar to my third case. See also Schroeder (2016). Turri (2010a) also argues that seeing that P does not entail knowing that P; but Turri's argument turns on the claim that fake barn cases do not undermine seeing that there is a barn—a claim that I reject, for reasons that will become clear in Chapter 5.

My first argument is simple. It goes like this:

P1   Necessarily, if S knows that P, then S believes that P.

P2   It is possible that S sees that P but does not believe that P.

C   Therefore, it is possible that S sees that P but does not know that P.

Premise P1 of this argument is part of the philosophical orthodoxy about knowledge, and Williamson himself does not deny it. Indeed, he takes great pains to explain how it could be true that knowledge entails belief, even if belief is not part of the analysis of knowledge. On Williamson's preferred view, belief is to be analyzed in terms of knowledge, rather than conversely, in a way to preserve this entailment. Belief is a state that *aims at* knowledge. So P1 is a good place for an argument to start.[23] I'll return to the plausibility of P1 and to Williamson's attitude toward it shortly.

But premise P2 is also compelling. I'll give several kinds of example. A first kind of example derives from the fact that perception represents many more things than we ever form beliefs about. Suppose that you are walking to your lecture, consumed with an obscure question about Kant interpretation. You pass a classroom with an open door, and see that the door is open, but since you are preoccupied with Kant, you do not form a belief that the door is open. You may remember nothing about the door a moment later, as with most things that you see but do not attend to. Or alternatively, if pressed a few minutes later, you may be able to imaginatively rehearse your walk down the hallway, and come to realize then that you saw that the door was open. Either way, at the time that you see that the door is open, you do not believe that the door is open.

What makes examples like this one possible, as I have noted, is that perception represents many more things than we ever attend to or are recorded as beliefs. It follows from this that such examples are not only possible, but they are ubiquitous. Even now, as you read this note, you see that many things are the case without believing them to be the case. A second kind of example in support of premise P2 is also ubiquitous. It turns on the observation that it takes *time* to form a belief. Even if you believe everything that you see, you see it *first*. This is a simple consequence of the fact that we are finite creatures with limited cognitive capacities, or more prosaically, that the neural realizers of belief are at least partly downstream from the neural realizers of perceptual states.

Both of my first two sorts of examples might be resisted, as in French (2012), on the grounds that factive perceptual verbs like 'sees that' do not pick out a purely perceptual relation, but only a state that obtains at least partly in virtue of belief—a

---

[23] Not that it has not been denied! Compare Radford (1966) and Farkas (2015) for very different approaches.

sort of hybrid combination of perception and belief. French is not thinking about my sorts of example, however, because he is responding to a different sort of case, due to John Turri (2010a). And unfortunately, I don't see how French's claim would make the problem posed by my cases go away. For even if 'sees that' expresses such a hybrid state, there are still purely perceptual relations to the world that underlie this state, and these perceptual relations happen only if the world is as they represent it to be. Such relations would be factive attitudes to the world, whether or not we have verbs for them in English.

Still, there is also a third, epistemologically important, kind of case that supports P2. In the two kinds of cases that I have surveyed so far, it is *rational* for a subject to believe what she sees, but she doesn't—either simply not yet, because too few milliseconds have elapsed for the proper neural signals to travel, or because she is attending to something else and can't form beliefs about everything. But it is also possible for a subject to see that P and not believe that P, because even though she sees that P, it is not *rational* for her to believe that P. This happens, I believe, in cases of *subjective perceptual defeat.*[24]

If you rationally but falsely believe that you are wearing rose-colored glasses, then even if you see that there is something red in front of you, it is not rational for you to believe that there is something red in front of you. If you *were* wearing rose-colored glasses, then you would not count as seeing that there is something red in front of you. But you are not really wearing rose-colored glasses—you just rationally believe that you are. So you really do see that there is something red in front of you. But if you are rational in such a case, you will not believe that there really is something red in front of you. So cases of subjective perceptual defeat are cases in which it is not even *rational* to believe what you see.[25]

You might doubt whether someone who believes that she is wearing rose-colored glasses can really count as seeing that there is something red in front of her. So suppose that you are in this case—you are looking at something red, it looks red to you in the normal way, but because you are wearing rose-colored glasses, you suspend belief. I ask you if there is something red in front of you, and you say that you aren't sure. Bewildered by this answer, I point out that you are wearing perfectly good glasses and looking right at them in good lighting. You take off your glasses and realize that the lenses are clear. You say, "Oh! I saw that it was red, but since I thought that I was wearing rose-colored glasses, I didn't trust my eyesight."

The appropriateness of this report supports the view that you really did see that there was something red in front of you. In contrast, the following, alternative, report does not sound so good: "Oh! I couldn't see that it was red, because I thought that I was wearing rose-colored glasses." You weren't actually wearing

---

[24] Compare Pritchard (2012).
[25] Indeed, it may be rational for you to believe that there is *not* anything red in front of you. But it is implausible to describe this as a case of inconsistent beliefs.

rose-colored glasses, so of course you *could* see that it was red. The fact that you believed otherwise at the time is neither here nor there. So I conclude that subjective defeasibility does not undermine seeing something to be the case.

This allows us to construct a second argument:

P3   Necessarily, if S knows that P, then it is rational for S to believe that P.

P4   It is possible that S sees that P but it is not rational for S to believe that P.

C   Therefore, it is possible that S sees that P but does not know that P.

The case of subjective perceptual defeat supports premise P4 as well as premise P2. But our second argument does not rely on premise P1. It relies instead on premise P3. But premise P3 is also independently compelling.[26] I noted above that Williamson does not deny premise P1. But Williamson positively affirms premise P3. According to Williamson (2013), the only rational norm governing belief is to believe only what you know. But from this, P3 follows.

Of course, Williamson's grounds for accepting P3 would lead him to reject my example in support of P4. Because he holds that belief is rational just in case it is knowledge, he would deny that it is possible to rationally but falsely believe that you are wearing rose-colored glasses. Still, even on this view, you could believe that it is 99 percent likely that you are wearing rose-colored glasses. But if this is what you believe, then it is not plausibly rational for you to believe that there is something red in front of you, given only your visual experience as evidence. So my second argument survives. Moreover, even if it is not irrational to believe that there is something red in front of you in this case, it is certainly intelligible for a cautious believer to suspend belief in such a case. So this case can still be used to support P2 of my original argument.

We can also use cases of subjective perceptual defeat to support a stronger conclusion. So far I have been arguing only that seeing does not entail knowing. But it is compatible with this thesis, that seeing *does* entail being *in a position to know*. But necessarily, if you are in a position to know that P, then it is rational for you to believe that P. This assumption is at least as compelling as premise P3. So cases of subjective perceptual defeat show that seeing does not even entail being in a position to know.

In *Knowledge and Its Limits*, Williamson briefly entertains the possibility that someone might deny that seeing entails believing, or that seeing entails rationality of (he says, 'justification for') belief, citing Steup (1992). Here is what he says:

> However, such cases put more pressure on the link between knowing and believing or having justification than they do on the link between perceiving or remembering and knowing. If you really do see *that* it is raining, which is not

---

[26] Again, of course, not that it is undeniable. Compare, prominently, Lasonen-Aarnio (2010).

simply to see the rain, then you know that it is raining; seeing that A is a way of knowing that A   (Williamson 2000, 38).

Here Williamson is saying that he finds it more plausible to reject my premises P1 and P3 than to reject the view that knowledge is the most general factive stative attitude or that *seeing* counts as a factive stative attitude. But other than simply asserting his view, he gives no reasons why it is more plausible than either P1 or P3, and he goes on to devote much ingenuity to making sense of both P1 and P3. This is hard to understand if Williamson does not find P1 and P3 to be at least *prima facie* compelling.

For all that I have said here—and there are reasons to suspect that it may not generalize—knowledge itself is entailed by all *non-perceptual* factive stative attitudes, including attitudes like *remembering* and emotive factives like 'is pleased that'.[27] We should also allow that there is *something* in common between perceptual factive stative attitudes, and we can allow that Williamson may even be right about many of its features—perhaps it requires safety and satisfies margin-for-error principles, and perhaps it is a distinctive mental state that is not shared with hallucinations or illusions. Perhaps it is even a necessary condition, in order to have the kind of evidence that we need in order to have knowledge.[28] Perhaps, in short, Williamson is right about almost everything about the nature of this state— indeed, I am myself very sympathetic to this conclusion. But this state is not knowledge.

4.4 Digression: A Model

In Chapters 3 and 4 I have been arguing that the problem of unjustified beliefs is intimately connected to puzzles about how perceptual experience could be a privileged source of evidence about the external world. If we assume that perceptual experiences themselves do not count as knowledge and cannot be justified or rational in and of themselves, then the orthodox answer to the problem of unjustified beliefs, which builds in a justification or knowledge restriction into the nature of subjective reasons, rules out the possibility that perceptual experiences can themselves be a source of evidence. But if we follow Williamson in allowing, on the other hand, that perceptual experiences can count as knowledge in and of themselves, then we are stuck in the grips of the best motivation for the view that subjective reasons must be factive, which plays such a central role in our puzzles from Chapter 4 about how perceptual experience could be a privileged source of evidence about the external world.

---

[27] Compare Unger (1975).   [28] I will argue precisely this in Chapter 5.

To get out of these difficulties, we must embrace a non-orthodox solution to the problem of unjustified beliefs.[29] We must be able to give some explanation of how the basic intuition that drives the problem of unjustified beliefs could be true, even though there is no justification or knowledge restriction on the act-oriented factors that compete with one another in the determination of what it is rational for an agent to do, or to believe. What we need, in short, is to know enough about the *mechanics* of how subjective reasons compete with one another, in order to be able to see how it could turn out that irrational beliefs will have no net effect on what it is rational for the agent to believe, even if we allow them into the mix.

This sounds like a strange abstract possibility—that we can allow irrational beliefs into our weighing calculus without fear that they will bias the results. But it is not, in fact, so strange. The magic is all in the mechanics of how our calculus for weighing reasons actually works. In this section, I will build on work by Jeff Horty (2012) to give a simple model for the calculus of how an agent's subjective reasons weigh together in order to determine what it is rational for her to believe. The model that I will give is highly idealized, and some of these idealizations are inconsistent with claims that I will go on to argue for in Parts III and IV of this book. But my purpose in stating the model is not to give the definitive account of how reasons combine in order to determine what it is rational to believe—a task which would be difficult for a lengthy book in its own right, not least because it would involve dealing with many other unsolved problems[30]—but rather, simply to demonstrate that the magic is, indeed, in the mechanics: it is an existence proof that there are simple and natural mechanics for the way in which subjective reasons combine to determine what it is rational for you to believe that predict that irrational beliefs will not affect what it is rational for you to believe, without needing to hard-wire this conclusion by restricting the nature of subjective reasons.

It turns out that Jeff Horty's work, developed and exposited in his wonderful book, *Reasons as Defaults*, and in a set of related papers,[31] is designed to do *most* of these things that I need from such a model, and can be adapted to do all of them. In the remainder of this section I'll summarize some of the central features of this system and offer this adaptation; readers who are willing to take my word for it may profitably skip to Section 4.5.

---

[29] The solution in this section is intended to be consistent with, but is not committed to, the argument in Schroeder (2011a).

[30] For example, a general account would need to deal with the arduous problem of how reasons *accrue*, as discussed by Nair (2016).

[31] Horty (2007a, 2007b, 2012, 2014). I will set aside the question of whether Horty's framework requires making *defaults* out to be prior to and explanatory of reasons, and if so, whether that challenges Reasons First. By the standards laid out in Chapter 2, defaults are going to count as reasons for my purposes in this book—and unlike the idea of Evidence as Reasons, it does not make some other familiar normative concept like *ought* analytically prior to reasons.

In his book, Horty develops a rigorous formal system for thinking about how a set of reasons comes together to support a conclusion about what to believe. His system, which is developed using tools from nonmonotonic logic, is carefully designed in order to shed light on the mechanics of the defeasibility of reasons, and it is flexible enough that it can be interpreted as allowing reasons to come both from belief and from perceptual appearances.[32] The most straightforward interpretations of his framework do not allow us to start with incompatible reasons, but as I will show, it can easily be adapted to do so, provided that we interpret it in a slightly different way from Horty's own interpretation.

The key concepts of Horty's framework are *defaults*, *priorities*, *scenarios*, and *extensions*. The framework itself is an extension of Reiter's (1980) default logic, whose idea was to model nonmonotonic or defeasible reasoning by supplementing deductive logic with additional, defeasible, inference rules, which are known as *defaults*. For example, the proposition (B) that Tweety is a bird intuitively defeasibly supports the conclusion (F) that Tweety can fly, and so this can be modeled by a default rule δ_1 of the form B→F. Reiter's idea was to be able, starting with a given consistent body of background beliefs, to characterize how those background beliefs could admissibly be *extended* through defeasible, non-deductive inference. Since he was interested in modeling reasoning that is non-monotonic, or having conclusions that might be given up upon learning something new, rather than in modeling reasoning that is irreflexive, i.e., that gives up some of the premises that it starts with, Reiter assumed that the background beliefs are consistent and that default reasoning would always *extend* those background beliefs. Hence, default logic is typically characterized as concerned with how to characterize *extensions* of a starting set of premises.

In Reiter's original default logic, each default rule contains a built-in condition that specifies when it is defeated. If you know (B) that Tweety is a bird but nothing else, it is reasonable to conclude (F) that she can fly. But this inference is defeasible; if you also know (W) that she has a broken wing, then it is more reasonable to conclude that she cannot fly. In Reiter's logic, we get this because the default rule explicitly tells us what its exceptions are. But intuitively, this is like building in a medical emergency as an exception to the principle to always keep your promises, rather than treating it as a balance of reasons, as Ross did. After all, in addition to the way that (B) defeasibly supports (F), the proposition (W) that Tweety has a broken wing also defeasibly supports the conclusion (~F) that Tweety cannot fly, and so this also can be modeled by a default rule δ_2 of the form W→~F.

So Horty's framework instead works by assigning a *priority* relationship among defaults. It models the way that the support given for (~F) by (W) outweighs the support given for (F) by (B) by assigning δ_2 a higher *priority*, which he writes,

[32] For discussion of the general challenges in and importance of exploring such models, see Nair and Horty (2018).

$\delta_1 < \delta_2$. The mechanics by which defaults are put together to determine reasons guarantees that defaults with higher priorities always win, which corresponds, roughly, to the idea that you should always believe what is better supported by reasons. In the full version of Horty's framework, the priorities on defaults are not fixed, but can themselves be reasoned about. But for our illustrative purposes here, we will require only a simpler version of the view, on which priorities can be assumed to be fixed by background facts.

So the goal of Horty's default logic is to get us from a set of background propositions W, a set of defaults D, and a priority ordering $<$, to one or more *extensions* or supersets of W that correspond to admissible conclusions to draw, given W as your starting point. Since the inputs to this process always consist in a $\langle W,D,< \rangle$ triple, Horty introduces a name for such triples, calling them *default theories*. Horty's default logic consists in a recipe by which default theories determine extensions.

Finally, the concept of a *scenario* plays a central role in Horty's mechanics for *how* default theories determine extensions. It helps to think of a scenario, very roughly, as a candidate for the reasons that are active in supporting conclusions. Formally, a scenario based on the default theory $\langle W,D,< \rangle$ is just a subset of D. Scenarios play a crucial role in the mechanics of Horty's default logic, because the way we get to an extension or set of conclusions is to first select a privileged set of reasons—what is called a *proper scenario*—from among the defaults with which we begin. Intuitively, the conclusions that we should draw are the ones that are supported by such a privileged—or *proper*—set of reasons.

Formally, proper scenarios are characterized in terms of the concept of a *binding* default. Intuitively, binding defaults are ones that are *good* reasons to rely on. Defaults are defined as binding or not relative to a scenario. To be binding in a scenario S, a default must satisfy three important conditions, which correspond to ruling out each of three ways in which a reason could be a bad one to rely on. First, its premise must be one that you could be in a position to believe if you relied on the reasons in S. Formally, a default is *triggered* just in case its premise is a logical consequence of the background information W together with the conclusions of all of the defaults in S. Second, its conclusion must be consistent with what you know—if accepting a reason would lead you to conclude something that you started off knowing not to be the case, then that can't be a good reason to rely on. Formally, a default is *conflicted* just in case its conclusion is inconsistent with the background information W together with the conclusions of each of the defaults in S. And finally, in order to be binding, a default must not be outranked by some other good reason. Formally, a default δ_1 is *defeated* in S just in case there is some default δ_2 that is triggered in S, such that $\delta_1 < \delta_2$ and the conclusions of δ_1 and δ_2 are not jointly consistent with the background information in W. So a default is *binding* in a scenario S just in case it is triggered in S, but not conflicted or defeated in S.

Finally, Horty's first-pass characterization of proper scenarios, which it will suffice to rely on here, as he does for most of his book, is that a scenario is proper just in case it contains all and only the defaults that are binding relative to it. Proper scenarios are therefore *stable*—they are *fixed points* of the process of checking a set of reasons over to see if there is some better set of reasons. And extensions are just what follow from the conclusions of a proper scenario, together with the propositions in W. So once we have a proper scenario in hand—a set of reasons that is a stable way to reason—the framework says that we are allowed to rely on those reasons—to draw the conclusions that the defaults in that scenario support.[33]

We can see how all of these elements come together with a simple example. Suppose that we have a case with the abstract structure $W=\{A,B\}$, $D=\{\delta_1=A\rightarrow C$, $\delta_2=B\rightarrow\sim C$, $\delta_3=C\rightarrow D\}$, and > specifies only that $\delta_1>\delta_2$. For example, you might start with the information (A) that Alice says that Caroline said that D and (B) that Bob said that Caroline did not say that D, where Alice is more trustworthy than Bob, which is reflected in the ranking of Alice's testimony (δ_1) over Bob's (δ_2). This default theory has only one stable scenario, which is $\{\delta_1,\delta_3\}$. If you reason on the basis of these reasons, you conclude that Caroline did say that D, and hence that D, and the reason provided by Bob's testimony is defeated, because it asks us to believe something incompatible with a more reliable source.

Now that we have the basic elements of Horty's framework on the table, we can see that it gives us a fruitful way of thinking about how potential inputs from belief come together to support answers to what it is rational for a subject to believe on that basis. To employ the framework, what we need is a way of thinking about how to fill in each of the roles in a default theory: W, and D, and <. On the simplest orthodox interpretation of the framework, which I relied on in the illustrative example above, we assume that W includes the beliefs or knowledge that the agent starts with—something that we do not expect to change, upon further reflection or the receipt of further information. And we assume that D and < somehow represent the subject's epistemic priors, or perhaps a set of objective support relationships that we should expect any rational agent's thinking to respect. Holding fixed D and <, the framework allows us to define a nonmonotonic consequence relation ⊨ between sets W of propositions and propositions. This consequence relation exhibits the property of nonmonotonicity, meaning that for some sets W and some propositions P and Q, W⊨P but it is not the case that W∩ {Q}⊨P. So it is on this interpretation that Horty's framework is naturally thought of as characterizing a nonmonotonic logic, and this is the sort of default interpretation that he assumes when applying this system to cases of reasoning with belief.

---

[33] Here I simplify slightly; Horty's framework allows for multiple extensions, in some cases, and interesting issues arise about what an agent should believe when there are multiple extensions, or about what further constraints might be added in order to eliminate multiple extensions. The cases that I will discuss are all cases with unique extensions.

But unfortunately, we can't adopt this orthodox interpretation for our purposes. The problem is that like most consequence relations studied in nonmonotonic logic, Horty's consequence relation is *reflexive*, meaning that if P∈W, then W⊨P. So everything that we put into W will come out as something it is admissible to believe (this is why we call them 'extensions'). But in order to address the problem of unjustified beliefs, what we are looking for is a mechanics for how reasons come together which does *not* build in the assumption that all of our inputs are things that it is rational for the agent to believe. So in order to use Horty's framework to model the apparent factive attitude view, we will need to interpret its components—W, D, and <—differently.

It turns out that there is an easy trick in order to do so. Instead of thinking of the beliefs that the subject starts with as nonnegotiable, we can think of them as a kind of *default* information. So to model the reasoning of a subject for whom it is presumed but not assumed a priori that she will retain her initial beliefs after rational reflection, we should not build the contents of her beliefs into W; rather, we should take W to be the empty set, and add defaults of the form T→P to D (where T is a tautology, so these are automatically triggered defaults), whenever she believes that P.[34]

So if we know the epistemic priors D and < that we would use to model the reasoning of an agent on the orthodox interpretation, and we know what a given agent believes to be the case and what appears to her to be the case, this allows us to construct a default theory ⟨W,D*,<*⟩, where W=∅, D* is the union of D together with defaults of the form T→P, for each content P of the agent's beliefs or appearances, and <* is < supplemented with appropriate rankings to apply to the additional defaults in D*. This default theory will have its own stable scenarios, resulting in extensions which can be thought of as characterizing possible rational belief sets that are rationally supported by the beliefs and appearances with which the subject begins, given those epistemic priors. If an extension includes all of the propositions that the subject initially believes, then we may conclude that all of her beliefs are rational for her to have. But if no extension includes one of the contents of her initial appearances, then we may conclude that it is not rational for the subject to believe that things are as they so appear to her. And since the mechanics builds in that no scenario is stable unless all of its defaults are *triggered*, it follows from this view that no unjustified belief ever makes a downstream difference for what it is rational for the agent to believe.

We can again illustrate with a simple example. Suppose that Edmund believes that Alice said that Caroline said that D, that Bob said that Caroline did not say

---

[34] More generally, we add a default of the form T→P whenever the proposition that P counts as among the agent's subjective reasons—whether by being what she believes, what she perceives, or in some other way.

that D, that Caroline said that D, and that Bob is more reliable than Alice.[35] One way in which this could be true can be modeled with the set of defaults $\delta_1 = \top \to A$, $\delta_2 = \top \to B$, $\delta_3 = \top \to C$, $\delta_4 = A \to C$, $\delta_5 = B \to \sim C$, $\delta_6 = C \to D$, with $\delta_5 > \delta_4$ and $\delta_5 > \delta_3$, where again A="Alice said that C", B="Bob said that $\sim$C", and C="Caroline said that D". The only stable scenario for this default theory is $\{\delta_1, \delta_2, \delta_5\}$. Defaults δ_1 and δ_2 are triggered by the trivial proposition $\top$, and δ_4 and δ_5 are triggered by the conclusions of δ_1 and δ_2. And only δ_4 is defeated. But δ_6 is not triggered unless δ_3 is, so it cannot be a member of a stable scenario unless δ_3 is. And δ_3 cannot be a member of any stable scenario, because it always conflicts with a triggered default of higher priority—δ_5. So the extension for this default theory is the set $\{A, B, \sim C\}$.

But we are interpreting the extension as telling us what Edmund rationally should believe. So what this tells us is that what Edmund rationally should believe is (A) that Alice said that Caroline said that D, (B) that Bob said that Caroline did not say that D, and ($\sim$C) that Caroline did not say that D. So even though Edmund starts off believing that Caroline said that D, which would otherwise support the conclusion that D, it is *not* rational for Edmund to believe that D, and this is *because* it is not rational for him to believe that Caroline said so, either—for he has decisive evidence that Caroline did not, in fact, say so. And so this is what we were looking for—without excluding irrational beliefs from the get-go, some beliefs are nevertheless judged to be irrational, and if they are, they don't get to lend any support.

In this section I've introduced the very basics of Horty's prioritized default logic and explained how, by interpreting it in the right sort of way, we can use it to model the reasoning even of subjects who are starting with inconsistent reasons. I don't claim that this adaptation of Horty's system is adequate to modeling every important feature of the way in which reasons support rational belief—on the contrary, in Part III of this book I will be arguing for a picture on which there are reasons that matter for the rationality of belief that cannot be modeled at all in this interpretation of Horty's system.[36] Nor do I mean to claim that there are not many further questions that would need to be resolved in order to fully interpret this system—Horty himself takes up some particularly interesting such questions in his book, whose first two chapters I have barely scraped here.

What I do claim is that by adapting Horty's framework in this way, we can see that there is at least one natural way to think about how subjective reasons come together in order to determine what it is rational for a subject to believe that does not *build in* up front that the inputs to this weighing must be rational, justified, or knowledge. Indeed, once we see how this picture works, it is not hard to see that similar points could be made about *any* non-reflexive model for reasoning—

---

[35] Note the contrast with the earlier version of this example, in which Alice is more reliable.
[36] I don't deny that they can be modeled in any interpretation of Horty's system—see Schroeder (2018b) for discussion.

though the treatment given here has the virtue of making explicit the competing role that reasons play in determining what is rational.

4.5 The Problem of Unjustified Belief Revisited

Recall from Chapter 1 that the problem of unjustified belief concerns what happens when a belief that might otherwise ground a subjective reason is unjustified. It is implausible that we can bootstrap ourselves into having sufficient subjective reasons to rationally believe something, simply by irrationally believing things from which it follows. So, unjustified beliefs do not seem to help to make their consequences more rational to believe. Nor, intuitively, does it feel right to say that one reason you have to believe a conclusion is your unjustified belief in a proposition from which it follows. The conventional solution to this problem is to suppose that it must be built into what it is to be a subjective reason that it is something that you know or rationally or justifiably believe—or even which you *know*.

But this is a problem for Reasons First because then subjective reasons cannot be both explanatorily and analytically prior to each of justification and knowledge—assuming that knowledge is normative. And as we saw in this chapter, it is a further problem for the idea that by adopting a non-factive account of subjective reasons, we could make sense of how perceptual experiences directly provide world-implicating subjective reasons for belief about the external world without incurring a difference between minimal pairs like C_1 and C_2, because perceptual experiences cannot themselves satisfy a justification condition; but if subjective reasons must be known, then that entails a factivity condition on subjective reasons, which is precisely what we've been trying to avoid.

My answer to the problem of unjustified beliefs weaves together two strands: first, the Horty-inspired model of how reasons support conclusions, from Section 4.4, and second, the minimal characterization of reasons as act-oriented competitors, from Chapter 2. The role that is played by the Horty-inspired model is that it gives us a way of thinking about how it could be that even irrational beliefs go into the weighing process that determines what it is rational for you to believe. It allows this without generating inappropriate bootstrapping, because the mechanics itself guarantees that beliefs whose rationality is not validated by the mechanics itself cannot ultimately play a supporting role, in supporting further conclusions. It cannot, I admit, be the full picture, but it helps us to see at least the outlines of how a fuller picture might go.

Given the minimal characterization of reasons from Chapter 2, this is enough to defend the idea that the fundamental explanatory concept of what I have been referring to as 'subjective reasons' does not need to be constrained by rationality or knowledge in order to be able to do its job properly. It may be, for all that I have said, that natural language restricts the word 'reason' to those act-oriented competitors that are rational to believe. But that does not change the fact that there is an underlying competition among factors that does not build in this constraint—and so it does not affect whether reasons come first, in the sense in which I am interested in this book.

5

The Apparent Factive Attitude View

5.1 Making Good

In Chapter 4 I showed that the options in theorizing about the way in which perceptual experiences provide us with evidence for beliefs about the external world have been sharply constrained by the background assumption that only a *truth* can rationalize. And in Chapter 5 I rebutted the best arguments I could find for thinking that this background assumption is true, which included defending an alternative solution to the problem of unjustified belief—one that is consistent with the thesis of Reasons First. This opens up the possibility of a view that makes good on the characteristic attractions of disjunctivist accounts of basic perceptual evidence, without their characteristic commitments. But it is not sufficient to *make good* on this possibility. For it turns out that not all ways of occupying this space are equally defensible.

In Chapter 3 we distinguished between four views on which perceptual evidence is world-implicating. According to the factive content view, which is accepted by Williamson, your evidence is the *content* of a perceptual state, and this gets to be your evidence because you stand in a factive perceptual relation to that content. According to the factive attitude view, which we saw that Comesaña and McGrath attribute to McDowell, your evidence is the proposition *that* you stand in a particular factive perceptual relation to the world, and this gets to be your evidence just because it is true. We also saw that each of these views has non-disjunctivist analogues. According to the non-factive content view, your evidence is the content of a perceptual state, and it gets to be your evidence whether or not that perceptual state is veridical. And according to the apparent factive attitude view, your evidence is that you stand in some particular factive attitude to the world, and this gets to be your evidence just because it *appears* to you to be true, given the right non-factive *appearance* relation.

The simplest way to hold that perceptual evidence is world-implicating but shared between the good and bad cases is clearly to go with the non-factive content view. This is the view that I have endorsed in earlier work—both in Schroeder (2008) and in Schroeder (2011a).[1] But what we will now see (Section 5.2), is that

---

[1] Compare Pryor (2005b), who notes that this is one way of defending non-inferential perceptual justification that is consistent with what he calls the *premise principle*, but argues that it is not necessary. I agree that it is not necessary; in Chapter 4 I argued that what it offers that Pryor's view does not, is an

Reasons First. Mark Schroeder, Oxford University Press (2021). © Mark Schroeder.
DOI: 10.1093/oso/9780198868224.003.0005

this view cannot be true, because it fails to deal adequately with the *defeasibility* of perceptual reasons. In fact, quite strikingly, its failures in dealing with defeasibility are matched by corresponding successes on the part of both the factive content view and the factive attitude view. This shows that both sorts of disjunctivist views about perceptual reasons get something importantly right that the non-factive content view misses—the importance of factive perceptual relations to the world.

Fortunately, as I will argue (Section 5.3), the apparent factive attitude view easily avoids these problems about defeasibility. By borrowing *more* from its disjunctivist alternatives, it can take on board their treatments of the defeasibility of knowledge, and in fact, I will argue, it actually results in a *better* treatment of the defeasibility of perceptual evidence than either the factive content view or the factive attitude view. What all of this shows, is that it is not enough, in order to make good on the promise of Chapters 3 and 4, to settle for the view that perceptual evidence is world-implicating but not necessarily true. We must also defend the specific commitments of the apparent factive attitude view. In Section 5.4 I'll show that there are at least two initially plausible interpretations of the commitments of this view. In Section 5.5 I'll compare the apparent factive attitude view to the other views that we have encountered along the way, in order to illustrate both its strengths, and why a number of other views can be thought of either as near-misses or as filling in an important part, but not all, of the story. And finally, I'll close in Section 5.6 with a comparison to another serious competitor.

5.2 Defeasibility

In Chapter 3, we sought an answer to how it is that having perceptual experiences is a particularly privileged way of coming to acquire evidence about the external world. We saw that phenomenal views of perceptual evidence struggle to explain how perception is a *privileged* or even particularly *good* source of evidence about the external world. They divide, roughly, into those on which perceptual experiences do not provide particularly good evidence (skepticism), those on which it needs additional support of some kind (coherentism, rationalism), and those which give up on or at least reject explaining how perceptual experiences are a

---

explanation in evidentialist terms of why these basic perceptual beliefs are justified, and not others, that does not open up Armstrong's In. Huemer (2001, 2006, 2007) defends the thesis of *Phenomenal Conservatism*, according to which you have prima facie justification to believe that P *when* it seems to you (perceptually or otherwise) that P. Huemer's arguments for and elaborations of this thesis are consistent with, but do not entail, the non-factive content view—to Huemer's view about *when* there is prima facie justification, the non-factive content view adds an explanation of *why*, in terms of the quality of the evidence.

way of having evidence in favor of explaining the justification of basic perceptual beliefs in non-evidential terms (pure externalism).

In contrast, world-implicating views of perceptual evidence are distinguished by offering particularly clean explanations of why perceptual experiences, at least in the good case, are ways of having particularly *good* evidence about the external world. What I have been trying to make room for, in Chapters 3 and 4, is a way to accept this sort of explanation of why perceptual evidence is so good, in a way that extends to the bad case, of non-veridical perception. But the problem we need to confront in this chapter is that we need to avoid perceptual evidence turning out to be *too* good. We don't want our explanation of how good basic perceptual evidence is to be *so* good that it cannot account for the ways in which basic perceptual evidence can be *defeated*.[2]

There are at least two different important ways in which it is important to allow that basic perceptual evidence can be defeated: what I will call *objective* defeat, and *subjective* defeat. A leading though controversial example of objective defeat is someone who is driving, oblivious, through fake barn country and encounters the only barn around for many miles, among dozens of barn façades.[3] Given that this person does not realize, and has no evidence, that they are in fake barn country, their perceptual experience as of a barn may make it rational for them to believe that there is a barn in front of them, but perceptual experiences like this cannot ground *knowledge*. So objective defeaters, like the fact that you are in fake barn country, are objective features of your circumstances that undermine the capacity of your perceptual experiences to ground knowledge.

In contrast, the paradigm of subjective defeat is someone who is driving through ordinary countryside, but who has rationally come to believe that she is in fake barn country.[4] For example, she may be following the signs to fake barn country, but some of the local teenagers switched the signs. When this person sees a barn in front of her, she rationally believes that most nearby things that look like barns are really only barn façades. So it is not rational for her to believe, in the absence of other, non-visual, evidence, that there is a barn in front of her. And since it is not rational for her to believe this, her belief cannot be knowledge. So subjective

---

[2] I originally learned the structure of the problem in this section from Scott Sturgeon; Ryan Walsh and Shyam Nair pressed versions of the problem for the factive content view, and Whiting (2015) develops an objection to Schroeder (2015b) that is based on this problem for the factive content view.

[3] Goldman (1976). The example is controversial because some theories of knowledge treat fake barn cases differently from cases like unknowingly wearing red-colored glasses. We will see one important such example later in this chapter. I'll continue to use it as my leading example of objective defeat, however, since I share the intuitive judgment in the case, and because my favored account can yield this verdict.

[4] As will become apparent, it has become contentious whether knowledge admits of subjective defeaters like this one, and many externalist views have come to reject this. Sosa (2009) and some who follow him will say that in this case *reflective knowledge* is defeated, but not *animal knowledge*. And Williamson and others who follow him will describe cases of apparent subjective defeat as cases in which you know but it is not rational for you to believe that you know, or in other similar terms.

defeaters are things you rationally believe that undermine the rationality of taking your perceptual evidence at face value, and hence which also undermine knowledge on the basis of perceptual experience.

Before going on to discuss how different views deal with both objective and subjective defeasibility of perceptual evidence, it is important to comment briefly on this example—of fake barn country. In discussing the fake barn country case as a case of *perceptual* defeasibility, I am assuming for the sake of discussion that you actually have a *perception* as of a fake barn, and not just that you have a perception as of something red and rectangular. In fact, however, whether perceptual experience itself ever directly represents things as barns is highly controversial,[5] and even assuming that it does, there are many reasons to think that such *high-level* perceptual experiences require some further kind of epistemic standing that is not required for *low-level* perceptual experiences.[6] Everything that I say in this book is intended to be neutral about these issues, and I discuss fake barn cases only for convenience. It is possible to construct perfect analogues of fake barn cases using low-level perceptual contents,[7] and there are other examples of both objective and subjective defeaters—such as wearing rose-colored glasses when making color-judgments—but I will sometimes discuss the fake barn country examples as if they are simple cases of perceptual defeat.[8]

It turns out that phenomenal views of basic perceptual evidence offer very elegant treatments of both objective and subjective defeasibility. On phenomenal views, your perceptual evidence that there is a barn in front of you is something like that it *seems* or *looks* to you like there is a barn, that you are being appeared to barn-wise, or the like. But while it may be reasonable to infer that there is a barn from the fact that it looks to you like there is, it is not reasonable to infer that there is a barn from the fact that it looks to you like there is *and you are in fake barn country.* So the phenomenal view of evidence can explain why it is that if you rationally believe that you are in fake barn country, that is a subjective defeater for your visual evidence that something is a barn. Similarly, the phenomenal view of evidence can plausibly extend this explanation to explain why it is that if you *really are* in fake barn country, your visual evidence alone cannot provide you with knowledge that there is a barn in front of you. This is because, as I will argue in Chapter 10, there is a close correspondence between propositions whose truth

---

[5] Siegel (2006, 2010); contrast Logue (2013), Prinz (2013).   [6] Siegel (2012, 2013).

[7] Compare Schroeder (2015c). For example, distance is one property that is uncontroversially represented in visual experience, but there are systematic environmental conditions under which visual distance perception is unreliable, as in mountain air.

[8] In general, what I really care about is that perceptual experiences can be defensibly associated with some kind of non-factive evidence about the world *or other* which supports external-world conclusions without the need for privileged priors.

defeats knowledge and propositions such that rational belief in them defeats rationality of belief.[9]

The factive content view gives a different, but also elegant, treatment of the defeasibility of basic perceptual evidence—at least, of its objective defeasibility. According to this view, recall, your visual evidence is the content of what you see, on a factive reading of 'see'. So when you see that there is a barn in front of you, your evidence is that there is a barn in front of you, and it is your evidence because you see it to be the case. But if you are in fake barn country, then you do *not* see that there is a barn in front of you, and so on this view, you do not have any visual evidence that there is a barn in front of you. Since you don't have any evidence, you can't know. So this is an elegant explanation of the objective defeasibility of basic perceptual evidence.

The factive attitude view is capable of giving a similar explanation of objective defeasibility. On this view, your visual evidence is always that you see that there is a barn, and this is your evidence only if it is true. But if you are in fake barn country, then you don't see that there is a barn, and so on this view, you don't have any visual evidence that there is a barn. So the reason that you can't know that there is a barn is that you don't have any evidence that this is so—and a similar treatment applies to other cases of objective defeat, such as unknowingly wearing rose-colored glasses.

Strikingly, both the factive content view and the factive attitude view yield funny results about subjective defeasibility, and in two different ways. First, their explanation of why your visual evidence of barns cannot ground knowledge when you are in fake barn country generalizes to predict that it is not *rational* to believe, on the basis of perceptual evidence, that there is a barn in front of you, if you are in fake barn country—*even if you have no evidence that you are in fake barn country*.[10] This is because on both of these views, whether your perceptual experience gives you evidence depends only on whether you *are* in fake barn country, and not on whether you realize that you are. So both the factive content view and the factive attitude view make it *too easy* for the rationality of your belief to be defeated. This is just a generalization of what we have already observed about these views—that they only explain how belief is rational in the good case.

---

[9] For an appealing but naive version of this observation, see Klein (1971). Lehrer and Paxson (1969) develop this observation into a paradigmatic defeasibility analysis of knowledge. For more on the defeasibility tradition in the analysis of knowledge, see particularly Annis (1973), Ackerman (1974), Johnsen (1974), Swain (1974), Barker (1976), Olin (1976), and Levy (1977). I will return to discuss what I will argue are the insights of this defeasibility tradition in Chapters 9 and 10.

[10] Strictly speaking, this is a consequence of these views together with the assumption that rationality is determined by subjective reasons—as we have been assuming, here. Views like these are sometimes instead paired with the idea that rationality is a kind of shadow cast by the objective case. For example, a very simple and natural version of this view is that a belief is rational just in case it is indistinguishable from knowledge. In keeping with our Core Hypothesis, it is worth pointing out here that this view does not extend very well to action, since actions are often rational when they are clearly distinguishable from the correct thing to do (so long as it is not clear what the correct choice is).

But we can now see the flip side of this observation. Since on these views whether your visual experience provides evidence depends only on whether you are in fake barn country, and not on whether you believe that you are, these views both predict that your evidence still provides just as strong rational support for either knowledge or rational belief—*even if you rationally believe that you are in fake barn country*—provided that you are not actually in fake barn country. These views can explain why it may be rational for you to believe that it is not rational to believe that there is a barn in front of you (after all, you believe that you don't have visual evidence), but your visual evidence is still just as good as ever.[11]

In contrast to all of these views, the non-factive analogue of Williamson's view—the factive content view—struggles to say anything plausible about either objective or subjective defeasibility. According to the non-factive content view, after all, all that it takes in order to have the proposition that P as part of your visual evidence, is to have a visual experience—even a non-veridical one—as of P. As with the other world-implicating views of basic perceptual evidence, this view explains why vision is such a privileged way of acquiring perceptual evidence about the world—for no evidence that P could be better than P itself. But its explanation is *too* good. If your evidence that there is a barn in front of you is *that there is a barn in front of you*, this evidence is so good that it is hard to see how it could possibly be defeated by learning that you are in fake barn country. So it is hard to see how rationally believing that you are in fake barn country could defeat the strength of your subjective evidence that you are in fake barn country.

Similarly, if you really are looking at a barn, then it is *true* that there is a barn in front of you. And no objective evidence that there is a barn in front of you could be better. But this objective evidence is so good that it is hard to see how it could be diminished by the fact that you are in fake barn country. After all, the fact that you are in fake barn country but *this is a barn* supports the conclusion that this is a barn just as well as the fact that this is a barn all by itself. And this is not a special feature of fake barn cases—which some views treat differently from other examples of defeasibility. The prediction is general, and applies also to visual evidence that there is something red in front of you given that you are wearing rose-colored glasses. So the non-factive content view does not yield plausible results about the objective defeasibility of basic perceptual evidence, either.

There are a number of tricks that we could try to pull out of our sleeves, in order to try to resuscitate the non-factive content view. We could, for example, try to assimilate believing that you are in fake barn country to other much-discussed cases of higher-order evidence.[12] It would take a full chapter or more to follow up every such possible move that might be made in its defense. And if the non-factive

---

[11] Compare especially Lasonen-Aarnio (2010)—also see Williamson (2011).
[12] Compare, for example, Christensen (2010), Lasonen-Aarnio (2014), Schoenfield (2015), and Worsnip (2018).

content view *could* be fixed to successfully deal with both objective and subjective defeasibility, that would be fine with me—after all, I have defended it in print more than once.[13] But I don't think that we should be optimistic; the problem is a *structural* one. The evidence that the non-factive content view attributes to perceptual experience is just *too* good.[14]

5.3 The Apparent Factive Attitude View

In Section 5.2 I gave the first half of my argument that it matters *which* form of non-factive, world-implicating view we take about basic perceptual evidence. This is because the non-factive content view has deep difficulties accounting for the defeasibility of basic perceptual evidence. To complete my argument that it matters which form of non-factive, world-implicating view we take, I must there-fore show that not all views that occupy the space that I have been trying to make room for in Chapters 3 and 4 share this problem. And they do not. I will now show that the *apparent factive attitude view*, the non-factive analogue of the view of basic perceptual evidence that Comesaña and McGrath attribute to John McDowell, not only does not face the factive content view's problems with perceptual defeasibility, but it actually provides a *better* treatment of subjective defeat than either of the factive world-implicating views.

The apparent factive attitude view is motivated by a simple thought—a diag-nosis of what the factive content view and factive attitude view get *right* that the non-factive content view gets *wrong*. Both the factive content view and the factive attitude view build on a privileged role for factive perceptual relations to the world—relations like *seeing that* something is the case, *hearing it to be* the case,[15] or *tasting that* it is the case. Each of these relations entails the truth of their contents, but also more—it is not enough to see that a hand before you is pressing down a button, to have a visual experience a of a hand pressing down a button, and for it to be true that a hand before you is pressing down a button. If the visual experience is caused by a hologram of a hand pushing down a button, for example, rather than by an actual hand pushing down a button, then you don't see that a hand is pushing down a button, even though you have a visual experience as of a hand pushing down a button and it is true. Nor is being caused by the hand pushing down a button enough to make your visual experience one as of a hand

---

[13] Schroeder (2008, 2011a).

[14] It is worth contrasting once more Huemer's (2006) "Phenomenal Conservatism". Phenomenal Conservatism, like the non-factive attitude view, says that we have reason to believe what seems to us to be the case. I have been arguing in earlier footnotes that non-factive evidential views offer a deeper and more powerful explanation than Huemer's view, but by explaining less, it may also remain free of the defeasibility objection leveled in this section.

[15] In English "hear that" most naturally expresses hearsay, which is both non-perceptual and non-factive, rather than a factive perceptual relation.

pushing down a button—for if the hologram is caused by the button being depressed, then you still do not see that a hand is pushing down a button.[16]

Both the factive content view and the factive attitude view take this kind of factive attitude to the environment, paradigmatically exemplified by the good case of actually seeing that a hand is pressing down a button, to be central to the way in which perceptual experiences justify beliefs. And this is what gives them great explanations of why perceptual reasons suffer from objective defeat—for objective defeaters are facts that undermine these very factive perceptual relations to the environment. For example, when you are in fake barn country, you *can't* see that there is a barn in front of you.[17] Since objective perceptual defeaters are the right kind of thing to defeat factive perceptual relations, *that* is why they are the right kind of thing to defeat perceptual evidence.

But the *way* that the factive content view and the factive attitude view bring in factive perceptual relations is what gives them trouble. Both views hold that factive perceptual relations matter for the *possession* condition on subjective reasons. According to the factive content view, this is because the possession condition for evidence is that you bear a factive perceptual relation to the evidence. And according to the factive attitude view, factive perceptual relations make it into both the *content* of your evidence *and* the possession condition for that evidence. This is because it says that your evidence is that you see that there is a barn, and you have this evidence just in case it is *true*.

In contrast, the apparent factive attitude view places the role for factive attitudes in the *content* of your evidence *rather than* in its possession condition. According to this view, your basic perceptual evidence always takes the form that you bear some factive perceptual relation to the environment—for example, that you see that there is a barn—and it gets to be *your* subjective evidence because it *appears* to you to be the case. More will need to be said about exactly what this appearance relation is, and I will return to it in Section 5.4. But what is important in order to appreciate the logical space that the apparent factive attitude view occupies, is simply that it is a relation that you can stand in to propositions that are false.

To see how elegantly the apparent factive attitude view deals with the defeasibility of perceptual evidence, let's take the case of objective defeat first. You are in fake barn country, but have no evidence that this is so. It appears to you that you see a barn, and so according to the apparent factive attitude view, you have the following subjective evidence that there is a barn in front of you: *that you see that there is a barn in front of you.* This subjective evidence is not defeated, and so it is as good as subjective evidence can be. So it makes it rational for you to believe that there is a barn in front of you—as it should be, since you have no evidence

---

[16] Compare Lewis (1980).

[17] Note that this is precisely the assumption needed by both the factive content view and the factive attitude view, in order to explain defeat. Though contrast Turri (2010a) for a dissenting view.

whatsoever that you are in fake barn country. But since you *are* in fake barn country, your evidence is not *true*. People who are in fake barn country cannot see that there is a barn in front of them. And we know from false lemma cases in the Gettier literature that false evidence cannot ground knowledge.[18] So being in fake barn country is an objective defeater for your visual evidence that there is a barn.

Notice that the apparent factive attitude view gets all of the same virtues of the accounts of defeat given by the factive content and factive attitude views, in that it completely borrows their accounts of why being in fake barn country objectively defeats your visual evidence. It defeats them because being in fake barn country is incompatible with seeing that something is a barn.[19] But it does *better* than these views, because it does not overgeneralize to predict that your *subjective* evidence is also defeated. Whereas the factive content and factive attitude views say that you have no subjective evidence that there is a barn in front of you, the apparent factive attitude view separates its treatments of rationality and knowledge by separating its treatments of objective and subjective reasons. It is rational for you to believe, because you have excellent subjective reasons, but you lack knowledge, because your subjective reason is false.

Moreover, in contrast to the factive views, the apparent factive attitude view also deals elegantly with subjective defeasibility. If you believe that you are in fake barn country, and it appears to you that you see a barn, then according to the apparent factive attitude view, your evidence is inconsistent. It includes both the proposition that you are in fake barn country and the proposition that you see that there is a barn, but those cannot both be true.[20] But it will plausibly never be the case that a single set of evidence rationalizes believing each of inconsistent things.[21] So either this inconsistent set of evidence will make it rational for you to believe that you are in fake barn country but *not* rational to believe, in the absence of further evidence, that there is a barn in front of you, or it will make it

---

[18] I'll offer my explanation of why this is true in Chapter 11.

[19] In the main text I am proceeding on the assumption that you can neither see nor know that something is a barn merely by visual inspection of its façade while you are in fake barn country. But in fact the apparent factive attitude account is committed to neither of these verdicts—it is also compatible with the assumption that you can both see and know that something is a barn by visual inspection of its façade even while in fake barn country. All that it requires is that these two things go hand-in-hand, so that your visual evidence turns out to false just in case knowledge is defeated.

Some philosophers, including as I've already noted Turri (2010a), have contended that you can see that something is a barn even without knowing that it is. This combination of views would pose trouble for the apparent factive attitude account, as they would undermine its treatment of defeat in this case. But I believe that this is a mistake that conflates seeing *that* something is a barn with seeing a barn.

[20] Again, notice that even if you disagree with this verdict about fake barn cases, we can still see that subjective defeasibility conditions will match objective defeasibility conditions, because the explanation of subjective defeasibility turns on the very same claim as the explanation of objective defeasibility.

[21] In addition to being plausible, this is a consequence of the simple Horty-inspired model from Section 5.4. If we generalize that model to allow appearances as well as beliefs to give us inputs to the model, then either the proposition that you see that there is a barn makes it into the extension, or the proposition that you are in fake barn country does, but not both. So it is rational to form the perceptual belief that there is a barn only if it is not rational to believe that you are in fake barn country.

rational for you to believe that you see that there is a barn in front of you but *not* rational to believe that you are in fake barn country. If the former, then your perceptual evidence is subjectively defeated, and if the latter, then you don't satisfy the conditions for subjective perceptual defeat—only a *rational* belief that you are in fake barn country can undermine the rationality of trusting your eyes—not an irrational belief that you are in fake barn country.

So the apparent factive attitude view deals elegantly with the case of subjective perceptual defeasibility. In contrast, as we saw in Section 5.2, neither the factive content view nor the factive attitude view allows rational beliefs about being in fake barn country, or about wearing colored glasses, or indeed about anything whatsoever, to defeat the rational support provided by veridical perceptual experiences for their contents.[22]

The successes of the apparent factive attitude view come through its diagnosis both of what the factive content and factive attitude views got *right*, as well as what they got wrong. What they got *right*, is that the justification provided by perceptual experience is intimately connected to factive perceptual relations to the environment. But what they got wrong, just as with their disjunctivist commitments in general, is that they tried to place the significance of these factive perceptual relations in the *possession* condition for subjective reasons, rather than in the *content* of basic perceptual evidence. What the successes of the apparent factive attitude view in dealing smoothly with perceptual defeasibility show, is that this was the wrong choice.

Finally, now that we have seen how the apparent factive attitude view deals with these kinds of objective defeasibility, we can see one more reason to think that it is on the right track, by seeing how it avoids another, even worse, problem about defeasibility that is faced by the non-factive content view. This problem derives from the fact that in some cases, different perceptual modalities can have the same contents. For example, you might have a visual appearance as of something square in front of you, and you might have a tactile experience as of something square in front of you. According to the non-factive content account, in each case your perceptual reason is the same—namely, that there is something square in front of you. But now suppose that, contrary to what I argued in Section 5.2, we had a good account of how learning that your current visual experiences are a hallucination could defeat your visual perceptual reasons. Then we would have an explanation of how learning that your current visual experiences are a hallucination defeat *that there is something square in front of you* as a reason to believe that there is something square in front of you. But on the non-factive content view, that is your *tactile* reason to believe that there is something square in front of you. So the

---

[22] Daniel Whiting has observed another important constraint on the appearance relation in the apparent factive attitude view—it cannot be closed under entailment, if this treatment of defeasibility is to work. Otherwise when it appears to you that you see that P it will also appear to you that P.

non-factive content view can explain why your visual reason is defeated only by also explaining how your tactile reason is defeated.

This further problem for the non-factive content view shows that perceptual reasons must somehow be marked for perceptual modality, in order to avoid this problem. Notice that the factive content account avoids this problem, because on this account, the fact that you are having a visual hallucination entails that you don't see that there is something square in front of you, but does not entail that you don't feel something square in front of you. And the factive attitude account easily avoids the problem, because on this account your reasons based on vision and touch are different—the former is the fact that you see that there is something square in front of you (which isn't true if you are having a visual hallucination), and the latter is the fact that you feel that there is something square in front of you.

In order to avoid these problems, basic perceptual reasons must be marked by perceptual modality. This is what the apparent factive attitude view does—it marks basic perceptual reasons for perceptual modality. That is yet another reason to think that it is on the right track. So I conclude that the apparent factive attitude account of basic perceptual reasons offers an account of the defeasibility of basic perceptual reasons that is superior not only to the non-factive content view, but also superior to both forms of factive world-implicating account. If we truly want an account of basic perceptual reasons on which they are world-implicating, the apparent factive attitude view is the way that we need to go.

5.4 Defending the Appearance Condition

In Section 5.3 I argued that the apparent factive attitude view is vastly superior to the non-factive content view of basic perceptual reasons on grounds of its treatment of the defeasibility of basic perceptual reasons. In fact, I argued that it gives such an attractive account of the defeasibility of basic perceptual reasons that it does better than the factive world-implicating views. But the apparent factive attitude view is not a freebie. It comes with particular commitments about the nature of perceptual experience. It holds that having the right sort of visual appearance as of something square in front of you in order to ground a subjective reason to believe that there is something square in front of you requires that it *appears* to you that you see that there is something square in front of you.

Apparent factive attitude view	Where ψ is a factive perceptual relation...
possession condition	It appears to you that you ψ that P.
your evidence is	That you ψ that P.

Since subjective conditions require that the possession condition be satisfied, this means that it is not enough to rationalize the belief that P that you see that P. It must also *appear* to you that you see that P.

Before I appreciated the problems with defeasibility that are faced by the non-factive content account, I thought that this additional condition required by the apparent factive attitude account was a fatal problem. In Schroeder (2008, 69), for example, I argued that it wouldn't help if *appearing* is just *belief*, because that just explains how we have evidence about the external world at the cost of accounting for how we have evidence about our own factive attitudes.

Fortunately, however, we haven't said anything yet about what the *appearance* relation that is invoked by the apparent factive attitude account is supposed to be. When I introduced the relation, it was semi-stipulative, picking out the relation that a subject must bear to the proposition that she sees that there is something square in front of her, in order for that to be among her subjective reasons. So it would be premature to jump to the conclusion that this relation is belief, or that it comes apart from actually seeing that P freely enough to generate intuitive counterexamples. Instead, we should see the idea that we want all typical cases of actually seeing that P to count as ways of having perceptual evidence as a *constraint* on how to interpret the *appearance* relation. In this section I want to outline two distinct defensible strategies for interpreting the *appearance* relation that I think arguably satisfy this constraint.

The first strategy for interpreting the *appearance* relation in the apparent factive attitude view is to interpret it as a kind of conscious *access*. There are different ways of developing this strategy, but what they have in common is that they grant that it may be possible to see that P without it appearing to you that you see that P, but contend that non-apparent seeings do not provide perceptual evidence that can rationalize belief.

For example, we might say that *appearing* is phenomenal consciousness. Given that in the vast majority of cases, if you see that there is a barn in front of you, this is a phenomenally conscious visual experience, it follows from this view that in the vast majority of cases, people who see that P do in fact satisfy the condition of it appearing to them that they see that P, and so they have excellent evidence about the world. So the cases in which this account predicts that you can see that P without having reason to believe that P are very rare. The exceptions are zombies, and arguably, blindsight[23]—one of which is rare, and the other of which is usually claimed only to be *possible*.[24] But the proponent of this view can also argue on independent grounds that perceptual experiences that are non-conscious do not rationalize beliefs. Philosophical zombies are obscure enough that judgments about what it is rational for them to believe are not the right kind of thing to be obvious, and it is plausible to maintain that blindsight does not rationalize belief in the same way as phenomenally conscious perceptual experiences do.[25]

---

[23] As argued by Brogaard (2011).   [24] Compare Chalmers (1996).
[25] The phenomenal consciousness view is consistent with Huemer's (2006) *phenomenal conservatism*, though it adds a twist that Huemer does not himself accept.

If you don't think that phenomenal consciousness is the right kind of constraint on perceptual experiences in order for them to play a role in rationalizing beliefs, then you might consider an alternative way of developing this strategy, by appealing to *access* consciousness.[26] Again, the strategy is to allow that we may have some perceptual experiences of which we are not access conscious,[27] but argue that these experiences do not provide us with *reasons*. For example, Smithies (2011) argues that *attention* is a particular mode of access consciousness, and attention is required in order to make information available for use in rationalizing thought or action. So Smithies's arguments might be used in order to justify restricting the role of perceptual experiences in rationalizing beliefs to cases of the right kind of conscious access. Similarly, Hatcher (2017) argues that access consciousness is *person-level* awareness—awareness of something that you count as having not simply in virtue of the fact that some part of you is aware of it. If rational response to reasons requires person-level awareness (as Hatcher also argues), then it requires access consciousness.

There are other ways of developing this strategy. What they have in common is that they interpret the *appearance* relation in the apparent factive attitude view in such a way that it is always present in *paradigmatic* cases of perceptual experience, and seek to close the gap between seeing and appearance by arguing that cases in which you see that P but it does not appear to you that you see that P are not ones which perceptual experiences actually justify.

But there is also a second, more ambitious, way of interpreting the *appearance* relation, which I call the *self-presenting* interpretation. On this second interpretation, it is actually *impossible* to see that P without it appearing to you that you see that P. This interpretation is more ambitious, because it aims to make good on the claim that seeing that P *always* gives you a reason to believe that P. In order to attain this ambition, the second interpretation requires two parts: first, the thesis that what *appears* to you is just the *representational content* of your perceptual experience; and second, the thesis that each perceptual experience represents itself as a factive perceptual relation to the world. The first of these theses is stipulative—it is an interpretation of what 'appears' is to mean, in our preferred version of the apparent factive attitude view. But the second thesis is substantive. It is a claim about the nature of perceptual experience.

In order to get a grip on the self-presenting interpretation of the apparent factive attitude view, it helps to compare a thesis that Searle (1983) defends in *Intentionality*. Searle claims that perceptual states represent themselves as *caused* by their contents. For example, a visual experience as of something a hand pressing down a button has the content that it *itself* is caused by a hand pressing down a button. Searle's argument for this is simple. A perceptual experience

---

[26] Block (2008).
[27] As argued by Block (2011), though compare Gross and Flombaum (2020).

cannot be *absolutely veridical*, he claims, unless it is caused by what it represents. Even if there is a hand pressing down a button, that is not enough to make your visual experience as of a hand pressing down a button absolutely veridical, because it is consistent with your having the visual experience as of a hand pressing down a button and there really being a hand pressing down a button that your visual experience is caused by something else, such as a hologram or a hallucination. So, Searle claims, it is part of the content of your experience, in the sense that it is part of its *absolute veridicality conditions*, that it is *caused* by a hand pressing down a button—not just that a hand is pressing down a button.

But now we can see that if Searle's argument works at all, then it generalizes. For as we observed before, we know that your visual experience can be caused *deviantly* by a hand pressing down a button—for example, if it is caused by a hologram of a hand pressing down a button, which is triggered by the button on which a hand is pressing down. David Lewis (1980) calls these cases of *veridical hallucination*. In this case, you don't see that a hand is pressing down a button any more than you do in the case where your experience is caused by a hologram with some other cause. So if Searle's example is not absolutely veridical, then this one is not, either.

It follows that Searle's argument can be used to motivate the idea that perceptual experiences represent themselves as factive perceptual relations to the world. When you have a visual experience as of something red, you are in a state that represents itself as a *seeing that* something is red. So if your reasons come from the representational content of your experiences, then among your reasons will be the proposition that that very experience is a seeing that something is red. Importantly, on this view *all* visual experiences represent themselves in this way, which is why you cannot see that there is something red without it appearing to you that you see that something is red. So on this view, unlike our first strategy for making sense of the apparent factive attitude view, seeing that there is something red *is* sufficient for having a visual reason to believe that there is something red.

The self-presenting interpretation of the apparent factive attitude view also has another nice virtue, in that it illustrates that nothing about the apparent factive attitude view requires that the *perceiver* be part of her visual evidence. Initially, we described the apparent factive attitude view as the view that when you see that P, your visual evidence is *that you see that P*—a proposition which involves not only a factive attitude to the world, *seeing that*, but a *perceiver*—you. It is natural to worry that this over-intellectualizes perceptual experience, in that it only allows perceptual experiences to justify for agents who are able to think of themselves first-personally. But the self-presentational interpretation of the apparent factive attitude view does not need to build the perceiver into the content of perceptual experiences—it only needs to build the *perception* itself into that content. Perceptual experiences represent *themselves* as veridical perceptual relations to the world.[28]

---

[28] This view is closely analogous to Joshua Crabill's (2015) theory of *authority*. Crabill follows Marmor (2011) and Hershowitz (2011) in arguing for an institutional theory of political authority, on

My main goal in Chapters 2, 3, and 4 has been to make room for and to argue for the attractions of world-implicating but non-factive accounts of basic perceptual evidence, as a way of illustrating this book's Core Hypothesis. In this chapter, I've conceded that not just any way of occupying this logical space is equally good—in order to deal adequately with the defeasibility of perceptual reasons, we must reject the non-factive content account. But my approach is ecumenical. It is important for my task in this book that there are *versions* of the apparent factive attitude account that are interesting and defensible, but not important *which* one is true. So I have been focused, in this section, on showing that the apparent factive attitude account can be developed in multiple ways, each of which have some promise to explain why perceptual reasons are present in all of the right cases.

Still, I am inclined to go further, and endorse the self-presentational interpretation of the apparent factive attitude view, on the grounds that it makes sense of some puzzling features of cross-modal perception. There are a variety of cases that illustrate this phenomenon, but a striking and simple one comes from an experiment performed by Young (1928). In the experiment, subjects are equipped with a device called a *pseudophone*, which directs sound coming from each side of the subject to the opposite ear. When subjects had their eyes closed, they reported hearing a voice on their right side as coming from their left, and a voice on their left side as coming from their right. But when the subjects *opened* their eyes and could see who was speaking, the effect vanished, and subjects heard the voice on their right as coming from the right, and similarly for the left.

In the open-eyed version of this case, subjects hear sounds as coming from their correct locations. The sense in which they *hear* them as coming from their correct locations, however, does not have anything to do with their ears or their cochlear nerve. Nor is it adequately captured by the claim that the representation happens at higher levels of auditory processing. What is distinctive and striking about the experiment and others like it, is that subjects *experience* the information as auditory—their auditory experience *changes* when they open their eyes, and they do not experience a conflict between where the sound looks and sounds to

which there is a non-normative, institutional notion of authority that is shared both by legitimate authorities and by illegitimate authorities, and legitimacy is a further condition. Crabill notes that Marmor and Hershowitz, like other positivists, accept what disjunctivists in the philosophy of perception would call a "common factor" argument for this conclusion, and interprets competing views of political authority, such as that of Darwall (2006), as analogous to disjunctivist theories of perceptual experience. On views like Darwall's, there is no common factor to legitimate authority and illegitimate authority—an illegitimate authority is just someone who purports to be or passes for a legitimate authority, just as on disjunctivist views of perceptual experience, hallunicatory perceptual experiences don't share a common factor with veridical ones, but are just states that are subjectively *indistinguishable* from veridical states. According to Crabill, Darwall and others are right that legitimate authority is *conceptually* prior, but wrong to think that it is *ontically* prior. He says that part of what it is to be an authority in general—whether legitimate or illegitimate—is to *represent* oneself as being a legitimate authority, but what is it to *be* a legitimate authority is to be an authority and to be legitimate. Similarly, what the self-presentational view of perceptual experience claims is that veridical perceptual experiences are central in that every perceptual experience represents itself as a veridical one.

be coming from. So this is not intuitively, I think, an absolutely veridical perceptual experience. The experience, in this case, is an illusion as of being in an auditory perceptual relation to the world. The self-presentational view can explain this—the subject's experiences don't just represent information about the world; they also represent themselves as having an auditory source. So I am inclined to think that the self-presentational view of perceptual experience is independently on the right track.

5.5 Putting it Together

Throughout Part II, I have been arguing that we get confirmation for this book's Core Hypothesis from consideration of the question of how perceptual experience could be a privileged sort of evidence about the external world. The theoretical options have been constrained, I showed, by the pervasive assumption that in order to have a subjective reason for belief, you must stand in a cognitive relation to a *truth*. It is only in the company of this assumption that we have to face a choice between views on which perceptual evidence is world-implicating and views on which non-veridical perceptual experiences also rationalize beliefs. Perhaps we can talk ourselves into accepting either of these consequences, but my question throughout has been: why?

In contrast to the pervasiveness of this assumption in epistemology, moral philosophy and the theory of rational action have been pervaded, until recent cross-fertilization from epistemology, with the assumption that what it is rational for an agent to do depends on her internal state—on what she rationally believes, independently of whether it is true. The sharp contrast between these two perspectives on the possibility of false beliefs justifying is evidence, I think, that one of these two areas of inquiry has been compromised by insufficient attention to the other.

The view taken by authors like Hawthorne and Magidor (2018) is that moral philosophers should have paid more attention to the insights of epistemology. Just as we assume, in epistemology, that to have subjective evidence, you must have knowledge, we should conclude that the same goes for subjective reasons for action, more generally. But once we draw into focus how much unnecessary trouble this view causes in epistemology, I think that a more reasonable conclusion to draw is that it is *epistemology* that has suffered, here, by insufficient attention to the parallel with moral philosophy. And this is our Core Hypothesis.

The view that we make room for in epistemology, if we give up on the problematic assumption that subjective reasons must be truths, is the apparent factive attitude view. This view borrows much from familiar disjunctivist theories about the epistemology of perception, which should not be surprising, since its core aspiration is to seize their virtues with a non-factive conception of subjective reasons. Like familiar disjunctivist theories, it holds that in the good case, perceptual experiences are a particularly privileged source of evidence about the external world, because perceptual experience is a way of acquiring evidence that actually *entails* things about the world outside of our experiences, as our experiences represent it to us. Like familiar disjunctivist theories, it holds that in paradigmatic cases, this evidence can both rationalize belief and be a firm basis for knowledge. And like familiar disjunctivist theories, it holds that what makes this possible is the intimate relationship between perceptual evidence and factive perceptual relations to the world—relations like *seeing that* something is the case.

The apparent factive attitude view holds, moreover, that the disjunctivist is right that the sort of rational standing required for *knowledge* differs between the good case and the bad case. And it holds that the disjunctivist is *also* right that merely adding the truth of the worldly content of perceptual experiences to what rationalizes belief in the bad case does not suffice for knowledge. This makes it consistent, I think, with the main theses of McDowell's (1995) article "Knowledge and the Internal", which is a sort of manifesto for epistemological disjunctivism about perception.

But where the apparent factive attitude view departs from familiar disjunctivist views is in its treatment of *subjective* reasons. Subjective reasons alone are not sufficient for knowledge, but they *are* sufficient for the *rationality* of belief.[29] By distinguishing between the reasons that rationalize and the reasons that can ground knowledge, the apparent factive attitude view not only can explain why false perceptual experiences can rationalize belief, but why true experiences under objectively defeating conditions can, as well. And even though it was not designed to do so, it can also explain why there can be *subjective* defeating conditions on knowledge and rationality—why even veridical perceptual experiences can fail to ground knowledge or rationality, when the agent rationally but falsely believes that she is in some defeating condition.

The apparent factive attitude view also has much in common with familiar *dogmatist* views about perceptual epistemology. Like familiar dogmatist views, it holds that being in the right perceptual state is sufficient, in and of itself, and independent of background or mediating beliefs, to rationalize corresponding beliefs about the external world, in the absence of defeat. This justification is non-inferential, in the sense that it is not a matter of inferring one belief from any other; on the contrary, it is a way in which the justification of beliefs can be grounded directly in perceptual experience.

But where the apparent factive attitude view departs from familiar such views is that it doesn't just argue that we *need* such a view, and that the view is *defensible*;

---

[29] Compare Schellenberg's (2013, 2014) distinction between factive evidence and phenomenal evidence. Schellenberg argues for why we need some such distinction, and the apparent factive attitude view situates it in the general distinction between objective and subjective reason.

the explanation that it provides is elegant and deeply continuous with the structure of *rationalizing explanations* in other domains. They justify, because being in these perceptual states is a privileged way of having *evidence* about the external world, and evidence is reason to believe. When you have a visual experience as of P, for example, it appears to you that your experience is a *seeing that P*. And so this puts you in possession of the very best sort of evidence that P—evidence that entails that P. So, perceptual experiences justify because they are a way of *having reasons*, because evidence is reason to believe, and because entailing evidence is the best sort of evidence.

This is a thoroughgoingly evidentialist, intuitively satisfying, explanation of why these perceptual states justify, because being grounded in evidence is our *best case* for what might justify beliefs. And so it closes off Armstrong's In. It demonstrates how an explanation can be *rationalizing*, without needing to be within the grasp of the subject whose beliefs are being rationalized. And it does so not by treating the rationalization of perceptual beliefs as something that requires defense of a special novel normative principle that breaks the evidential symmetry between external world hypotheses and brain-in-vat hypotheses, but simply by acknowledging that perceptual experience already breaks this symmetry.

Another way of seeing the same point is to see why the apparent factive attitude view does not require defending a privileged set of *priors*. It is natural to suspect that dogmatist views, because they distinguish the rational status of drawing conclusions about the external world from the rational status of drawing conclusions about the intentions of the evil demon or the arrangement of ones and zeros in the matrix, must be committed to a privileged set of priors, according to which external world conclusions are more probable, conditional on perceptual evidence, than conclusions about the evil demon or about the matrix.[30] But the apparent factive attitude view needs only that the probability that P, conditional on the proposition that you stand in a factive perceptual relation to the fact that P, is high. But of course this probability is high, since the fact that P is *entailed* by the fact that you stand in a factive perceptual relation to the fact that P. Hence, it is codified by *any* probability function.

And this same feature is why the apparent factive attitude view also provides an illuminating treatment of the *bootstrapping* problem for dogmatist views.[31] The bootstrapping problem is the worry that dogmatism makes it *too easy* to 'bootstrap' the rationality of believing that your perceptual capacities are arbitrarily reliable, simply by employing them over and over. The basic thought is that since dogmatism says that it is rational for you to form the belief that something is blue

<hr />

[30] White (2006), Silins (2007).

[31] For the original bootstrapping argument, see Vogel (2000), and for the application to dogmatism, Cohen (2002). Cohen (2010) and Wedgwood (2013) argue that it can be extended to a priori justification for the reliability of perceptual experience. The answer that I give here on behalf of the apparent factive attitude view extends to the a priori versions of the argument.

whenever you have the right visual experience—for example, that it visually appears blue to you—you can presumably do this over and over again, coming to form arbitrarily many beliefs of the form, "x visually appears blue to me and it is blue". But this gives you, the argument goes, excellent inductive evidence that every time something visually appears blue to you, it is blue.

The apparent factive attitude view cuts the bootstrapping argument off at its source. According to this view, your visual evidence that something is blue is always the proposition that you see that it is blue. So if this view is right, then as you do this over and over again, the inferences that you draw look like this:

I see that x_1 is blue.

So x_1 is blue.

So I see that x_1 is blue, and x_1 is blue.

I see that x_2 is blue.

So x_2 is blue.

So I see that x_2 is blue, and x_2 is blue.

I see that x_3 is blue.

So x_3 is blue.

So I see that x_3 is blue, and x_3 is blue.

. . .

But this process does not give you any inductive evidence that every time it visually appears to you that something is blue, it really is blue—it only gives you inductive evidence that every time you *see that* something is blue, it really is blue. But that, of course, is a necessary truth, since seeing that is a factive perceptual relation.

We might try to fix the argument in the following way—by also inferring that it visually appears to you that the thing is blue, at each step.

I see that x_1 is blue.

So x_1 is blue and it visually appears to me that x_1 is blue.

I see that x_2 is blue.

So x_2 is blue and it visually appears to me that x_2 is blue.

I see that x_3 is blue.

So x_3 is blue and it visually appears to me that x_3 is blue.

. . .

This style of reasoning gives us the right *pattern* of conjunctions to inductively draw the conclusion that every time something visually appears blue to you, it really is blue, but unfortunately, reasoning inductively in this way is no longer *justified*, because you now have a *non-representative sample*, and inductive reasoning is only justified, at best, in the absence of any reason to think that your sample is non-representative (and possibly only in the presence of reason to believe that it is positively representative).

Compare the following example. Vanya works in a call center in India, handling complaints about customer service for a retailer in Western Europe. Her job gives her knowledge about many customers of this retailer, all of whom have complaints. So she reasons as follows:

x_1 is a customer of the retailer and is unhappy with their service.

x_2 is a customer of the retailer and is unhappy with their service.

x_3 is a customer of the retailer and is unhappy with their service.

. . .

Clearly it would not be reasonable for Vanya to conclude that every customer of the retailer is unhappy with their service—even though she knows of many such cases, and does not know of any customers who are happy with their service. And this is because her sample is non-representative—since she doesn't have a way of coming by cases in which customers are happy with their service, the cases in which she believes that someone is unhappy with their service are not representative of whether all customers are unhappy. Similarly, according to the apparent factive attitude view, visual evidence is unrepresentative about the reliability of vision, and in *precisely the same way*. Seeing is only one way of coming by cases of visual experience. So even though these are all cases in which you have visual appearances, it is a non-representative sample of such cases.

It should not be surprising, I think, that the apparent factive attitude view has interesting things to say about bootstrapping and about the objection that dogmatists require a privileged set of priors. This is because although it is a version of dogmatism, it is focused on answering the fundamental question of *why* perceptual experiences justify. It should not be a surprise that looking further afield to offer an account with more continuities with rationalizing explanations elsewhere should have more promise to help us understand how this particular rationalizing explanation works.

5.6 Comparing and Contrasting

The apparent factive attitude view, I have been claiming in this section and throughout Part II, lies in a particularly sweet spot in perceptual epistemology. It captures what is right about disjunctivist theories but without disjunctivist commitments about rational belief. It captures what is right about dogmatism, but with a satisfying evidentialist explanation, and actually provides a satisfying, elegant solution to one of the ongoing puzzles about dogmatism, the bootstrapping problem. And it captures what is right about disjunctivist theories—without their disjunctivism.

Nevertheless, the apparent factive attitude view is the thing that I am least confident about in this whole book. I am least confident about it not only because I am unsure about all of its consequences and about its specific commitments about the philosophy of perception, but particularly because my arguments leading in its direction have been contrastive, rather than direct. Since I first introduced the possibility of world-implicating perceptual evidence in Chapter 3, we considered only two main candidates for what that world-implicating evidence might be—the worldly contents of perceptual experiences, or that one bears some particular factive perceptual relation toward that content. But these are of course not the only two possible world-implicating candidates for basic perceptual evidence.

Another promising candidate—one that I had not really managed to get my head around when I first began working on this book—is Matthew McGrath's (2017, 2018a) view that perceptual evidence consists in objective *looks* propositions—such as that this looks like a book. On this view, *looks* propositions count as world-implicating in my sense because they are not just about how things look *to* someone, but rather about how things really are in the world—some things really do look like books (most but not all books do, for example, and some clever cigar cases do, as well).

It is possible to take the looks view in a disjunctivist direction, by insisting that looks propositions can be your perceptual evidence only when they are true. But it is also possible to take it—and McGrath does take it—in a non-disjunctivist direction, by allowing that looks propositions can be your perceptual evidence when things look *to you* to be some way, even if they do not, objectively, actually look to be that way.[32]

This view has much in common with the main points that I have been emphasizing in Chapters 2, 3, and 4. So by the standards employed here, it does very well. It occupies the space that I argued in Chapter 3 is important—of distinguishing between objective and subjective dimensions of support and allowing for non-factive, reasons-based, rationalization of beliefs. But because its candidate for perceptual evidence is different, its treatment of defeasibility is somewhat different as well. On the looks view, if something looks red to you only because you are wearing rose-colored glasses, then it does not really look red—and so the perceptual evidence that it looks red is not good objective reason

---

[32] See also Comesaña and McGrath (2015).

to believe that it is red. This is very much like the treatment of objective defeat given by the apparent factive attitude view. And if you *believe* that something looks red to you only because you are wearing red-colored glasses, then you will *believe* that it does not really look red—and so the perceptual evidence that it looks red will be excluded by your belief that it does not look red—again, much like the treatment of subjective defeasibility given by the apparent factive attitude view.

But this is as far as the similarities go. The looks view leads to a very different conclusion about fake barn cases, because the fact that you are in fake barn country is not inconsistent with something looking like a barn. So on the looks view, your perceptual evidence that something is a barn remains just as objectively good, even when you are in fake barn country—it is not objectively defeated. And similarly, believing that you are in fake barn country should not subjectively defeat your knowledge either, because again, that is perfectly consistent with your perceptual evidence.

As I've already noted, fake barn cases have come to be perceived by some as a matter of taste. So if you are persuaded by the original examples, then you may like the apparent factive attitude view better, whereas if you are unpersuaded by them, then you may like the looks view better.[33] But I think that the resources of the two views to account for defeat come even further apart than this. And that is because even in the case of rose-colored glasses, if you are looking at something that really does look red, and it looks red to you because you are wearing rose-colored glasses, on the looks view your perceptual evidence is still *true* and not subject to any objective defeat. But this is bad! You *can't* know that something is red merely by looking at it, if you are wearing rose-colored glasses.

Now, the looks view has more resources to appeal to, to try to explain what is going on in this case. After all, the proposition that something looks red is far from entailing that it is red. And McGrath makes much of this distance in his ingenious arguments for the looks view. So, more needs to be said. But more importantly, although I am pulled toward the apparent factive attitude view, I want to re-emphasize that the most important lesson from these three chapters, as far as I am concerned, is about the factivity of subjective reasons.

The apparent factive attitude view does not usurp the contributions of other important traditions in epistemology. It deepens and clarifies, rather than replaces, dogmatism. It finds a great deal of truth in prominent disjunctivist approaches. And it leaves a large role to be played by externalist accounts of perceptual content and of factive perceptual relations to the world.

The cost of accepting either the looks view *or* the apparent factive attitude view is that we allow that an agent can have a subjective reason without needing to stand in a cognitive or perceptual relation to a truth. And this, I have argued, is no

---

[33] Just a reminder that the apparent factive attitude view can go either way on fake barn cases, so long as seeing that and knowing that go together.

cost at all. Whenever philosophers have theorized about rationality, either of belief or of action, without thinking about it directly in terms of reasons or of evidence, they have generally assumed without thought that what it is rational to do or to believe does not need to be grounded in truths. It is only when people have tried to ground rationality in *reasons* or *evidence* that it has seemed hard to resist the conclusion that rationality must be grounded in truths. But we should reject this conclusion—both on the Moorean ground that it is less plausible than our prior assumption that rationality is a matter of perspective, rather than truth, and on the ground that all of the arguments that subjective reasons must be truths rest on mistakes.

PART III
HOW EVIDENCE RATIONALIZES BELIEF

We have sinned against you in thought, word, and deed.
Book of Common Prayer

6

Balance in Epistemology

6.1 Where We Stand

This book is about the role of reasons in epistemology. Together, we are exploring our Core Conjecture that in at least some cases, substantive and central issues in epistemology have been distorted by a neglect to take seriously the common normative subject matter of normative inquiry in epistemology and in moral philosophy. And we are particularly interested in the thesis of *Reasons First*, which has come to be at least perceived as having a kind of orthodox status within contemporary moral philosophy, but does not have the same status in epistemology. But since epistemology is, as I have argued, a thoroughgoingly normative discipline, the thesis of Reasons First can be true at all only if it is true of the central normative concepts of epistemology—including rationality, justification, and, as I will eventually argue in Part IV, knowledge. Yet we saw already in Chapter 1 that epistemology poses distinctive obstacles to the thesis of Reasons First—the problem of unjustified belief, and the problem of sufficiency.

Part II was devoted to the problem of unjustified belief. I argued, there, that the orthodox move in response to the problem of unjustified belief—the move that creates the problem for Reasons First—is actually at the heart of a very general set of problems about how perceptual experience could be a privileged source of evidence about the external world. This move—along with other assumptions about reasons—plays a central role in making invisible what I argued ought to be a surprisingly attractive view about the nature of basic perceptual evidence—one on which such evidence is *world-implicating* but can still rationalize belief even when it is not veridical. It may not be that this is ultimately the *correct* view about basic perceptual evidence, but since it shares the central attractions of disjunctivist theories without their costs, it deserves to be taken seriously, and the factors that have made it invisible deserve to be called into question.

Part III, in turn, will be devoted to the problem of sufficiency. Just as Chapter 3 raised general problems in epistemology, which Chapter 4 showed could be avoided with an alternative, Reasons First-respecting, solution to the problem of unjustified belief, and Chapter 5 showed that this could be defended and developed into an interesting and defensible view, the *apparent factive attitude view*, Chapter 6 will raise a general problem in epistemology, which Chapter 7 will show can be avoided with the correct, Reasons First-respecting, solution to the problem

Reasons First. Mark Schroeder, Oxford University Press (2021). © Mark Schroeder.
DOI: 10.1093/oso/9780198868224.003.0006

of sufficiency, and which Chapter 8 will show can be defended and developed into an interesting and defensible view—a view that I will call *Pragmatic Intellectualism*. Chapter 9 extends this view further and applies it to moral questions about belief.[1]

The problem of sufficiency, recall, arises from the fact that the kinds of reasons in favor of belief that seem to matter in order for it to be rational include only *evidence*. Paradigmatically, *Pascalian* considerations like those offered by Pascal in favor of believing in God do not help to make belief in God rational in the way that is required for knowledge, and the idea that only properly *epistemic* reasons matter for the rationality of belief, and that epistemic reasons include only evidence, explains this fact. But if the reasons that matter with respect to belief are only evidence, then that makes it very hard to say what it takes for reasons for belief to be *sufficient*, without simply saying that they are good enough that they make it rational to believe. But if the only way to understand what it is for reasons to be sufficient is in terms of rationality or justification, then reasons cannot be used in order to both analyze and explain rationality and justification.

My solution to the problem of sufficiency is simpler than my solution to the problem of unjustified beliefs. It is that the problem turns on the assumption that the only reasons that matter for the rationality of belief are evidence. So to solve the problem in a way that is friendly to Reasons First, we should reject this assumption. We should say, instead, that there are some reasons either for or against belief that are not evidence either for or against the content of the belief. The version of this claim that I will endorse will be, in particular, that there are some reasons *against* belief that are not evidence for or against its content.

I will offer several different converging sources of evidence for this view, but at the heart of these motivations is the observation that if we do not allow that non-evidential reasons can matter for the rationality of belief, then we create deep and puzzling problems about how it is that evidence can play a role in explaining what it is rational for us to believe—the same puzzles that make it hard to characterize the sufficiency of reasons without explaining it in terms of rationality or justification. This chapter is about these puzzles about how evidence can justify. In Section 6.2, I will outline several distinct ways in which facts about evidence seem to underdetermine what it is rational for someone to believe or what she is rational in believing. In Section 6.3 I'll show that some, but not all, of these puzzles can be dissolved by distinguishing reasons to deliberate or make up one's mind from the reasons that matter within deliberation, and in Section 6.4, I'll sketch the structure of my solution—the view that there are epistemic reasons against belief that are not evidence.

---

[1] As we'll see later, deciding what to do is different from acting, and actually more like belief.

6.2 Seven Puzzles about the Sufficiency of Evidence

The problem of sufficiency is the challenge of how reasons could explain justification or the rationality of belief, given that the reasons that matter in epistemology
are *evidence*. The problem is hard, because it is hard to see how to generalize from
facts about evidence to facts about rational belief. If reasons for and against belief
are evidence—and there is nothing independent and general that we can say about
what facts about evidence determine facts about rationality—then the problem is
that perhaps the only thing to be said about what it is for reasons for belief to be
sufficient to justify, appeals to rationality or justification, and hence cannot be used
to *explain* rationality or justification.

So the problem of sufficiency gains currency from observations about how hard
it is to generalize to conclusions about rationality on the basis of facts about
evidence. I will be introducing several such observations in what follows. But these
observations constitute problems in their own right. For it *is* natural to think that
evidence plays an important role in explaining the rationality of beliefs. That
conviction, of course, played a central role in motivating the attempt, considered
in Chapters 3 through 5, to understand how perceptual experience could be a
privileged source of evidence about the external world, and hence how perceptual
experience could play an intelligible role in justifying external world beliefs. But if
it is puzzling—and as I will go on to argue, here, it *is* puzzling—how facts about
evidence alone can predict and explain what it is rational for a subject to believe,
then that is itself a very general problem about how it could be that evidence plays
a central role at all in explaining rational belief or knowledge.

The first puzzle that I want to consider about how evidence rationalizes belief is
very simple. I take it from Gilbert Harman (2002), and I call it the problem of *near
ties*. The problem is this. When reasons for competing actions are equally good—
when they are *tied*—it is rationally permissible to act in either way. But when the
evidence for and against P is tied—when you have equally good evidence that
P and that ~P—it is not rationally permissible to have either belief. On the
contrary, in general it is arguably always rationally impermissible to have either
belief, when the evidence is tied, and indeed, even when the evidence is even close
to being tied. Hence, the problem of *near ties*. With respect to action, the reasons
may be sufficient to justify belief when they are *at least as good* as the competing
reasons. So in the case of action, it may seem that we can appeal to an independent
standard for what makes reasons sufficient, in order to explain what it is rational
for an agent to do in terms of her reasons and their competition. But in the case of
belief, this does not appear to be possible, because evidence is not sufficient just
because it is at least as good as competing evidence.

The problem of *near ties* makes the problem of sufficiency sharp. It appears
to—and Harman argues that it does—show that epistemic rationality is very

different from the rationality of action, and in particular, that there is a very different relationship between reasons and rationality in the cases of belief and of action. But the problem of near ties is also puzzling in its own right. How good *does* evidence have to be, in order to make belief rational? Exactly how much better than competing evidence must it be? It turns out that several problems make it very hard to give a general answer to this question.

We might try to measure evidence in terms of how *probable* it makes a conclusion. On this perspective, the problem with tied evidence is that when evidence is tied or close to tied, both P and ~P are equiprobable or close to equiprobable. But the belief that P will be rational when the evidence that P makes it sufficiently probable. But in addition to general problems about further answering how the threshold for sufficient probability is to be non-arbitrarily set, this approach faces the problem that beliefs can be arbitrarily probable without being rational, as illustrated by cases involving *lotteries*.[2] If you know that a lottery involving *n* tickets with an equally good chance of winning has just been conducted, but do not yet know which ticket was selected as the winner, then you know that each ticket is $\frac{n-1}{n}$ likely to be a loser, which can be arbitrarily close to 1, for large enough values of *n*. So for any probabilistic threshold for rational belief short of 1, there is a lottery in which it is rational to believe, of each ticket, that it is a loser. Yet it is also rational to believe—indeed, I stipulated that it is one of the things that you know about the lottery—that one of the tickets is a winner. And it is rational to believe that you have considered all of the tickets. But from this we get the conclusion that each of a set of inconsistent beliefs is rational.

In principle one could, of course, avoid inconsistent beliefs by believing only *some* of the things that it is rational to believe. To do this, you would have to withhold either belief about whether the lottery has a winner, or about whether you have considered all of the tickets, or about at least one of the tickets. But I stipulated that you *know* that the lottery has a winner and you know which tickets are in the lottery. So it would be strange indeed if it were rational to withhold belief about either if these things, simply in order to consistently believe, of each ticket, that it is a loser—as if you could rationally come to doubt that the lottery has a winner or which tickets are included, simply by noting that each one is a probable loser. But to believe of some tickets that they are losers while withholding about other tickets would be rationally arbitrary—for we can stipulate that the tickets are symmetric in how you relate to them (for example, that none of them is the one that you bought[3]). So there is no rational way to believe of some tickets that they will be losers, while retaining consistent beliefs. From this

---

[2] Kyburg (1961). Compare also Ryan (1996), Nelkin (2000), and Smith (forthcoming).

[3] The intuition that it *is* rational to believe of a ticket that you have the opportunity to buy that it will lose is what originally drew me to the thesis of pragmatic encroachment in epistemology, as an undergraduate; and as we'll see in Chapter 8, I still think this is essentially right.

I conclude that lottery cases show that there is no threshold short of 1 for probability that is sufficient for rational belief.

In stating this problem, I have been focusing on probability thresholds of less than 1. But it does not help to avoid this problem, I believe, to try to set a threshold of a probability of 1, either. This is because on any natural conception of probability, it sometimes *is* rational to believe things that are merely probable, but not certain. There is, of course, one not-so-natural conception of probability that might be thought to get around this problem. Timothy Williamson (2000) appeals to what he calls the *evidential* probability of a proposition, which is the probability of that proposition, conditional on your evidence. He defends the view that it is rational to believe a proposition just in case its probability conditional on your evidence is 1. But this does not really get around our problem. For our problem is that it is rational to form some beliefs that do not follow deductively from the evidence that you already possess. Williamson will say about such cases that *once you form* the belief in question, if it is really rational, then it is knowledge, and hence its content is part of your evidence, and so it follows that its probability conditional on your evidence really is 1. But that gives us no explanation in terms of the evidence that you have *before* forming this belief, of why it is a rational one for you to form. So on Williamson's view, evidence simply *drops out* in the explanation of what it is prospectively rational for you to believe.[4]

So far, I have been arguing that it is difficult to say how much evidence is required in order to rationalize belief in probabilistic terms. But it is also difficult to answer this question in terms that appeal to the *quantity* or *preponderance* of the evidence. And that is because there are some cases in which beliefs are rational that are based on very little evidence, or evidence that only slightly outweighs the counter-evidence, but there are other cases in which it is not rational to believe, even though we have collected much more evidence, and our evidence is more decisive.

Let us take the problem about the *quantity of evidence* first. This problem can be illustrated by comparing the appropriate evidential standards for beliefs about subject matters where very little evidence is possible to subject matters where it is easy to collect decisive evidence. Examples of the former types of subject matter include ancient history, theoretical physics, and philosophy. For each of these subject matters, there are limits to our methods of evidence collection, and in some cases there may only be a very restricted range of possible evidence that could bear either way on a question. Yet it is sometimes—arguably, often— rational for practitioners of these fields to form beliefs about their subject matter. In contrast, for some subject matters, evidence is easy to come by. The very same questions that can be asked about what was going on in the room where Socrates

---

[4] For discussion, see Cohen and Comesaña (2013b).

drank his hemlock or where Brutus and Cassius plotted the assassination of Julius Caesar can be asked about what is going on in the room next to you as you read this. But the evidence that could rationally convince a historian about Socrates or Brutus could not rationally persuade you—for you are in a position to go next door and check for yourself. The bare availability of further evidence can therefore make it irrational to believe things that would otherwise be rational to believe.

Similar, though more controversial, points go for the *preponderance* of the evidence. This can be illustrated by comparing pairs of cases that differ in what are commonly known as the *stakes* of being wrong. A classic case illustrating this problem of *stakes* goes like this:[5] you are driving home from work on Friday, with the plan to stop at the bank along the way to deposit your paycheck before meeting your spouse for a dinner reservation. But when you pull up to the bank, you can see that the line for the teller goes well out the door, making it unlikely that you could make it through the line and still make your dinner reservation. Luckily, you have some evidence that the bank will be open on Saturday morning—for example, you seem to remember getting a flyer mentioning that they would soon have Saturday hours, and you've seen the door open a few times on Saturday morning while driving past. Now consider two versions of the case just described. In the first version, it doesn't matter very much whether your paycheck is deposited over the next week—and in particular, it matters less than whether you miss your dinner reservation with your spouse. But in the second version, it matters a great deal whether your paycheck is deposited before Sunday, when it is needed for your mortgage payment to clear, in order to keep your house from going into foreclosure—and hence in particular, it matters far more than whether you miss your dinner reservation with your spouse.

It is natural, at least pre-theoretically, to think that more evidence is required, in the case in which your mortgage payment is coming due, in order for it to be rational for you to form the belief that the bank will be open on Saturday morning, than in the case in which it doesn't matter if your paycheck is deposited before Monday. And if this is right, then there is no fixed preponderance of evidence that is either necessary or sufficient to rationalize belief, since a greater preponderance of evidence is required when the costs of error—sometimes colloquially referred to as the 'stakes'—are high. This idea—which has come to be known as *pragmatic encroachment*—is controversial and I will not depend on it in what follows, but I think that it is correct, and I will go on to defend it in Chapters 8 and 9.

In addition to these kinds of problems with understanding how evidence rationalizes belief, there are several further ways in which what it is rational for someone to believe seems to come apart from her evidence. For example, the problem of *arbitrary closure* is that all evidence that P is evidence in support of the

---

[5] Bank cases are originally due to DeRose (1992), and mine is loosely adapted from Stanley (2005). Similar cases are discussed by Fantl and McGrath (2002) and many others.

consequences of the proposition that P, but not all evidence against P is evidence against all of its consequences.[6] So every consequence of the proposition that P is at least as well-supported by evidence as it is. Yet intuitively, we are not rationally required to believe every logical consequence of everything that we believe—indeed, it would be irrational to bother doing so. So this seems to suggest another way in which the rationality of a belief cannot depend only on how well it is supported by the evidence.

The rationality of belief can also depend on the costs of deliberation. Lin and Min may have exactly the same evidence in support of the proposition that Lin should go to graduate school in Los Angeles, for example, but if Lin has spent all of the time since acquiring this evidence on the phone with her mother-in-law while her fire alarm is going off in the background and her toddler is breaking glassware, it may be rational for Min to take account of this evidence and believe that Lin should go to the University of Southern California, but not rational for Lin to believe this, since there are more pressing matters at hand. Again, this is a way in which what it is rational to believe comes apart from bare facts about the balance of the evidence.

Moreover, the order in which evidence is acquired can also make a difference. For example, Will and Phil both do research in the same field, and have both read all of the same studies that bear on whether P. But Will has been in the field for a long time, and Phil has just finished graduate school. When Will first entered the field, all of the evidence supported the thesis that P, and so, like most researchers at the time, he concluded that P. Over time, however, contrary evidence has occasionally trickled in, and more recent evidence has tended to tell against the hypothesis that P. Taken one-by-one, none of the new studies were significant enough to push Will to reconsider his view, and so he still believes that P. Phil also recognizes that the evidence that P is better than the evidence to the contrary. But since Phil is younger, he never formed a belief that P, and he considered all of the evidence at once. He concluded that although it is more likely that P, the totality of the evidence isn't good enough to close the question, and so he remains agnostic about whether P.[7] If cases like Will and Phil's are both possible and rational, then belief has a kind of rational *inertia*. And if belief exhibits rational inertia like this, then again, which beliefs are rational cannot be solely determined by the balance of the evidence.

---

[6] This point is somewhat more subtle than it looks, especially as I have been taking care throughout this book not to make any direct claims about how to measure evidence, either in terms of quantity or in terms of force. One important complication is that a particular piece of evidence, E, may make many consequences of P *less* likely even while making P *more* likely. So depending on how we measure evidence, it may not be true that a particular piece of evidence, E, supports the consequences of P just as well as it supports P. Nevertheless, the posterior probability of the consequences of P has to be at least as high as the posterior probability of P.

[7] Compare the cases discussed in Podgorski (2016a) and the explanation offered in Podgorski (2016a, 2016b). See also McGrath (2007).

6.3 Two Stages of Reasons

In Section 6.2 I assembled a variety of puzzles about the way in which evidence rationalizes belief. All of these puzzles are interesting, I think, but they fall into at least two very different categories. *Some* of them can be readily dealt with by distinguishing the *external* question about *whether* to deliberate whether P from the internal question of what to conclude, *within* deliberation about whether P. And this is important. For if all of the non-evidential factors affecting the rationality of belief could be explained away as bearing on the external question of whether to deliberate, rather than on the internal question of what to conclude within deliberation about whether P, then the idea that evidence alone plays a role in determining the rationality of belief could be preserved as applicable to the reasons *internal* to deliberation. But in this section I'll show that once we see why this is the *right* treatment of the problems of arbitrary closure, costs of deliberation, and cognitive inertia, we are also in a position to see that it is *not* the right treatment of the problems of statistical evidence, quantity of evidence, costs of error, or the problem of *near ties*. So focusing on the contrast between these two families of puzzles about how evidence rationalizes belief draws into focus what an adequate answer to the full class of problems would have to look like.

Let's take the problem of arbitrary closure first. What the setup of the problem of arbitrary closure shows, is that arbitrary consequences of a proposition are at least as well-supported by evidence as it is. And the worry that this raises is that it might turn out to be at least as rational to believe the arbitrary consequences of any proposition, as to believe that proposition itself. So, for example, yesterday it was at least rational for you to believe that either you are alive or 'avada kadavra' is an effective killing curse as for you to believe that you are alive. But intuitively, the worry goes, it is *not* as rational to believe every arbitrary consequence of the proposition that you are alive—and in particular, we could rightly criticize you if yesterday you had not believed that you were alive, but we could not rightly criticize you for not having believed yesterday that either you were alive or 'avada kadavra' is an effective killing curse.

But notice that this example is more compelling when it is described as being about yesterday, before you read these words, than if it is described as being about today. Though you are not criticizable for failing yesterday to believe that either you were alive or 'avada kadavra' is an effective killing curse, now you are. The reason for this is that yesterday you had not considered this disjunction and had no reason to, but today you have.[8] Perhaps today you had no special reason to consider it either, but now that you have, there is no going back, because the only reasonable conclusion to consideration of the question as to whether either you

---

[8] Compare Cohen (unpublished).

are alive or 'avada kadavra' is an effective killing curse is 'yes'. So the reason it was rational to lack this belief yesterday was that it was rational to have not considered the question—not because there is any other reasonable answer to the question. So for all that cases of arbitrary closure show, the reasonability of answers to questions always hangs solely on the evidence for and against, but the question of what it is rational to believe depends both on what questions it is rational to consider and on what answers it is reasonable to give to those questions.

The idea that rationality of belief must be carved up in this way, between the rationality of considering a question and the reasonable answers to that question, is an important and familiar one. It is the idea that there are *two levels* of rational assessment of belief, or two *stages* of reasoning, deriving from the interaction of *external* reasons for or against considering a question and *internal* reasons within the process of deliberating about that question. This idea has been endorsed and developed by Owens (2000), Hieronymi (2013), Hubbs (2013), and Shah and Silverstein (2013), among many others, and as Cohen (unpublished) has argued persuasively, it *fits* with the case of the problem of arbitrary closure.

Distinguishing between reasons external to doxastic deliberation and reasons internal to it also helps with the problems of costs of deliberation and of cognitive inertia. Lin's problem, for example, is not that the reasonable answer to the question of whether she should go to graduate school in Los Angeles is something different than it is for Min—her problem is that she should be thinking about something else right now—her fire alarm and her mother-in-law's phone call and the broken glass near her toddler's bare feet.

One way of testing the claim that it is whether *deliberation* is rational that is at issue in this situation, rather than which conclusion to that deliberation is reasonable, is that if we change the status quo of Lin's beliefs about whether she should go to graduate school in Los Angeles, we change the effects of her distracting circumstances. For example, compare a version of the case in which Lin has not yet formed a belief about where she should go to graduate school when the fire alarm starts going off, with one in which she had earlier concluded that she should go to graduate school in New York. In both cases, once the fire alarm starts going off, the status quo becomes rationally entrenched. It is not rational *now*, as the fire alarm is going off and her mother-in-law is on the phone and her toddler is about to step on broken glass—to change her view about where she ought to go to graduate school, and so whatever view she already has about that question is one that it is rational for her to keep, at least for now. The fact that distracting circumstances entrench the rationality of the status quo *whatever that is*, strongly supports the view that the distracting circumstances do not affect which

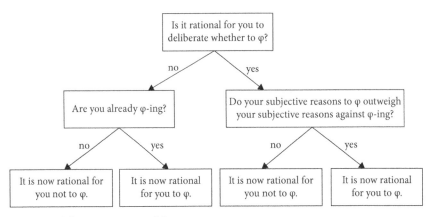

Figure 6.1 The two-stage model

conclusion is reasonable *within* doxastic deliberation, but only *whether* to open or re-open deliberation, at all.[9]

Finally, as Abelard Podgorski (2016a) has ably argued, the problem of cognitive inertia is also plausibly dealt with by distinguishing between reasons whether to deliberate and reasons within deliberation. If it is rational for Will to retain his belief that P even though the appropriate response for Phil, who has considered the question afresh, is to be agnostic, then that is because the further evidence that has come in against this proposition has never been significant, by itself, to require Will to reconsider his view. Since it has never been significant enough to require reconsideration, he is rational to retain his existing view. And so the status quo is supported. Again, we see that what makes this a compelling case to be handled by a distinction between the rationality of considering the question and the reasonability of answers within that consideration is the status quo. Will does not get grandfathered in, just because he is older—if Will has a colleague who never made up her mind about whether P until the newer evidence came in, it is not any more rational for her to believe that P. What makes it rational for Will to have this belief is that it is the status quo and it is rational not to reconsider—not just the order in which he has acquired evidence.

In this section we have seen that there are some important ways in which the evidence under-determines what it is rational for someone to believe that drop out of the fact that what it is rational to believe is a product of the status quo of what you believe, the question of whether it is rational for you to consider some question, and the question of what conclusion it is rational or reasonable to draw about that question—of how it is rational to *conclude* deliberation. The

---

[9] Compare Schroeder (2013). In Schroeder (2012b) I made the mistake of holding that cost-of-deliberation cases pattern with cost-of-error and availability-of-evidence cases, but Shah and Silverstein (2013) convinced me that this was an error.

case of arbitrary closure shows that it matters what questions you are considering and it is rational for you to consider, and the cases of costs of deliberation and of cognitive inertia illustrate what we should expect, if there are separate questions of whether it is rational to deliberate, and what it is reasonable to conclude within that deliberation—we should expect reasons against deliberation to prop up the rationality of retaining the status quo—whatever that is.

6.4 Limits of the Two-Stage Strategy

I have been focusing in Section 6.3 on what the two-stage strategy gets *right*, in order to make vivid how different these cases are, from the other group of problems that I canvassed in Section 6.2—the lottery problem, the problem of the availability of further evidence, the problem of costs of error, and Harman's point about the problem of near ties.

Let's take the lottery problem first. Recall that this problem arises in cases in which you have arbitrarily good statistical evidence regarding each ticket, that it will not win, but you know that one of the tickets will win. Something about this setup somehow makes it irrational to believe of an arbitrary ticket that it will win, even though the probability of that ticket winning may be much higher than other things that it is totally rational for you to believe. If this is a product of the two-stage strategy, then that must be because it is irrational to deliberate about whether a lottery ticket will win, rather than because believing that it will not win is not the most reasonable conclusion to such deliberation.

But this gets things wrong. As we saw in the case of arbitrary closure, even when it is not particularly rational to deliberate about some question, if you find yourself thinking about the question and the answer is immediately obvious it is not rational to not accept the answer to that question. Applying the same principle to the lottery case, we should expect that if you find yourself thinking explicitly about whether some ticket will win, then the only reasonable response is to conclude that it will not—and perhaps, to stop yourself from thinking about the other tickets, before you get stuck with a contradiction. But this is not right—in the lottery case, the symmetry between the tickets makes it unreasonable to conclude that any given ticket will not win, *even if you find yourself thinking about whether that ticket will win.*

Similarly, we saw from the cases of the problem of costs of deliberation and the problem of cognitive inertia that reasons not to deliberate will prop up the status quo. If it is irrational to open deliberation, then it will be rational to retain whatever view you already have about the question. But it is *not* rational to retain views that you have about whether particular tickets in a lottery will win. For example, if you made the mistake a few hours ago of concluding that ticket 354 will not win, it does not become rational to retain that belief, simply because you shouldn't reconsider the question. And even more clearly, if you formed a belief on a hunch that ticket 1192 *will* win, it doesn't become rational to retain that belief, simply because you shouldn't reconsider the question. So we can see that so far from propping up the status quo, cases of purely statistical evidence don't care about the status quo at all—they always make it unreasonable to have *either* belief.

Similar reasoning extends to the problem of the availability of evidence. Earlier I noted that with respect to many questions about philosophy or about ancient history for which evidence is sparse and difficult to come by, it is completely rational to draw conclusions, even when similar quantities of evidence would not rationalize a conclusion about how many people are in the next room over—or other questions for which it is easy to gather additional, decisive, evidence. The relevant difference between the cases, I argued, is a matter of *how much* further evidence is available. When there is much better evidence available, and it is easy to gather, it is less rational to form a belief, than if there is no further evidence available. In order to explain this case, the two-stage strategy would have to contend that when there is more evidence available, it is irrational to deliberate.

But as we have already seen, even if there is no point in deliberating about whether either you are alive or 'avada kadavra' is an effective killing curse, once you find yourself considering the question—simply because you read it in a book called *Reasons First*—there is only one reasonable response. Similarly, we should expect that even if you made a rational mistake to *begin* reasoning about how many people are in the next room, once you have made that mistake, you are rational *going forward* in concluding that there are twelve (say), provided that that is the answer that is best-supported by the highly circumstantial evidence that you do have. But this, I think, is not right. Even if you find yourself wondering how many people are in the room next door, the correct way for this reasoning to *proceed* is for you to recognize that the best way to find out is to *look*.

We also used support for the status quo as a test for the effects of reasons for or against deliberating. And again, we can see that the availability of further evidence cannot be a feature of only such external reasons. If the fact that further evidence is available only counts against opening the question, then it would tend to prop up your status quo belief, no matter what it is. But that means that if you *earlier* formed the belief that there are twelve people in the room next door on the basis of your paltry evidence, though you were irrational *then*, you are *now* being rational to *retain* that belief, since it is not a question that you should be deliberating about. And worse, it means that if you earlier formed the belief that there are eight people in the room next door completely on a hunch and even though it conflicted with your weak circumstantial evidence, you are still rational now in retaining that belief, simply because it is not rational to reconsider the question. This is not right. The availability of evidence is not just something that we need to think about when deciding *whether* to consider a question—it is also one of the things that you need to think about *in the course* of considering that question. And concluding that you don't have enough evidence to settle the question isn't just an *interruption* of considering the question—it is one of the natural *conclusions* of deliberation. So the effects of the availability of further evidence cannot be subsumed to a two-stage treatment.

In the case of the problem of costs of error, the failures of the two-stage treatment are even more obvious. Recall that in cost-of-error cases like the bank case, one popular and reasonable view is that more evidence is needed in order to rationally form a belief, if the costs of acting on that belief if it is false are high. In order to treat this case, the two-stage strategy would have to postulate that costs of error are a reason not to deliberate. But as with the arbitrary closure case, that would seem to suggest that even if deliberating was a bad idea, once you find yourself in the middle of deliberating about whether the bank will be open on Saturday, the only reasonable conclusion is that it is. But this is not right—if you find the bank case plausible at all, the fact that you are already thinking about whether the bank will be open on Saturday does not seem to get you off of the hook for having more evidence, if you are in the high-stakes case. Cost-of-error cases also do not seem to prop up the status quo. If you start off believing that the bank will be open on Saturday, realizing that your mortgage payment is coming due should prompt you to reconsider your evidence—not to clamp down on your belief.

But even more tellingly, cost-of-error cases are transparently asymmetric in a way that cannot be accounted for by any two-stage treatment. This is because in cases like the bank case, the costs of relying on a false belief that the bank *will* be open on Saturday are high, but the costs of relying on a false belief that the bank *won't* be open are *low*.[10] So though more evidence is required in order to rationally believe that the bank will be open, more evidence is *not* required in order to rationally believe that the bank will *not* be open. It follows from this observation that if your evidence supports the view that the bank will not be open on Saturday, nothing about the fact of your knowledge of your impending mortgage payment makes you required to seek out more evidence before concluding that the bank will not be open. In other words, the costs of error are *selective*—they tell against the conclusion that the bank will be open, but they do not tell against the conclusion that the bank will not be open.

No facts about the rationality of deliberation or about reasons for or against deliberation could be selective in this way. If costs of error count against deliberation, then they count against deliberation full-stop—regardless of the outcome of that deliberation. If it is irrational to deliberate about whether P, then we get the same indictment of the conclusion that ~P as we do of the conclusion that P—both are indicted by the same problematic deliberative history. In order to account

---

[10] See Schroeder (2012a).

for the way in which costs of error affect the rationality of belief, we therefore need to see them as playing a role *within* deliberation—they must compete directly with the evidence. And as we saw in Chapter 2, this is a familiar observation from ethical theory going back all of the way to Ross—if greater evidence is required to overcome greater costs of error, then that is likely because evidence and costs of error are competing *directly* in the determination of what it is most reasonable for someone to believe.

In this section I have been arguing that the problem of purely statistical evidence, the problem of availability of evidence, and the problem of costs of error are all different in kind from the problems of arbitrary closure, of costs of deliberation, and of cognitive inertia that I showed in Section 6.3 can be safely set aside as products of the fact that there is a distinction between whether it is rational to deliberate and what is the reasonable conclusion of deliberation. I emphasize each of these problems, because they are the specific phenomena of which I think an adequate account of how evidence supports reasonable conclusions owes us an account, and in order to make clear that each phenomenon rightly belongs *within* doxastic deliberation. But it is possible to see even more quickly that the two-stage strategy must fail somewhere. This is shown directly by the problem of *near ties*.

The problem of near ties, recall, is that it is never rational to believe either that P or that ~P, if the evidence is perfectly tied—and typically not rational to have either belief when the evidence is *nearly* tied. When it comes to action, actions are rational just in case they are supported by reasons that are *at least as good* as the competing reasons, and so it is a puzzle that beliefs do not seem to be rational when they are supported by evidence that is at least as good as the competing evidence— assuming that the only reasons that matter for the rationality of belief are evidence.

The problem of near ties is not even a remotely plausible candidate for a two-stage treatment. It is transparently a fact about how evidence determines what it is reasonable to believe that near ties do not suffice. And there is no prior way of determining, *before* you consider a question, whether the evidence is nearly tied, in order to decide whether it is worth deliberating about that question. The conclusion that the evidence is nearly tied is something that can only emerge *within* deliberation—by weighing the evidence itself. All of this is in addition to the facts that near-ties still matter even if you find that you are already deliberating about some question, and the fact that they only support agnosticism, rather than propping up the status quo indiscriminately.

Whereas the lottery problem, the problem of further evidence, and the problem of costs of error are all *specific* phenomena which exhibit the under-determination of the rationality of belief by the evidence, the problem of near ties is highly general. In Section 6.5, I will argue that it is the *central* problem about how evidence rationalizes belief, and holds the key to the solutions of at least two of the other problems.

6.5 A Solution

The problem of near ties lies at the heart of all of our problems about how evidence justifies belief. If the only reasons that matter for the rationality of belief are evidence for and against its content, then the problem of near ties shows us that we need some *independent* conception of what makes evidence sufficient—we cannot simply read it off as the product of its weighing against competing reasons. And this is what drives the problem of sufficiency. But the problem of near ties is *also* the most general case of the puzzles that we have been discussing about how evidence rationalizes belief. My argument for this will consist in showing how a solution to the problem of near ties immediately reveals solutions to the other problems.

What drives all of our puzzles is the assumption that the only reasons that matter for the rationality of belief are evidence for or against its content. So we can solve all of these puzzles by rejecting that assumption. Though evidence that P is always reason to believe that P, evidence whether P may not be the *only* source of reasons for or against believing that P. And the problem of mere ties gives us an *argument* that there are other such reasons—and in particular, for what role they play.

When Harman introduces the problem of near ties, he notes that with respect to action, an action is rational when the reasons in favor of it are *at least as good* as the reasons against. But the problem of near ties is that a belief is not rational whenever the evidence in favor is at least as good as the evidence against. So Harman concludes that the rationality of belief is very different from the rationality of action. We can precisify his reasoning in the following way:

P1   All evidence that P is reason to believe that P.
P2   *Only* evidence that ~P is reason against believing that P.
C1   So if the evidence is tied, then the reasons to believe that P are at least as good as the reasons against believing that P (from P1 and P2).
P3   It is never rational to believe that P when the evidence is tied.
C2   So if the evidence is tied, then the reasons to believe that P are at least as good as the reasons against believing that P, but it is not rational to believe that P (from C1 and P3).
P4   The evidence is sometimes tied.
C   Sometimes the reasons to believe that P are at least as good as the reasons against believing that P, but it is not rational to believe that P (from C2 and P4).

But in this book we are taking a very different approach. I have argued very early on that epistemology is just as much a normative discipline as moral philosophy, and that we should expect differences between epistemology and moral philosophy to flow from the difference of their subject matter—the differences between belief and action—rather than from the fact that there simply fail to be parallels between normative concepts like reasons and rationality as they apply in these two domains. And the Core Hypothesis of this book is that we should expect to see *problems* that arise when people think about questions in either ethics or episte-mology in isolation from how they arise across the board. Harman's conclusion illustrates the Core Hypothesis perfectly.

If we start with just a slightly higher prior credence than Harman does in the hypothesis that reasons interact in the same way with respect to belief and with respect to action, then we should take seriously the idea that one of Harman's premises is less compelling than the negation of his conclusion. We can then reason as follows:

P1   It is rational to believe that P just in case the reasons to believe that P are at least as good as the reasons against believing that P.

P2   All evidence that P is reason to believe that P.

P3   All evidence that ~P is reason against believing that P.

C1   So if the evidence is tied, then it is rational to believe that P just in case there are no reasons against believing that P that are not evidence that ~P (from P1, P2, P3).

P4   It is never rational to believe that P when the evidence is tied.

C2   So if the evidence is tied, then there are reasons against believing that P that are not evidence that ~P.

If we turn Harman's argument on its head, therefore—as Harman himself famously recommends is often the appropriate response to arguments[11]—we get an argument not only that there *can* be reasons against belief that are not evidence against its content, but that there must *always* be such reasons, whenever the evidence is closely tied. What I want to suggest, is that this is true because there are always reasons against belief that are not evidence, *regardless* of whether the evidence is tied.

This conclusion follows if the costs of error and the availability of further evidence are always reasons against belief that are not evidence against its content. In general, there are always some risks of relying on a false belief—if only because it is not possible to tell in advance how it might infect your beliefs about other topics, if you rely on it.[12] And there is nearly always some possible way of acquiring further evidence. So if these sorts of factors can count as reasons against belief, there will *always* be reasons against belief that are not evidence against its content. And since this is so, it *follows* that near ties in evidence will not be sufficient to rationalize belief—even though all it takes to rationalize belief is to be

---

[11] Harman (1986).   [12] See *Slaves of the Passions* (Schroeder, 2007, ch. 6).

at least as good as the reasons against. This is because once we allow for reasons against belief that are not evidence, the evidence in favor needs to outweigh the *combination* of evidential and non-evidential reasons against belief.

This gives us an elegant solution to all of our problems at once.[13] More evidence is required to rationalize belief when the costs of error appear to be high for the *very same reason* that a greater conflicting obligation is required to justify breaking a more important promise and more evidence in favor is required to rationalize belief when there is also ample *contrary* evidence. It is because these are reasons that compete directly with one another in the determination of what it is rational or appropriate for someone to do or to believe. Similarly, more evidence is required to rationalize belief when more evidence is available, because the amount of additional available evidence *competes directly* with the amount of evidence for P, in determining whether it is rational to believe that P. Since both of these reasons against belief are always present, they are always present in cases in which the evidence is tied, and so in all cases of near ties, they tip the balance against believing. And since all of this is determined directly by the competition between reasons, we do not need to appeal to any prior account of the nature of sufficiency, or of rationality, in order to use the competition between reasons to determine what it is rational for someone to believe, thus solving the problem of sufficiency.[14]

In Chapter 1, I laid out some of the circumstantial evidence that evidence and reasons are closely related, and distinguished between the hypotheses of Reasons as Evidence and Evidence as Reasons. I argued there against the view that reasons are just evidence of a particular kind of thing, and in favor of the view that evidence matters in epistemology by being reason to believe. But now we can see that the argument in this chapter constitutes a much more direct argument in favor of Evidence as Reasons. The answer that I have been giving to the most central problems about how evidence can rationalize belief depends essentially on the idea that evidence can compete directly with reasons against belief that are not evidence against its content.

Similarly, in Chapter 2, I introduced the Rossian diagnosis of why there are few or no simple absolute rules about what is wrong or what you ought to do. According to this diagnosis, there are no such absolute rules, because what is wrong, and what you ought to do, are simply determined by the balance of competing reasons. We can now see that my answer to the puzzles about how evidence rationalizes belief is the same as Ross's. This seems complicated, but the

---

[13] At least, to most of them. I remain agnostic whether this is also helpful in solving the lottery problem or instead some different tool is appropriate for that problem—see note 15, below.

[14] Interested readers will find it fruitful to contrast the treatment offered here to those in Schroeder (2012a), which poses but fails to adequately address the problem of near ties, and in Snedegar (2017, ch. 6), which offers an alternative, contrastivist, treatment of the problem of near ties. I have tried here to do with a primitive distinction between reasons for and against belief like that appealed to by Greenspan (2005) what Snedegar accomplishes by appeal to essentially contrastive reasons.

complications that we see are simply a predictable result of the interaction between simple, competing factors. And those factors are reasons.

In this chapter I have laid out both the difficult problems about how evidence can play a role in rationalizing belief, and the essentials of my solution. The solution that I have advanced is that though evidence that P is the only kind of properly epistemic reason in *favor* of believing that P, evidence that ~P is *not* the only kind of properly epistemic reason *against* believing that P. In particular, facts about the availability of further evidence and about what is at stake, I suggested, can be properly epistemic reasons against belief.[15]

This is the core of my answer to these problems within epistemology, and it is also the core of my answer to how this makes good on the Core Hypothesis of the book, and the core of my answer to why the correct solution to these problems shows us the way to a solution to the problem of sufficiency that is not only consistent with the thesis of Reasons First, but actually vindicates it, as doing powerful explanatory work in epistemology. On this view, explaining what it is rational to believe in terms of the competition between reasons has exactly the same virtues as the Rossian diagnosis of explaining what you morally ought to do, all things considered.[16]

So far, I've argued *that* this is true, but I haven't yet explained how it *could* be true. And indeed, an important part of why this solution has not seemed more obviously available within epistemology is precisely that most have not seen how it *could* be available. After all, we initially characterized the domain of properly *epistemic* reasons, in Chapter 1, by contrast with Pascalian considerations—cases in which you stand to gain or lose, in some way, if you have some particular belief, because you will be rewarded or punished by some exterior or interior psychological mechanism, such as eternal damnation, monetary rewards, or even just feeling better about yourself. And certainly *one* obvious difference between these cases is that our paradigms of normal reasons for belief are all evidence, and Pascalian reasons are all practical. So the diagnosis that the epistemic/non-epistemic distinction classifies only evidence on the 'epistemic' side and

---

[15] I do not take a stand, here, on whether the lottery problem can be accounted for in this way. Although I have argued that it is not adequately treated by the two-stage strategy, a third possibility is that the problem of merely statistical evidence turns out to actually not be very good evidence, because strength of evidence is tied to explanatory relationships, rather than probabilifying relationships. So I will not take a stand on how this problem is best treated, and will not return to it in the next few chapters.

[16] It follows from this solution that belief is epistemically rational just in case it is supported by sufficient evidence—since evidence that P is the only epistemic reason for believing that P. Evidentialists sometimes formulate their thesis in this way. But other times they say that evidentialism is the thesis that whether a belief is epistemically rational (or justified) is determined wholly by the evidence (compare Conee and Feldman (2004) for both formulations). These two formulations are compatible only if what makes evidence sufficient is wholly determined by the evidence. But that depends, in turn, on what sorts of epistemic reasons there are against belief.

everything remotely practical-sounding on the 'non-epistemic' side is a highly natural one.

Still, despite the fact that this is a natural *hypothesis* about the distinction between paradigmatic reasons for beliefs and Pascalian cases, it does not follow that this is the most *relevant* distinction between the two cases. Since it is a *possible* distinction, of course, it is open for theorists to stipulate that they will use 'epistemic reasons' stipulatively to refer only to evidence. But to use the word stipulatively in this way is to leave open whether the epistemic/non-epistemic distinction carries any general relevance for epistemology. So I suggest that it is more helpful to use the term 'epistemic' in a way that holds fixed that it is relevant for epistemology, and leaves open which reasons count as *epistemic*. Epistemic reasons, in the sense that I intend, are whatever reasons bear on epistemic rationality, where epistemic rationality is the *strongest kind of rationality entailed by knowledge*.[17]

Whether there are epistemic reasons against belief that are not evidence against its content cannot, therefore, be a terminological issue. It is a substantive issue to be decided by looking more closely at the kinds of reasons that can bear on the strongest kind of rationality entailed by knowledge. That is the task to which we turn in Chapters 7 and 8.

---

[17] Schroeder (2015d). Compare Cohen (2016), and note that this definition still works if there is only one kind of rationality of belief—it simply does not presuppose it.

7

Epistemic Reasons as Right-Kind Reasons

7.1 Locating the Epistemic/Non-Epistemic Distinction

In Chapter 6 I argued that the key to both solving the outstanding problems in
epistemology about how evidence can explain what it is rational to believe, and
solving the problem of sufficiency for Reasons First, is to recognize that there are
epistemic reasons *against* belief that are not evidence against its content. We saw
that this possibility cannot be ruled out by terminological fiat, but rather is a
substantive issue that must be investigated by seeing which reasons bear on the
strongest kind of rationality entailed by knowledge.

This way of framing the question leaves open whether there are epistemic
reasons that are not evidence, without closing off the possibility that there are
not. It is a question to be settled by looking at what reasons bear on the strongest
kind of rationality entailed by knowledge. This is, in turn, a question that we can
get leverage on from different directions. For example, in Chapter 6 we already
approached this question directly. If you can know anything about philosophy or
ancient history, then it can be rational to believe things about philosophy or
ancient history in the strongest way required for knowledge. Yet I contend that
you cannot know the number of people in the next room on the basis of similar
evidence to that we have in philosophy or about ancient history. And the reason
that you cannot know this is that it is not even rational to believe these things.

The direct path is one way to seek evidence about which kinds of considerations
can be epistemic reasons. But it is not a particularly illuminating source of
evidence. There is no independent leverage that we can get, in this way, on
thinking about what kinds of considerations are epistemic reasons, other than
thinking directly about what matters for knowledge. And at least one of the
important kinds of cases that we have been discussing—cases involving high
'stakes', or costs of error—are themselves highly controversial. Fortunately, it is
not the only way that we can get leverage on this question. As I will now argue,
epistemic rationality—that is, the strongest kind of rationality that is entailed by
knowledge—has much in common with distinctive dimensions of rational evaluation appropriate to *other* attitudes, including intention, fear, admiration, and
others. If this is right, and epistemic rationality is to belief what the distinctive
rationality of intention is to intention and the distinctive rationality of fear is to
fear, then we will be able to get leverage on the question of which reasons for and
against belief are properly epistemic by comparing it to analogous questions of

Reasons First. Mark Schroeder, Oxford University Press (2021). © Mark Schroeder.
DOI: 10.1093/oso/9780198868224.003.0007

which reasons are the proper ones for and against intention, and which are the proper reasons for and against fear.

The idea that there is something analogous between the distinction between epistemic and non-epistemic reasons, and corresponding distinctions that can be drawn with respect to reasons for and against other attitudes, does not originate with me. Many philosophers have observed that just as there is something funny about believing something because you have been offered money to do so, there is something funny about intending to do something just because you have been offered money for having the intention (independently of whether you actually act on it), something funny about admiring someone just because you have been offered money to admire them (things are potentially different if they themselves are the ones offering the money, which is a kind of gumption, to be sure), and something funny about fearing something just because you have been offered money to fear it.[1]

Let's take the case of reasons for admiration, first. Typical reasons to admire someone are that she is funny, generous, or talented at playing the piano. Typical reasons *not* to admire someone are that she is selfish, cruel, or vindictive. To the extent that someone has the former features and *not* the latter features, she is an appropriate object of admiration—it is correct to admire her. And to the extent that you rationally believe her to have the former features and do not rationally believe her to have the latter features it is *rational* to admire her. It makes sense to admire someone you think is funny and talented at playing the piano. It could be a mistake, if unbeknownst to you it turns out that she is also selfish, cruel, and vindictive. And if you learned those things about her, it would be rational for you to stop admiring her. But in the absence of being aware of those traits, whether it is rational—whether it *makes sense*—for you to admire her depends on what you *do* believe about her.

Indeed, whether it is rational for you to admire her depends on *which* of her features you are aware of. If you know only that she is funny, it may make sense to admire her, but not if you realize that she is also selfish. But if in addition, you learn how amazing she is at the piano, it may make sense to admire her despite her selfishness. Yet it would not make sense for someone else who was also aware of her cruelty and vindictiveness to admire her. So the question of whom it is rational to admire, like the question of what you ought to do, is subject to *competition*. Different factors—funniness, talent, cruelty, selfishness, and vindictiveness—all bear on whether it is rational to admire someone, and seem to count in different ways, for and against it.

Our second characteristic of reasons, from Chapter 2, was that they are *act-oriented*, rather than *outcome-oriented*. The same clearly goes for these

---

[1] For example, D'Arms and Jacobson (2000a, 2000b), Owens (2000), Hieronymi (2005).

reasons to admire. If you could persuade several other people to admire someone by *not* admiring them, the fact that she is funny does not make this a more rational to thing to do. Similarly, if you find yourself in this situation, the fact that someone is cruel does not make it make more sense to admire them, just because that could prevent others from admiring her. So reasons for and against admiration do not count in favor of or against *outcomes* in which they are admired, but just in favor of or against *admiring them*.

Finally, our third characteristic of reasons, from Chapter 2, was that they can be *acted on*. In the case of reasons for admiration or belief, of course, the sense in which these reasons can be acted on is not literally that they can lead to *action*, but that they can be the reasons *for which* you believe, or *for which* you admire. And ordinary reasons to admire *can* be the reasons for which you admire. When you admire someone, you typically admire them *for* their sense of humor, or *for* their generosity. And when you do so, the reason for which you admire them is that they are funny, or that they are generous.

So our intuitive examples of ordinary reasons for or against admiring someone satisfy our key characteristics of reasons. They are paradigmatic reasons, in the sense of 'reason' employed in this book. The same is not at all obvious of benefits and costs of admiring someone, in general. Suppose that someone offers you a great deal of money to admire her daughter. In some sense that 'counts in favor' of admiring the daughter—if you could get yourself to admire her, you would benefit. Or suppose that someone threatens your family on the condition that you admire her rival. In some sense that 'counts against' admiring the rival—for doing so will come at a steep price.

Costs and benefits like these can be weighed against one another. If you are offered US$1,000 to admire someone but your family's lives are threatened if you do, the costs clearly count against admiring them. So they satisfy the first characteristic of reasons. But they do not satisfy ourother two characteristics of reasons. As many philosophers have observed, it is not possible to admire someone just because her mother has offered you money to do so. To do so would be to admire her for her mother's offer; and having a mother who would offer you money to admire her is not itself an admirable trait. It is easy to respond to the mother's offer by trying to learn more about someone, or concentrate on seeing her in a sympathetic or positive light, hoping that this will lead one to learn about her admirable features and hence to come to admire her. But it is not so easy to respond immediately to the monetary offer by admiring her, in the way that you can spontaneously respond to watching her play the piano with admiration. So, arbitrary costs and benefits of admiring someone do not satisfy our third characteristic of reasons.

They also, arguably, do not satisfy our second characteristic. Suppose that *each* of us experiences benefits to admiring someone, because her mother has offered to donate US$1,000 to a worthy charitable cause for everyone who admires him. But now suppose that two of your friends will not admire the daughter unless you *don't* admire her—so that if you admire her, only US$1,000 will be donated to charity, but if you don't, they will, and hence US$2,000 will be donated. Clearly, whatever can be said in favor of your admiring her in the case where your admiration has no effects on your friends can be said against it, in the case where you *can* influence their admiration. After all, the effects of your admiration on your friends' admiration does not differ in kind from its effects on charitable donations. So it seems the arbitrary benefits and costs of admiration are outcome-oriented, rather than act-oriented—again, unlike our chief characteristics of reasons.

Similar points go for paradigmatic reasons for and against belief, in contrast to Pascalian cases of being offered money to have some belief, threatened with punishment for not having it, or where the belief is merely unpleasant. Paradigmatic cases of reasons for and against belief are evidence for or against its content. As we saw in Chapter 1 when I argued for the hypothesis of *evidence as reasons*, evidence can weigh against each other—it may be rational to believe something given some evidence in favor of it, no longer rational to believe once you learn of some evidence against it, and rational again once you learn of yet more evidence in favor.

Evidence is also act-oriented, rather than outcome-oriented. If you could get your friends to believe something by not believing it yourself, that bears in no way on what it is rational for you to believe in any way that is required for knowledge. Otherwise it could turn out that the mere existence of stubborn friends with beliefs that are anti-correlated with yours can prevent you from knowing. And evidence satisfies our third characteristic of reasons as well—you can believe on its basis. The fact that she is smiling can be the reason for which you believe that she is happy.

Like arbitrary costs and benefits of admiration, Pascalian considerations about belief are arbitrary costs or benefits of having some belief. And like arbitrary costs and benefits in general, they can be weighed or compete with one another, satisfying the first characteristic of reasons. But they also famously fail the characteristic of being something that can be acted on. Though it is easy to be motivated to spend more time reading scripture if you become convinced by Pascal's wager, hoping thereby to influence your beliefs indirectly, it is not so easy to become directly convinced that God exists, as you might if They spoke to you directly out of the burning bush, or you came to accept the ontological argument. And Pascalian considerations are also outcome-oriented, rather than act-oriented. If there are charitable donations to be gained by people's believing something, it does not matter whether you are the one believing it or someone else is. So like arbitrary costs and benefits of admiration more generally, Pascalian considerations about belief do not satisfy our key characteristics of reasons.[2]

---

[2] Compare Hieronymi (2005), Shah (2006), and Way (2012).

In this section I've been attempting to lay out at length some of the key parallels between reasons for and against belief and reasons for and against admiration. But similar points can be drawn for other attitudes for which we can have reasons. The bare offer of money to have an attitude, or threat of punishment for having it, *never* creates an act-oriented competitor bearing on the rationality of that attitude which is the kind of consideration to which someone can immediately respond, making it the reason *for which* one holds that attitude. For each attitude, we can call the *normal* reasons that exhibit all three of our characteristics of reasons the *right* kind of reason, and the arbitrary costs and benefits that are created by bare offers or threats the *wrong* kind of reason.[3] My suggestion, given the unity of this phenomenon, is that it must have some unified explanation. The hope is that we can *use* that unified explanation in order to get leverage on the question of whether there are epistemic reasons against belief that are not evidence.

7.2 The Object-Given/State-Given Theory

As I noted already in Section 7.1, I am not the first to observe parallels between Pascalian reasons and the case of arbitrary costs and benefits of other attitudes. Yet if this is a common observation, and it is *uncommon* to recognize the existence of epistemic reasons against belief that are not evidence, something must be preventing people from seeing this. That something is an assumption about *what* uniform phenomenon is going on across the cases of reasons for belief, admiration, and other attitudes. This assumption has come to be called the *object-given/state-given* theory.

According to the object-given/state-given theory, the only proper or *right-kind* reasons in favor of any attitude are considerations that bear on its *object* or *content*.[4] Anything that does not count for or against the content of the attitude, according to this theory, must count in favor of it only by constituting a benefit or cost of the *state* of having that attitude. And all benefits or costs of being in the state of having the attitude, like the arbitrary benefits and costs considered in Section 7.1, must be the *wrong* kind of reason for or against having that attitude.

If the object-given/state-given theory could be motivated in a way that is independent of its consequences for reasons for and against belief, then it would

---

[3] This terminology comes from Rabinowicz and Rønnow-Rasmussen (2004). But it is important to note that Rabinowicz and Rønnow-Rasmussen were concerned in that article in the first instance with a different problem—the problem of isolating which reasons are to be weighed in what is known as a *fitting attitudes* analysis of 'good' in terms of the balance of reasons for and against desire. The use of this vocabulary spread in part because the reasons that you want to go into a fitting attitudes analysis of 'good' are very closely related to the ones that bear on the rationality of desiring something. But it is still important to keep these two problems separated.

[4] Compare Parfit (1997), Piller (2001, 2006), Olson (2004), Stratton-Lake (2005), Danielson and Olson (2007), and Skorupski (2007).

be a way of using the parallels that I began to document in Section 7.1 in order to get leverage *against* my claim that there are epistemic reasons against belief that are not evidence. So if this were right, then it would turn out that so far from *helping* to defend my suggestion in Chapter 6, this would actually be a way of learning that I am wrong.

But it turns out that the object-given state-given theory is *not* actually motivated independently of the specific view that the only reasons for or against belief are evidence. On the contrary, the best way to think about where the object-given/state-given theory comes from, is that it is an attempt to *generalize* the orthodox view that the only epistemic reasons for or against belief are evidence for or against its content, in order to formulate a view that is applicable to reasons for or against attitudes, in general.

The terminology of the object-given/state-given theory comes from Parfit (2001), who applied this distinction to reasons for desire, as part of an attempt to argue that desire-based theories of reasons cannot make sense of how desires could themselves be rational or irrational. According to Parfit, when a desire is *intrinsically* rational, and not just instrumentally rational for its good effects, there are reasons in favor of this desire that bear on its *content*, rather than on the state of having the desire. For example, the fact that it would be good to φ is a reason that bears on the *content* of the desire to φ, whereas the fact that it would be good to desire to φ is, intuitively, a reason that bears on the *state* of desiring to φ.

Though this terminology is intuitive as applied to this particular example, many have noticed that it is very hard to see how it generalizes. In particular, it is not clear what it means for an arbitrary reason to bear on the object of an arbitrary desire, much less how this generalizes to states like fear, admiration, or liking. Some attitudes, like admiration and liking, don't have contents at all in the propositional sense, but rather are directed toward individuals.[5] So to bear on the objects of these attitudes, reasons must be somehow related to the individuals who are the possible objects of fear, admiration, or liking. But it is very hard to see what this comes to in a way that does not overgeneralize.

In contrast, the best case for the object-given/state-given theory, the one that is most similar to the case of reasons for belief, and the one that lends it credence, is the case of reasons for intention. In the case of intention, it is a little bit harder to construct examples analogous to Pascalian considerations, but Kavka's (1983) toxin puzzle has come to be accepted by many as analogous to the case of Pascalian reasons for belief. In the toxin puzzle, you are offered a large monetary prize by an eccentric billionaire for intending to drink a mild toxin at noon tomorrow. At midnight tonight, you will undergo a brain scan to verify whether you genuinely

---

[5] Grzankowski (2015, 2016).

intend to drink the toxin or not, and if you do,[6] the money will be wired directly into your bank account. Consequently, when the time comes to drink the toxin at noon tomorrow, there will no longer be any benefit to be gained from drinking the toxin—and much to lose, since it will make you sick for the afternoon.

The toxin puzzle is designed to be a case in which the benefit to be gained from intending to drink the toxin is worth the cost of actually drinking it, but that benefit accrues only to *intending at midnight* to drink the toxin, and not to actually drinking it. Many philosophers believe that it is *not* possible to rationally form the right intention in the toxin puzzle, and *one* explanation of why not, is that mere arbitrary *benefits* of having an intention are not right-kind reasons to form it. On this view, the only right-kind reasons to intend to φ are reasons to actually φ. And this has been observed by many to have strong parallels with the idea that the only epistemic reasons to believe that P are evidence that P. In each case, the only right-kind reasons in favor of an attitude are reasons for its content.

Now, it is worth observing that even if we accept that it is impossible to intend in the toxin puzzle case, this impossibility can be explained without grounding it in the impossibility of there being reasons for intention that are not reasons to do the thing intended. For example, it is usually assumed that it is not rational to intend to do something that you believe that you will not do. Yet in the toxin puzzle case, you can know in advance that if you are rational, you will not drink the toxin when the time comes, because by then you will either have gotten the money or not, and drinking the toxin will make no difference. So you can't rationally intend at midnight to drink it unless you think you are going to be irrational. Since this explanation of why it is irrational to intend to drink the toxin has nothing to do with whether you have a genuine reason to do so, it follows that the difficulty in getting the toxin does not tell us directly that there are never right-kind reasons to intend that are not reasons to do as intended.

Yet the claim that the only reasons to intend are reasons to do as intended is still plausible, and like the claim that the only epistemic reasons in favor of belief are evidence in favor of its content, I will not contest it, here. Instead, I think that the problems with the object-given/state-given theory come out most clearly when we try to generalize these *plausible* ideas to the *implausible* ideas that the only epistemic reasons *against* belief are evidence against its content, and correspondingly, that the only right-kind reasons against intention are reasons against its content.

If it were really true that the only reasons for and against intending to φ are reasons for and against φ-ing, then we would expect that it is rational to φ just in case it is rational to intend to φ. But this is wrong. There are fiddly reasons why it

---

[6] The case also requires stipulating that you are not allowed to place side bets; otherwise you can give yourself a reason to intend to drink the toxin by giving yourself *another* reason to actually drink it when the time comes, tomorrow.

is wrong as stated—for example, it could be rational to do something spontane-ously, but intending to do it would prevent it from being spontaneous. I'll set these aside and not worry about whether they pose a deep obstacle, because there are also deep reasons why this equivalence is a mistake.

The deep reasons why it is a mistake derive from the fact that in forming an intention to do something, you are committing yourself to doing it when the time comes. But it is always possible that you will get more information that is relevant to whether to φ in between now and the time of action. Sometimes, in fact, you can even know in advance that you will get more important information before the time comes to act. It's a consequence of this fact that it can be rational given your *current* information to φ, but not rational to commit in advance to φ-ing, because that would preclude acting on better information.[7] So it is often the case that your current reasons support φ-ing at some later time but do *not* support intending to φ at that time.

Suppose, for example, that I am considering whether to drive to Los Angeles tomorrow. The benefits of doing so include the pleasant scenery and the chance of seeing my brother, and the costs include the traffic. Suppose that right now I estimate the chance that I will be able to see my brother at only 10 percent, and that does not make it worth the traffic—even counting the pleasantness of the scenery. I *could* decide now not to make the drive tomorrow, and if there were no more to the story, then that might be rational. But if I also know that my brother will call tonight to let me know whether he will be available tomorrow, then it does not make sense to decide in advance not to go. Even though I am fairly confident that he will tell me that he will not be available, if I decide in advance not to go, then I am ruling out the possibility that I will later decide to go if he tells me that he will be available—and to do so is to miss out on the chance of seeing him.

My explanation of this case is simple. It is that the availability of further evidence is a reason *against* intention that is not a reason against the thing intended. The object-given/state-given theory is wrong. And it is no wonder that it is wrong, I suggest, just like it is no wonder that it is wrong about epistemic reasons for and against belief. For whereas with respect to action, there are only two choices—either to go, or not to go—with respect to my forward-looking intention, there are *three* options. I may intend to go, I may intend not to go, or I may have neither intention. Consequently, the question of which of these three options is rational cannot be settled by considerations that only count in favor of two of them. This is precisely analogous to the case for belief, where we saw in Chapter 6 that deep puzzles about the rationality of belief arise because with respect to belief, there are

---

[7] This puts the point a little bit too strongly. It wouldn't preclude in the sense of making impossible, but it would be to decide in advance *not* to, which is all that I need here.

three options: to believe that P, to believe that ~P, or to have neither belief, whereas evidence only counts in favor of two of these options.

In both cases, I suggest, the interesting characteristics of rational belief and rational intention derive from the fact that with respect to each we face tripartite choices. These interesting characteristics become confusing if we try to think about them through a binary lens, but there is no good reason to accept that we must impose a binary lens. On the contrary, I suggest, in both cases we can understand the rational conditions on belief *and* intention much better if we appreciate how it accords simply with the balance of reasons—so long as we recognize reasons for *all* of the available options.

The fact that my brother will call tonight is not a reason to drive to LA tomorrow. It is not a reason to stay home. So it is not an *object*-given reason against intention— it does not bear either way on the object of this intention. Moreover, intuitively, this reason matters because it lays out a *benefit* of being undecided whether to drive to LA. If I am undecided whether to drive, then I will be open to incorporating the information that I get from my brother when he calls, and making a more informed decision in that light. Since this is intuitively a benefit of being in the state of lacking the intention, it is intuitively a *state*-given reason against intention. So it fails the object-given/state-given criteria on both sides.

Nevertheless, the fact that my brother will call tonight *is* a reason to put off my decision whether to drive to LA. And unlike the Pascalian considerations of arbitrary costs or benefits of intention, it satisfies all of our key characteristics of reasons. It competes with contrary considerations—for example, if my wife needs to know whether she can use our car tomorrow or arrange in advance for a ride, then I may need to make up my mind before tonight's call after all. It is also act-oriented, rather than outcome-oriented. There is nothing to be gained by me going ahead and deciding not to drive to LA so that two of my friends will be able to put off their decision in order to get my brother's information. And most importantly, it is a reason that can be *acted on*. If I am about to decide not to drive to LA when my brother texts, "I'll let you know tonight", it is not hard to put off my decision—on the contrary, doing so is entirely natural.

The object-given/state-given theory, I conclude, is just as poor a fit for reasons for intention, its other best case, as it is for reasons for belief. Far from being dissuaded that there are epistemic reasons against belief by comparison to the analogy with reasons for and against intention, our confidence in the conclusion of Chapter 6 should be reaffirmed.

7.3 The Nature of Attitudes

Still, if the object-given/state-given theory is wrong, what is true instead? What generalizations can we draw about the nature of right-kind reasons which might help us to determine which sort of right-kind reasons there are for and against belief, giving us yet another way of triangulating on our conclusion that there are epistemic reasons against belief that are not evidence?

A good answer, I suggest, needs to pay close attention to the differences between attitudes.[8] The right kind of reasons for and against an attitude must have something close to do with what makes that attitude the kind of attitude that it is. Notice that this suggestion contrasts sharply with the chief idea behind the object-given/state-given distinction. That theory is driven by the idea that we can determine whether a consideration is a right-kind reason for or against an attitude without even knowing what kind of attitude we are talking about—all that we need to know is whether the consideration bears on its content.

This commitment is, I think, absurd. Although there is something in common between *wrong* kinds of reasons for attitudes, there is nothing obvious in common between *right* kinds of reasons for attitudes. Wrong kinds of reasons for attitudes, as I have been suggesting, are just arbitrary benefits or costs of having those attitudes. There is a simple recipe: imagine that an evil demon or an eccentric billionaire cares which attitudes you have, and has both some way of detecting the answer and the means to reward or punish. Or more realistically, imagine that believing something or fearing something makes you feel good (or bad) about yourself, or has positive or negative consequences for your relationship with someone. These cases clearly have much in common. In contrast, it is hard to say what reasons to believe that Athens is the capital of Greece, to admire Beethoven, and to fear death all have in common. It would be strange indeed if we could say what they have in common without having to factor out the distinctive differences between belief, admiration, and fear.

I am following Pamela Hieronymi (2005, 2006, 2013) in holding that in order to understand which kinds of considerations are right-kind reasons for or against a given attitude, you need to understand the nature of that attitude. But according to Hieronymi's view, the only attitudes that we can have reasons directly for or against—as opposed to states of mind that we can cultivate for reasons, but not have directly for reasons—are what she calls *judgment-constituted attitudes*. An attitude is *judgment-constituted*, in turn, just in case it has some associated *constitutive question*, such that answering that question amounts to forming that attitude. For example, the constitutive question of the belief that P is whether P—in answering the question whether P in the affirmative, you are *ipso facto* forming the belief that P. Similarly, the constitutive question of the intention to φ is the question of whether to φ. You count as intending to φ just in case you answer that question in the affirmative. More generally, according to Hieronymi, reasons for and against each attitude are reasons that *bear on the question*[9] constitutive of that attitude.

---

[8] Compare Nolfi (2015), though Nolfi's account is much more permissive about epistemic reasons than mine.

[9] Or questions.

Since the question that is constitutive of the belief that P is the question whether P, it follows from Hieronymi's view that the only reasons for or against the belief that P are considerations which bear on whether P. So she concludes, as I think she is right to do given her view, that only evidence can be reason for or against belief. Similarly, since the question that is constitutive of the intention to φ is the question whether to φ, only considerations that bear on the question of whether to φ can be reasons for or against intention. So she concludes, as I think she is right to do given her view, that the only reasons for or against intention are reasons for or against the action intended.

I have already argued directly against these consequences, both for the case of belief, and for the case of intention. But I think Hieronymi's view only becomes more strained when we begin to consider the cases of other attitudes. Belief and intention are the best cases, I think, for the concept of judgment-constituted attitudes—we should all agree at least that believing that p is equivalent to answering the question whether p in the affirmative, and that intending to φ is equivalent to answering the question of whether to φ in the affirmative, even if we disagree about the constitutive relationships between them. But the model is much less plausible when we try to extend it to other attitudes.

Take, for example, the case of admiration. Which question is it, exactly, such that admiring Beethoven is constituted by some answer to that question? Suppose, I think most plausibly, that it is the question of whether Beethoven is admirable. This is *also* the constitutive question for the belief that Beethoven is admirable. So since admiring Beethoven is answering the question whether Beethoven is admirable in the affirmative, and believing that Beethoven is admirable is answering the question whether Beethoven is admirable in the affirmative, it follows that admiring Beethoven is the *same* as believing that Beethoven is admirable.

This, I suggest, is wrong. Admiring Beethoven is not identical to having *any* particular belief about him—not even that he is admirable. It is possible to believe that someone—for example, a rival—is admirable without being at all able to bring yourself to admire them. And it is possible to admire someone—for example, someone particularly charismatic—without believing that they are in fact admirable, or even while affirmatively believing that they are not. The same points go, I think, for the relationship between admiring someone and *any* other belief or set of beliefs about them. Yet for every question of the form *whether* P, there is a belief that is constituted, on Hieronymi's view, by answering that question in the affirmative. So I don't see how to avoid the mistaken conclusion that the only attitudes that we can have reasons for or against are either identical to beliefs, or identical to intentions. Although it is a virtue worth appreciating of Hieronymi's account that it draws a clean line between the kinds of attitudes for which we can have reasons and the kinds of mental states that we do not directly have reasons for, I therefore suggest that her account draws this line much too narrowly.

In contrast, if we want to avoid embracing over-strong commitments about the nature of attitudes, then we can think of different attitudes like belief, intention, hope, admiration, fear, and disgust as all playing distinctive functional *roles* in our psychologies.[10] On the view that I will defend here, the right kind of reasons for and against each attitude are the considerations whose truth an attitude needs to be sensitive to, in order to most successfully fulfill its distinctive role.

Take, for example, the case of fear. Fear, I suggest, plays the role of triggering fight-or-flight systems of heightened awareness, in order to enable us to respond quickly to threats. In order to play this role, fear needs to be sensitive to evidence of possible danger, unusual circumstances, or the unknown. Being triggered by these kinds of circumstances will enable fear to play its role of preparing you for threats should they arise. But the adrenaline response associated with fear cannot be effective if it is active at baseline, and so fear needs to also be tempered in the safest circumstances. So fear also needs to retreat given evidence of relative safety. Consequently, it is no wonder that reasons to fear include not just actual danger, but evidence of possible danger, unusual circumstances, and the unknown. It is no mystery that children fear the dark, or that many of us fear death, even when we don't take it itself to be any longer a harm.

Similarly, consider anxiety. Anxiety plausibly, I think, plays something like the role of directing attention towards things that might help us to solve important problems. In order to play this role well, it needs to be sensitive to whether something is important—and it normally is. Anxiety over things that we ourselves acknowledge to be unimportant is pathological. But it must also be sensitive to whether there is anything that we can do to make a difference. If we can't make a difference, then there is no problem to be solved. Yet in order to play this role it does not have to be sensitive to whether it is distressing to be anxious. On the contrary anxiety in humans works precisely by being distressing. So we can draw an intuitive distinction between two seemingly state-given reasons against anxiety—that we can't make a difference and that is doing more harm (in the form of distress) than good—and that distinction seems, I think, to capture something right about which considerations anxiety is really responsive to and really matter for the internal rationality of anxiety.

Or take admiration, which I used as my example in my argument against Hieronymi. Admiration plausibly plays the role of giving us role-models to emulate. So it makes sense that in order to play this role well, it will have to be sensitive to features that matter for whether someone's life is worth emulating or aspiring to. Being offered money to admire someone is not something that

---

[10] It is common in the philosophy of mind to define the functional role of an attitude in terms of its causal inputs and outputs. This understanding of role won't do for my purposes. I instead need a teleological or quasi-design conception of role. I will rely here only on what I take to be intuitively clear cases, but much more would need to be said to fill this out.

admiration needs to be sensitive to, in order to do its job, because people who have the feature that other people offer third people money to admire them are no more worth emulating than anyone else, at least on that basis.

And as a final illustration, consider the case of intention. Intention, I claim following Michael Bratman (1987), plays the role in our psychologies of allowing us to commit to decisions about what to do ahead of time, so as to better distribute our decision-making resources over time. It is because of intention, for example, that we are able to spread wedding planning out over a year of weekend afternoons instead of having to confront choices on the fly as they arise over the course of a single day. In order to play this role, intentions must be sensitive to reasons for and against actually acting as intended. There is no advantage to deciding to do something early that it is a bad idea to actually do, and so reasons against φ-ing are all things that should tend to lead one not to intend to φ. And conversely, reasons to φ are all advantages of intending to φ, since in the absence of interfering effects such as changing one's mind, when one intends to φ, that will result in one's actually doing so.

But in order to do their job well, intentions must *also* be sensitive to the availability of better information. You can't use intentions in order to coordinate your decision-making to happen at the most efficient times to decide, if you make decisions at low-information times that could easily instead have been made at high-information times. So it is no surprise that the fact that my brother will call later is a reason against intending now not to drive to LA tomorrow, or that it is so easy and natural for me to respond to this reason by putting off making up my mind. This is because this ability is actually crucial for intentions to be able to perform their job well.

Nor are these the only right-kind reasons for and against intention. Given their role in coordinating decision-making over time, we also rely on the assumption that we will act as we intend in order to make other decisions, in the meantime. So future-directed intentions, such as the intention not to drive to LA tomorrow, can simplify reasoning about other questions, such as whether to offer my wife the use of our car for the day. Consequently, intentions will not be able to perform their role of coordinating decision-making over time well unless they are also sensitive to the need to be able to rely on a stable answer to what one can be expected to do. That is why the fact that my wife and I need to coordinate who will have the car tomorrow can be a reason for me to decide now whether to drive to LA tomorrow.

Notice that all of these kinds of reasons are considerations that it is advantageous, in some sense, to be sensitive to. Fear and intention cannot play their roles well in our psychological economies, unless they are sensitive to these considerations.[11]

---

[11] Of course, a thinker can only respond to considerations like these in ways that are *mediated* by some representation or indication of them. But this doesn't mean that the thinker is only responding to her own beliefs. On this way of talking, responding to her own beliefs would have to be mediated by higher-order representations of those very beliefs.

And that is just another way of saying that there is an advantage of being sensitive to them—whatever advantage is accrued by having well-functioning fear or intention. And advantages of being sensitive to these considerations are very closely related to advantages of being in the states, in the presence of those conditions. That can make my explanation of right-kind reasons feel very much like an explanation of *state-given* reasons to have attitudes.

But recall that I have already argued that there is nothing inherently wrong with state-given reasons to have attitudes. What *is* wrong, is reasons that derive only from arbitrary advantages or costs to having attitudes that have nothing to do with the nature or role of that attitude, but only with money or punishment that accrues from having or lacking some particular state. And we can now see why being offered money to fear something, or to intend something can never be a right-kind reason for fear, or for intention. That is because being sensitive to monetary offers plays no role whatsoever in making fear more effective at playing its role of triggering heightened awareness and preparedness, in order to enable us to respond more quickly to threats. Indeed, fears would be worse at doing this job, if they were also sensitive to monetary offers. And similar points go for intention.

Much cleaning up is required, in order to make this account of reasons precise. Yet I believe that its outlines are clear enough, from the cases that we have considered, in order to be clear that it is productive, offering something illuminating to say about why a range of factors might affect the rationality of both fear and intention—and plausible views about each. It is clear enough that it successfully allows some benefits or costs of having attitudes in, without allowing *arbitrary* benefits or costs in. And in the remainder of this chapter, I will argue both that it is the *right kind* of view to make sense at least of both the *availability of evidence* and *cost of error* types of epistemic reason against belief that I argued for directly in Chapter 6, but also that it does not *entail* the existence of both kinds of non-evidential epistemic reason against belief. Which kinds of epistemic reasons there are against belief will depend on what we say about the nature of belief—about its role in our cognitive economy.

7.4 A Toy Theory of Belief

According to a simple account of belief along the lines of that advocated in Stalnaker (1984), the role of beliefs in our psychologies is to allow one to act in such a way as to fulfill one's desires. On this view, the actions that you choose are those that will maximize your desire-satisfaction in worlds in which your beliefs are true. As we will see later, this is in many ways an overly simple conception of belief. But it has the right ingredients in order to help us to see why it is that evidence against its content, the availability of further evidence, and the costs of error can all be right-kind reasons against belief.

Let's take the case of evidence, first. Beliefs will clearly not do well at allowing us to act in such a way as to fulfill our desires, if the beliefs themselves are unhinged from the truth. They will do better at this, to the extent that we form them in the presence of evidence that they are actually true. But more importantly, they will fail at this role unless we tend to *avoid* them in the presence of evidence *against* their truth. So evidence that P seems like the right kind of thing on the basis of which to form the belief that P, on this view, and even more clearly, evidence that P seems like the right kind of thing on the basis of which to *not* believe that P.

The toy Stalnakerian theory of belief also offers a clear explanation of why we should expect high costs of error to be right-kind reasons *against* belief. Unless your beliefs are sensitive to the costs of error, you will form beliefs to the effect that you have no allergy to penicillin just as easily as you form beliefs about whether it will rain tomorrow. But if you believe falsely that you have no allergy to penicillin, and that belief plays its role in your cognitive economy of being that on which you act in order to fulfill your desires, it will lead you to reason in the normal way to accept penicillin as an antibiotic. But accepting penicillin as an antibiotic can have drastic consequences for someone who is allergic to it—by the lights of one's own desires.

Finally, the toy theory even allows for a first pass at an explanation of why the availability of further, better, evidence should be a right-kind reason against belief. And that is because forming a belief on the basis of less information is a less reliable way of forming beliefs than forming beliefs on the basis of more information. And so only a creature whose beliefs are capable of being sensitive to the difference between the quality of her current evidence and the quality of the easily available evidence will be able to form beliefs in the most reliable way available, without giving up on the prospect of having any beliefs to go on at all, in the cases where little evidence is available. So again, beliefs that are sensitive to the comparison of quality between your current evidence and the available evidence will do much better at fulfilling their role.

The toy Stalnakerian theory of belief therefore illustrates exactly what I propose that we should want from an account of belief, in order for us to be able to see how its nature could give rise to the right sorts of epistemic reasons against belief— including both evidence and non-evidential reasons. Nonetheless, it is not exactly right, and I do not accept this theory. The problem is that it is too simple. On Stalnaker's official view,[12] the simple belief-desire model is a kind of heuristic simplification of real human psychologies. It captures part of the correct picture well, because our psychologies really are organized out of a map-like, mind-to-world directed component something like belief, and a shopping-list-like, world-

---

[12] Compare Stalnaker (2008).

to-mind directed component something like desire, and it is the job of the former to allow us to do well with respect to the latter.

But both of these attitudes are actually more fine-grained than in the toy theory. The job of beliefs is instead played by *credences* or *degrees of confidence*, which can be modeled not in terms of a *set* of propositions believed or not believed, but instead by a probability function that assigns each proposition to a value between zero and one. And the job of desires is instead played by *preferences* or *utilities*. In turn, Stalnaker's simple account on which the way that beliefs and desires interact is that we do whatever will achieve our desires in worlds where our beliefs are true, with the apparatus of something like orthodox decision theory, according to which the function of credences and preferences is to cooperate so that we do what will maximize expected utility.

The change from the flat representation of belief corresponding to sets of worlds to the graded one corresponding to the credal, probabilistic, picture can seem like a difference of degree, rather than kind. On both pictures, there is a map-like state of mind whose role is to allow us to pursue a directive-like state of mind. The two pictures merely differ over the fineness of grain of the map-like state of mind. But in fact, the credal picture completely upsets the rationale for taking both availability of evidence and the costs of error as considerations to be right-kind reasons bearing on the rationality of belief.

Take the case of costs of error first. If belief is an ungraded, all or nothing, state, and it plays its role in your cognitive economy when you act on the assumption that it is true, then it is clear why being wrong can have high costs. For even if it is very unlikely that you are wrong, if the cost of being wrong outweighs its unlikeliness, then having a belief carries more risks than rewards. But in contrast, if the role of belief is instead played by the graded state of *credence*, then there are no costs at all to having high credence in such cases. For on orthodox decision theory, you don't act on the assumption that everything you have high credence in is *true*; rather, you weight the utilities that you place on outcomes by your credence in those outcomes. So the burden of avoiding bad consequences is carried instead by your *preferences* or *utilities*. There is therefore is no cost associated with having a high credence that you are not allergic to penicillin as such; whenever given the opportunity to act on the information about whether you have such an allergy, you may trust that if your credences play their role successfully, and you attach low enough utilities to bad outcomes, then you will accept penicillin as an antibiotic only if the probability that you are not allergic is so high that it outweighs the costs of taking penicillin and being allergic.

Similarly, the credal picture loses the explanation given by the toy Stalnakerian picture of why facts about the availability of better evidence can be right-kind reasons against belief. On the Stalnakerian picture, it made sense to form beliefs in the presence of better quality evidence. But on standard assumptions about probabilistically graded belief, it makes sense instead to incorporate *all* evidence, *all the time*. The orthodox view about how we should update our credences in response to evidence is that you should *always* incorporate new evidence. The reason that there are no costs to incorporating small amounts of evidence into our credences in comparison to incorporating large amounts of evidence, later, is that the orthodox assumption is that we are to update our credences by Bayesian conditionalization, and Bayesian conditionalization is *commutative*, so it never matters which order we add evidence in—we will always end up in the very same place. Consequently, the best way to incorporate the most possible information into credences is to *always* incorporate *all* of the evidence.

So even when we start with a simple picture on which a belief-like state has the role of cooperating with a desire-like state in order to produce action, it turns out to matter a great deal, for purposes of understanding whether there are epistemic reasons bearing on the rationality of the belief-like state that are not evidence, exactly what that belief-like state is like. If our psychologies are organized much like the toy Stalnakerian picture says that they are, then there are real contrasts between believing that P, believing that ~P, and having neither belief, and both costs of error and the availability of further evidence could be properly epistemic reasons against belief, despite not being evidence against the content of that belief. But if our psychologies are organized much like the classical Bayesian picture takes them to be, the *very same* view that I have been defending about the nature and source of right-kind reasons for attitudes predicts that only *evidence* should count as a right-kind reason pertaining to our only belief-like state, credence.

7.5 Earning It Back

So far, I've argued that we can get independent leverage on the question of which kinds of reasons bear on the distinctively epistemic rationality of belief by comparison with trying to understand which reasons bear on the distinctive rationality of other attitudes. According to the proposal that I've defended, these are the considerations that each attitude needs to be sensitive to, in order to perform its function well. And we saw, in the form of the toy Stalnakerian account, that this is the right *kind* of thing to at least *make room* for epistemic reasons against belief that are not evidence. But the fact that this consequence rapidly disappears when we shift from the toy belief-desire model of our psychology to the more fine-grained credence/preference model shows that our work is not done.

From the perspective of Chapter 6, the fact that the credal/preference picture of our psychology eliminates the non-evidential reasons should actually not be terribly surprising. We saw in Chapter 6, after all, that a wide variety of problems arise for understanding how evidence can play a role in rationalizing belief. The *source* of these problems, I argued, both there and in this chapter, was the *ternary* structure of belief with regard to any binary question—you can believe that P, believe that ~P, or have neither belief, and it is the fact that there are three choices, but evidence is reason for only two of them, that was the source of the most difficult puzzles. Since credence construed in probabilistic terms does not have a ternary structure, but a *comtinuum-valued* structure, allowing for continuum-many distinctions in the doxastic attitude you take toward any proposition, it is clear that this diagnosis does not apply to credences.

Moreover, on reflection, it is also clear that none of the problems discussed in Chapter 6 is a problem for credences, in any case. Harman's problem of near ties, for example, was the problem that it is never permissible to believe either that P or that ~P, and that in fact when the evidence is close to tied it is never permissible to believe either. Even this bare statement of the problem is already infected by the distinction between all-or-nothing belief and credence. To formulate something similar in terms of credence, we would have to say that it is never permissible to have a credence in a proposition when the evidence is near to tied, which is incompatible with orthodox Bayesianism according to which it is *always* rational permissible to have a credence in every proposition, and almost certainly false. Similar points go for each of the other problems considered in that chapter.

So I conclude that if credences are psychologically real and function much like they are traditionally conceived to, then there may well be no non-evidential reasons for or against credences, or for revising credences in one way rather than another. If there is a role for non-evidential reasons in epistemology, it is in what is sometimes called *traditional* epistemology—the epistemology of binary, all-or-nothing, belief. So to take seriously the problems from Chapter 6, we need to take seriously the idea that there is such a state as believing that P, a binary state that you can be in or not be in, and hence which admits of a corresponding ternary distinction between believing that P, believing that ~P, and having neither belief.

Some extreme Bayesians deny that there is any such thing as binary belief.[13] But most philosophers accept that even if our psychologies are fundamentally structured around a probabilistically graded state of credence, it can still make sense to talk about all-or-nothing belief. But as to what, exactly, binary belief is, there is an abundance of views. *Credal reductivists* hold that facts about belief reduce without remainder to facts about credence. There are many forms of credal reductivism. The thesis known as *Lockeanism* maintains that there is a fixed threshold τ such that anyone who has a credence that P greater than τ counts as believing that P. Lockeanism, moreover, is just the simplest possible threshold view. According to other threshold views, there are different thresholds for different propositions, or the threshold varies from context to context so that what counts as 'belief' is context-sensitive, or both. And according to *pragmatic credal reductivism*, the

---

[13] Compare Jeffrey (2002).

threshold varies between propositions in a way that is set, at least in part, by the stakes of relying on that proposition.[14]

According to credal reductivism, therefore, belief does not have a function in our cognitive economies, over and above the function of credence. So if right-kind reasons are the considerations that attitudes must be sensitive to, in order to best fulfil their functions, it follows from all forms of credal reductivism that there are no right-kind reasons relevant to belief, over and above those relevant to credences. So if facts about belief reduce to facts about credence in this way, I don't believe that we should be optimistic about making sense of any of the puzzles about how evidence can play a role in rationalizing belief, from Chapter 6.

In contrast, if belief is itself a psychological state with its own role and significance, then our story about right-kind reasons for and against belief can come into play. Now, if belief is such a state, there are three remaining possibilities. It could be, as credal eliminativists claim, that the representational role in our psychologies is played by belief *rather* than credence, and we do not have states worth calling credences at all. Or it could be, in a flip of credal reductivism, that facts about credences themselves reduce to facts about beliefs.[15] Or finally, it could be, as dualists claim, that neither belief nor credence reduces to the other, but they play complementary roles in our psychologies.[16]

Now, there is a master argument against the thesis that there is any such state as belief that plays a distinctive role in our psychologies, and it works by elimination against these three alternatives.[17] The argument is that credences *are* real (which I think we should grant), and *cannot* be reduced to beliefs (which is more complicated but again I think we should grant for our purposes, since the simplest ways of making the reduction work look bad), so the only real possibility, if beliefs play their own psychological role, is dualism. But, the master argument alleges, there is a twin challenge to dualism. Dualists must be able to say what role is left for beliefs to play, that is not already played by credences; and they must explain why positing both beliefs and credences is not simply positing two completely redundant representational systems.

Good answers to what beliefs are, and what role they play in our psychologies, have answers to these two challenges. For example, according to Justin Dallmann (2016), to believe that P is simply to have a *stable high credence* that P. On Dallmann's view, facts about belief do not simply reduce, psychologically, to facts about credence, because forming a belief is a genuine psychological event that engenders a genuine psychological change, independently of a change in

---

[14] Weatherson (2005), Ganson (2008), Fantl and McGrath (2010). For critical discussion, see especially Brown (2013, 2018) and Ross and Schroeder (2014).

[15] Compare Easwaran (2016).   [16] Weisberg (2020).

[17] Weatherson (2005) gives I think the most forceful statement of this challenge.

credence. When you form a belief, you are adopting something like a plan or a commitment to treat your credence as settled, rather than continuing to update in response to additional evidence. But on Dallmann's view, belief is not a separate, redundant, representational system from credence—on the contrary, to believe something is just to have a high credence in it *plus* an additional commitment not to revise that credence.[18]

Dallmann's view also has an answer to what role is played by belief that is not played by credence. It disposes you to treat some of your high credences as *settled*—as not subject to further investigation or necessary to be continually updated with new information. This is what explains, according to Dallmann, why it is *incorrect* to have a false belief—why false beliefs are in some interesting sense *wrong*, whereas it is hard to make sense of how any intermediate credence could count as being wrong. When you are 95 percent confident that it will rain tomorrow but it does not, you may not have been wrong at all—in particular, if that only happens to you 5 percent of the time, you are perfectly calibrated. But in contrast, if you predict that it will rain tomorrow but it does not, then you *are* wrong. Dallmann's account explains *why* there is something normatively significant about false belief that is not normatively significant about high credence, because according to his account, when you have a belief, you are *committed* to the truth of a proposition, in a way that you are not committed to the truth of a proposition that you merely have a high credence in—after all, having a high credence is also a way of hedging, by also having a positive credence in the alternative.

And finally, Dallmann's account of belief can explain *why* there is a need, in addition to credences, for commitments to treat some high credences as settled. He argues, in particular, that imperfect, cognitively limited creatures like us, who cannot update instantly by conditionalization, can do better with respect to the goal of expected accuracy of our credences, by treating some issues as settled. Once enough evidence has come in about some questions, Dalllmann argues, we do better to devote our limited cognitive resources to other questions. And we do so, solely with respect to the expected accuracy of our credences. According to Dallmann, this both helps to explain why some of the biases revealed in psychological research could be valuable, and actually helps to defend the view that we do in fact have and reason with credences, by providing the basis for an answer to a variety of objections to the effect that Bayesian constraints on credal revision are overly demanding.[19]

---

[18] On this view, clearly, though belief is something over and above facts about credence, it is not a *lot* over and above facts about credence. This makes it unsurprising that Dallmann referred to an earlier version of his view in a paper title as a "normatively adequate credal reductivism" (Dallmann (2014)).

[19] Dallmann (2017).

Dallmann's theory is therefore a kind of dualism, in my sense—it allows for the psychological reality of both belief and credence, which together play complementary roles in our psychologies. But so far from being a radical alternative to the idea that credences are real or psychologically fundamental, it is actually a kind of *defense* of this claim. Yet because commitments to non-reconsideration play a functional role in our psychologies, Dallmann's account gives us the ingredients to test out our general account of the right kinds of reasons for and against attitudes.

In particular, since the role of commitment to a credence is to allow for better distribution of cognitive resources, these commitment states will do better at doing their job, if they are sensitive to the relative comparison between the value of evidence that has already come in and the further evidence that might be available. It makes sense to form a commitment to stable credence, and commitments to stable credence will best do their job, when you form them in just the cases where the highest quality evidence has already come in. So Dallmann's stable high credence theory of belief has exactly the right structure in order to explain why it is that facts about the availability of further evidence can themselves be epistemic reasons against belief.

In contrast, Dallmann's stable high credence theory does *not* explain why costs of error could be epistemic reasons against belief. On the contrary, it predicts that they will not be, for the very same reason that they are not epistemic reasons on the simple Bayesian picture. There is no benefit to being reluctant to commit to a stable high credence in cases in which the costs of error are high, because the role of the commitment involved in belief is not to *rely* on something's truth, but merely to relieve oneself of the burden of thinking more about it. Consequently, there is no risk of having a high stable credence in a proposition where the cost of relying on that proposition will be high if it is false, because even though you have that stable high credence, you will *not* rely on it—you will instead reason with expected utilities, and when the costs are high enough, those will swamp the probabilities in your reasoning.

Dallmann's stable high credence theory, I suggest, is therefore a kind of proof of concept of my strategy, in this chapter, of trying to understand how there could be epistemic reasons against belief that are not evidence against the content of that belief, by triangulating through a general theory of what kinds of things are right-kind reasons for and against attitudes in general, together with a theory about the nature of belief, in particular. It shows that a defensible theory of the nature of belief can account for one of the main classes of examples that I have given of epistemic reasons against belief that are not evidence.

And moreover, it shows how to account for these, less controversial, examples, *without* accounting for my second, more controversial, class of examples, which regard the costs of error. So this proves that there is nothing about my answer to the puzzles from Chapter 6 or my argumentative strategy in this chapter in support of that answer which requires endorsing the thesis that there is any form of *pragmatic encroachment* in epistemology. I therefore offer Dallmann's account of belief to those who are attracted to my answer to the puzzles in Chapter 6 but skeptical about pragmatic encroachment, in general.

However, once we have seen the attractions of coming this far, we should grant that whether or not there are cost-of-error related epistemic reasons against belief depends, essentially, on what kind of state belief is, and what role it plays in our psychologies. In Chapter 8 we'll therefore turn to my own view, which is that we should in fact go further—for cost-of-error related epistemic reasons are both defensible and compelling in their own right, and flow from an even better account of the nature of all-or-nothing belief. I call the resulting view *Pragmatic Intellectualism*.

8

Pragmatic Intellectualism

8.1 The Default Reliance Account

In Chapter 7 we saw how to ground an account of the right kind of reasons for and against belief in an account of belief's nature. We found an account that did *not* result in the controversial thesis of pragmatic encroachment, but still allowed us to give answers to the other problems raised in Chapter 6—Justin Dallmann's view that belief is *stable high credence*. This shows that my fundamental answer to these problems does not require a commitment to the idea that there is pragmatic encroachment on the epistemic rationality of belief. Nevertheless, it constitutes a defense of a framework that *opens up* the possibility that there is pragmatic encroachment on the epistemic rationality of belief—a possibility that could be made good on, with a different account of the nature of belief. In this chapter I will develop such an account, lay out some of its consequences, and show why it results in a particularly attractive version of the thesis of pragmatic encroachment in epistemology. I call the resulting package of views *Pragmatic Intellectualism*.

The account of the nature of belief that forms the basis for Pragmatic Intellectualism is what I call the *default reliance* account. According to the default reliance account, the role of belief is to give you something to rely on *by default*.[1] So on this view, beliefs are general-purpose, default *assumptions* about what is true.

The default reliance account is helpfully illuminated by comparison to the attitude that is sometimes called *acceptance in a context*. When you are building a bridge, for the sake of your calculations it helps to assume the truth of Newtonian mechanics. Even though you know that Newtonian mechanics is not a true description of the universe, when you are doing your calculations about the load-bearing capacity of your bridge, it is helpful to assume that it is true. We may say that you *accept* this theory for purposes of your calculations. Acceptance, so understood, is something that you *do* at a time. When you accept a proposition, you treat it as true in your reasoning at that time.

But if you design bridges often, you may come to *automatically* accept the truth of Newtonian mechanics whenever you are calculating its load-bearing capacity. If

---

[1] In Ross and Schroeder (2014), Jake Ross and I defended an account of belief that we called the *Reasoning Disposition* account. The Reasoning Disposition account can be thought of as the dispositionalist version of what I am here calling the Default Reliance account. Compare the objections to the dispositionalist account in Ross and Schroeder (2014) given by Brown (2018).

Reasons First. Mark Schroeder, Oxford University Press (2021). © Mark Schroeder.
DOI: 10.1093/oso/9780198868224.003.0008

you do so, you have acquired a kind of habit or custom. This custom *disposes* you, whenever you are designing bridges, to accept the truth of Newtonian mechanics. But like all dispositions, this disposition can be masked. Though you are disposed to accept Newtonian mechanics when designing bridges, a friend who is a novelist may ask you to design a bridge that occupies a central place in her novel that is set in a world governed by Aristotelian celestial mechanics. So you won't *always* accept the truth of Newtonian mechanics when you are designing bridges, but you will do so automatically in the absence of interfering factors.

But perhaps you don't just design bridges. Maybe you are frequently required to perform calculations about the expected behavior of medium-sized objects, of which bridges are only one example. So instead of having a habit of accepting Newtonian mechanics only when you are designing bridges, you develop a habit of accepting Newtonian mechanics whenever you are predicting the behavior of medium-sized objects. This habit disposes you, by default, to accept Newtonian physics whenever you are interested in the behavior of medium-sized objects, but again, like all dispositions, this one can be masked. Your nephew could interrupt your calculations, asking why you wrote down some formula, given what his physics teacher told him about quantum mechanics.

Belief, on the default reliance account, is just the limiting case of this progression from limited to more general habits of acceptance. To believe that P is to have a *perfectly general* habit of accepting that P.[2] This habit will dispose you to accept that P by *default*, but like all dispositions, it will by no means guarantee that you accept that P. For example, you might have the *general* habit of accepting that Newtonian mechanics is false, but the *specific* habit of accepting that it is true when you are calculating the behavior of medium-sized objects. In that case, your more specific habit will override your general habit, and you will not accept that Newtonian mechanics is true. There is nothing puzzling about having each of these habits, or about the more specific habit overriding the more general one; you may similarly have the habit of speaking to people in English but also the habit of speaking to people in French when in Paris. (And this may even be the correct description of you if you are living in Paris.)

The default reliance account has an answer to how belief and credence can cooperate together in our psychologies, because it assigns them complementary roles. When you reason about what to do, you will begin with what you accept to be true, in your situation. Sometimes, in simple decisions, that will be enough to determine what to do, but in other cases, you will need, in addition, to consider probabilities.[3] In that case, your credences and what you accept will cooperate to determine what you do. In the simplest such cases, if you are reasoning well, then

---

[2] Compare Holton (2014).   [3] Compare Lin (2013).

you will choose the action with the highest expected utility—conditional on what you are accepting to be true.

Reasoning with credences against a background of things that are assumed to be true is in effect what Julia Staffel (2019) has called *pseudo-conditionalization*. When you *pseudo-conditionalize*, you don't actually update your credences or degrees of belief to new credences, as you do when you learn something. Rather, you generate an alternative set of probabilities that are relevant to action, *from your credences proper, by* applying the operation of conditionalization to those credences and the things that you are *accepting*. Ralph Wedgwood (2012) calls this the shift from your *intellectual* credences to your *practical* credences.

Both Wedgwood and Staffel make the shift from your credences to the probabilities that are actually active in practical reasoning seem like they are just as cognitively demanding as updating your entire probabilistic credence function by conditionalization. But it need not be so demanding. On *any* conception, the expected value of an action is calculated by taking a weighted sum of the utility of each of the conjunctive states of affairs of your taking that action and each possible resulting state of affairs. So instead of calculating the expected utility conditional on what you accept by first conditionalizing on what you accept and then using those probabilities to calculate expected utility, you can instead calculate it by simply leaving possibilities you accept won't happen off of your decision table.

For example, suppose that you face the choice of whether to bring an umbrella. There are two choices: to bring it, or not to bring it. If you live in Southern California, as I do, then much of the year, your decision table looks like this (I represent choices as columns and world states as rows for layout purposes):

	bring umbrella	don't bring umbrella
it doesn't rain	benefit=0 + cost=–1 =–1	benefit=0 + cost=0=0

Since you take for granted that it won't rain, the decision whether to bring an umbrella is straightforward—there are only costs, and no benefits. Choosing not to bring the umbrella *dominates* choosing to bring it, in the sense that it comes out better on every row of your decision table. It's not that your credence is zero that it will rain—anything is possible, after all, and indeed, it does sometimes rain in Southern California—usually when you are not expecting it. I certainly get caught without a much-needed umbrella at least once a year as a result of reasoning like this. Nevertheless, it is a fairly accurate reflection of how I actually think about whether to bring an umbrella, on most days.

But sometimes it is important to take account of the risk of rain. This can happen because it is January, and so you don't actually believe that it won't rain. Or it can happen because today you have to carry the elaborate paper sculpture that your daughter has been working on for weeks a block from the parking lot to her school, so greater caution is appropriate. Either way, when you take account of the risk of rain, your decision table might look something like this:

	bring umbrella	don't bring umbrella
it rains	benefit = 101 + cost = –1 =100	benefit = 0 + cost = 0 = 0
it doesn't rain	benefit = 0 + cost = –1 = –1	benefit = 0 + cost = 0 = 0

In this case neither decision dominates the other, and so this is the kind of case in which you need to think about how likely each possible row of your decision table is. So if your credence in rain is above 1 percent it will make sense for you to decide to bring the umbrella—whether or not you believe that it will rain. Again, this is more or less an accurate reflection of how I think about whether to bring an umbrella—although I usually believe it won't rain, sometimes in January or when it is particularly cloudy I don't positively believe that it won't rain on that day, and I decide whether to bring an umbrella on such days by thinking about what I'll be doing and what I'm wearing, and the resulting costs of getting wet.

One thing that I typically don't do, however, is to think about whether to bring an umbrella by considering the following decision table:

	bring umbrella	don't bring umbrella
it rains, car crash	benefit = 200 + cost = –1 = 199	benefit = 0 + cost = 0 = 0
it rains, no car crash	benefit = 101 + cost = –1 = 100	benefit = 0 + cost = 0 = 0
no rain, car crash	benefit = 0 + cost = –1 = –1	benefit = 0 + cost = 0 = 0
no rain, no car crash	benefit = 0 + cost = –1 = –1	benefit = 0 + cost = 0 = 0

Of course, it is true that having an umbrella in the rain is particularly useful if you have been in a car crash. But in tallying the benefits of having an umbrella in the rain, I typically don't consider the benefits that it may have should I be in a car crash at all. After all, on any given day, I take for granted that I won't be in a car crash that day when reasoning about most matters. I promise to meet someone for lunch without worrying that a car crash will cause me to break my promise, and I don't go to special lengths to arrange for someone to be on call to stand in for my lecture in the afternoon, just in case.

The default reliance account of belief explains why I don't consider or need to consider the possibility that I will have a car crash, when I decide whether to bring an umbrella, without having the mistaken result that it will make sense for me to leave this possibility out of consideration when I decide whether to carry insurance or what kind of insurance to carry. Because I believe that I will not have an accident on a particular day, I am disposed by default to accept that I will not have an accident. And when I accept a possibility, I leave its negation off of my decision table. The explanation of why I don't consider the possibility of a car crash in deciding whether to bring an umbrella is therefore *exactly the same* as the explanation of why I don't consider the possibility of rain on a typical day in Southern California.

As a result, it is subject to exactly the same sorts of qualifications: in variations of the case in which I don't believe and am not accepting for some other purpose that I will not have an accident, I *will* need to include it on my decision table. And similarly, even when I believe that there will be no accident, my disposition to accept that there will not will sometimes be defeated—as by a sense of caution, when I am reasoning about whether to buy insurance, or how much insurance to carry.[4]

8.2 Epistemic Reasons

The default reliance account of belief identifies an intelligible role for belief that complements the role of credences, rather than replacing it. Indeed, it seems that there *must* be something that plays such a role. For most of the possible information about which state of affairs will result from a choice is ultimately irrelevant for the decision that you will make. The possibility that you will have a car crash is small enough on any given day that differences in the utility of having an umbrella with you conditional on your having a car crash in the rain are small enough, once weighted by probabilities, to not make any difference. And car crashes are only one of hundreds of possibilities of comparably equal likelihood that do make a difference to the relevant expected utilities, but not a relevantly significant one.

If making any decision as simple as whether to take an umbrella required employing full decision tables, then decision-making must be a cognitively complex process, indeed. And if we ever make any decisions like this, the process is certainly incredibly opaque to us—I am quite confident that I have never considered the possibility of a car crash in connection with the decision to bring an umbrella until writing this chapter (though now it is a bit hard to get out of my head). So there are great benefits to be gained, by anything that can allow us to reap the benefits of a simpler decision-making process that can ignore these complicated considerations that ultimately rarely make any difference, if ever.

Yet you can't treat the decision of which features to leave out of your decision table as itself simply one more thing to deliberate about, on a case-by-case basis.

---

[4] Note of course that even if I believe each day that I will not have an accident that day, decisions whether to carry insurance and how much to carry typically concern the possibility of an accident over a much longer period. So *some*, though not all, similar such cases might be covered by a failure of rational belief to obey an arbitrary conjunctive closure principle, or because the difference between today and arbitrary future days makes it rational to believe things about today without believing similarly evidentially supported similar things about arbitrary future days.

To do so, you would have to either consider all of the relevant possibilities in any case, which would undermine the benefits, or you would have to have decided on the basis of a yet prior decision to leave some of them out, on pain of regress.

The alternative, obviously, is that you can have a *policy* of non-consideration. A *policy* of non-consideration of some possibilities could be formed once, and hence not require separate, redundant, consideration of all of the possible costs and benefits in each possible case. Yet a policy of *never* considering a possibility would be dangerous—and unnecessary to garner the benefits of having a policy. All that you need in order to get these benefits is to have a policy of *default* non-consideration. And that, essentially, is what the default reliance account says that belief is. So it is hard to see how to garner the benefits of simplifying our decision-making in cases where the gains to be made in correct decision-making are miniscule in relation to the immense computation costs of reasoning, without ending up with something very much like the default reliance account. Everyone, I suggest, needs something to play something like this role.

The default reliance account also predicts that beliefs will have what Michael Bratman has called *rational inertia*. According to Bratman (1987), who first discusses this property in connection with intentions, a state has rational inertia when the conditions under which it is rational to *form* this state are not the same as the conditions under which it is rational to *persist* in the state. If a state has rational inertia, then once you have entered that state, it will often be rational to continue in it even when you learn things that, had you learned them before entering the state, would have made it irrational for you to enter it in the first place. According to Bratman, some of the principal benefits of having a psychology in which intentions play an important role complementary to beliefs and desires accrue to the fact that since intentions are not subject to constant reconsideration, they provide a way of organizing our decision-making over time.

Beliefs are also plausibly subject to rational inertia. The psychologist Arie Kruglanski (2004) calls the descriptive version of this phenomenon *seizing and freezing*, and it is supported by a wide variety of experiments in which subjects who have made up their minds about some question are less susceptible to being influenced by further evidence than subjects who have not yet made up their mind. Kruglanski's experiments are both evidence that there really is a state of having 'made up one's mind' that is part of human psychology—just as the 'folk' idea that there are such things as binary beliefs maintains—and also evidence that this state is subject to inertia.[5]

And it is plausible that this inertia is *rational*. The rational inertia of beliefs underlies the puzzle from Chapter 6 about *order of evidence*. It can be rational for a senior professor who considered a question very carefully early in her career to

---

[5] Kruglanski's results are prominently discussed in greater detail by both Nagel (2008), who is responsible for introducing this important work to philosophers, and Weisberg (2020).

have continued to maintain her view over the course of several intervening decades despite occasionally encountering small but suggestive pieces of evidence to the contrary, even if the only rational course for a graduate student considering all of the available evidence today is to remain agnostic.[6]

The default reliance account predicts that beliefs should have rational inertia. After all, according to the default reliance account, when you believe something, you have a *perfectly general* disposition to rely on it in your reasoning—to leave the alternative off of your decision table. So when the question comes up of whether to reconsider your belief that P, by default your decision table will look like this:

	reconsider	don't reconsider
P	benefit = 0 + cost = −1 = −1	benefit = 0 + cost = 0 = 0

On the assumption that P, reconsidering whether P will involve wasted time and effort and lead you, at best, back to the same place, and at worst, to giving up a true belief. So it's a no-brainer, so long as you are accepting that P, not to reconsider your belief that P. Yet so long as you believe that P, this will be your default attitude toward reconsideration. So it will be no wonder that it will be rational for you not to reconsider—that beliefs will have rational inertia. But this will not keep you from *ever* reconsidering your beliefs—for belief itself is not a commitment to *always* accept that P, but only a commitment to accept that P by *default*. So you can still rationally reconsider, so long as something overcomes this default.

Note that this gives us an account of belief's rational inertia that contrasts with the one that we might get from Dallmann. For Dallmann, all belief is a commitment not to deliberate further. But for the default reliance account, there is no commitment at all not to reason further—it just turns out that if you do believe, then you can only come to a decision to reason further by already overcoming your default disposition. This, I think, gives us not just *some* account of the rational inertia of belief, but a more plausible account of its extent.

It is a consequence of the fact that belief is subject to rational inertia that like intention, it is better to form beliefs when more of the relevant evidence has come in. In both cases, if you form the state too early, then you cannot take advantage of later reasons. If I form an intention now not to drive into Los Angeles tomorrow, then I preclude[7] myself from being able to take advantage of the better information that my brother's phone call will provide about the key issue on which the

---

point of driving to Los Angeles depends—namely, whether he will be there. Similarly, if you form a belief about how many people are in the next room now, on the basis of your current, circumstantial, evidence, then you preclude yourself from forming a belief on the basis of the better evidence that is provided by simply going ahead and taking a look.

In both cases, facts about the availability of relatively much better evidence are reasons *against* the relevant states—against intention, and against belief. And they satisfy my account of right-kind reasons from Chapter 7, because the state of belief can do a better job of playing its role in allowing you to simplify decision-making, if it is sensitive to the availability of relatively superior evidence. When much better evidence is easily available, the thing to do is to first seek it, and *then* settle on a cognitive policy of what to accept by default, and a creature who reasons in this way will do much better, overall, at simplifying their reasoning in ways that carry the benefits of simplification without the costs of mistakes, than a creature who is not so sensitive.[8]

Similarly, it is clear why evidence that P is the right sort of thing for a creature to be sensitive to, in forming the belief that P, and evidence that ~P is the right sort of thing for it to be sensitive to, in *not* forming this belief. This is because the more likely that it is true that P, the smaller the expected costs of relying on the assumption that it is true in decision-making. And finally, since the belief that P is like a kind of long-range policy for assuming that P by default, a creature who is sensitive, in forming her beliefs, to the expected costs of error will do better at achieving the simplifying benefits of belief without the costs associated with making mistakes.

So the Default Reliance account of belief provides us with the right ingredients, I suggest, to make good on both the *orthodox* reasons for and against belief, and on both important classes of non-evidential reasons against belief that I defended in Chapter 6: availability-of-further-evidence reasons, and cost-of-error reasons. This combination is what I call *Pragmatic Intellectualism*.

8.3 Virtues of Pragmatic Intellectualism

Pragmatic Intellectualism is a form of *pragmatic encroachment* in epistemology. It is a view according to which what it is epistemically rational to believe can depend, among other things, on seemingly practical features of one's situation,

---

[8] Note that this explanation also predicts—correctly, I think—that the decision of whether to *accept* a proposition is not itself sensitive to the availability of further evidence bearing on that proposition. It can make perfect sense to accept a proposition even when you know that you are about to get much more decisive evidence whether it is true—for example, in reasoning by *reductio*. This follows because acceptance does not by itself have rational inertia, and that in turn is because only a *perfectly general* habit of acceptance will apply to even the circumstances of deciding whether to reconsider that habit.

and in particular on the costs of error. And since epistemic rationality is the strongest kind of rationality entailed by knowledge, it follows from Pragmatic Intellectualism that there is pragmatic encroachment on knowledge, as well—what you know can depend, among other things, on practical features of your situation.[9]

But Pragmatic Intellectualism isn't just a view on which this *is* true. It offers a deep explanation of *why* it is true. It is true because on the *best explanation* of why evidence matters for rational belief, evidence matters by being reason to believe. But in addition to reasons *to* believe, there are also reasons *against* belief. And on the best account of the nature of reasons for and against attitudes in general, together with the best account of the nature of belief in particular, we get the result that among the reasons against belief are some with an intuitively practical flavor. They are reasons which concern the potential costs of erroneously relying on a belief.

Let us set aside, for now, the relationship between Pragmatic Intellectualism and knowledge, since knowledge is the topic of Part IV of this book, and focus for now on the virtues of Pragmatic Intellectualism as a theory about the epistemic rationality of belief. There are many such virtues. A simple one—not proprietary to Pragmatic Intellectualism, but quite important—is that Pragmatic Intellectualism is not only consistent with, but even entails, the classical evidentialist thesis that it is epistemically rational to believe something just in case it is supported by adequate evidence.[10] This is one dimension among many along which Pragmatic Intellectualism is philosophically *conservative*. It is not a wild and liberal thesis about what can affect the rationality of belief—rather, it is tightly constrained, and the nature of the constraints that it endorses provides us with an explanation of why so many theorists could have made the mistake of coming to accept stronger constraints. And as I'll argue in Chapter 12, one of the most important desiderata for philosophical theories is to be able to offer explanations of how familiar views could have gone wrong while seeming right.

Another important virtue of Pragmatic Intellectualism is that it helps us understand what could motivate pragmatic encroachment in epistemology without accepting strong knowledge-action principles, such as those endorsed by Fantl and McGrath (2010) and by Hawthorne and Stanley (2009).[11] According to these authors, knowing that P should put you in a rational position to act under the

---

[9] The only point that I am making here is that since knowledge entails rational belief, pragmatic encroachment on knowledge will yield pragmatic encroachment on rational belief. This captures cases in which the stakes are *believed* to be high. But proponents of pragmatic encroachment on knowledge have typically claimed also or instead that knowledge can be defeated when the stakes are *actually* high—independently of whether the agent realizes it. These are what Stanley has called *ignorant high stakes* cases. I will return to explain ignorant high stakes cases in Chapter 11.

[10] Compare Foley (1993), Owens (2000), and Conee and Feldman (2004).

[11] For purposes of exposition and framing, my co-author and I also used a knowledge-action principle in order to motivate the thesis of pragmatic encroachment in Ross and Schroeder (2014). As we'll see in what follows, I don't believe that principle is true.

assumption that P. Since the costs of error can affect whether it is rational for you to act under the assumption that P, they argue, it follows that whether you know can depend on the costs of error. Most philosophers have taken this to be one of the most forceful arguments for pragmatic encroachment in epistemology, and to offer hope of providing the best *explanation* of why pragmatic encroachment is true—it needs to be true, on this view, for knowledge to play its proper role as the rational basis for action.

The problem with this line of reasoning is that all of the knowledge-action principles that have been employed in such arguments appear to be *false*. There are all sorts of things that we know, that we can't take for granted in every decision. We've already seen such a case. If I can know anything about the near future, I know that I won't be in a car crash today, but I can't count on that in considering whether to buy insurance. But there are even better cases. I certainly know that my name is 'Mark' but I wouldn't take a bet of a penny against my life over it. Surgeons often know which operation their patients require, but they always double-check before actually making the first incision.[12]

Pragmatic Intellectualism provides the basis for an explanation of the close connection between knowledge and action without committing to any such strong knowledge-action principle. According to Pragmatic Intellectualism, you know only if it is rational for you to believe something, and belief is a kind of policy of *default* reliance, but you can believe something without actually relying on it, and it can even be rational to believe what you know you can't rely on, so long as you can also be reasonably confident that you won't, in fact, rely on it.[13]

So long as the *policy* of default reliance remains reasonable, you can still count as knowing something even if it is not rational, in your current circumstances and with regard to the current decision that you are making, to rely on it. And this is what we see happening with each of the cases that I've mentioned. It is reasonable to have a policy of default reliance on the proposition that I won't be in a car crash today, because it is reasonable to be confident that if I *am* in a car crash today, I will change my mind about whether I would, and in the meantime, the chances that I am in a car crash are low enough as not to make a significant difference to most of my decisions. It is reasonable to have a policy of default reliance on the proposition that my name is 'Mark' even when confronted with a bet of a penny against my life on this proposition, because it is reasonable to be confident that I will not now take the bet, despite the policy, and that I am not likely to get many such bets in the future. And it is reasonable to have a default policy of believing that she is scheduled for a left-sided mastectomy despite the need to double-check, because I know that I have a policy of double-checking that is more specific than, and will override, my general default to rely on this belief.[14]

---

[12] Brown (2008a, 2008b), Lackey (2010).

[13] Or at least, not too much to outweigh the benefits of making up your mind now.

[14] Compare Jackson (2019).

The fact that Pragmatic Intellectualism is not committed to a strong knowledge-action principle, therefore, means that it is not vulnerable to one of the common ways in which the thesis of pragmatic encroachment has been attacked. But better, since it actually offers an explanation of *which* sorts of cases will be counterexamples to knowledge-action principles, Pragmatic Intellectualism's fit with these cases is even better.

In rejecting strong knowledge-action principles, Pragmatic Intellectualism divorces the stakes-sensitivity of epistemically rational belief from the decision facing you in any particular moment.[15] Since belief is a long-term strategy, not just a short-term answer to what to leave in or out of deliberation at the moment, it does not automatically cease to be rational to cease to believe a proposition just because it ceases to be rational to decide on the assumption that it is true. This has the more general consequence that belief is rationally *stable*.

In contrast, most proponents of pragmatic encroachment in epistemology endorse views on which what it is rational to believe is incredibly unstable—shifting from moment to moment as the choices available to one shift. This is a consequence of knowledge-action principles, because what it is rational to *do* can shift easily from moment to moment as the alternatives available to one shift, and so knowledge-action principles engender a corresponding shift in knowledge and the epistemic rationality of belief. Indeed, on one class of views—*pragmatic credal reductivist* theories such as those endorsed by Weatherson (2005), Ganson (2008), and Fantl and McGrath (2010)—there is pragmatic encroachment on knowledge because there is pragmatic encroachment on *belief*. On these views, which credal states *count* as belief itself shifts automatically as the choices available to one shift. Hence, on these views, what you *do* believe shifts automatically and frequently as the choices available to you shift, without anything else needing to happen to you, psychologically.[16]

The instability of traditional forms of pragmatic encroachment is one of their greatest weaknesses. Baron Reed (2012) pushes this point forcefully by drawing out how it engenders a susceptibility to Dutch books. As your beliefs shift from situation to situation, if beliefs make any difference at all psychologically for which choices it is rational for you to make, then we will be able to construct cases in which you will be rationally willing to pay in the low stakes situation to undo choices that you make in the high stakes situation. This allows us to let the two

---

[15]   Compare the objections to pragmatic encroachment in Brown (2013, 2018).

[16]   McGrath (2018b) argues that everyone has a similar problem with instability in when it is okay to rely on a belief in reasoning, but I don't think that this is the same kind of problem, as it is a question of what to *do*, and what to do can clearly reasonably change as your circumstances change in this way. So I do not find this attempt to generalize the problem persuasive. Fantl and McGrath (2019) also provide reasons on the basis of the significance of emotions to think that their view is actually much more stable. If this is right, then this issue between us will turn out to be much more subtle than I will be able to adjudicate, here.

situations oscillate freely, pumping you of money at will, as Dutch bookies are reportedly wont to do.[17]

Rational instability of belief also runs afoul of plausible *reflection*-like constraints on rational belief. The original principle of Reflection, formulated by van Fraassen (1984), concerns the rational relationship between your current credences and what you expect your credences to be in the future.[18] But many have been persuaded that reflection-like principles apply outside the domain of credence. For example, it is plausible that it is not rational to now intend to do something that you expect not to do when the time for action comes—earlier we saw why this principle could explain the irrationality of intending to drink the toxin in Kavka's toxin puzzle. Similarly, I suggest, it is not rational to now believe something that you expect not to believe in the future when you are better informed. Pragmatic encroachment views that allow for the rational instability of belief violate this constraint not only in selected cases, but easily and often, making it puzzling why it would even *seem* plausible.

Another important virtue of Pragmatic Intellectualism is that it is a kind of *single-tier* pragmatic encroachment. It allows for pragmatic encroachment on the rationality of binary belief, that is, without allowing for pragmatic encroachment on the rationality of *credence*. This is a virtue that it shares with pragmatic credal reductivist views—for on those views, the only thing that changes in high-stakes situations is which credences we count as 'beliefs', and so there are no rational effects of stakes on the credence that it is rational to have.

In contrast, Jason Stanley (2005) and others who are sympathetic to the view that your evidence is what you know are led to conclude that if credences should be rationally responsive to evidence, but your evidence is given by what you know and what you know depends on the stakes, then which credence it is rational to have may also depend on the practical stakes. This, I think, is a very bad result. As I argued in Chapter 7, credences will perform their job only very poorly if they are subject to easy manipulation by raising or lowering the stakes, and especially so if all it takes to raise or lower the stakes is to affect immediately available options and their consequences.

In addition to all of these virtues, Pragmatic Intellectualism employs a well-defined conception of stakes that does not bleed into the idea that everything practical matters for the rationality of belief and can explain away many putative counterexamples to pragmatic encroachment theses. Pragmatic encroachment arises not because of advantages or disadvantages of belief *per se*, but only because of *costs of error*—costs of believing something falsely. But not all costs of believing something falsely count—Pascal's wager itself, after all, is a cost that accrues in the

---

[17] I give what I think is an improved version of Reed's Dutch book case in Schroeder (2018c).
[18] For a helpful discussion of Reflection, see Weisberg (2007).

cell of your decision table where you believe God doesn't exist but that is false.[19] Only the costs of the belief playing its normal role in your psychology—of leading you to leave the alternative out of your decision table—are the right sorts of costs to be epistemic reasons against belief, because only they are the ones that belief needs to be sensitive to, in order to perform its function well.

It turns out that a surprisingly large number of attempts to offer counterexamples or other objections to pragmatic encroachment turn on examples that do not fit this schema. And even where proponents of those objections believe that they can be recast using examples that do fit it, these alternative examples are much less intuitively forceful. This gives the proponent of Pragmatic Intellectualism a powerful strategy for countering a vast range of current and future objections.

I'll illustrate with just one example, though this dialectic could be rehearsed at exhausting length. Baron Reed (2018) offers the objection to the thesis of pragmatic encroachment that it creates a kind of easily abused power to rationally persuade someone out of some belief not by offering counterevidence, but merely by raising the stakes. Reed's example is of someone who has been stealing lunches from co-workers, and then reminds the person who he is worried has begun to suspect him that he is looking forward to recommending her for a promotion— hence raising, Reed suggests, the stakes for her over the question of whether he is in fact the culprit.[20] This does sound like an easily abused power, if raising the stakes is something that it is easy for someone to actually do. But remember that for Pragmatic Intellectualism, the stakes do not go up just because it is not rational to rely on something *now*, because the epistemic reasons against belief concern the costs of belief as a long-term strategy. In contrast, pointing out that allergic reactions to penicillin can actually be quite dangerous *does* seem like the right sort of thing for one to be able to do, in order to persuade her to drop her belief.

As I'll argue in Chapter 9, close interpersonal friendships *are* the right sort of thing to raise the stakes for negative beliefs about the other, and so one way in which you could raise the long-term stakes for someone and hence rationally persuade them to come to doubt a negative belief about you, is to form a long-term friendship with them. But that hardly looks like an abuse—indeed, coming to be friends with someone seems like just the kind of thing that might rationally lead you to come to doubt some of your negative first impressions of them.[21]

I have no way of guaranteeing, of course, that there are not some cases in which someone has so much power over someone else that they are able to unilaterally

---

[19] This is the feature that Benton (2018) exploits to try to generalize Pascal's argument.

[20] Reed (2018, 207).

[21] In the same vein, compare MacFarlane's (2005) objection that theories allowing for pragmatic encroachment will allow for *knowledge laundering*. Essentially, that they face a dilemma between denying that you are in a position to learn by testimony from someone who knows, or allowing that you can learn by testimony from someone whose source of evidence is no better than your own, simply because the stakes are lower for her. But pragmatic intellectualism does not face this dilemma. The stakes for action for one person can raise the stakes for others, as well.

and abusively change the long-term stakes. If you control someone's life so much that you can make them despair of escaping situations in which they will be punished for error about some topic, then that *is*, on my view, the right sort of thing to be able to rationally persuade them out of some view, and I agree with Reed that it would be an abuse. But I suggest that since this kind of power can only exist in imbalanced and abusive relationships to begin with, rather than seeing it as an objectionable consequence of the theory, we should see the theory as helping us to see at a deeper level more of what has been so objectionable about power imbalanced abusive relationships all along.

The response that I have been giving to Reed illustrates a pattern that I suggest is common. A critic of pragmatic encroachment uses an example that is intuitively forceful but not a genuine counterexample to Pragmatic Intellectualism, because it relies on an uncareful setup or the wrong conception of what makes stakes high. In some cases there are *versions* of the same case that can be constructed using the proper notion of costs of error, but these cases are less intuitively forceful, and can be resisted, in some cases instructively. It gives us a powerful recipe for handling critical discussions of pragmatic encroachment.

Finally, the greatest virtue of Pragmatic Intellectualism is that it is well-motivated from plausible, independent, highly general constraints. We've started from the most general approach to the rationality of belief, assuming that what goes for the rationality of belief is just what goes for rationality more generally, together with what is distinctive of belief. And then we've supplied an account of what is distinctive of belief. This is the territory over which this issue should be fought—for the rationality of belief *must* be what we get when we put rationality together with belief.

This illustrates, therefore, the Core Hypothesis of this book, according to which the comparison to other branches of normative inquiry does sometimes make a difference—indeed, an important difference—for even very core topics of traditional epistemology. The explanatory virtues of Pragmatic Intellectualism come from the *continuity* it finds between the rationality of belief and the rationality of other attitudes, and its key move is the same as Ross's—by understanding rational belief as the *balance* between competing factors, we get an elegant and explanatory account of one of the most central questions in epistemology—when belief is rational in the way required for knowledge.

8.4 Recap

In Part III I've taken up the problem of sufficiency, one of the two chief obstacles to Reasons First in epistemology that we encountered in Chapter 1. In keeping with our Core Hypothesis, I have argued that the problem of sufficiency, and the hasty, Reasons First inconsistent, response to it, is actually at the core of many central puzzles in epistemology about what role evidence could actually play in rationalizing belief. By seeing past this hasty conclusion and paying more attention to what is distinctive of belief, we can see our way to answers to each of these central problems about how evidence can rationalize belief, by making room for epistemic reasons against belief that are not evidence against its content.[22]

The view that I have developed and defended in these chapters has three layers. The first and most important layer is the observation that one of the most important differences between belief and action is that whereas with respect to action we can make binary choices, with respect to belief, there is always an alternative to believing that P or believing that ~P—having neither belief. It is from this ternary structure that many of the most important differences between belief and action flow, and it is that idea that is captured in the jacket illustration for this book. Out of everything that I say in this book, this is the claim in which I have the greatest confidence.

The second layer of the view developed in these chapters is my proposal that we need to evaluate the scope of what qualifies as epistemic reasons for or against belief by deriving it from a general account of what makes reasons count as the characteristic reasons for or against attitudes of different kinds, together with an account of the nature of belief. I defended this principle both on general grounds and by showing that it can be developed and defended independently of the stronger commitments of pragmatic intellectualism.

Finally, the third layer of the view developed in these chapters was the *default reliance* account of the nature of belief, from which I argued it follows that among the epistemic reasons against belief are those which derive from the potential costs of error. Together, these three layers constitute the view that I have called *Pragmatic Intellectualism*—a view which incorporates a role for pragmatic factors in the epistemic rationality of belief—and as I'll argue in Chapter 11, for knowledge—in a way that is surprisingly conservative along many other dimensions.

Pragmatic Intellectualism is, I think, an incredibly natural view. The fact that it could count as strange, surprising, or even creative, is I think a testament to the powerful grip of the assumption that the distinction between Pascalian considerations and normal reasons for belief is just the distinction between evidence and 'practical' considerations. Since that is the assumption that is required to drive the sufficiency problem for Reasons First in epistemology, I conclude that there is no good sufficiency problem for Reasons First. We can all benefit by setting this assumption aside.

---

[22] It bears reminding, here, that I have not actually defended an answer to the problem of merely statistical evidence, which we originally raised with lottery cases. It is possible that this problem could be answered in parallel to the cases of further available evidence and of costs of error, but I suspect that it is not best answered in this way.

9

Doxastic Wrongs

9.1 The Ethics of Belief

The main arguments of Chapters 6, 7, and 8 have concerned the ethics of belief, in the very broadest sense that is familiar from epistemology—the question of what you should believe, and why. I have been at pains to argue that we should understand what makes beliefs rational or irrational in terms of the balance of reasons, rather than understanding reasons as sufficient or not simply on the basis of whether they make or would make beliefs rational. This is what is required in order to answer the problem of sufficiency, and all that my answer requires is to somehow make sense of the possibility of epistemic reasons against belief that are not evidence.

Nevertheless, I have been arguing at length that not only *can* we make sense of such reasons, but once we allow ourselves to think in terms of them, we actually get access to a powerful way of understanding the contours of the epistemic rationality of belief. And part of my evidence for that was that I've shown how we can actually be led to contrary views about *which* non-evidential epistemic reasons against belief there are by adopting different hypotheses about the nature of binary belief and its role in our psychologies. Although I've been clear about my preference for the default reliance account of belief and Pragmatic Intellectualism's identification of both availability-of-further-evidence and cost-of-error reasons against belief, the approach that I've been arguing for throughout Part III is ecumenical about pragmatic encroachment in epistemology. You can buy into everything else that I've said here while rejecting pragmatic encroachment by adopting Justin Dallmann's attractive *stable high credence* account of the nature of binary belief, for example, and other natural views will be possible, as well.

In a sense, that completes the arguments of Part III of this book. And so if you are content with those conclusions, or dogmatically skeptical about pragmatic encroachment in epistemology, it is possible to skip the remainder of this chapter and continue directly to Part IV, where I will show how to leverage the insights of Parts II and III in order to answer the Gettier Problem and provide an attractive analysis of knowledge, and where I will show how knowledge and moral worth constitute the best cases for the hypothesis of Reasons First.

But if you have the patience to bear with me, in this slightly tangential chapter I want to turn to the ethics of belief in the *narrow* sense—the question of whether

Reasons First. Mark Schroeder, Oxford University Press (2021). © Mark Schroeder.
DOI: 10.1093/oso/9780198868224.003.0009

there are ever moral issues at stake over what to believe. Although I have offered converging lines of evidence for Pragmatic Intellectualism in Chapters 6, 7, and 8, the greatest fruits of Pragmatic Intellectualism, I will be suggesting in this chapter, are that they allow us to make sense of genuinely moral constraints on belief—and in particular, of the possibility that we can wrong each other by what we believe about one another. I call such wrongs *doxastic wrongs*.

In the remainder of this chapter, I will argue that we *can* wrong one another by our beliefs, that Pragmatic Intellectualism is the key to defending this claim from its most obvious obstacles, and that the most plausible examples of beliefs that wrong are also among the most intuitively compelling examples of cases in which the costs of error raise the standards for what is required in order for evidence to be sufficient for rational belief. It would have been easy, for the sake of balance and continuity, to have left this chapter out of this book, since the most important lessons of Part III for the overall dialectic of the book do not turn on whether we accept Pragmatic Intellectualism or not. Nevertheless, it is my own conviction that the issues raised in this chapter are at the very heart of why it is so important to get these issues right, and why they are much larger than the bare question of whether there is a viable concept of sufficiency that is analytically prior to rationality, or conversely.

9.2 Beliefs That Wrong

Among contemporary analytic philosophers, it is anathema to suppose that there are genuinely ethical questions, in the narrow sense, about what it is permissible to believe. Much of my thinking about this topic is influenced by my former student and collaborator Rima Basu, and we both have found that when we have explained to philosophers that our view is that there are some doxastic wrongs—some cases in which someone wrongs someone directly by virtue of what she believes about them—we have often been gently corrected that we must surely mean that there is some wrong either *upstream* from the belief or *downstream* from it—that the believer failed to consider the matter in a cool or fully reflective light, or that she acted on this belief when she should instead have bracketed it for purposes of action.

In contrast, ordinary moral thinking, Basu and I believe, is full of the idea that there can be doxastic wrongs. Rightly or wrongly, it is part of lay common sense that racism is both morally wrong and at least partially *constituted* by what one believes either about race or about particular individuals on the basis of their race. Certainly we treat the things that someone says or seems to think as evidence that they are racist. And similar points go for sexism, anti-Semitism, and other prominent isms. A common though not constitutive thought in credal religions is that it is possible to err in creed, and not merely in deed[1]—and indeed, that creed is in some way central. But for simplicity, I'll focus on a case of a doxastic wrong within a close relationship, as I believe that the greatest potential for doxastic wrongs lies in the closest of interpersonal relationships.

Suppose that after several unsuccessful attempts to get over my alcohol problem, I have now been sober for several months.[2] Tonight I manage to stay away from drinking even after the visiting colloquium speaker spills wine on my arm, forcing me to smell alcohol for the whole evening, so it is my greatest achievement, yet. But when I get home, my wife smells the alcohol on me and concludes that I have fallen off of the wagon. If I see the look in her eye, I will rightly be upset—her belief wrongs me.

Of course, we should all be more confident that there is *some* wrong in the neighborhood of my wife's judgment than we should be about exactly what this wrong consists in. And so philosophers who have general cause to doubt that beliefs can ever wrong in and of themselves have a ready strategy available for explaining away apparent counterexamples like this one—they can point to wrongs that take place either *upstream* from the belief formation, such as the care that she takes in forming her belief, or *downstream* from it, such as the way that she acts on it, or takes insufficient care not to reveal to me that this is what she thinks. And part of what makes both of these plausible strategies is that she *does* plausibly owe it to me to think carefully before forming negative beliefs about me, and it *does* hurt me to find out what she thinks. So it is easy to see how both the upstream causes and downstream effects of the belief could themselves constitute wrongs.

But one surefire way to tell that it is the belief that wrongs me, and not the look in her eye or the care she took in forming the belief, is that I will not be satisfied if she apologizes for what she did *after* forming the belief, such as giving it away with that look in her eye, and what she did *before* forming the belief, such as the care that she took in forming it. What bothers me is the way that her estimation of the situation brings me down—the way in which it minimizes my achievement. So long as she refuses to apologize for *that*, I suggest, I am right to feel wronged by her judgment. And I suggest that you would feel that way, too.

Perceived need for apology is a good test for directed wrongs, because directed wrongs are precisely what demand apology. You can wrong someone without acting in a way that is wrong all things considered, but when you do, even though you should have no regrets or guilt over doing what is right all things considered, you still owe them an apology. Sometimes, of course, it is wise to lubricate interpersonal relationships by apologizing even when you have not, in fact, wronged someone, because it is better to apologize unnecessarily than for them

---

[1] In the *Common Book of Prayer*, for example, the congregation confesses to have sinned against God "in thought, word, and deed".
[2] This example comes from Basu and Schroeder (2019).

to think that you have wronged them without apologizing. But even this explanation of why this is better turns on the assumption that apologies truly are owed just in case you have wronged someone—and that your friend merely disagrees with you about whether you have wronged them. So I infer that it truly is possible to wrong someone by what you believe about them.

The spilled wine case constitutes, in the first instance, an argument that we can wrong one another by what we believe about them. It is an attempt to triangulate on a *directed* wrong of belief. But in general, where there are directed wrongs, there are things that are wrong *simpliciter*. Even if it is not always wrong *simpliciter* to wrong someone—some wrongs may be justified by the wrongs that they prevent, but are still wrongs nonetheless—it is *presumptively* wrong to do so. So if there are doxastic wrongs, I infer, by and large there will also be substantive moral questions of what it is morally wrong to believe. There will be, in other words, an ethics of belief in the *narrow* sense.

Once we open our eyes up to this possibility, I suggest, we can find doxastic wrongs all over the place. In keeping with the case that we have already been discussing, one important class of cases arises within *friendships*. For example, Simon Keller (2004a) and Sarah Stroud (2006) have each argued much more generally that it is incompatible with the demands of friendship that we apply the same evidential standards to conclusions about our friends as to similar conclusions about strangers, or to conclusions about the weather supported by similar evidence. Neither Keller nor Stroud quite endorses the thesis that we *wrong* our friends by what we believe about them, if we treat them just like the weather, but their reasoning suggests it.

For example, Billy and Stan are driving through Alabama, and are arrested for the murder of a convenience store clerk. When he is arrested, Billy confesses that they did it, and there are eye-witnesses to two young men of their description hopping into a mint-green convertible that looks just like theirs. There is even forensic evidence showing that the getaway car from the crime wore the very same tires as the car they are arrested driving. Billy and Stan's only defense is that when Billy confessed, he thought he was being arrested for stealing a can of tuna—which he had—and that there must have been another mint-green convertible with two similar-looking young men that drove by at the same time. When Vinny—Billy's cousin who is studying for the bar exam—arrives in Alabama to take up their legal defense, he owes it to Billy not to respond to the evidence of guilt in the same way as local bystanders do.[3]

Even outside of the context of close interpersonal relationships, there are positive/negative asymmetries in how we form beliefs about others. For example,

---

[3] These, of course, are the circumstances in the 1992 film *My Cousin Vinny*. Of course, Vinny *does* give Billy and Stan the benefit of the doubt, and this is taken for granted in the film as requiring no special explanation.

Tamar Gendler (2011) considers the case of the distinguished African–American historian John Hope Franklin, who was awarded the Presidential Medal of Freedom in 1995. The night before he received the award, he hosted a small party with friends at the Cosmos Club in Washington, D.C., a historically white club of which he was one of the very first black members, and where most staff were black. While walking through the club, a woman calls him out, presents him with her coat check, and asks him to bring her his coat.

Given that all of the club attendants were in uniform and Franklin was not, it is clear that she has formed a belief that he is staff on the basis of his race alone. This is a statistically promising basis, given the underlying demographic statistics at the club. But that doesn't make it an okay thing for her to think—on the contrary, Franklin would be right to feel wronged by the woman—even though they have no special relationship. As before, we can try to locate the wrong either upstream or downstream from the belief, but again, though her asking him is what *causes* him to be bothered, I don't think Franklin is bothered, at least primarily *about* what she says, so much as he is bothered by her *presumption*.

In addition to beliefs that wrong other people, I think that we can also wrong *ourselves* by what we believe about ourselves. Consider the case of judgments of self-worth. Falsely believing yourself to be better than you are at, say, playing chess, or the piano, is a vice. But falsely believing yourself to be much worse than you really are is not a virtue—modesty, which is a virtue, is concerned with how you comport yourself, and perhaps what you *attend* to in thought, not with what you actually believe about yourself.[4] In fact, falsely believing yourself to be much worse at something than you actually are is quite tragic. Compare the example of Virgil, who devotes seven years of his life to writing a PhD dissertation that documents the influence of the Cambridge Platonist Ralph Cudworth on Immanuel Kant's thinking. Years later, news comes to light on DailyNous.com of hitherto-undiscovered correspondence in which Kant asks, in 1794 "Wer ist diese Cudworth Person, die du in deinem letzten Brief erwähnt hast?"[5] If Virgil now concludes, along with other casual readers of DailyNous.com that his dissertation was worthless, this isn't modesty, but tragic. Given his personal investment, he surely wrongs himself not to hold out for better authentication of the letter.

Or consider a case from Marušic (2012). You are a long-time smoker and are trying to work up a resolution to quit. The empirical evidence is compelling that it takes the vast majority of smokers many attempts before they successfully quit. But if you believe that you will be unsuccessful, you won't be able to intend to quit. Marušic argues persuasively that what makes quitting even possible, in such circumstances, is that quitters *don't* believe that they will fail. He actually goes farther, and argues that it is rational for someone trying to quit smoking to believe

---

[4] Though contrast Driver (1999).
[5] "Who is this Cudworth person who you mentioned in your last letter?"

that they will succeed, but we needn't follow him so far in order to appreciate the force of the point that you *wrong* yourself, to sell yourself short.[6]

9.3 Overcoming Obstacles

I don't claim that any of the examples that I have given of doxastic wrongs are incontrovertible—though I do find the spilled wine case particularly compelling. But the possible examples are easy enough, and prevalent enough that we should need some good reason not to take any of them at face value. It turns out that there are at least two obvious philosophical challenges to the idea that beliefs can wrong—but also that both of them are addressed by Pragmatic Intellectualism.[7]

The first challenge is the *problem of control*. It arises because many epistemologists have doubted whether we have sufficient control over our beliefs for it to turn out that there are any beliefs that we ought to have *at all*, even in some restricted *epistemic* sense of 'ought'. If whether there is anything we ought or ought not to believe can be cast into doubt even setting moral wrongness aside, it will be no wonder if philosophers are especially shy about attributing *moral* wrongness to beliefs.

At a first pass, the problem of control for the idea that beliefs can wrong is just the parallel of the problem of control for the idea that there are any beliefs that we ought to have at all, even in a restricted epistemic sense. But in fact the problem of control becomes much more forceful once we consider some of the most promising answers to why there *can* be some things that we ought, or ought not, to believe, despite our lack of any ability to believe, in Bernard Williams' (1973a) terms, 'at will'.[8] For example, Nishi Shah (2002) points out that to believe at will is to believe what you intend to believe. So to be able to believe at will would be for our intentions to be able to control our beliefs. But there can be things that we ought to intend even if our intentions are not in control of our intentions, so this condition is clearly too strong.

What is much more plausible, is that in order for an 'ought' to apply to beliefs, that 'ought' must derive from reasons to which our beliefs are actually sensitive.[9] Yet our beliefs *are* sensitive to the evidence. And evidence is reason to believe *par excellence*. So insofar as what we epistemically ought to believe is derived from the evidence, we have exactly the right sort of control over our beliefs in order for such *oughts* to apply to us. Yet if this is the best sort of answer to why we do have the right sort of control over what we believe for there to be things that we ought or

[6] Marušic (2015).
[7] The points in this section follow Basu and Schroeder (2019) and Schroeder (2018d), where they are developed at greater length, but I should note that Basu (2018) does not accept Pragmatic Intellectualism or restrict her conception of moral reasons bearing on belief to costs of error, as I advocate.
[8] Compare Bennett (1990).   [9] Shah (2006).

ought not to believe, that might make us only *more* skeptical of whether there are any things that it is *morally* wrong to believe. For though it is highly plausible that our beliefs are sensitive to the evidence, it is much less plausible that our beliefs are sensitive to just any old moral consideration—for example, learning that it would be utility-maximizing to believe something is not the right sort of thing to convince us that it is true.

So the problem of control, it must be admitted, is a serious challenge to the idea that beliefs can wrong. But getting the problem fully into view also allows us to see why Pragmatic Intellectualism already answers it. For according to Pragmatic Intellectualism, our beliefs *are*, in fact, sensitive to the *right* kinds of moral considerations. Not to the moral *benefits* of beliefs, but to the moral *costs* of *error*. It would wrong your spouse to mistakenly believe that he has fallen off of the wagon if in fact he has managed to stay sober despite adverse circumstances. Knowing that doesn't just require us, but also makes it possible for us, to hold out for better evidence, before jumping to that conclusion. Similarly, we are perfectly capable of taking more care—of holding ourselves to higher evidential standards—before coming to draw conclusions about someone simply on the basis of racial statistics. So if sensitivity to the reasons that go into determining an 'ought' is all that is required for that 'ought' to apply to us, then I see no reason why there cannot be moral 'oughts' governing belief that apply to us, so long as they are constrained to only depend on such reasons.

Pragmatic Intellectualism gives us a qualified defense of the possibility of doxastic wrongs, in the sense that it maintains that our moral beliefs really *are* sensitive to some moral considerations—considerations that turn on the cost of error. So in keeping with its overall conservative stance in epistemology, it does *not* allow for arbitrary moral standards governing belief, or for the utilities or con-sequences of beliefs themselves to matter—at all. The only moral reasons bearing on belief that it allows for, are cases in which there are moral costs of error. But I contend that all of our leading examples *are* like this.

The other important general philosophical challenge to the possibility of doxastic wrongs is what Rima Basu and I have called the *coordination problem*. The problem is that if there are moral norms governing belief but these are not coordinated with the epistemic norms governing belief, then these two sets of norms will come into an objectionable kind of tension. This tension may manifest itself in different ways, depending on what more specific assumptions we make about each of the moral and epistemic norms governing belief. For example, if there are some things that you morally ought not to believe but that you epistemically ought *to* believe, then this is a kind of deontic *conflict*, and so you will have to choose between being rational and being good. Indeed, that we face this choice is just what both Keller (2004a) and Stroud (2006) have argued about friendship, and similarly, what Gendler (2011) has concluded about what she calls the "epistemic costs of implicit bias".

But epistemic and moral norms could come into an objectionable sort of tension even if we don't assume that there are any outright deontic conflicts. For example, if we accept my appeal to Pragmatic Intellectualism in order to defend doxastic wrongs from the problem of control, then we will conclude that though there are moral reasons *against* belief, there are no moral reasons in *favor* of belief. So on this view, it may sometimes be morally wrong to positively believe something of someone, but it is never morally wrong to *lack* some belief about someone.[10] And Mark Nelson (2010) has argued that though there are things we have epistemic duties *not* to believe, there is nothing that we ever have a positive epistemic duty *to* believe. If Nelson is right about epistemic obligations, and what we have said so far is right about the moral obligations governing belief, then there *won't* be any proper deontic conflicts between moral and epistemic norms—there will be nothing such that you are morally required to do it and epistemically required not to, or conversely.

But even this should not put us at ease about a lack of coordination between epistemic and moral norms governing belief. For the fact that a belief satisfies every epistemic standard required for knowledge looks like a pretty good justification for holding it. When I challenge my wife about her belief that I have fallen off of the wagon, it would be disingenuous for her to both apologize for it but also insist that the only thing keeping it from being knowledge was that it was false. This is disingenuous, because satisfying everything required for knowledge short of truth looks like it *answers* the moral charges against the belief.

So I conclude that the problem of coordination is again a serious challenge to the possibility of doxastic wrongs. If there are doxastic wrongs at all, I conclude, the moral and epistemic norms governing beliefs must be *coordinated*. And there are two ways in which these two sets of norms could be coordinated. It could be that doxastic wrongs are simply restricted to be just a special case of epistemically unjustified beliefs. But our leading examples of doxastic wrongs do not fit this mold—they are cases where the quality of the evidence is quite comparable to the quality of the evidence on the basis of which we rationally form beliefs about the weather all of the time. So the problem of coordination suggests, again, that we can capture the most compelling intuitive examples of doxastic wrongs only if we accept that there is what has come to be called *moral encroachment* on the epistemic rationality of belief.

Again, Pragmatic Intellectualism tells us how this can be so. It can be so, so long as the only moral reasons bearing on belief are a special case of the costs of error allowed by Pragmatic Intellectualism to be epistemic reasons against belief. And

---

[10] Note that both Keller (2004a) and Stroud (2005) appear to think that positive beliefs can also be required for friendship. But I would argue that none of their arguments that this is so pay sufficient attention to Pragmatic Intellectualism's alternative.

again, I suggest that our best examples of doxastic wrongs can all be construed in this way—as special cases of the costs of error.

9.4 The Picture

On the picture that I think is correct, moral beliefs can wrong, but the truth of Pragmatic Intellectualism guarantees the harmony between the moral and epistemic norms directly governing belief. It can do this, I suggest, because only *false* beliefs wrong, and the way that Pragmatic Intellectualism makes room for pragmatic encroachment is precisely through the consequences of false beliefs. It is worth spelling out more carefully how this package of views hangs together.

In Part II we saw that it is important to distinguish objective and subjective modes of evaluation of belief. In the objective mode, the reasons that matter are objective reasons, which must be truths.[11] But in the subjective mode, the reasons that matter are subjective reasons, which need not be truths. So in order to discuss whether and how the moral and epistemic norms governing beliefs might be harmonized, we need to consider contrasting questions about objective and subjective moral and epistemic modes of evaluation.

When I say that a belief wrongs you, I mean that it constitutes an objective wrong—a wrong in what Parfit (2011) calls the "fact-relative sense". So whether a belief wrongs you will depend—like whether it is correct—on how things are in the world, and not just on your evidence. The harmony of objective moral and epistemic norms on belief is therefore guaranteed directly by the assumption that only false beliefs can wrong. Since only a false belief can wrong, wronging someone can only be an *additional* demerit to a belief—over and above being a mistake. So there is never a conflict between objective moral and epistemic norms governing belief.

It is controversial, of course, whether only false beliefs can wrong. Some thinkers, including Basu, incline toward the view that true beliefs can wrong just as false beliefs can. And Keller's and Stroud's important discussions of the epistemic requirements of friendship suggest that friendship can require you to believe good things of your friends, and not just not to believe bad things about them. But I think that all of the best and clearest examples of wrongful beliefs *are*, in fact, false ones. This is so in the spilled wine case, it is so in the John Hope Franklin case, it is so in the self-worth case, and it is so, I believe, even in the clearest cases from Marusic and from Keller and Stroud. The evidence is much better that we can wrong one another by having false beliefs about one another than that we can wrong one another through true beliefs. So I conclude that we

---

[11] Again, please translate as appropriate into your preferred ontology for reasons.

can protect the harmony of objective moral and objective epistemic norms by accepting the assumption that only false beliefs can wrong.

But beliefs, like actions, can be subjectively wrong even when they do not constitute objective wrongs. I do not wrong you by grabbing my own luggage off of the carousel, but if I was trying to steal yours and took my own by mistake, then I am blameworthy. Similarly, the woman at the Cosmos Club does not wrong the staff when she presumes them to be staff, but she is equally blameworthy as when she presumes this of John Hope Franklin on similar evidence. Acting or believing in a way that is blameworthy is not morally awesome—on the contrary, there is an important kind of moral criticism that we can make of it—that it is subjectively morally wrong. But we shouldn't confuse this kind of criticism with the criticism that it constitutes an objective wrong any more than we should confuse the criticism of an act or belief as irrational with the criticism of it as incorrect.

Whereas the harmony of the objective moral and epistemic norms on belief is guaranteed by the assumption that true beliefs cannot wrong, the harmony between the subjective moral and epistemic norms on belief is guaranteed by Pragmatic Intellectualism, together with the assumption that makes a conflict worrisome—that satisfying everything required for knowledge short of truth looks like it *answers* the moral charges against the belief.

Let's take the first side, first. Since beliefs can objectively wrong when they are false, the risk of wronging someone is a candidate to count as one of the costs of error that create stakes-based epistemic reasons against belief. Now, we know from Chapter 8 that not all costs of being wrong count as genuinely epistemic reasons against belief—not even costs that are distinctive costs of being wrong. After all, we can imagine a version of the Pascalian argument that relies on a God who punishes atheism but not agnosticism with eternal damnation. According to Pragmatic Intellectualism, however, the distinction between costs of error that constitute epistemic reasons against belief and those that do not is that the former must proceed from the belief's playing its normal role in our psychologies. So Pragmatic Intellectualism can go either way on whether it accommodates moral encroachment—depending on what we say about whether beliefs that wrong do so by playing their normal role in our psychologies.

But the best case that beliefs wrong is not that they do so by means of their effects—after all, any cases in which beliefs have effects are cases that do not successfully screen off the hypothesis that the wrong is downstream from the belief. So the costs of wrongful beliefs are not *caused* by the belief—in its normal role or otherwise. But they may be *constituted directly* by beliefs. Insofar as the kinds of possible relationships that we are capable of entering into one another are shaped directly by what we believe about one another, it may be true that wrongful beliefs directly constitute costs of error. And that is what I believe.

So when a belief carries a risk of wronging someone if it is false, that creates extra subjective reasons not to believe it, thus raising the bar for how much evidence is required in order to make it epistemically rational to believe. This is how moral encroachment works, by the lights of Pragmatic Intellectualism. Meanwhile, since evidence *can* outweigh the cost-of-error reasons against belief to make it rational to believe, in order for the moral and epistemic to be fully in harmony, we need to also assume that being epistemically rational constitutes a subjective *moral* justification for belief.

Together, these assumptions can be represented in Figure 9.1, which shows how the objective (left to right) and subjective (top to bottom) dimensions of evaluation of belief cross cut, while the moral (bottom and right) and the epistemic (top and left) are coordinated within the objective and subjective modes of evaluation, but not across them:

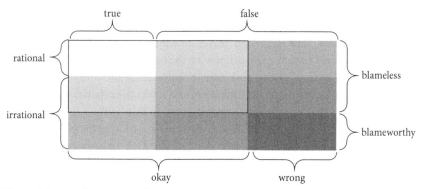

Figure 9.1 Moral–epistemic harmony

As we can see from Figure 9.1, the hypothesis that beliefs can wrong merely enlarges the space of possibilities over the top-left rectangle of familiar options. Paradigmatic cases of wrongful beliefs are ones that are also blameworthy and can be found in the lower right-hand corner. But beliefs can still wrong but be rational and blameless (top right-hand corner)—as my wife's belief may well be in the spilled wine case if the evidence that I have fallen off of the wagon is overwhelming enough. Or they can be blameworthy but true (lower left-hand corner)—as with the woman at the Cosmos Club who by luck gives her coat check to an actual attendant instead of to John Hope Franklin. They can be blameworthy and false but not wrong (bottom middle)—for example, if my wife believes that I have been drinking tonight, and I have not, but unbeknownst to her I have secretly been drinking at other times. And they can be blamelessly wrong but irrational (middle right)—for example, if someone who doesn't realize that I am a recovering alcoholic believes that I have had a drink even though there is no good evidence of this. And finally, of course, knowledge can be morally criticized in none of these ways, because it is a special case, as I have been assuming, of rational true belief.

So together with the assumption that only false beliefs can wrong, Pragmatic Intellectualism provides a powerful and conservative explanation of how it could be that beliefs wrong without creating conflicts with epistemic norms. If beliefs *can* wrong, then this would be a very reasonable way to expect them to do so.

9.5 The Best Examples

I now want to argue that the very best examples of doxastic wrongs are also, as it turns out, among the very best cases for pragmatic encroachment in epistemology, to begin with—and that this is precisely what we should expect, if Pragmatic Intellectualism is true, given Pragmatic Intellectualism's emphasis on *long-term*, rather than merely *immediate*, costs of error.

Traditionally, pragmatic encroachment in epistemology has been motivated by variants of so-called 'bank' and 'train' cases, in which someone needs to act now, and the costs of error accrue if you act now on the basis of that belief, but it is false. We considered a version of the bank case in introducing the problem about the preponderance of the evidence, in Chapter 6, and it was the original way in which I introduced the idea of pragmatic encroachment, in this book.

Bank and train cases fit perfectly with knowledge-action principles. They are cases in which what matters is what to do *now*, and in high-stakes versions of these cases, what it makes sense to do *conditional* on the assumption that the bank will be open differs from what it makes sense to do *unconditionally*, given the high costs of error. But in Chapter 8 I argued that we should reject strong knowledge-action principles. What you know, and what it is rational to believe, is *not* perfectly sensitive to how it is rational to act in the situation of the moment. Because belief is like a long-term plan, what it is rational to believe will depend more on the expected *long-term* costs of error than on the *immediate* costs of error. Consequently, I argued, often it is rational to believe something but *not* take it for granted in deciding how to act. And in particular, this is rational when the costs of error are largely in the present.

In the simplest versions of the bank case, it turns out, the costs of error *are* mostly in the present. Once you stay in line for the bank on Friday afternoon instead of going home with the plan to return on Saturday, it may never be important for you again whether the bank was open that Saturday—and there will no longer be high costs of error. It follows that we should not expect bank and train cases to be the best cases for pragmatic encroachment. I don't say that they *cannot* be cases of pragmatic encroachment—arguably, since it will likely never be important to you whether the bank was in fact open on this particular Saturday, there is not much to be gained from believing that it was, either. And there are *some* potential costs of error that stretch into the future. For example, if you stand in line just to be safe despite believing that the bank will in fact be open on Saturday, it won't make sense on Sunday to regret standing in line on the grounds that the bank was open, without having checked in the meantime about whether it was in fact open.

So I want to allow that at least *some* bank and train cases may in fact be genuine examples of pragmatic encroachment in epistemology. But if Pragmatic Intellectualism is true, we should not expect them to be the *best* examples. And indeed, I suggest, they are not. The most intuitively forceful examples of pragmatic encroachment in epistemology, I contend, are examples of *stable high stakes*— cases in which the predictable costs of error pertain not simply to a current decision, but also to a pattern of possible decisions or the role of belief extended over time into the indefinite future. And the *least* intuitively forceful examples of pragmatic encroachment are the cases in which the stakes are most transparently unstable.

Take, for example, the case in which I am offered a credible bet of a penny against my life on the proposition that my name is 'Mark'. I am as confident as I can be in anything that my name is 'Mark', but I wouldn't wager my life on that proposition merely for the prospect of a penny, and I would be irrational to do so. No matter how confident I might be about my name, the disparity in payouts is still too great. This case, recall, was my leading counterexample to strong knowledge-action principles. It is a case, I claim, in which I know, and hence it is epistemically rational for me to believe, that my name is 'Mark', but not rational to take that proposition for granted in reasoning about what to do. And it is a case in which it is *clearest* that the costs of error are transient—even if you can wrap your head around imagining that I am actually offered a credible such bet, it is not likely that I will soon enter an environment in which bets like these are typical of situations in which it matters what my name is, or that I would be at risk to actually take them. But cases that are leading candidates to be counterexamples to a principle are *ipso facto* the least intuitively forceful examples of that principle.

And on the flip side, the *best* examples in support of pragmatic encroachment in epistemology are cases in which the stakes are stably high and transparently so. My leading example of such a case is the belief that you are not allergic to penicillin. Since allergy to penicillin is typically a persistent state, whether you are allergic to penicillin will be just as important, and with respect to the very same kinds of decisions, at any point in your future, as it is now. And the kinds of situations in which it will matter for your decision whether you are allergic to penicillin are also likely to be dominated by cases in which you must decide whether to accept penicillin or another antibiotic in the penicillin family for medical treatment. That makes it hard to resort to the fallback strategy of believing that you are not allergic but having a habit accepting that you are when seeking medical treatment. So with respect to this proposition, the costs of error are not just high, but stable, and they predominate expected future cases in which this belief may be relevant.

All of these features combine to make it one of the clearer cases of pragmatic encroachment, according to Pragmatic Intellectualism, and I contend that it *is* intuitively forceful. Stewart Cohen (2012), (unpublished), for example, has forcefully emphasized the plausibility that the rational thing to do in typical bank cases is to believe that the bank will be open on Saturday, but to wait and stand in line anyway, just to be safe. It is much less plausible that the thing to do is to believe that you are not allergic to penicillin but to decline it anyway. So, I suggest, the most forceful examples of pragmatic encroachment on knowledge and the rationality of belief are cases involving stable high stakes.

It turns out that the best examples of doxastic wrongs are also all grounded in stable features of situations. When you are friends with someone, you expect that friendship to continue indefinitely into the future. Of course, not all friendships do continue. But in contrast to what we might call merely 'being friendly', they don't come with expiration dates, either. Once you have an idea of when the friendship will expire, it has already begun to expire. The contrast between merely being friendly with someone, which is compatible with foreseeing an expiration, and being their friend, which is not, corresponds, I suggest, to the distinction between cases in which you are not in an elevated position to wrong someone by what you believe about them, and cases in which you are. And since being a friend is not inconsistent with epistemic rationality, I suggest that cases like our *My Cousin Vinny* case are just as forceful support of pragmatic encroachment in epistemology, as they are as examples of what is required by friendship. And I think they are forceful examples indeed of what is required by friendship.

Now, the features that elevate the stakes of racist or sexist beliefs, such as the assumption that John Hope Franklin is staff at the Cosmos club simply because he is black, are not grounded in persistent relationships like friendship, because of course John Hope Franklin and the woman who hands him her coat check are not friends. According to some philosophers, what they owe to one another may nevertheless still be grounded in features of their relationship, but if it is, this relationship is the most stable one of all, because it holds between any two people whatsoever.[12] But whether doxastic wrongs between strangers are just an attenuated case of doxastic wrongs between friends or not, the explanation of why this particular belief wrongs John Hope Franklin is deeply rooted in the historical racial divide in the United States, and in Washington, D.C., in particular, where the Cosmos club is located in the middle of a swanky neighborhood that excluded blacks except in service roles until far too recently and is still dominantly white.

---

[12] Compare Bero (2017).

All of these features of the case are paradigms of stability, because they are rooted in facts about the past, and the past is fixed.

So this shows that Gendler's John Hope Franklin example has the right features to be a leading case of pragmatic encroachment by the lights of Pragmatic Intellectualism. But it is also, I contend, a particularly forceful case for pragmatic encroachment in epistemology, in its own right. The woman who hands Hope Franklin her coat check *is* being epistemically irresponsible to believe that he is staff. And she is being epistemically irresponsible in spite of the fact that in the case, the statistical evidence provided by his race and the background distributional facts about race at the Cosmos Club is just as good as statistical evidence that it is fine to use in other cases.

Similarly, with respect to beliefs by which you can wrong yourself, I considered the case of negative beliefs impinging on your own self-worth. Part of why these wrong you, I suggest, is your relationship with yourself. But since that is permanent, of course it makes a stable contribution to how these beliefs matter. Similarly, though facts about what matters to your self-worth can change over time, as your understanding of yourself changes, they don't change straightforwardly in accordance with our *expectations*. But not only does Virgil wrong himself by jumping to the conclusion that his entire dissertation was based on a mistake, I think it is clearly irrational for him to so easily be led to this conclusion without pressing harder on the data.

And finally, the same goes with respect to cases like Marusic's example of trying to quit smoking. Whether you would succeed if you tried does not only matter at the time at which you are about to try, it also matters for how you should feel about your effort or lack of effort, when you look back at it from the future, and for your prospects for trying again.[13] And Marusic (2015) himself has forcefully argued at length that these are cases in which what it is rational to believe about your own future must be sensitive to non-evidential facts.

In all of these cases, I suggest, not only do we get examples that fit better with the structure of Pragmatic Intellectualism's distinctive account of the nature of pragmatic encroachment in epistemology, we also get cases that are more forceful in their own right in lending support to the idea that what you know or what it is epistemically rational for you to believe may in some cases depend on intuitively 'practical' features. But more: these cases show us, in a way that simple transient bank cases do not, why the thesis of pragmatic encroachment in epistemology is so *important*. For it helps to open up rich and fertile questions about the ethics of belief in the *narrow* sense that would otherwise be invisible. This is something, I think, that is worth getting right and not dismissing out of hand.

---

[13] Compare Schroeder (2019).

PART IV

KNOWLEDGE AND MORAL WORTH

[W]hen the holding of a thing to be true is sufficient both subjectively and objectively, it is *knowledge*.

Immanuel Kant, *Critique of Pure Reason*, A822/B850

10

Acting and Believing Well

10.1 Key Lessons So Far

At the beginning of this book, I set out to support our Core Hypothesis that epistemology has suffered through comparative neglect of the continuity between epistemology and moral philosophy by investigating the thesis of Reasons First. The thesis of Reasons First, we saw, is relatively prominent in moral philosophy—claimed by some, even, to be orthodox—yet it does not have a similar status in epistemology. And we saw that there are good reasons why, for there are at least two prominent objections to Reasons First that are highly visible within epistemology—so visible, even, as to fundamentally shape how epistemologists frame the options available in trying to answer some of their most central questions—yet are not so visible in moral philosophy.

Consequently, in Parts II and III I have endeavored to argue that the way in which these visible problems have shaped epistemology are problematic in their own right. And I have argued that by rejecting those answers, we can get much *better* answers to the central questions in epistemology about how perception can rationalize belief and what role evidence can play in rationalizing belief. Doing so is not only *compatible* with Reasons First, we have seen, but the key virtues of the resulting views—both the apparent factive attitude view about basic perceptual justification and Pragmatic Intellectualism about the relationship between evidence and the rationalization of belief—*rely essentially* on claims about how rationality is grounded in facts about the balance of reasons. This isn't quite an endorsement of Reasons First in its full generality, but it is very much in the spirit of the idea that proponents of Reasons First take to generalize.

One of the key takeaways from Part II was the importance of distinguishing between objective and subjective reasons. Epistemology, I suggested, has been deeply shaped by the assumption that in order to *rationalize* belief, reasons must be *true*. But truth, I argued, is a more appropriate constraint on the kinds of reasons that make beliefs *correct*, than on those that make belief *rational*. If reasons are just act-oriented competitors that can be acted on, nothing guarantees that talk about the reasons 'there are' and the reasons 'you have' are about the same kind of reasons, one of which is out there to be grasped, and one of which is somehow in your possession.

Reasons First. Mark Schroeder, Oxford University Press (2021). © Mark Schroeder.
DOI: 10.1093/oso/9780198868224.003.0010

On the contrary, we saw, since 'has' talk is pleonastic, we can make sense of this talk perfectly well as talk about cross-cutting 'reason' relations, perfectly analogously to how some moral philosophers have long distinguished between what you ought *subjectively* or rationally to do and what you ought *objectively* to do, in the sense of what it is correct for you to do. And once we make this distinction, we don't have to let the *true* things that we want to say about the defeasibility of knowledge force us to say *false* things about the defeasibility of rational belief, which is what I charged epistemological disjunctivists with doing, despite offering us an otherwise deeply attractive picture of the nature of perceptual justification.

So one way of identifying the key payoff of Part II, was that it allowed us to attain the attractive features of familiar disjunctivist views of perceptual justification—at least, what I claimed those virtues are—without their most obvious apparent costs—or at least, what I have taken those costs to be. But another way of identifying the payoff was that it showed us how to separate the goal of providing a *rationalizing* explanation of basic perceptual justification from the goal of giving an account of basic perceptual justification that needs to be in the grasp of the believer herself. The apparent factive attitude view is a kind of dogmatism, but it neither abhors explanations of *why* some basic ways of forming beliefs are rational, nor resorts to purely externalist explanations in terms of reliability. Its explanation is *mediated* by an account of why this way of forming beliefs is supported by the agent's reasons.

So the apparent factive attitude view shows us not just how to avoid some of the pitfalls of other views about basic perceptual justification, but how reasons can play valuable explanatory work, by offering the kind of rationalizing explanation that we can see traditional internalists as hankering for, without committing to the full commitments of misguided traditional internalist conceptions of what it would take, in order to provide such a rationalizing explanation. The vocabulary of reasons gives us a diagnosis, in other words, of what familiar forms of epistemological externalism such as process reliabilism and subjunctive theories are rightly felt by internalists to leave out, without validating internalists' own conception of what is worth striving for.

The key upshot of Part III, in contrast, was that answering the problem of sufficiency does not require understanding what makes reasons *sufficient* by reference to a *prior* notion of rationality, justification, or knowledge. Rather, we can understand *rationality* in terms of a prior account of what makes reasons *sufficient*. For facts about sufficiency are simply facts about the balance of reasons.

This showed us that the hypothesis of *evidence as reasons*, originally motivated in Chapter 1, can have powerful explanatory benefits in helping us to understand many of the most curious features of what it seems rational to believe and when, provided only that we supplement it with an adequate account of what makes something an epistemic reason either for or *against* belief. This lesson is in effect simply a special case of Ross's diagnosis of the surprisingly complex phenomena concerning when you *ought* to do something. Ross observed that despite this apparent complexity, all of these phenomena can be explained as the product of balancing between simple competing factors. Once you understand which factors are in play, you can understand what is going on in complex situations.

So the key lesson from Part III constitutes, in effect, a special case of what we in Chapter 2 called the *classical argument* for Reasons First. The classical argument, recall, was in the first instance an argument that reasons are *locally* fundamental, explanatory of some particular normative property or relation. The argument is that the hypothesis that facts about that property or relation are exhaustively grounded in facts about the balance of reasons offers the best explanation of the observed facts about the behavior of that property or relation. So in Part III, I was in effect offering a *classical argument* that epistemic rationality is grounded in the balance of epistemic reasons for and against belief.

My goal in Part IV is to bring all of these lessons together, in order to argue that the greatest benefits of Reasons First in epistemology concern its power to help us understand what is arguably epistemology's most central problem: the nature of knowledge. We will see that the lessons that we have already covered help us to avoid mistakes in the analysis of knowledge that were entered into by otherwise initially promising views. But more importantly, we will illustrate the Core Hypothesis yet again by seeing how appreciating the continuity between epistemology and moral philosophy leads to a powerful and illuminating perspective on knowledge, and how the case of knowledge lets the hypothesis of Reasons First shine most brightly.

In order to unpack this bold agenda, we'll start at the end, by seeing why everything that we have said so far about reasons and in support of their explanatory role in normative theory quite surprisingly leaves one of the most important and central characteristics of reasons on the table. Then in the rest of this chapter we'll see that this characteristic of reasons is especially well-suited to be important in the analysis of knowledge. In Chapter 11 I'll introduce and defend my preferred analysis of knowledge—which I call the Kantian Account—and see how it is made possible by avoiding the pitfalls in Parts II and III. Finally, in Chapter 12 we'll explore what the Kantian Account says about basic perceptual knowledge when combined with the apparent factive attitude view, what it says about pragmatic encroachment when combined with Pragmatic Intellectualism, and what it has to say about its competitors.

10.2 The Deliberative Role of Reasons

In order to understand why reasons are so closely suited for understanding knowledge, it helps to begin by seeing why everything that we have said about reasons so far leaves one of the most important and central features of reasons on the table. Recall that in Chapter 2 I did not characterize reasons in terms of what is picked out by the word 'reason', either semantically or pragmatically, even holding fixed the right kind of context. Nor did I characterize them ostensively, though I have used examples periodically throughout this book to illustrate. Rather, I characterized reasons in terms of the way that they *compete*, the fact that they are *act-oriented* rather than *outcome-oriented*, and the fact that they can be *acted on*.

Yet despite characterizing reasons in terms of these three chief characteristics, only the first two characteristics of reasons have played any significant role anywhere in our discussion. Take, for example, the classical argument that what we ought to do must be grounded in facts about reasons, which I attributed to Ross in Chapter 2. This argument relies essentially and transparently on the competitive nature of reasons, and as I argued in Chapter 2, in order to successfully rule out pluralist forms of consequentialism, it must also rely on the act-oriented character. But it requires no assumptions about whether reasons can be acted on.

Similarly, in Part II I considered how it could be that perceptual experience makes belief rational, by offering a source of *reasons* for belief. Essentially nowhere either in this question or in my preferred answer to it did we ever need to advert to the claim that reasons can be acted on.[1] And in Part III I considered how evidence makes belief rational. Again, although I could have supplemented my arguments that there are non-evidential epistemic reasons against belief with further circumstantial support by documenting how such considerations can be acted on in a way that is very similar to how we act on reasons, that is not the strategy that I actually employed in Chapter 7.[2] Nowhere in Part III did I actually place weight on the claim that we can act for reasons or require it to do substantial philosophical work either in framing our problems or in my answers to them.

Consequently, if we think of the project of this book so far as a kind of defense of a central explanatory role for reasons in epistemology and moral philosophy, there is a very palpable sense in which it is leaving important argumentative resources on the table, by not appealing to the third and final characteristic of reasons, their *deliberative role*. Indeed, this is quite surprising. For as we saw already in Chapter 2, the idea that normative reasons play a role in deliberation or reasoning, or that when we are reasoning well, the reasons for which we act *are* or

---

[1] The lone exception was in my backup argument against the good case bootstrapper in Section 3.4, which Errol Lord calls the "new new evil demon problem".

[2] Compare my argumentative strategy in Schroeder (2013). Though note that in Section 9.3 I did discuss our ability to respond to non-evidential epistemic reasons against belief in the context of responding to an objection to the idea that beliefs can wrong. Since it is the objector who relies on the claim that reasons can be responded to, however, it the burden of pragmatic intellectualism to accommodate it, not to use it to do any interesting philosophical work.

are closely associated with the normative reasons for us to act, is quite pervasive. Bernard Williams (1981), for example, famously maintains that it is central to the concept of a reason that there must be a *sound deliberative path* from recognizing that reason to acting on it. Similarly, building on but qualifying what Williams says, Christine Korsgaard (1986) equally famously maintains that if there is a reason for you to do something, then insofar as rationality has influence on your actions, you will be motivated to act for this reason.

A whole family of newly popular views now maintains that this deliberative role for reasons is central, and indeed that the nature of reasons can be analyzed in terms of it. For example, according to both Kieran Setiya (2014) and Matty Silverstein (2016), who develop this idea in different ways, this is what reasons *are*—they are premises of sound deliberative inferences.[3] According to Jonathan Way (2017), reasons are premises of good reasoning. And according to Alex Gregory (2016), normative reasons are simply good motivating reasons.

The exact shape of the deliberative role for reasons is highly contested. For example, in *Slaves of the Passions* I argued that there are some normative reasons that *cannot* be good motivating reasons, cannot be premises of good reasoning, cannot motivate you if you are rational, and cannot be the subject of beliefs which trigger good dispositions of practical thought.[4] This is because some reasons are what have come to be called *elusive*, in the sense that finding out about them makes them go away. For example, for someone who loves successful surprise parties thrown in his own honor, but hates unsuccessful surprise parties, the fact that there is a hitherto-unsuspected surprise party waiting for him in the next room is a reason to go into the next room, in the sense that it is an act-oriented competitor that contributes to the advisability of his going into the next room. But it can't be a reason for which he could rationally act, because he couldn't learn about it without making it false. So I am clearly on the record as skeptical about whether the deliberative role for reasons could be used in order to provide an *analysis* of reasons' nature.

Nevertheless, even I have insisted on the importance of this role—for example, in *Slaves of the Passions* I argued that forceful objections can be leveled against many explanatory moral theories on the basis of the deliberative role of reasons.[5] If a normative theory is committed to the claim that X, Y, and Z are reasons for someone to act, but it would be objectionable in some way for her to be thinking about any of X, Y, or Z in deliberating about what to do, then that, I argued, is a significant strike against that theory, because in normal cases, at least, complete

---

[3] This is Setiya's (2014) informal gloss on his account, which he goes on to spell out more precisely in other terms, but the idea of sound inferences forms the backbone of Silverstein's (2016) account. This difference makes it likely that Silverstein's account has better prospects to avoid the objection from *elusive* reasons explained below. See also Asarnow (2016, 2017) and Silverstein (2017).

[4] Schroeder (2007, ch. 2).   [5] Schroeder (2007, ch. 2), contrast Railton (1984).

and non-enthymematic reasoning *should* involve attention to one's reasons.[6] So even I, as sort of an arch critic of making too much of the deliberative role of reasons, am committed to the claim that there is some genuine deliberative role of reasons, and that it is an important one.

If reasons have a deliberative role, and that role is important or central, it would be quite strange if the centrality of reasons in normative theory did not offer any place for that deliberative role. So given that none of the key virtues of appeals to reasons in normative theory so far—either in epistemology or in ethics—have made use of reasons' deliberative role, we should expect that we have still left some of the most distinctive features of reasons on the table. As I'll now try to show in the remainder of this chapter and in Chapter 11, I think that this is correct.

The deliberative role of reasons is important, because it matters not just *what* you do, or what you believe, but also *how* you do or believe it. The contrast between what you do and how you do it is brought out by Aristotle's important distinction between acting *from* virtue and acting *in accordance with* virtue. Someone who acts from virtue and someone who acts in accordance with virtue may do the same thing in the same situation, but acting from virtue is a more demanding condition—it is not just doing as the virtuous person would do, but doing it from the motives of the virtuous person. And this distinction is crucially important for Aristotle. Acting in accordance with virtue is a good thing, to be sure, and it is an essential part of the moral education required in order to acquire virtue. But acting from virtue is even better.

Kant follows Aristotle in making a similar distinction in the opening passages of the *Groundwork* (2002) between acting from duty and merely acting in accordance with duty. Like Aristotle's distinction, for Kant acting from duty is a more demanding condition than merely acting in accordance with duty. Both the person who acts from duty and the person who acts in accordance with duty do the right thing—both do their duty. But only one of them acts well. The contrast is brought out by Kant's famous example of the prudent shopkeeper, who charges the same prices to inexperienced shoppers as to anyone else—therefore doing the right thing—but does so in order not to lose customers. For Kant this distinction is so important that it is literally where moral philosophy starts—understanding what it is to act *from* duty, and not merely in accordance with duty, is the key to identifying the nature of the good will, and hence to understanding why the categorical imperative lies at the basis of morality.

---

[6] This thought is both plausible in its own right, and makes sense of the intuitive pull of 'objectionable reasoning' objections to many different normative theories. For example, Williams (1973b) argues that it is incompatible with integrity, the structure of personal relationships, and having genuine projects to be moved by the kinds of considerations that the utilitarian takes to matter for what to do. And similarly, desire-based or 'Humean' theories of reasons are often accused of making practical reasoning out to be objectionably self-regarding. Likewise, ideal Kantian agents are sometimes accused of being overly concerned with universalizability.

Both Aristotle and Kant, I will say, distinguish between doing the right thing and acting *well*. When you act well, you do the right thing, but you don't *just* do the right thing. Acting well imposes a constraint on your motives. For Kant as for Aristotle, acting well means acting according to a certain kind of motivation. This renders acting well immune to some kinds of luck. Because the motives of the person who acts well are connected to what is the right thing to do in the right sort of way, it is no coincidence that the person who acts well does the right thing. In contrast, the prudent shopkeeper does the right thing only because morality and prudence happen to coincide, in his case.

As we saw in Chapter 2, Aristotle's and Kant's distinctions can rapidly be generalized. We can distinguish between doing what it is rational to do, and acting rationally. For example, if it is rational for someone to buy life insurance and she buys it, but just because the salesperson flirts with her, she does the rational thing to buy the insurance, but does not act rationally. So someone who acts rationally does what it is rational to do, but not only that; she also does it in the right way, and it is no coincidence that what she does is rational. We can therefore identify this as another instance of the same kind of distinction that Aristotle and Kant made.

Stretching the natural meanings of the terms somewhat, we can say that when you do what it is rational to do, you meet a standard of *rightness*, but when you act rationally, you go further, and act *well*. In short, following this stipulation we can say that the distinction between doing what it is rational to do and acting rationally is a *right/well pair*. Since this use of both 'right' and 'well' is stipulative, it is important not to read too much into the intuitive meanings of either of these terms. In particular, strictly speaking we should distinguish between what is rational and what is right, but I am referring to doing what is rational as the 'right' member of this pair.

Similarly, and importantly, someone whose action is praiseworthy but based on a mistake may intuitively count as acting 'well' even though she does not do the 'right' thing, but this way of talking should not lead us to think that this counts as a *right/well* pair in our sense—it does not. Acting in a way that is praiseworthy is the 'well' member of the pair in which it contrasts with doing the thing that it would be praiseworthy to do, and doing the morally right thing is the 'right' member of the pair in which it contrasts with acting with moral worth—which is not just acting in a way that is praiseworthy.

With this terminology on board, we can see that what goes for rational action also goes for rational belief. If it is rational for Bert to believe given his evidence that the Republicans will win the election, and he does so believe, but only because his gut tells him so, Bert believes what it is rational for him to believe, but he does not believe rationally. Like acting rationally, believing rationally imposes a constraint not only on what Bert does, but on how he does it, and when Bert believes the thing that it is rational for him to believe, this is no coincidence. So believing what it is rational to believe and believing rationally are another right/well pair.

And similar points go for other emotions or attitudes, to the extent that they are subject to rational assessment. It may be rational to fear the man chasing you with a knife, but if you fear him because of his clown suit and not because of his knife, then although you fear the thing it is rational for you to fear, you do not fear rationally.

The standard distinction in epistemology between propositional and doxastic justification is also a distinction between believing rightly and believing well. Someone with doxastic justification for their belief also has propositional justification, but she satisfies a stronger condition as well—one that constrains the *grounds* for her belief, or the way that she believes it, and which makes it no coincidence that she believes what she has a propositional justification to believe. And indeed, we can find distinctions between right/well pairs everywhere there are norms. We can distinguish between complying with the law and following the law, between complying with the rules of games and following the rules of those games, and between making the right (as in winning) move in a game and playing the game well. In every case it is more significant—a higher achievement—to act, believe, or feel well, and not merely to do, believe, or feel the right thing.

Knowledge has much in common with each of these other properties of acting, believing, or feeling well. Knowing entails believing the correct thing, but knowledge is not mere correct belief; it is a stronger condition that imposes a constraint on *how* or *why* you believe. And famously, this constraint rules out many forms of believing the right thing merely by luck or coincidence. So far, this isn't enough to prove that knowledge should be understood in parallel with all of the other concepts of acting, believing, or feeling well—the similarities could be superficial—or other properties of acting, believing, or feeling well could inherit some of their distinctive properties from those of knowledge. But the parallels are striking enough that we should think about them together, if we are going to think seriously about the nature and role of knowledge.

10.3 Artificial Norms and Well First

In Section 10.2 we saw that the deliberative role of reasons—the fact that reasons can be *acted on*—is both important and played little positive role—other than as an earmark—in the main virtues of Reasons First that we encountered in Parts II and III of this book. And we recalled from Chapter 2 and expanded on the diverse range of contrasting concepts of doing, believing, or feeling the right thing, and acting, believing, or feeling *well*. The deliberative role of reasons comes into its own in helping us to understand the nature and significance of the various concepts of acting, believing, or feeling *well*. Each of the *well* properties imposes a constraint not only on what you do, believe, or feel, but on the reasons *for which* you do, believe, or feel it.

So now we're in a position to see where we are going: once we take this seriously, we will see why every normative standard that is determined by the balance of reasons admits of a corresponding standard of not just meeting this standard, but of doing *well* by it. Since normative standards so generally do seem to be accompanied by corresponding standards of doing well by them, this will in turn give us an argument by inference to the best explanation that normative standards generally must be determined by the balance of reasons. I call this the *fundamental argument* for the priority of reasons, since in contrast to the classical argument, which we have seen in action in Chapters 2 through 9, the fundamental argument draws on each of the central distinctive features of reasons.

The simplest way to think about the fundamental argument for Reasons First is in terms of the kind of explanation that we should expect of why we see so many *right/well* pairs. It could be that this is because *right* properties are prior to and explanatory of their corresponding *well* properties—for example because to act well is just to do the right thing *and* satisfy some further condition. Or it could be that it is because *well* properties are prior to and explanatory of their corresponding *right* properties—for example because to do the right thing is just to do what would be done by someone who was acting *well*. But in this and in Section 10.4 I am going to argue against both of these possibilities, and in favor of the claim that the relationship between *right* and *well* properties of all stripes follows from the way that both are explained in terms of reasons. I'll begin, in this section, by taking on the view that *well* comes first.

We'll need to start by setting aside a familiar but bad argument that *well* properties cannot come first. Since in each case of a pair of contrasting right/ well properties, acting well entails doing the right thing, there is a tempting but over-hasty argument that acting well *must* consist in doing the right thing plus some further condition. This over-hasty argument has the same form as *common factor* arguments in many other places in philosophy. The most familiar common factor argument is that since there is something in common between veridical

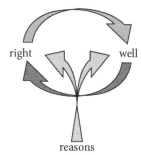

Figure 10.1 Well first

perceptual experience and hallucination or illusion, veridical experience must consist in what is going on in hallucination or illusion together with some further condition. Another familiar example in epistemology is the common factor argument that since knowing entails believing, knowing must consist in believing plus some further condition on belief.[7] In the philosophy of law, many legal positivists argue that since unjust laws are still laws, the concept of law must be prior to and independent of the concept of just laws, and being a just law must consist in being a law plus some further condition. And in political philosophy, a similar argument contends that since having legitimate authority entails having authority, but not all authority is legitimate, legitimate authority must consist in authority plus a further condition—legitimacy—and hence that the correct analysis of authority in general must not give any special pride of place to legitimate authority.[8]

But philosophers of perception have led the way in noting that each of these arguments falls substantially short of deductive validity. Although one candidate explanation of the fact (if it is a fact) that veridical and non-veridical perceptual experiences have something in common may be that having a veridical experience consists in this common factor plus a further condition, a competing explanation is that what they have in common is something that is itself analyzed in terms of veridical perception. For example, I suggested in Chapter 5, as one possible way of elaborating on and defending the apparent factive attitude view, that both veridical and non-veridical perceptual experiences represent themselves *as* veridical perceptual experiences.[9] Similarly, although one candidate explanation of why knowledge entails belief is that knowledge is belief plus a further condition, a competing explanation is that to believe is to be in a state that is subjectively indiscriminable from knowing.[10] And similar moves are possible in legal philosophy, political philosophy, the philosophy of action, and many other places where common factor arguments might be offered.

So we should not be swayed by common factor arguments—they are the kinds of arguments that look good only to someone who already believes their conclusions. Some philosophers, once they appreciate the fallacy lying behind common factor arguments, have become correspondingly quite critical of the kinds of views that *could* be motivated by common factor arguments.[11] But we should be cautious not to do so. The fact that common factor arguments are fallacious tells us nothing about which strategy of explaining the entailments in each of these cases is more promising—the one that prioritizes the wider property, or the

---

[7] Contrast Williamson (2000). [8] Compare the discussion in Crabill (2015).

[9] Disjunctivist views, on which strictly speaking the only thing the good and bad cases have in common is that they satisfy a disjunction, are also possible in each case.

[10] Williamson (2000). [11] Compare Lord (2018, ch. 7).

one that prioritizes the narrower one. We need to consider each of them in their own right, and to look for better arguments on each side.

With respect to the case of pairs of contrasting right/well properties, both priority views are possible, and deserve taking seriously. Indeed, we can plausibly find instances of each priority view throughout both moral philosophy and epistemology. As we've seen, Kant's famous example of the prudent shopkeeper illustrates the difference between acting in accordance with duty and acting from duty, and Kant held that the example shows that the only thing that is good without qualification is the good will. This led him to endorse the view that what morality primarily concerns are the *maxims* for which you act, and only second-arily what you actually do on the basis of those maxims. This seems to be a view on which acting well is primary, and acting rightly is just its shadow—what we get when we ask which actions *could* be done well. Similarly, we saw that Aristotle famously distinguished between acting in accordance with virtue and acting from virtue. On the views of some prominent virtue ethicists such as Rosalind Hursthouse (1999), therefore, doing the right thing is a sort of *shadow* of acting well—a matter of doing what someone who acts well *would* do, in that situation.[12]

Similarly, in epistemology, although the more common way of understanding the relationship between propositional and doxastic justification is to hold that doxastic justification consists in propositional justification plus some further condition, John Turri (2010b) argues that doxastic justification is prior, and entails propositional justification because propositional justification is its shadow—roughly a state of what one is in a position to be doxastically justified in believing. Similarly, although the historically conventional view is that knowing is believing the right thing plus some further condition, many philosophers have recently defended the view that the value of believing the right thing is just a shadow or consequence of the value of knowing. On such views, it turns out that knowledge, although it is certainly a normatively *important* property, need not be itself a normative property at all. This is because we don't need to incorporate any norm *into* knowledge, so long as the fundamental norm *concerns* knowledge and *valorizes* knowledge. So as long as this holds, we will get the norms on what is the right thing to believe in the same way that Kant and Aristotle seem to hold—as shadows of what it is to believe well.[13]

But each of these views is wrong. Right properties cannot in general be shadows of well properties, because they are more fundamental. The best way to see this is

---

[12] I don't want to commit to an interpretive claim about either Kant or Aristotle, here, just to the naive plausibility of seeing this thought in their work.

[13] Similarly, this is how Neil Mehta (2016), for example, thinks of non-truth-entailing norms governing belief. For Mehta, they are not reflections of the norm of *knowledge*, but of the norm of *knowability*. But he does claim that knowability is the central norm governing belief, and that other norms are derivative from it.

to focus, not on controversial cases of epistemic norms governing belief, or moral norms governing action, but on artificial norms, as in games, since these are the clearest case. Chess, for example, is a game constituted by a set of rules for the movement of pieces, and the victory condition that the opponent's king be captured. Given the victory condition and the movement rules for the pieces, however, it follows that some moves are better than others. Indeed, in many positions, particularly in the endgame, there is a unique best move. If you break the rules of chess, you are not really playing chess, but if you fail to make the best move, you are still playing chess—you are just more likely to lose, depending on the strength of your opponent, because you are not making the right move. But it is not enough to play well, that you make the right move. If you make the right move because of an error in calculation, or through a combination of blunders, although you make the right move you are not playing well. Playing well is an achievement that goes over and above making the right move.

It would be absurd to conclude on this basis that there is some fundamental norm governing chess that says to play well. And it would be even more absurd to say that the norms which tell us which move is the right one are just a shadow of which move would be made by someone who is playing well.[14] On the contrary, we *know* where the norms which tell us which move is right come from—they are a straightforward (though in many cases, quite laborious) calculation from the tree of possible moves, given the underlying rules of the game. So the norms on right moves *can't* come from some prior norms on playing well.

We know this, because we know how chess endgame theory works.[15] It does not begin with a set of standards on playing chess well, but rather from axioms about the admissible moves for each piece and the victory conditions for the game. But we can also demonstrate it in independent ways. Although the rules of chess are fixed, we can consider how modified versions of the game would affect the right move to make in each situation. We modify the game by changing either the victory conditions or the rules of play.[16] *That* changes the strategy of the game, and thereby changes the right move to make in each situation. And so it changes what it takes to play the game well. But one thing that we definitely do not do, is to directly change our standards on what counts as playing well. Of course, we do not often create alternative versions of the game of chess. But many card games do involve easy variants, changing rules about trump suits, bidding practices, partners, order of suits or order of cards, or many other features of game play or of

---

[14] Similarly, it would be absurd to conclude, following Mehta (2016), that the fundamental norm governing chess playing is to make the move that could be an instance of playing well. On the contrary, it is only because there is an independent ideal of *getting in a stronger position to win* that some moves even count as playing well.

[15] Compare Silman (2007) for an instructive introduction.

[16] Or the layout of the board or the number of players, as in the jacket illustration for this book.

victory conditions that are easy to toggle. Indeed, adapting to variations like these is one of the pleasures of many forms of card playing.

It is true, of course, and not inconsistent with what I am saying here, that sometimes we modify the rules of a game with the *goal* of changing what it takes to play the game well. For example, we might shorten the clock in a chess game in order to encourage riskier play. Or we might add new ways for pawns to capture in order to create a more open style of play. But the fact that we can sometimes anticipate how changes in the rules will affect what it will take to play well does not change the fact that we effect those changes in the standards of playing well *by* changing the rules. Our goal may be to change the standards of playing well, but that change is itself still grounded in our change in the rules of play. Similarly, an engineer may choose to make a phone out of metal rather than glass *in order* to make it less fragile, but what makes the phone unfragile is still its material constitution, rather than conversely.

The case of chess, I claim, proves that it is a mistake of insufficient generality to think that we can get norms of right action from norms of acting well. On the contrary, because we know where the norms on moves in chess come from, we *know* that they are not a mere shadow of norms on how to play chess *well*. On the contrary, as soon as we generate a standard on better and worse moves, we *get* a standard on the extent to which someone is playing well. The standards on playing well come *from* the standards on whichever move is the right one to make. If we invent a new game with new rules and new victory conditions, we *get automatically* an achievement of playing that game well; and what counts as playing the game well comes from the features that advance victory—an independent standard of right moves—rather than conversely.[17]

To the extent that we find it plausible that things go the other way around, therefore, as suggested by Kant and by Hursthouse's take on virtue ethics, or by Turri's account of propositional justification, that can only be because we have given ourselves a restricted diet of examples. And that is in turn further evidence for this book's *Core Hypothesis*—that it matters for us to consider the problems of epistemology in *continuity* with other normative subject matters.

10.4 The Well Principle and Right First

So far, I have argued against views that attempt to analyze right properties in terms of their corresponding well properties, by arguing against a special case of

[17] This gives us the sort of view of acting well that is defended by Hills (2009), Markovits (2010), and Arpaly and Schroeder (2014), on which acting well requires acting in a way that stands in the right relationship to the *reasons* that support acting in that way.

such analyzes—the case for artificial games. Symmetry, I suggested, should lead us to expect that if this order of explanation is not right for the cases of contrasting right/well properties that we can find in the case of artificial norms as in games, then it is not right for other cases, either. But considerations of symmetry are not the only reason to think that what goes for chess must also go for acting well and for believing well.

The fact that we *get* standards for playing chess well as a *consequence* of the standards for which moves are best—and that there are similar consequences in the cases of every other artificial set of norms—tells us that there must be some *generative principle* that generates whatever else is good about playing chess well on the basis of the norms of which moves are right. Let us call this principle the *Well Principle*.

Well Principle   Wherever there is a primary norm, there is a secondary standard of performing *well* which entails complying with the underlying primary norm, but also imposes constraints on motive and rules out complying merely by coincidence or by luck.

Even if moral and epistemic norms have a different order of explanation between doing the right thing and acting well than artificial norms, we can still apply the Well Principle to them. If there are primary norms of acting from virtue or duty, of believing with doxastic justification, or of knowing, then we should expect there to be corresponding achievements of not just *complying* with these norms, but doing *well* by them.

But this is not what we observe. Take, for example, the case of Kant's notion of acting from duty.[18] Someone who acts from duty achieves a higher normative standard than someone who merely acts in accordance with duty. But if acting from duty is the primary norm, then the Well Principle will generate a corresponding norm of not just acting from duty, but acting from duty *well*. If there were such a thing as acting from duty well, it would entail acting from duty, as playing well entails making the right move, but it would be possible to act from duty without acting from duty well, and someone who acted from duty without acting from duty well would act from duty for the wrong motive, or as the mere result of a coincidence or of luck. This does not make sense. And the problem is not just a grammatical one. There is no such thing as acting from duty well for us to have grammar to talk about—there is only acting from duty. Acting from duty *is* doing the right thing well.

Similarly, if the standard of doxastic justification were the primary norm, then the Well Principle would generate a standard of being doxastically justified *well*. If

---

[18] Compare Stratton-Lake (2000).

there were such a thing, then it would entail being doxastically justified, but it would be possible to be doxastically justified without being doxastically justified well, and someone in that state would be doxastically justified in the wrong way or for the wrong reasons, or as the result of a coincidence or luck. This again does not make sense. There is no such thing as being doxastically justified well—there is only being doxastically justified. Being doxastically justified *is* being propositionally justified well.

Let me summarize the argument so far. The case of artificial norms gives us not only evidence by parity that all well properties are grounded in their corresponding right properties, but also evidence that there is a generative principle—the Well Principle—that generates a corresponding standard of acting (believing, feeling) well, for any underlying standard of doing (believing, feeling) the right thing. There must be such a generative principle, because there is no extra work to do, to generate new standards of acting well, corresponding to artificial norms. We only need to create the underlying norms. But so long as the Well Principle is sufficiently general, that tells us how things have to go with non-artificial norms, as well. The only way to resist this argument is to hold that somehow the Well Principle is restricted to artificial norms, and by coincidence a quite different explanatory structure merely happens to yield very similar-looking phenomena for non-artificial norms. But there is no good reason to think that this is the case. So by casting a sufficiently general eye we gain the leverage of perspective to see what is wrong with what would otherwise be a very powerful idea—another example confirming the Core Hypothesis of this book.

The foregoing argument relies on the existence of the Well Principle. But the Well Principle suggests that the order of explanation between *right* and *well* properties goes in the other direction—from *right* to *well*. We can get a sense for at least some of the range of how philosophers might try to explain *well* properties in terms of *right* properties by turning to a recent expanding literature in moral philosophy, concerning the nature of what has come to be known as *moral worth*. The project of giving an account of the nature of *moral worth*—the distinctive kind of acting well that corresponds to doing the thing that is morally

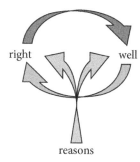

Figure 10.2 Right first

right, usually characterized by reference to Kant's remarks about acting from duty—has received a great deal of attention in recent moral philosophy. What most of this recent literature has in common, is that it presupposes that moral worth is to be accounted for *in terms of* rightness, rather than conversely. So, all sides in this debate are really, in our terms, attempting to characterize a special case of the Well Principle.

Some accounts of moral worth try to explain it in terms that are ecumenical, in the sense that they impose no constraints on the nature of moral rightness. Chief among these is the treatment of Paulina Sliwa (2016). According to Sliwa, acting with moral worth is doing what you know to be right out of a desire to do the right thing. Sliwa's account has many prominent virtues. Since knowledge is factive, it explains why acting with moral worth entails doing the right thing. Since it requires acting on the desire to do the right thing, it constrains the motives of someone who acts with moral worth, as we expect of all well properties. And since knowledge is immune to various important kinds of coincidence or luck, Sliwa's account explains why moral worth is immune to corresponding kinds of coincidence or luck. This offers her account—and those attracted to it—a way of treating knowledge and moral worth as *not* being strictly analogous, while still offering an explanation of why they are similar in some ways—moral worth simply inherits its luck-free properties from those of knowledge.

Importantly for us, Sliwa's account is also perfectly ecumenical, in that it can be plugged into absolutely any commitments about the nature or extent of moral rightness. And it offers us an account of why the Well Principle comes for free: for any normative standard, we can trivially construct the property of knowing what meets that standard and acting out of a desire to meet that standard. For example, it is easy to see how it would apply to new variants on chess and other artificial games—someone who plays well is someone who knows the right (winning) move to make, and makes it with goal in mind. On Sliwa's picture, the Well Principle, so far from being mysterious or having a strange source, consists in nothing other than the fact that we can act with any goal.

A number of objections have been leveled against accounts of moral worth like Sliwa's. The most prominent is that it makes moral motivation out to be what Michael Smith (1994) calls 'objectionably fetishistic'—focused on the goal of doing what is right, rather than on the underlying things that make actions right. It has also been objected to be too cognitively demanding,[19] and that applies the wrong kind of anti-luck principle to moral worth.[20] All of these objections have proved to be highly contentious, and I'll take no stand on them, here. My objection to Sliwa's account is that it is insufficiently general to apply to analogous well properties in other domains—even setting the analogy to knowledge aside.

---

[19] Arpaly (2002b).   [20] Howard (2019).

Take, for example, the analogous treatment of the property of acting rationally—the well property that entails doing the thing that it is rational to do. The analogue of Sliwa's account would say that acting rationally is doing the thing that you know it is rational to do out of the desire to do the rational thing. This account, I think, cannot be right. For one thing, we should worry about whether combining it with Sliwa's original account of moral worth rules out acting both rationally and with moral worth at one and the same time. For another, the whole reason that Sliwa thinks that acting with moral worth requires acting on the desire to do what is right is that she thinks that it requires acting on knowledge of what is right, and that the desire to do what is right is what you need, together with knowledge of what is right, in order to act rationally.

Similarly, the analogue of Sliwa's account for fearing appropriately would be that you fear appropriately just in case your fear is motivated by knowledge of what it is appropriate to fear and the desire to fear what it is appropriate to fear. Again, I think, this is a bizarre thing to think. It vastly overgeneralizes fear and requires that it be sensitive to beliefs about appropriateness, rather than just to perceptions and beliefs about things like danger. And the analogue of Sliwa's account for doxastic justification would be that you are doxastically justified when you believe what you know to be propositionally justified out of a desire to have propositionally justified beliefs. The objections to this principle can write themselves.

Sliwa's is not the only account of moral worth that is ecumenical with respect to the underlying structure of the norms to which it applies. Zoë Johnson King (2020), for example, argues that moral worth consists in doing something *in order* to do what is right—roughly speaking, keeping something like the desiderative component of Sliwa's account without committing to its doxastic component. Johnson King's account has many similar virtues to Sliwa's, but it also fails to generalize in similar ways. This doesn't show that Johnson King's account *cannot* be the correct account of moral worth, any more than the preceding remarks show that Sliwa cannot be right about moral worth. But just as this book's Core Hypothesis suggests that we can get into problems in epistemology by not thinking of it in parallel with ethics, similarly it is only to be expected, I think, that we will get into problems in considering the right account to give of moral worth if we do not consider them in parallel with other similar problems about other *well* properties—some of the paradigms of which come from epistemology.

The space of possible ecumenical accounts of moral worth in terms of moral rightness is potentially large, and I have no proof that any such account must fail to generalize as we saw with the cases of Sliwa's account. But we can give a more direct argument that we should expect the correct explanation of the Well Principle not to be ecumenical about the nature of rightness.[21] And that is that

---

[21] I gave a different and more involved argument for this same conclusion in Schroeder (forthcoming).

the Well Principle should not turn out to be recursive. Although there are such things as making the right move and as playing well, there is no such thing as playing well, well, or as playing well, well, well. And this is not simply because adverbs do not stack in English so this is ungrammatical—it is because there is no interesting further and more demanding standard that it would be helpful to have grammatical language to discuss.

Similarly, although there are such things as doing the right thing and acting with moral worth, there is no such thing as acting with moral worth well, or as acting with moral worth well, well. Although there are such things as fearing what it is rational to fear and fearing rationally, there is no such thing as fearing rationally well, or as fearing rationally well, well. And although there are such things as propositional and doxastic justification, there is no such thing as being doxastically justified well, or as being doxastically justified well, well. But because ecumenical accounts of the Well Principle impose no constraints on the nature of the underlying norm, they can't discriminate between whether they are being applied to a standard of making the right move, or a standard of playing well.[22]

10.5 The Fundamental Argument and Reasons First

In contrast, the other most prominent class of contemporary views about the nature of moral worth is not ecumenical. These accounts are what have come to be known as *right reasons* accounts.[23] According to right reasons accounts, very roughly speaking, you act with moral worth when you do the right thing *for the reasons that make it right*. Right reasons accounts explain why acting with moral worth entails doing the right thing. They explain why acting with moral worth constrains your motive, because they impose a condition on the reasons for which

---

[22] A possible response. Perhaps the proponent of Sliwa's account could argue that the reason the principle is recursive is that it is not possible to simultaneously satisfy Sliwa's cognitive condition of *knowing* that something would be (for example) a case of acting from duty, and also satisfy her conative condition, of doing that act out of a de dicto desire to act from duty. The naive thought behind this argument is that because knowledge is factive, in order to satisfy both conditions, someone would have to act from two motives: the desire to do what is *in accordance* with duty, and the duty to act *from* duty. So if it is impossible to act from both motives in the way required by Sliwa's theory, then we can get an explanation of why Sliwa's condition does not apply recursively. But unfortunately, this thought only poses us a dilemma. For in order for this explanation to go through, we have to interpret Sliwa's conative condition *exclusively*, so that someone cannot count as satisfying it for two desires at the same time. But this makes it impossible for someone to count as acting rationally and with moral worth at the same time, if we take her account to be a general treatment of the well principle. So I conclude that this response fails.

[23] Arpaly (2002a), Hills (2009), and Markovits (2010, 2012) are some of the most prominent recent statements of such views.

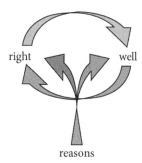

Figure 10.3 Reasons first

you act. They explain the lack of coincidence and luck in your doing the right thing in terms of your motive.[24]

But they are not ecumenical, because they only generate a standard of acting well corresponding to norms that are themselves determined by the balance of reasons. Only for standards that are themselves determined by the balance of reasons do right reasons accounts apply. Wherever we have such a standard, the Well Principle is a simple corollary of the fact that reasons can be acted on, and so the condition of doing something for the reasons that make it right is well-defined. But since the condition of doing something for the reasons that make it right is not itself a condition determined by the balance of reasons, the Well Principle is not recursive.

And this, finally, gives us the alternative, more powerful, argument for the normative priority of reasons that we have anticipated throughout this chapter. The deliberative role of reasons—that they can be acted on—grounds and explains the Well Principle—the fact that wherever there is a norm determined by the balance of reasons, there will be a corresponding standard of not just complying with that norm, but of doing well by it. And so the fact that we see corresponding standards of acting, believing, or feeling well throughout normative theory gives us an argument by inference to the best explanation that the underlying norms are all explained by the balance of reasons. I call this the *fundamental argument* for the priority of reasons.[25]

As we've observed, most of this book has been motivated by attention to the classical argument for the priority of reasons. But the fundamental argument is more powerful. It has more leverage to distinguish reasons from other things that could do similar work. And it can also help us to see that some norms are in fact determined by the balance of reasons, even in cases where those norms are so simple that we could otherwise account for them without appealing to reasons.

---

[24] It should be noted that right reasons accounts support and explain different kinds of anti-luck principles than, for example, Sliwa's account. Howard (2019) argues that Sliwa's account supports the wrong kind of anti-luck principles.

[25] See also Schroeder (forthcoming).

For example, simple games like chess are governed by absolute rules of play, and so we don't seem to need to appeal to reasons in order to make sense of what makes something a permissible move in chess. But we can make sense of someone who plays chess well in the minimal sense not that they are a good player or make the winning move, but merely in the sense that they follow the rules, and don't merely comply with them.

Similarly, it is common to think that with respect to belief, the correct thing to believe is just the truth. Since the truth is not determined by the balance of reasons, it seems that reasons are not needed in order to explain the norm of correctness governing belief. But if knowledge is believing well, and entails believing the correct thing, the explanation that I have advanced in this section tells us that even correctness of belief must itself be determined by the balance of reasons—albeit in a predictable enough way that only truths will turn out to be correct.

It is no coincidence that I have turned to moral worth and the many other closely analogous properties of acting, believing, or feeling well, in the course of trying to illustrate reasons' greatest virtues in epistemology. As I have already hinted, knowledge at least superficially has much in common with each of the other well properties. Knowledge entails believing the right thing, but it imposes a constraint on how or why you believe it. When you know you do not believe the right thing merely by coincidence or as a matter of luck.

Sliwa's account, I noted, can be thought of as an attempt to treat knowledge not as strictly analogous to moral worth (and by extension, to other well properties), but to take seriously the parallel features of knowledge and moral worth by reducing the properties of moral worth—in particular, immunity from luck—to those of knowledge. But as we saw, Sliwa's account doesn't generalize well to other well properties like acting rationally, fearing rationally, or doxastic justification. This point cannot be overemphasized. I am suggesting that knowledge is strictly analogous to the full range of *well* properties. Any account on which it is not, must confront the many similarities between knowledge and other *well* properties. Sliwa's account has the right structure, at least, to do this for the special case of knowledge and moral worth (though we can quibble about whether it gets exactly the right kind of immunity to luck). But since Sliwa's account does not generalize, we need something else that does, in order to resist a closer analogy between knowledge and other *well* properties. So my argument against Sliwa is, *ipso facto*, an argument that knowledge *is* analogous to moral worth.

But we can add to the case that knowledge is directly analogous to other well properties—and not something from which they can derive their features. In Section 10.4, I argued against the idea that non-artificial norms exhibit a different relationship between doing the right thing and acting well than artificial games, by showing that such a view would lead the Well Principle to over-generate. The same points can be made about knowledge. It is true that knowing is meeting a high standard. But if there were a norm that says to know then the Well Principle would generate a standard of knowing *well*.

If there were such a thing, then it would entail knowing, but it would be possible to know without knowing well, and someone in that state would know in the wrong way or for the wrong reasons, or as the result of coincidence or luck. As in the other cases, I believe that this does not make sense. Knowledge is already the state that imposes constraints on the reasons for which you believe and rules out coincidence or luck. So there is no state that stands to knowledge in the way that playing well stands to making the right move. There is no such thing as knowing well—there is only knowing. By parity of reasoning, this suggests that knowing *is* believing well.[26]

The idea that knowing is believing well can be taken in different directions. Ernest Sosa has long advocated the view that knowing is, in my sense, believing well—which he calls 'apt belief'. This, according to Sosa, is animal knowledge—the kind of knowledge that animals as well as reflective creatures like us can have, though we can also have more sophisticated kinds of knowledge. And I am merely following in Sosa's footsteps to take seriously the strict parallels among the full range of *well* properties.

But Sosa has a very different way of thinking about aptness than mine—and one of the consequences of my arguments so far is that it is far too ecumenical. Whatever you can do, on Sosa's account, you can do aptly—so long as you can be competent ('adroit') at doing it, and it can manifest your competence. Indeed, Sosa or his defenders are likely to object that I am mistaken to say in the preceding argument that there is no such thing as knowing well, because as Sosa argues in *Knowing Full Well*, in addition to believing aptly (having animal knowledge), you can have beliefs that are meta-apt—manifesting your competence at taking appropriate risks in believing correctly. If your belief is apt in both of these ways, then it is *reflective knowledge*.

Of course, reflective knowledge is *not* apt apt belief. It is simply belief that manifests two kinds of competence—competence at arriving at the truth, and competence at taking appropriate risks in arriving at the truth. So it does not exhibit a recursively applied well property; it merely exhibits two different *well* properties. But Sosa (2011) also defends an even more demanding standard for human knowledge to meet—which he illuminatingly dubs *knowing full well*. When you know full well, you don't just believe aptly and take appropriate risks

---

[26] Compare Greco's (2003, 2010) claim that knowledge is a kind of *achievement*—true belief for which the agent gets *credit*. I do think that 'achievement' is a natural word for what knowledge, acting with moral worth (in Kant's terms) or out of virtue (in Aristotle's terms), believing justifiedly, and playing well in chess all have in common (compare Lord [2018]). But so understood, achievement is a narrower notion that that discussed by Keller (2004b, 2009), Bradford (2013, 2015), and von Kriegstein (2014). However, see Lackey (2007) for reasons for thinking that 'credit' may not be exactly the right way to think about this.

in your belief aptly—the aptness of your belief *manifests* your aptness at taking appropriate risks in what to believe.

Knowing full well is a closer candidate to count as believing well, well, because it has the same structure as Sosa takes to apply to all cases of aptness—there is something that you do that manifests something else. The something that you do in this case is believing aptly—animal knowledge. So in order for believing full well to be identical to knowing aptly, we only have to assume that aptly taking appropriate risks in arriving at the truth *is* competence at believing aptly. But I don't see how this is true, even for Sosa. In general for Sosa, competences are traits or abilities, but on his definition of knowing full well, the thing that has to be manifested is what he dubs *meta-aptness*—the aptness of a particular case of taking appropriate risks with respect to arriving at the truth.

I also think that Sosa's account of aptness can be challenged on grounds of over-generality, even setting knowledge aside. If it is a general account of the class of what I have called *well* properties, then it should turn out that acting with moral worth is aptly doing the right thing and acting rationally is aptly doing the rational thing. And then there could be—at least in principle—a state of aptly aptly doing the right thing—a state that you would be in if you have a competence to do the right thing aptly and manifest that competence by doing the right thing aptly. And similarly for acting rationally aptly. But I am skeptical that either of these things makes sense. Perhaps with a thick enough notion of a competence my skepticism might be explained away on the grounds that few if any humans have such a competence, but again I worry that Sosa's notion of competence is too thin for this—and needs to be so thin, in order to cover other cases.

So knowledge, I conclude, *is* the analogue to playing chess well, not the analogue to making the right move. If you are playing chess and you accept a financial offer to move your knight to d6, then you are not playing well, even if that is the right move in your position. Similarly, if you believe that your friend is innocent because you would feel bad not to, then you do not know, even if that is the truth. If you are playing chess and you move your knight to d6 on the basis of a miscalculation about the future state of the board this will lead to, you do not play well, even if it is in fact the right move in your position. Similarly, if you believe that someone in the office owns a Ford on the basis of your assumption that Nogot owns a Ford,[27] you do not know, even though you believe the truth. And if you are playing chess and, relying on your experience in similar situations, move your knight to d6 because it feels right, you do not play well if it would also feel right to you in closely similar board situations in which the same move would be a mistake, for it is only luck that led you to make the right move. Similarly, if you believe that what you see is a barn, but it is in fact the only barn in fake barn

---

[27] Lehrer (1965).

country, then you do not know that it is a barn. Knowledge is the analogue of playing chess well.

In this chapter I have argued that reasons' greatest explanatory power will arise in cases where we can appeal to all three of their features—including their deliberative role. The deliberative role of reasons is most important, I have argued, with respect to the normative properties that I have called *well* properties—each of which involves acting, believing, or feeling *well* in some respect, corresponding to an underlying norm of rightness which is satisfied, but not just satisfied, by someone who is acting, believing, or feeling well in that respect. And I have argued that knowledge is among this family of well properties. Adequate views of both knowledge *and* moral worth will need to respect this. In Chapter 11 my goal will be to make good on that claim by making the right reasons account of the Well Principle more precise, showing us what kind of account of knowledge this yields, and illustrating some of its core attractions.

11

The Kantian Account of Knowledge

11.1 Right Reasons

In Chapter 10 I argued that there are many examples of *right*/*well* pairs of normative properties from many different areas of normative inquiry, and that each of these pairs has much in common. I offered two different arguments against the idea that the right properties can be analyzed in terms of their corresponding *well* properties, both of which drew on considering the consequences of artificial norms, including games. And I argued against indiscriminate ways of trying to analyze the well properties in terms of their corresponding right properties—both in detail, and on the general grounds that the *right*/*well* relationship is not recursive.

This led us to the conclusion that there has to be something special about *right* properties which make them eligible to have a corresponding *well* property. That special thing, I suggested, is being determined by the balance of reasons. And there is a whole class of familiar attempts to theorize about both moral worth and about knowledge that explain why a property that is determined by the balance of reasons will always have a corresponding well property—*right reasons* accounts.

The way that right reasons accounts do so is simple. They apply to properties that consist in the balance of reasons of two kinds—for example, the moral reasons for and against doing something. They say, very roughly, that when the reasons *for which* you do that thing match the reasons *for* you to do it in the right way, then you count as having the corresponding well property. Let's break this down.

When right reasons accounts of moral worth are discussed in the literature, it is not always acknowledged that they constrain our account of moral rightness in the way that I have argued that they must. And indeed, it is not *obvious* that they do. This is because we need to distinguish between two very different pictures of the relationship between reasons and rightness. On the reasons-first view, moral rightness consists in the balance of reasons. So on this view, not only are facts about moral rightness explained by reasons, they are explained by *facts about* reasons, and the *reason* relation itself is analytically prior to moral rightness. But on a competing view, facts about what is morally right are themselves explained by reasons, but they are grounded in the facts that *are* reasons, not in the facts *that* they are reasons. On this view, moral rightness turns out to be analytically prior to *reasons*—reasons are just the facts, whichever those facts are, that explain why some action is morally right. I call this latter view the *cleanup* package, both

Reasons First. Mark Schroeder, Oxford University Press (2021). © Mark Schroeder.
DOI: 10.1093/oso/9780198868224.003.0011

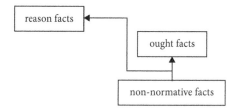

Figure 11.1 Cleanup Package

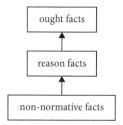

Figure 11.2 Reasons First Package

because it is thought by some to clean up the messiness of reasons and because its most prominent proponent is John Broome.[1]

In Chapter 10 I gave an argument that tells against the cleanup package. The promise of right reasons accounts lies in the fact that unlike Sliwa's knowledge-based account, they are too limited to apply recursively, and so they do not predict that there should be such a thing as acting well well, or acting well well well, or the like.[2] Since we do not observe interesting such properties, this is a virtue. But on the cleanup package, whenever something satisfies a normative standard, there will be things that explain why it does. And so if we combine right reasons views with the cleanup package, right reasons accounts will apply recursively. In contrast, on the reasons first-friendly interpretation of right reasons views, they apply only to normative standards that are themselves determined by the balance of reasons. That is why the fundamental argument supports the analytic priority of the reason relation over other normative properties and relations—and not just the explanatory of reasons.

In Chapter 2 I assumed that normative reasons, in the sense in which we are interested in this book, obey the deliberative property, meaning that they are the kind of thing that can be acted on. As with my other chief criteria for demarcating the concept of a reason in Chapter 2, the deliberative property does not distinguish objective reasons from subjective reasons. The fact that his glass contains

---

[1] Broome (2004, 2013).
[2] I give a different and more complicated but complementary argument against the cleanup package in Schroeder (forthcoming). This argument was hinted at in Chapter 2.

petrol is an objective reason for Bernie not to take a sip—one that he unfortunately does not know about but on which he could act, if he came to know about it. But likewise, Bernie's reasonable belief that his glass contains a gin and tonic gives him a subjective reason to take a sip—one that he unfortunately does act on. What makes Bernie's situation tragic is that acting on the reason that makes his act rational leads him astray from doing what would be correct.

Since both objective and subjective reasons can compete, there are both objective and subjective normative standards. Rationality of action is plausibly a subjective standard. What makes an action the rational thing to do, if it depends on reasons at all, is determined by the balance of *subjective* reasons for and against performing that action. Similarly, what makes a belief the epistemically rational thing to believe is the balance of subjective epistemic reasons for and against that belief, and what makes something the rational thing to fear is determined by the balance of the subjective right-kind reasons for and against fearing that thing.

In contrast, what makes an action the *correct* thing to do is determined by the balance of the *objective* reasons for and against performing that action. What makes a something the correct thing to fear is determined by the balance of the objective right-kind reasons for and against fearing that thing. And if the correctness of belief has anything to do with reasons at all, then by generalizing, we can conclude that what makes a belief the correct thing to believe, correspondingly, would be determined by the balance of the objective epistemic reasons for and against that belief.

In the case of belief, most theorists assume that what makes a belief correct is that its content is true, and so this treatment in terms of the balance of objective reasons is not obvious. But one of the lessons of the Core Hypothesis of this book is that sometimes we get better insight by casting our vision more widely. And the view that correctness of belief is determined by the balance of reasons is not inconsistent with the view that the correctness of belief is determined solely by whether it is true. The former can subsume the latter, if only we assume that the fact that it is false that P is always a better reason against believing that P than any reason in favor of it. This guarantees that it is never correct to believe something false. And if we want to accept, further, that it is always correct to believe what is true,[3] then we can add the assumption that the fact that P is always a better reason to believe that P than any reason against believing that P.

So on the balancing picture, normative standards can consist either in the balance of objective reasons or in the balance of subjective reasons. Right reasons accounts can be applied to either. They say that *whatever* reasons play a role in determining whether some standard obtains, matching the reasons *for which* you do something to the reasons *for* you to do it in the right way will make you count as meeting the corresponding standard of acting *well*.

---

[3] I will not assume this, but it is not inconsistent with anything that I say in this book.

Finally, we must say something about what this matching consists in. On one view—a natural interpretation of Julia Markovits's (2010) slogan that moral worth consists in "doing the right thing for the reasons that make it right", acting well requires that the reasons for which you do something must include *all* of the reasons for you to do it and *not* include anything that is not a reason for you to do it. But this condition is incredibly demanding. It means that no one can get moral worth for doing anything so long as there are redundant reasons to do it that they are unaware of or unmotivated by, and that likewise, no one can get moral worth for doing anything so long as they have any ulterior motive.

We get a more forgiving condition by relaxing this position in two ways. First, we can allow for not taking account of *all* of the reasons, so long as you take account of *enough* of them. Your action meets the standard of rightness just in case *all* of the appropriate reasons to do it outweigh *all* of the appropriate reasons against it. But you can meet the corresponding standard of acting well without being aware of or acting on *all* of the reasons for doing it, so long as the reasons for which you do act are sufficiently weighty appropriate reasons to outweigh all of the appropriate reasons against the action. And if we like, we can allow for you to have extra motives that do not detract from whether you act well, so long as *among* the reasons for which you act are some which are sufficiently weighty appropriate reasons to outweigh all of the appropriate reasons against the action. We can put these two lessons into a formula, as follows:

Right Reasons   Let N be a normative standard which is met by φ-ing just in case the N-reasons to φ outweigh the N-reasons against φ-ing. Then an agent X meets the corresponding standard of acting N-ly well just in case there is some subset S of the N-reasons to φ such that among the reasons for which X φs are the reasons in S and the N-reasons in S outweigh the N-reasons against φ-ing.

Right Reasons looks like a mouthful, but that is because it is formulated in order to be neutral among different right properties. What it says, in a nutshell, is that you believe rationally just in case among the reasons for which you believe are enough to make your belief the rational one to have. You fear appropriately just in case among the reasons for which you fear are enough to make your fear appropriate. And so on.

So now we can see a little bit of how the Well Principle is generated by Right Reasons. In order to apply this account to knowledge, we must identify whether knowledge consists in doing well by some subjective normative standard, or doing well by some objective normative standard. The answer, in the case of knowledge, is *both*. Knowing entails believing what it is rational to believe,[4] and it also entails

---

[4] Compare Cohen and Comesaña (2013a) on the subjectivity of the sort of rationality entailed by knowledge.

believing what it is correct to believe. So the S-reasons that are relevant for knowledge are epistemic reasons that are both objective reasons and subjective reasons. You know, just in case among the reasons for which you believe are some that are both objectively and subjectively sufficient.[5] Since this is exactly what Kant says about knowledge in the first *Critique* 1999), I'll refer to this as the *Kantian Account* of knowledge.[6]

11.2 Knowledge as Matching

We are now in a position to see that the Kantian Account of knowledge easily and elegantly predicts many of the most important features of knowledge that have made it seem difficult to analyze. For example, Williamson leads off *Knowledge and Its Limits* (2000) with an argument that knowledge is what he calls *prime*, meaning that it is not equivalent to any conjunction of internal and external conditions. Dialectically in that book, Williamson presents his argument that knowledge is prime as if it is supposed to discourage us about any prior conviction that we have that knowledge must have some analysis. Belief, after all, is typically supposed to be an internal condition, and truth is typically supposed to be an external condition. Truly believing that P is therefore a composite condition in Williamson's sense, and his argument shows that knowledge is not. He offers this argument as if it warms the ground for his assertion that knowledge has no analysis.

But primeness is actually a very easy condition for analyzable conditions to satisfy. It is so easy, in fact, that the condition of believing the truth about *whether* P is a prime condition in Williamson's sense. There is no pair consisting of a wholly internal condition and a wholly external condition, such that someone believes the truth about whether P just in case they satisfy both that internal condition and that external condition. We can see this in the very same way that Williamson argues that knowledge is prime. We take one agent, who believes the truth about whether P because she believes that P and it is true that P, and another agent, who believes the truth about whether P because she believes that ~P and it is true that ~P, and we simply mix and match their internal and external conditions,

---

[5] Just a reminder that in the main text I have assumed throughout that talk about 'justification' naturally lines up with the rationality of belief, which corresponds to the sufficiency of the subjective reasons for which you believe, and contrasts with correctness, which corresponds to the sufficiency of the objective reasons. I think this is the most natural way to interpret what Gettier (1963) must have had in mind when he offered 'justification' as a word for what Ayer's and Chisholm's third conditions on knowledge were each trying to capture. But given that the S-reasons for knowledge are those that are both objective and subjective reasons, another reasonable candidate for the reference of 'justified' is this intersective condition. Such a candidate might make 'justified' come out closer to the view of Littlejohn (2012) than the alternative reading that I prefer.

[6] Compare Chignell (2007a, 2007b).

considering an example of an agent who believes that P while it is true that ~P. The third agent satisfies any internal condition satisfied by the first and any external condition satisfied by the second, but she does not believe the truth about whether P. So no conjunction of internal and external conditions is sufficient for believing the truth about whether P.

But believing the truth about whether P is obviously an analyzable condition. It is the condition of being such that whatever the true answer is to whether P, you believe it. It is therefore analyzed, in part, in terms of belief, and of truth—an internal condition, and an external condition. But the reason why it is prime is that believing the truth about whether P requires a *match* between internal and external conditions. So it is no wonder, then, that every serious attempt to analyze knowledge since Gettier can be thought of as an attempt to impose some kind of *matching* condition between internal and external factors.

Right reasons accounts of well properties, including the Kantian Account, are a special case of matching conditions. According to right reasons accounts, you act well when there is the right kind of match between the reasons *for which* you do something and the reasons that make it the right thing for you to do. So since, as I argued in Chapter 4, the reasons for which you do something are an internal condition, but the reasons that make something objectively right for you to do are an external condition, right reason accounts of the well properties corresponding to any kind of objective standard of rightness involve a kind of match between internal and external factors—precisely as we should expect for an analysis of knowledge.

The Kantian Account also makes elegant sense of the duality of ways that knowledge can be *defeated*. As early as Chapter 5 we observed that knowledge can be systematically defeated by both objective and subjective factors, and that there is a striking *correspondence* between which kinds of objective factors can defeat knowledge, and which kinds of subjective factors can defeat it. For example, someone who is driving past the only barn in fake barn country does not know by visual inspection that it is a barn, even if she is unaware that she is in fake barn country—the mere condition of being in fake barn country defeats her knowledge. But similarly, someone who is not in fake barn country but rationally and reasonably believes that she is does not know that something is a barn by visual inspection, either. The same kind of thing that defeats knowledge when it is true also defeats knowledge when it is reasonably believed to be true.

Notice that in the fake barn cases, the objective defeater and the subjective defeater come paired. The very same proposition whose truth defeats your knowledge in the objective defeater case is one such that your mere belief in it defeats his justification in the subjective defeater case.[7] This turns out to be no

---

[7] There are important subtleties about what else needs to be held fixed in order for this correspondence to hold that I am ignoring here.

coincidence—it is an important and general fact that objective and subjective defeaters for knowledge *always* come paired. To see this, compare a different sort of case. The fake barn country case involves what has come to be known as an *undercutting* defeater. The fact that you are driving through fake barn country undercuts your justification for believing that you are looking at a barn, because it renders your visual evidence less useful. Undercutting defeaters are typically contrasted with *countervailing* defeaters, which involve contrary reasons.

For example, if you read in an academic article that a study has shown that axillary dissection is indicated for breast cancer, the fact that this study used an unrepresentative sample would be an undercutter for the conclusion that axillary dissection is so indicated, but the fact that there are several other studies which show no positive net effects for axillary dissection unless the sentinel lymph node tests positive for metastatic disease would be a countervailing defeater. Like undercutting defeaters, countervailing defeaters for knowledge come paired in matching objective and subjective varieties. If you form a belief that axillary dissection is indicated for breast cancer after reading only one article, then even if this is true, you don't really know it, if there is good research to the contrary. This is the objective defeater case. But if you *have* read the contrary literature and believe the first article anyway in spite of the evidence, then you don't know, either. That is the subjective defeater case.

The importance of the pairing of objective and subjective defeaters for knowledge is illustrated by the literature on *pragmatic encroachment* on knowledge. As we saw in Chapters 7 and 8, some authors have argued that knowledge depends not only on evidence and other truth-related factors, but also on what is at stake over a question for the believer.[8] But importantly, advocates of such pragmatic encroachment typically hold that high stakes can make it harder to know in each of two different ways. It can be harder to know either because the stakes are actually high, regardless of whether the agent realizes that they are, or because the agent believes the stakes to be high, regardless of whether they really are. The former cases—called *ignorant high stakes* by Stanley (2005)—are putative objective defeaters for knowledge, and the latter are putative subjective defeaters for knowledge.

It is no surprise that pragmatic encroachers like Stanley will think that there are two different ways in which stakes can make it harder to know, because it follows from our general principle that defeaters for knowledge always come paired in this way. Consequently, whether or not you follow Stanley and the others in believing that there actually *is* pragmatic encroachment on knowledge, the fact that those who are tempted to think there is are naturally led to postulate two

---

[8] See especially Fantl and McGrath (2002), Hawthorne (2004), Stanley (2005), Fantl and McGrath (2010), Schroeder (2012), and Ross and Schroeder (2014).

corresponding types of defeat is further evidence for the centrality of the phenomenon of defeater pairing.[9]

The fact that defeaters come paired in this way strongly suggests that there are parallel objective and subjective components of knowledge—components that knowledge requires to match in the right way. This is not an immediate consequence of the bare idea that knowledge is a kind of *well* property. Some well properties, like acting or believing rationally, do not have objective defeaters. And some, including arguably the property of playing chess well, do not have subjective defeaters. So not all well properties exhibit the specific kind of matched defeater structure for knowledge. But this *does* follow from the Kantian Account, according to which knowledge requires believing well along each of two dimensions—both subjectively, and objectively.

In contrast, we can use the pairing of objective and subjective defeaters on knowledge to test the idea, encountered earlier in Chapter 5, that apparent subjective defeaters of knowledge are not cases in which you don't know at all, but are instead cases in which although you know, it is reasonable for you to believe that you do not. If all of the defeating conditions on knowledge were uncontroversial, then this view could explain why we get objective and subjective defeater pairing—after all, whenever you have a subjective defeater, you believe that you are in a situation in which you have an objective defeater. Hence, it is reasonable for you to believe that you don't know.

But unfortunately, the defeating conditions on knowledge are *not* uncontroversial. And the problem with this view is that it filters the reasonability of the subject believing that they do not know through *the subject's* view about what is an objective defeating condition on knowledge. So, for example, this view predicts that if even if we as theorists think that there are practical, stakes-related objective defeaters of knowledge (ignorant high-stakes cases), we should still think that it is reasonable for subjects who do not believe in pragmatic encroachment to know and believe that they know when they believe themselves to be in high-stakes situations. And similarly, it predicts that even if we as theorists think that there are *no* stakes-related defeaters of knowledge, apparent high-stakes cases should still strike us in the same way as other cases of apparent subjective defeat of knowledge when their subjects are known to believe in pragmatic encroachment. But neither of these, I think, is what we observe. So I conclude that this is not an adequate diagnosis of the appearance of subjective defeating conditions on knowledge.

11.3 Standing Up to the Facts

We can get even more illumination from the Kantian Account when it comes to the distinctive explanatory properties of knowledge. In *Knowledge and its Limits*,

---

[9] For a similar observation about lottery cases, see Nelkin (2000).

one of the ways in which Williamson argues that knowledge is more important than belief is by arguing that it has a distinctive kind of explanatory power. Williamson argues for this distinctive explanatory power for his own distinctive dialectical reasons, and for our purposes we will not need everything that Williamson means to get out of this argument.[10] But what I do think is clearly correct about Williamson's point is that there are at least some cases in which the fact that someone knows provides a better explanation of their action than the fact that they believe, that they rationally or justifiably believe, or that their credence is high. Seeing how it provides a better explanation will help us to see what *kind* of match between internal and external factors we should expect knowledge to involve.

Williamson's (2000, 62) leading example of an explanation in which knowledge plays a distinctive explanatory role is the case of a burglar who "spends all night ransacking a house, risking discovery by staying so long". Williamson's explanation of why the burglar stayed so long is that he knew that there was a diamond in the house. Williamson rests on the intuitive force of this claim, but I think that we can say more. The burglar's behavior cannot be explained by the fact that he believed that there was a diamond in the house, because several hours of ransacking with no results to show for it would in most cases suffice to make it rational for someone who believes, but does not know, that there is a diamond in the house, to give up that belief. Similarly, the burglar's behavior is not explained by the fact that he justifiably believed that there was a diamond in the house—for even a very good justification to believe that there is a diamond in the house can be defeated by the accumulation of the kind of counterevidence one is bound to come by in the course of eight or nine hours of searching for it with no luck. And it is not explained by a high credence, since having a high credence does not explain why it stays high throughout the search. In contrast, Williamson claims, and I think that we should agree, the burglar's searching all night *can* be explained by the fact that he *knew* that there was a diamond in the house.

Williamson seems to think that knowledge can provide this distinctive kind of explanatory power because it is a different kind of psychological state from mere belief. But it is not clear why this should help. The distinctive kinds of cases in which knowledge offers distinctive explanatory power are cases like the burglar's in which an action is explained over time where the actor acquires more evidence than they started with about whether there is a diamond in the house. What requires explanation, here, is not what the burglar does, but why he *keeps doing it*. So the explanatory power that we need from knowledge is an explanation of why someone who knows would *continue to believe*, even under circumstances like these.

---

[10] Compare, for example, Molyneux (2007).

Williamson discusses the case of the burglar only briefly and suggestively, in order to go on and set it aside. So it's not clear to me exactly how he thinks of the extra explanatory power of knowledge as working in this case. But the natural principles to appeal to are Williamson's closely related claims that knowledge obeys *margin-of-error* principles, and that knowledge exhibits *safety*. Both safety and margin-of-error principles concern whether someone who knows could easily have been wrong—whether there are nearby cases in which the process that results in their knowledge results instead in a false conclusion. If the burglar knows that there is a diamond in the house, then he could not easily have been wrong.

But this does little to help us understand why the burglar *still* knows that there is a diamond in the house after several hours of ransacking, because surely the longer the burglar ransacks without finding the diamond, the more easily he could have been wrong to continue to believe that there is a diamond. Worse, according to Williamson, there can be cases of improbable knowledge.[11] So even if the burglar continues to know that there is a diamond all night long, the more evidence they accumulate that they could easily have been wrong—and so the more probable it is that they do not know that there is a diamond. And it is hard to explain why the rational response to expect from the burglar is to continue to believe the thing that looks increasingly unlikely to be knowledge—or to continue to act on it.

In contrast, I suggest that the reason the burglar's knowledge can provide a better explanation for his behavior than the fact that he believed, or even that he justifiably believed, is that knowledge involves a match between the burglar's belief state and the facts. It is because it involves such a match, that it can explain why the burglar *still believes*, and indeed still *rationally* believes, that there is a diamond in the house, even after eight or nine hours of looking for it with no luck. Here is an intuitive gloss on how it does this: it does it because knowledge is belief whose justification *stands up to the facts*. The fact that the burglar knows explains why he is justified in not ceasing to believe, even once he has acquired a fair bit of new evidence that there is no diamond in the house after all, because it involves having a justification that stands up to—and hence is robust in the face of—such evidence.[12]

How does this relate to our idea that knowledge is a match between the relationship between a belief and an agent's other beliefs, and the relationship between that belief and the world? It tells us something about what that relationship is. A belief's justification depends on its relationship to the agent's other beliefs. The idea of knowledge as match tells us that a belief must bear a similar relationship to the world, as it bears to other beliefs, in virtue of which it is

---

[11] Williamson (2011).

[12] It is not, of course, robust in the face of *any* such evidence—it is possible to lose knowledge by learning more things. More on this and its significance in Section 11.3.

justified. It's because of this match between the facts and one's justification, that because the burglar knows, his justification is robust in the face of the facts.

The Kantian Account, again, tells us that this is so. It says that the reasons for which an agent believes must be not only sufficient to make it rational to believe, but must, in addition, outweigh *all* of the objective reasons against belief—including any objective evidence that the burglar might learn while ransacking the house. So it is no wonder that the burglar spends all night searching. He does so because he still believes the diamond is there even after hours of not finding it; he still believes so because it is rational for him to still believe, and it is rational for him to believe because even before he started, the evidence on the basis of which he believed was good enough to outweigh the evidence that he has acquired in the meantime. His justification stands up to the facts.

The natural diagnosis of the explanatory power of knowledge in cases like that of Williamson's burglar, I have suggested, is that knowledge is belief whose justification is good enough that it *stands up to* the facts, in some important sense. The Kantian Account makes good on this diagnosis, and it does so in a way that is principled and well-motivated. But this idea is not in any way novel. On the contrary, it is at the heart of most of the first decade of responses to the Gettier problem and is the core insight that motivated much of the literature over the following decade, as well. Most of the distinctive problems of the Gettier literature concerned epicycles on what in retrospect we can now see as short-sighted strategies to make more precise the sense in which a justification must stand up to the facts, in order to amount to knowledge.

This intuitive idea not only provides an intuitive explanation of Williamson's observations about the explanatory power of knowledge, it also explains the simplest sorts of Gettier cases—'false lemma' cases like Gettier's (1963) original *Brown in Barcelona*, undercutting defeater cases like fake barn country, and even countervailing defeater cases like the breast cancer research case. In each of these cases, the reasons for which the agent believes are not objectively sufficient. In false lemma cases, the reasons for which the agent believes are not objectively sufficient because being false they are not objective reasons at all. In undercutting defeater cases like unwittingly being in fake barn country or unwittingly wearing rose-colored glasses or Russell's clock case, they are not objectively sufficient because the objective reason for belief that they provide is not as weighty as it seems. And in countervailing defeater cases like the breast cancer research case, they are not objectively sufficient because there is better objective reason against belief—in this case, the other evidence against belief that the agent is not aware of.

Similarly, if we accept the idea of Pragmatic Intellectualism that cost-of-error related considerations are reasons against belief that are not evidence, then the Kantian Account also predicts that ignorant high stakes cases are a special case of countervailing objective defeat. They are cases in which the reasons for which the agent believes are not objectively sufficient because there are even better objective reasons against believing.

And it even captures the truth condition on knowledge without imposing it as an extra condition.[13] In all of these cases, the subject rationally believes something, but there is a relevant truth of which they were unaware that makes the objective sufficiency of the reasons for which they believe something other than what it seems. And for the most part, this grounds the imperfect subjunctive gloss that if they were to come to be aware of this further truth, it would no longer be rational for them to believe what they do. The appeal of this sort of idea should therefore be clear, and it is no surprise that many authors in the early decades of research into the Gettier problem offered versions of the idea that knowledge is justified belief that stands up in some way to the facts.[14]

11.4 Surmounting Obstacles

The analysis of knowledge did not become the most famous failed project of analytic philosophy because it was mysterious how to get as far as the idea that knowledge is belief whose justification stands up to the facts. What became notoriously difficult was nailing down the details. Two issues, in particular, turned out to pose repeated challenges, no matter how theorists tried to contort the details of their accounts. Both can be illuminatingly illustrated with a particularly simple and natural account due to Peter Klein (1971) that fully captures the spirit of our guiding idea that knowledge is belief whose justification 'stands up to' the facts.

According to Klein (1971), S knows p (at time t_1) just in case at t_1 S truly believes p, p is evident to S, and "there is no true proposition such that if it became evident to S at t_1, p would no longer be evident to S" (1971, 475).[15] This captures very well the idea that knowledge is belief whose justification stands up to the facts. Klein captures the way in which belief must stand up to the facts by supposing that there must be no fact such that were it added to S's beliefs, S's justification for believing p (its 'evidentness') would go away. This account explains why knowledge involves the kind of match that makes it prime. It

---

[13] Though contrast Hazlett (2012), (unpublished). Capturing the truth condition requires the Kantian Account to assume that the fact that ~P is a better reason against believing that P than any possible reason in favor—the same condition that we saw earlier guarantees that it is never correct to believe something false, so that truth falls out as the correctness norm on belief.

[14] See, in particularClark (1963), Sosa (1964, 1970), Lehrer (1965), (1970), (1974), Lehrer and Paxson (1969), Klein (1971), Annis (1973), Ackerman (1974), Johnsen (1974), Swain (1974), Unger (1975), Barker (1976), and Olin (1976) for some of the highlights of this tradition.

[15] Just a reminder that though I myself do not use p as a variable over propositions in this book, I'll follow the usage of other authors when stating their views.

explains why we observe defeater pairing, because the objective conditions which defeat knowledge are just the things which, were they to be justifiedly believed, would subjectively defeat knowledge by defeating justification. And it explains Williamson's thesis about explanatory power, because it explains why someone who knows will in general continue to be justified in her belief even when she discovers new evidence, as the burglar does after spending the entire night ransacking the house in search of a diamond.[16]

Klein's account explains all of these observations because it makes good on the idea that knowledge is belief whose justification stands up to the facts. As we'll see, it is subject to predictable counterexamples. But it is important to keep clear on whether these counterexamples reflect poorly on the core idea that knowledge is belief whose justification stands up to the facts, or they only reflect poorly on the way in which Klein tried to make this idea precise. My suggestion is that the major problems besetting this account and others like it derive from mistakes in implementation, rather than from any failure of the core insight that knowledge is belief whose justification stands up to the facts in the right way. And we can fix these mistakes in implementation by taking more seriously the idea that knowledge is just a special case of a *well* property, and by taking on board some lessons from Part III of this book.

The first important class of counterexamples to Klein's account received the bulk of the attention for similar accounts in the late 1960s and throughout the 1970s. These counterexamples surround what we can call the *defeater* dialectic, in light of which refinements on views like Klein's came to be known as *defeasibility* analyses of knowledge. The most famous such counterexample and first important refinements on such views actually preceded the publication of Klein's article, in an article from 1969 by Keith Lehrer and Thomas Paxson. Suppose that you see Tom Grabit come out of the library, pull a book from under his shirt, cackle gleefully, and scurry off. In this case, absent further information, it looks like you know that Tom stole a book. But if Tom has an identical twin Tim from whom you could not distinguish him, then it seems that you don't really know after all. Tim would therefore be a defeater for your knowledge that Tom stole a book. Klein's account can capture this defeater for knowledge, since if you were to find out that Tom has an identical twin, then you would no longer be justified in believing that Tom stole a book solely on the basis of your visual evidence. So far, so good.

But unfortunately, just as knowledge can be defeated, defeaters for knowledge can also be defeated. Suppose, for example, that Tim's wedding was scheduled for today in another state. If this is the case, then it seems that you *can* know that Tom stole a book on the basis of your visual evidence alone, even though he has an

---

[16] Note, however, that it does not explain the *right degree* of robustness of knowledge in the face of new evidence. It predicts too much robustness.

identical twin. So the potential defeater for your knowledge is itself defeated. Klein's account is too strong, and gets this wrong. According to Klein, since finding out that Tom has a twin (without also finding out that Tim's wedding is scheduled to take place in another state) would make your justification go away, you don't know.[17]

In the early 1970s a great deal of published work on the analysis of knowledge went into trying to characterize the conditions on which a true proposition is a defeater that is not itself defeated. This turned out to be very difficult to do, in part because just as knowledge can be defeated and defeaters can be defeated, defeater-defeaters can also be defeated. For example, if Tim called off the wedding, then the fact that it was scheduled to be today in another state doesn't interfere with Tim's interfering with your visual evidence that Tom stole a book. And if the reason Tim called off the wedding was to elope to Bali instead, then it seems that you can know after all. But if all of the flights to Bali have been cancelled, then perhaps you don't. What cases like this show is that defeaters and defeater-defeaters can go on, ad infinitum.[18]

This means that it is not enough for an analysis of knowledge to predict the ways in which knowledge can be defeated. It must also be able to predict the ways in which the defeaters for knowledge can themselves be defeated, so that the agent knows after all. An analysis that fails to allow for defeaters will be too expansive, allowing for knowledge that there is not. But an analysis that fails to allow for defeater-defeaters will be too narrow, failing to account for knowledge that there is. And one that fails to allow for defeater-defeater-defeaters will be too expansive again. Just talking about the phenomenon is a bit dizzying; it's easy to see why so many attempts to analyze knowledge ended up with epicycles—the phenomenon seems to cry out for them.

In retrospect, I suggest, the literature about defeasibility analyses of knowledge looks so arcane because theorists were using the wrong analytical tools to make their analyses precise. And they were using the wrong tools, because they were insufficiently appreciative of the continuities with ethics. Understanding the defeasibility of reasons, I say, is a *general* problem for understanding how anything could be determined by the balance of reasons in *any* domain.

---

[17] In general, whenever there is a potential objective defeater for your knowledge that is itself defeated, learning the potential defeater without learning its defeater-defeater will undermine both justification and knowledge. Defeaters which are themselves defeated can thus provide *misleading* evidence, if you learn them without also learning of their defeater. This shows that the extra explanatory power offered by knowledge in burglar cases like Williamson's is limited. The fact that the burglar knows that there is a diamond when he enters the house helps to explain why he searches all night, but it doesn't guarantee it, since he could lose his knowledge during the night, by learning a defeated defeater for his knowledge, without learning its defeater-defeater.

[18] Compare especially Levy (1977) for discussion of this point. This case is a variation on a case introduced by Lehrer and Paxson (1969), variations on which are common in the literature cited in note 14.

The other major difficulty faced by many early attempts to analyze knowledge is the conditional fallacy. An account commits the conditional fallacy by attempting to analyze a categorical property in conditional terms. For example, we saw that on Klein's account you know if you justifiedly believe the truth, and moreover there is no true proposition, such that were you to (justifiedly) believe it, you would cease to be justified in your belief. This conditional account attempts to capture the idea that knowledge is true belief whose justification is good enough to 'stand up to' the facts, and uses the conditional in order to gloss what it is to be good enough to stand up to the facts. The idea is that it *is* good enough, if it *would still be* sufficient for justification, if the agent (justifiedly) had beliefs in those facts.

This account runs into trouble with the conditional fallacy. To see why in the abstract, note that the conditional analysis has us evaluate whether some justification *is* good enough for knowledge by looking at whether it *would be* good enough, at the closest world at which the agent has the other belief. But in some cases, the closest world in which the agent has the relevant belief will also be a world where other things happen. Perhaps the agent *would* know, in such a world, even though she actually does not. Or perhaps she would not, even though actually she does. Either of these scenarios can create conditional fallacy trouble for such an account.

Once we understand how the conditional fallacy works, it is easy to imagine what such counterexamples must look like, but the one offered by Shope (1983) is simple: suppose that S knows that she is not justified in believing that R. But suppose that it is true that R. Finally, add to the case that were S to justifiedly believe that R, this justification would be transparent to her, so that she would no longer be justified in believing that she is not justified in believing it. According to Klein's account, S does not know. But this is wrong. Importantly, our work in Part III allows us to sidestep this problem. Instead of relying on a subjunctive gloss on sufficiency, the Kantian Account relies on a categorical account that grounds these subjunctive conditionals when they are true. And it is able to do this, because it was able to draw on our Reasons First respecting solution to the problem of sufficiency.

A commonly endorsed more recent diagnosis of the difficulty of analyzing knowledge derives from Linda Zagzebski's influential treatment.[19] Zagzebski argues that Gettier problems will always be inescapable so long as truth is an extra, independent, condition on knowledge, in addition to justification, belief, and any 'fourth condition'. Her argument is simple: every way that these other conditions can fall short of truth leaves a gap that can be filled only through luck— and she offers a persuasive rundown of how to construct Gettier-style counter-examples to a wide variety of such views, drawing on precisely that gap. This is a

---

[19] Zagzebski (1994, 1996).

central motivation for the idea that any successful account of knowledge will need to involve an anti-luck condition—an idea that itself has seemed to obviate the need for evidence to play any essential role.

But the Kantian Account does *not* build in an independent truth condition that can be exploited by this analysis. On the contrary, the truth condition is entailed by the condition that the reasons for which the agent believes are objectively sufficient. This is because we have assumed that the fact that ~P is always a conclusive reason not to believe that P—so there can be sufficient objective reasons only for believing truths. And this, in turn, is what gives my version of right reasons analyses a kind of common cause explanation of the relationship between *right* and *well* properties—because the *right* condition is *always* only entailed by, and not itself a conjunct of, the analysis of its corresponding *well* property.

So by Zagzebski's own lights, the Kantian Account is not open to the very source that we should expect Gettier problems to come from. Of course, my own preference is to identify the condition of believing for reasons that are *subjectively* sufficient as the condition that counts as 'justification', and that is the way that I have talked throughout this book. And that condition *is* independent of truth, and captures Zagzebski's sense that few philosophers will want to endorse the view that justification actually entails truth. But the objective sufficiency condition is not independent of truth—there is no independent appeal to the truth of the belief in question that could happen merely by luck.

The defeater dialectic and the conditional fallacy are the two main problems for the analyses of knowledge canvassed by Shope (1983), which is cited by pessimists like both Williamson (2000) and Kvanvig (2003) as an authoritative treatment of the persistent problems facing analyses of knowledge. And Zagzebski's (1994) article is one of the most influential diagnoses of the difficulties involved in the Gettier problem. There is no guarantee that an analysis of knowledge that avoids these three problems without arcane twists and turns will also be free of other problems or objections, but if there is an independently motivated and natural account that is free of these three problems, that should at least make us question what grounds the failures of the Gettier literature give us for inductive pessimism about the Gettierological project.

11.5 The Kantian Account

It turns out that the defeater dialectic is very familiar to moral philosophers, as pushed by proponents of moral particularism. Whereas the defeater dialectic for knowledge starts with the problem that knowledge can be defeated in a range of ways, and then adds that defeaters can be defeated, and even defeater-defeaters can be defeated, the particularist dialectic in moral philosophy starts with the facts that the wrongness of an action can be defeated in a variety of ways, and even those defeaters can themselves be defeated. Just as the defeater dialectic in epistemology poses a problem for the analysis of knowledge, particularists argue that the defeater dialectic in moral philosophy poses a problem for the possibility of posing any informative generalizations at all about—let alone any analyses of— moral wrongness.[20]

In moral philosophy, the defeater dialectic is at the heart of the classical argument for the thesis of reasons first. The difficulty of formulating general principles about what is right or wrong is precisely what makes the idea that wrongness is simply determined by whatever is disfavored by the balance of reasons an extremely powerful explanatory hypothesis. So the defeater dialectic is exactly what we should expect, if the property of a belief being justified or rational is itself one of the normative properties that are determined by the balance of reasons.

I conclude that we have found yet another topic where epistemology has suffered by lack of comparison with moral philosophy, confirming once again the Core Hypothesis of this book. If the defeater dialectic for knowledge is indeed mirrored by corresponding dialectics for defeaters for wrongness, then we need to take seriously the hypothesis that both derive from the same source—even if we do not fully understand exactly how that source works. If knowledge is belief whose justification stands up to the facts, and justification is, at least in part, a matter of the balance of reasons, then knowledge will inherit the general features of everything else that is determined by the balance of reasons. In particular, not only will knowledge be defeasible because justification is defeasible, but since reasons themselves can be defeated, there will be defeaters for defeaters of knowledge.

The defeater dialectic is therefore not a puzzle that shows that knowledge is too complicated to be interesting or that it defies generalization. Rather, it is simply a pattern that must be captured at the right level of description, in the way that ellipses are well-captured by conic sections but only poorly captured by approximations in terms of triangles. It is exactly the pattern that we would expect if knowledge were justification that stands up to the facts and justification were, at least in part, a matter of the balance of reasons, and so rather than talking us out of either of these two claims, it should *reinforce* them. It should lead us to the Kantian Account of knowledge.

The work that we have done in Part III of this book is also what enabled us to cleanly evade the conditional fallacy. Klein's (1971) account was pushed to reach for a conditional analysis of what it is for a justification to be 'good enough' to 'stand up to' the facts, because he didn't have access to a categorical account of what it is for reasons or a justification to be sufficient. In this book, we have used

---

[20] Compare especially Dancy (2004), Schroeder (2011b) for discussion. See also Gert (2008).

another name for what is puzzling about how to give a categorical analysis of the sufficiency of reasons in epistemology—we have called it the *problem of sufficiency*, and it was the focus of Part III of this book. The problem of sufficiency is the problem of reading off conclusions about justification or rationality of assumptions about reasons or evidence in epistemology. In the absence of any way of reading off such conclusions, it has seemed like the only thing that we can say about what it means for reasons to be 'sufficient' is that they *suffice for justification*. But of course that cannot be circularly included in an analysis of justification in terms of reasons.

But what we can now see is that Klein's subjunctive account of what it takes for justification to stand up to the facts is just a special case of this circular account of the sufficiency of reasons. And so we are now in a position to see that Part III of this book gives us the resources to avoid the conditional fallacy. Reasons are sufficient, we said in Chapter 6, when they *beat all comers*. That is, when they outweigh the totality of all of the opposing reasons. So we can account for the way in which a justification must stand up to the facts by directly comparing the weights of reasons—the reasons involved in that justification, and the objective reasons against belief.

This is what the Kantian Account of knowledge does. It does not test the actual sufficiency of the reasons for which you believe by checking to see whether they would be sufficient to make your belief rational if you were aware of more facts. Rather, it tests the actual sufficiency of the reasons for which you believe by comparing them directly to your actual reasons against believing. This makes its account of sufficiency categorical in nature, and immune to the conditional fallacy.

So far, I've said that knowledge is a special kind of believing well—believing well with respect to both objective and subjective epistemic reasons. And I've both given evidence by *parity* that this is the right sort of thing for knowledge to be, and given evidence from *within* epistemology that this is what knowledge actually is. But this is only a sketch of an account, and further refinements are possible. For example, it is plausible that in order to know, it's not enough for the reasons for which you believe to be both objectively and subjectively sufficient (as Kant says and as I argued in an earlier paper); rather, some subset of the reasons for which you believe must be *jointly* objectively and subjectively sufficient. I've formulated the Kantian Account here to embrace this amendment, but the question is underdetermined by any evidence I've considered.[21] Both views are possible elaborations of the right reasons framework.

Another plausible constraint is that you must not just believe well, but your reasoning toward that belief must be done well as well—in the sense, for example, that when you discount some possible evidence, the defeater for it that you accept

---

[21] Note that this amounts to a revision of the view advocated in Schroeder (2015b).

must be an objectively and subjectively sufficient defeater for it. I'm happy to accept this as a plausible refinement as well. Or you might think that acting and believing well is subject to a *salience* constraint, so that you can't count as acting or believing well just because your reasons are objectively sufficient, if there were other reasons available to you that were obviously much better than the ones that you relied on. None of these refinements is inconsistent with the fundamental truths that knowledge is a special case of doing something well, or that the property of doing something well is a matter of a matching relationship between the reasons for which you do it and the reasons to do it—all that I maintain is that the issues about how to refine should go hand-in-hand for knowledge and for moral worth, as well as for other *well* properties.

So although I have sketched the outlines of a specific account of knowledge by sketching the outlines of a specific version of a right reasons account of the Well Principle, it should be clear by now that these accounts should stand or fall not on the basis of whether I can convince you of their details, but on the basis of whether what goes wrong with my treatment of knowledge can be traced to it going wrong in a similar way over its treatment of other well properties, including moral worth. My main thesis is that knowledge and moral worth must be wrapped up together and covered by the same encompassing theory. That theory, I have given some reasons to expect, will draw on both the deliberative and explanatory roles of reasons. But exactly how it does so is a matter for much further investigation and refinement.

11.6 Closing Parable

After Edmund Gettier published his famous article "Is Justified True Belief Knowledge?" in 1963, the question as to whether knowledge can be analyzed and if so, how, came to occupy a central place in epistemology. But after a couple of decades of intensive attempts to respond to Gettier or to tweak other responses to Gettier in order to bypass objections or counterexamples, most epistemologists moved on out of the kind of collective exhaustion that comes from a literature being explored to the point of inductive pessimism—or at least of boredom. Jonathan Kvanvig (2003) eventually offered one of the most striking takeaway lessons from the entire episode—an argument that whatever has a nature that is complex enough to get around all of the standard classes of kinds of counterexamples to analyses of knowledge could not possibly be natural enough to be interesting or important. So, Kvanvig concluded, knowledge is not interesting or important.

At around the same time that Kvanvig was developing these arguments, Timothy Williamson (2000) was advancing the flip side of the very same thought. Knowledge *is* interesting and important, Williamson argued. But that importance does not turn on its analysis or nature. On the contrary, according to Williamson, knowledge *cannot* be analyzed. It is interesting and important not because it has a complex nature that tracks complex intuitions in subtle cases, but because its nature is simple, obeying and grounding some simple generalizations.

I believe that each of these lessons from the Gettier literature has been a wrong turn. Contra Williamson, I have been arguing in this chapter and Chapter 10 that knowledge does admit of analysis—it is a special case of what in Chapter 10 I called a *well* property, and so admits of an especially interesting analysis that is of a kind with the analyses of other such properties. Contra Kvanvig, I have argued that this analysis captures the complex intuitive judgments about knowledge in a way that is simple and natural. There is nothing simpler or more natural than the notion of not just satisfying a normative standard, but of doing well by it. It is no wonder that knowledge is natural and important, because doing well by normative standards is always natural and important.

Both lessons emerge, I will argue, from an observation about where others went wrong. If you try to approximate the shape of an ellipse with triangles, you will fail, and more triangles will not help—except in the infinite limit. So watching people try to approximate the shape of an ellipse with triangles is bound to rationally result in inductive pessimism. And it is *right* to observe that any shape that is made only by a large number of triangles is probably not a very natural or interesting shape. But none of this tells us that ellipses are not a natural shape, or that they lack a simple or interesting analysis. It just tells us that we have been looking in the wrong place for such an analysis.

The point of this cautionary tale is simple: even when inductive pessimism about an analytical enterprise is clearly warranted, there remains a very legitimate question about the allowable *scope* of that pessimism. If the tools utilized in the analytical project are crude or clumsy or simply of the wrong kind, or if promising ideas in the course of the project are prematurely further analyzed using crude tools, then their failure is to be expected; this is even if a correct analysis is ultimately available, and even if the first steps of this analysis—such as the idea that knowledge is belief whose justification stands up to the facts—are on the right track.

My own view is that something broadly like this has happened in the real-life field of epistemology: that the tools applied in early Gettierological attempts were crude, that promising ideas were sometimes dismissed because they prematurely attempted to analyze the parts of their picture in unpromising ways, and that a correct analysis of knowledge *is* available, which both sheds light on why various previous attempts to analyze knowledge were overly crude and required amendment, and why knowledge plays some of the important roles that it in fact does.

I have tried to introduce such an analysis in this chapter. The correct analysis of knowledge, I have been arguing, is that it is a kind of believing *well*. That means that it is believing the right thing, for the reasons that make it the right thing to believe. Epistemologists and moral philosophers have a great deal to learn from one another.

12

Reasons First?

12.1 Bringing It Home

I now hope to have kept my promise to make good on this book's Core Hypothesis from Chapter 1—that epistemology is disadvantaged by considering its questions in isolation from those of neighboring normative disciplines, including ethics. I don't claim any particular novelty for this hypothesis—many others have tried to bridge this gap—but I do suggest that its effects are still apparent. But in this book I've tried to offer concrete arguments that though both fields have much to learn from one another, the lessons for epistemology are particularly important.

My main argument for these claims has taken the structure of following up on three of the places where epistemology has been most disadvantaged, I think, by a lack of consideration of how its problems may be continuous with those of other areas of normative inquiry—the case of basic perceptual justification, of under-standing how evidence justifies, and of the analysis of knowledge. Much of theorizing in epistemology has been driven by competing responses to the set of constraints set by the problem of basic perceptual justification, and for many years the question of how knowledge is to be analyzed and what further analytic or explanatory role it plays has been conceived of as central to one's approach to the field as a whole. Yet in all three of these domains, I have argued, we have a great deal to gain by taking seriously the analogy between epistemology and other normative disciplines.

In the case of basic perceptual justification, I argued that the major options are shaped at the most basic level by the unwarranted assumption that in order to justify, evidence must be a truth. Given the hypothesis of evidence as reasons, this is very closely related to the idea that subjective reasons must be truths. The best argument for this claim, I suggested, is the response that it gives to the problem of unjustified belief. But once we give a better, Reasons First-friendly, answer to the problem of unjustified belief, I argued, we can see our way to a view—the apparent factive attitude view—that evades the most familiar problems for the most familiar theories of the role of perceptual experience in justifying belief.

Indeed, the analogy to other normative domains is even more general. Conventional theories of the rationality of action and other choices have always distinguished between which actions are fully advisable given all of the relevant facts, and which actions are actually rational for a person to do. What it is rational

Reasons First. Mark Schroeder, Oxford University Press (2021). © Mark Schroeder.
DOI: 10.1093/oso/9780198868224.003.0012

for a person to do does not depend on what is true, but only on what she believes. So there is no reason to think that it needs to be fundamentally explained by some truths to which she has access. Parity of reasoning should lead us to expect that the same should go in epistemology.

In the case of the role of evidence in justifying belief, I argued that the puzzles are shaped by the unwarranted assumption that the only epistemic reasons for or against a belief are evidence for or against its content. But although this assumption is understandable, it is tenable only if we expect up front for there to be significant differences between epistemology and other normative disciplines. Once we take seriously the idea that there might be continuity between epistemology and other normative disciplines, that tells us immediately that there must be epistemic reasons against belief that are not evidence against its content. And I showed in Chapters 7 and 8 that this view is easily grounded in and explained by a better understanding of the nature of belief—an explanation whose shape is made visible by taking seriously the idea that the distinction between epistemic and non-epistemic reasons for belief is of a kind with similar right-kind/wrong-kind distinctions for other attitudes. And this is itself another, direct, illustration of the Core Hypothesis.

And in the case of the theory of knowledge, I have again been arguing that the continuity between epistemology and other normative disciplines has much to teach us in epistemology. Knowledge has much in common with other well properties from other areas of normative inquiry. And it cannot be established a priori, in advance of inquiry that we have the right leverage to get the right account of knowledge without considering any of its parallel properties and can then safely apply analogous theories to them. On the contrary, I have shown that we can get much sharper constraints by considering the case of artificial norms, including those of game play.

I conclude that the Core Hypothesis of this book has been validated. Even if many of the specific theses that I have advocated are mistaken, epistemology clearly has a great deal to gain from considering its questions in continuity with questions from related normative disciplines. And we should *not* assume without argument that whatever can be defended in epistemology can be safely cut and pasted wherever we go.

12.2 Competitors

If the Kantian theory of knowledge is anything close to being on track, then it, like the apparent factive attitude view from Chapter 5 and Pragmatic Intellectualism from Chapter 8, can offer a *diagnosis* of what has seemed to be attractive about so many of its competitors, together with a rationalizing answer to how they could have gone astray. Every philosophical theory tries to account for some class of phenomena, but the most promising theories offer illumination not only about what is true, but about what makes the most popular false theories seem so attractive, or even about the distribution or pattern of which false theories people have entertained or accepted.

The apparent factive attitude view has a simple diagnosis of how theorists about basic perceptual justification could have come to have accepted the views that they have. We have already seen the diagnosis in Chapters 3 and 4. According to this view, perceptual experience rationalizes belief only by providing *evidence* for the content of that belief. But epistemologists have been trapped by the assumption that evidence must be factive—that only a truth can be evidence. This assumption, as we saw, forces a dilemma. Either the evidence that you acquire when you have a perceptual experience entails something about the world outside of your head, or it does not.

If your basic perceptual evidence is not world-entailing, then there is a large gap between any evidence available to you in perceptual experience and any conclusions about the external world. This gap, we know, is what creates the specter of skepticism. To improve your evidential position with respect to external world conclusions without improving it with respect to brain-in-vat conclusions or evil-demon conclusions, therefore, we would need to rely on background assumptions. But if those background assumptions are themselves grounded in perceptual experience, then we get circularity or regress. And if they are not grounded in perceptual experience, then we get a strong form of rationalism, according to which even empirical knowledge must be grounded in something a priori. On the other hand, if your basic perceptual evidence *is* world-entailing, then it is evidence that you can only have in the good case. For in the bad case, anything that entails something about the external world could be false. So this fork leads to a form of epistemological disjunctivism.

So all of these views—coherentism, rationalism, and disjunctivism—are motivated by getting something *right*. What they get right, is that perceptual experience rationalizes belief by being a source of evidence. Where they go wrong is simply by making the very simple mistake of thinking that in order to rationalize, evidence must be *true*—a special case of the assumption that in order to rationalize, *reasons* must be true.

Of course, not everyone thinks that perceptual experience has to rationalize by providing evidence. But the best reason why not, I have suggested, is that following Armstrong's In, it has looked like avoiding coherentism, and rationalism will require anyone to appeal to non-evidential explanations. Pure externalism in epistemology, on this diagnosis, has become widespread not because it is close to the truth, but because Armstrong's In has looked like such a compelling argument, and coherentism and rationalism have seemed to be such unpalatable alternatives. But according to the apparent factive attitude view, pure externalists *are* right that an ultimate explanation of basic perceptual justification will be grounded in an external relationship to one's environment. That is because external conditions will play a role in the theory of content determination, and plausibly in determining which mental states count as ways of possessing reasons.

The apparent factive attitude view also credits major forms of epistemological disjunctivism with getting a great deal right. Disjunctivists have appreciated better than others the way in which the options are shaped by which assumptions we make about basic perceptual evidence. And they have been more self-conscious about realizing how their views have been shaped by the assumption that evidence must be *true*. Finally, disjunctivists have rightly emphasized the importance of factive perceptual relations to the environment, and the way in which the good case is prior to the bad case. All of these things are *true*, according to the apparent factive attitude view.

So the apparent factive attitude view has an explanation of why philosophers have been led to accept the views that they have about basic perceptual justification. This explanation makes sense of the specific alternatives that philosophers have been led to endorse, and of why they have continued to endorse them in the face of objections. All of these views are attempts to get as close to the truth as possible, hindered only by the false assumption that evidence must be factive in order to rationalize belief.

Pragmatic Intellectualism also has a diagnosis of why other philosophers have come to accept the views that they have, about the role of evidence in rationalizing belief. According to Pragmatic Intellectualism, evidence rationalizes belief by being reason to believe. Indeed, evidence is the *only* kind of reason to believe, so no belief can be rationalized in the absence of evidence. But all of the insights of Pragmatic Intellectualism come from the space that it occupies between this claim and the subtly stronger claim that evidence is the only kind of reason for *or against* belief.

So the virtues of Pragmatic Intellectualism arise not only from what it says about evidence and belief, but from its diagnosis of what subtle thing other theorists have missed, which set them off track even though they may otherwise have started with promising or even true insights.

Finally, the Kantian Theory of knowledge also provides an illuminating diagnosis of where other theories of its subject matter—in this case, of knowledge—have gone astray. As I showed in Chapter 11, the Kantian Theory belongs to the family of *defeasibility* theories of knowledge explored in the 1960s and 1970s. Defeasibility theories correctly identified that knowledge is belief whose justification stands up to the facts in the right way. Where they struggled was in identifying the way in which justification must stand up to the facts. And they struggled to do so, I've argued, because they lacked an adequate understanding of the nature of justification itself. This left them appealing to tools that were too coarse-grained to capture their target. They were susceptible to the conditional fallacy and to the increasingly arcane counterexamples that form a part of the defeater dialectic.

So everyone, I say, is a little bit right. Aristotle took this virtue of philosophical theories quite seriously, in his *endoxastic method*. When we do philosophy by the endoxastic method, we consider not only the first-order phenomena that we are anxious to understand, but also what others have said about them. We then look for what each existing theory gets right, and what it gets wrong. Seeing what other theories get right, or what true observation they draw mistaken inferences from, lends support for the theory that we do end up accepting. After all, one of the things that we know about our subject matter is that it is the one that we are theorizing about. So there must be some explanation of how intelligent people could have come to accept the views about it that they have. Views that can offer such an explanation are more promising to track the truth than those that cannot.

12.3 Combining

Each of the three views that have emerged in Parts II, III, and IV of this book are interesting in their own right. But they are especially interesting, I think, when they are combined. When we combine the Kantian Theory with the apparent factive attitude view, for example, we get an attractive account not only of the *rationality* of basic perceptual beliefs, but of basic perceptual *knowledge*.

The apparent factive attitude view explains how it is that perceptual experience justifies basic perceptual beliefs in the bad case as well as the good case. It does so by holding that perceptual experience justifies belief by providing *subjective reason* to believe, and subjective reasons do not need to be truths. The subjective reason that you have for belief, when you have a visual perceptual experience as of P, is that you see that P. Since seeing that is factive, this reason entails that P, and hence there is no skeptical scenario consistent with your perceptual evidence. It is, as we would expect from direct perceptual evidence, the best sort of evidence that you can get as to whether P. But it is still defeasible, because if you believe that you are in conditions that are misleading with respect to vision as to whether P, then not all of your reasons bearing on belief can be true, and so some—perhaps including this one—may need to be rejected. But since subjective reasons do not need to be truths, you can have this very subjective reason even if you are in the bad case—we have a unified explanation of the justification of basic perceptual beliefs.

In the bad case you have a visual experience as of P but do not see that P. The apparent factive attitude view insists that in one sense, your perceptual evidence is still quite good—it is an excellent *subjective* reason to believe that P. But in another sense, we should allow, your perceptual evidence is not good at all. For it is no *objective* reason to believe that P. Objective reasons, unlike subjective reasons, must be truths. So whereas your subjective reasons are the same in the good case and the bad case, your objective reasons are always different. So that gives us a diagnosis of what might seem appealing about epistemological disjunctivism.

All of this can be said by the apparent factive attitude view all by itself. But when conjoined with the Kantian Theory of knowledge, we get a deeper explanation of why it is so important what your objective reasons are. This is important, because knowledge requires sufficiency of *objective* reasons. When you are in the bad case, your basic perceptual reasons for belief are false. That is why they are not objective reasons at all. And since they are not objective reasons, you are not in a position to know, at least on the basis of perceptual evidence, if you are in the bad case.

The Kantian Account also deepens our explanation of what goes wrong with competing disjunctivist accounts of defeasibility. We saw in Chapter 5 that the disjunctivist views that we considered—the factive content view and the factive attitude views—both offered better treatments of defeasibility than the non-factive content view. Both of these views can explain why your visual evidence can be *objectively* defeated, for example, when you are in fake barn country. According to the factive content view, this is because when you are in fake barn country, you fail to satisfy the possession condition for this evidence. And according to the factive attitude view, this is because when you are in fake barn country, your putative evidence is false, and hence not evidence at all.

But as we also saw in Chapter 5, both of these views struggle with subjective defeasibility. On both views, so long as your visual evidence is true and you satisfy the possession conditions for that evidence, that evidence should be able to ground knowledge. So if you see that there is a barn in front of you, both views are committed to the verdict that you are in a position to know that there is a barn in front of you, even if you rationally but falsely believe that you are in fake barn country. But this verdict seems false. You can't know by looking that something is a barn, if you believe that you are in fake barn country.

The Kantian Theory of knowledge explains where these verdicts go wrong. They go wrong by not distinguishing between the subjective and objective dimensions of knowledge. Objective and subjective reasons support belief in different, complementary ways, *both* of which are required for knowledge. The factive content view and the factive attitude view get the objective defeasibility of knowledge right because they are focused on the way that perceptual experience provides *objective* reasons for belief. The diagnosis that these views are really focused just on objective reasons for belief therefore explains why these views' under-prediction of rational belief in 'bad' cases and their over-prediction of rational belief and of knowledge in cases of subjective defeasibility are just two sides of the same coin.

Just as the Kantian Theory of knowledge lends strength to the apparent factive attitude view, the apparent factive attitude view also lends its support to the Kantian Theory. It is a commitment of the Kantian Theory that all knowledge and rational belief are grounded in the reasons for which we believe. But this is the commitment that sets the puzzles of Part II of this book about the nature of basic perceptual justification. If we don't follow the apparent factive attitude view in allowing subjective reasons to rationalize beliefs even though they are false, then the Kantian Theory puts us under extra pressure to navigate the choices among factive evidentialist theories.

So the Kantian Theory of knowledge plays well with the apparent factive attitude view. But it also plays nicely with Pragmatic Intellectualism. When we add the Kantian view to Pragmatic Intellectualism, we get an elegant explanation of pragmatic encroachment on not just the rationality of belief, but on knowledge. On this view, there is pragmatic encroachment on knowledge because there is pragmatic encroachment on the epistemic rationality of belief, and knowledge is just belief whose epistemic rationality stands up to the facts in the right sort of way.

According to Pragmatic Intellectualism, the reason why pragmatic factors that can intuitively be described as what is 'at stake' can affect how much evidence you require in order for it to be epistemically rational for you to believe is the very same as the reason why more evidence is required in order for it to be epistemically rational for you to believe about matters where evidence is easily acquired. In both cases it is because these factors—the costs of error and the availability of decisive further evidence—are epistemic reasons against belief. When you are aware that it is easy to acquire more evidence, you have a subjective countervailing defeater for your evidence. Similarly, when you are aware that the costs of error are high, you have a subjective countervailing defeater. Subjective countervailing defeaters are just reasons on the opposite side of the competition that determines what it is epistemically rational for you to believe. Since what it is epistemically rational for you to believe is determined by the balance in this competition, in order for it to be epistemically rational for you to believe in these cases, the evidence must be even stronger.

Since perceived costs of error and the perceived availability of further evidence are subjective epistemic reasons against belief, actual costs of error and the actual availability of further evidence are *objective* epistemic reasons against belief. And that means that they are potential *objective* countervailing defeaters. According to the Kantian Theory, knowledge requires belief for reasons that are both objectively and subjectively sufficient—that win the balance of objective reasons and also win the balance of subjective reasons. So on Kantian Pragmatic Intellectualism, knowledge can be defeated either by the perception of costs of error or by the actual costs of error. These are simply two sides of the same coin, in the very same way as other forms of defeater pairing. Similarly, knowledge can be defeated either by the perception of the easy availability of further evidence or by its actual availability.

This explanation predicts the duality between objective high stakes and subjective high stakes cases, and it does so in a way that is principled, rather than ad hoc—because they are a special case of the phenomenon of defeater pairing *in general.* Significantly, on this view there is pragmatic encroachment on knowledge *because* there is pragmatic encroachment on rational belief. In contrast, Hawthorne (2004), Stanley (2005), and Fantl and McGrath (2010) all make it look like there is pragmatic encroachment on the epistemic rationality of belief, if there is, because there is pragmatic encroachment on knowledge.

Each of these views offers insight into why we might expect there to be pragmatic encroachment on knowledge, but not into what *makes* knowledge pragmatically encroached on. Kantian Pragmatic Intellectualism therefore offers a stark contrast. Kantian Pragmatic Intellectualism grounds the explanation of pragmatic encroachment on knowledge in the very simple fact that knowledge is a kind of well property, and all well properties consist in a match between the reasons for which someone does something and the sufficiency of the reasons to do it. Given this background, all it takes to explain pragmatic encroachment is the fact that some epistemic reasons against belief are practical in nature, turning on the costs of error. And that is exactly what we should be led to expect, given the right understanding of the role that belief plays in our psychological economy. In contrast to knowledge-based ways of thinking about pragmatic encroachment, this view not only offers a much deeper and more general explanation, but it does so without appealing to overly strong forms of knowledge-action principles.

And just as the Kantian Theory deepens the explanation of pragmatic encroachment on knowledge offered by Pragmatic Intellectualism, we've already seen that the central features of Pragmatic Intellectualism are what make room for the Kantian Theory of knowledge. It is Pragmatic Intellectualism's recognition of the importance of non-evidential epistemic reasons against belief that allowed us to make sense of the sufficiency of reasons as a categorical property, and allowed us to make sense of the defeater dialectic as exactly what we should expect given the balancing nature of sufficiency. As I showed in Chapter 7, you can accept these insights without following Pragmatic Intellectualism in allowing that some epistemic reasons against belief are *practical* in nature—for example, by accepting an account of the nature of binary belief along the lines of Dallmann's. So the Kantian Theory is still independent of Pragmatic Intellectualism. But it is a natural partner.

12.4 The Fundamental Argument for Reasons First

In this book we have observed many of the central features of reasons at work in explanatory normative theorizing. The competition of reasons against one another allows us to make sense of the behavior of many seemingly intractable phenomena. Ross observed that the competition between *prima facie duties* was exactly the right structure to explain both the apparent force of many generalizations in normative ethical theory and at the same time explain the predictability of the kinds of counterexamples that they face, and the impossibility of constructing strict generalizations, even ones that are considerably ad hoc. As we saw in

Chapter 11, many of the main themes that emerged in the Gettier literature are strikingly similar to those Ross was concerned with. So it should be no surprise that the balancing structure of reasons explanation turns out to be fruitful in the analysis of knowledge, for many of the same reasons, at the heart of the classical argument, that it is fruitful in normative explanations more generally.

The balancing structure of reasons, we saw, also illuminated the complex ways in which what it is rational to believe can depend on many features of your situation other than the pure balance of your evidence—including how much further evidence is available. As soon as we appreciate that binary belief formation is not a binary choice, but a ternary choice, the very fact that the only thing that matters *for* forming belief is evidence for its content requires us to identify something *other* than evidence that counts against belief. It was the balancing role of reasons in normative explanations that lent power to the explanations that we provided in terms of this ternary structure and the various forms of non-evidential reasons against belief.

In Part IV, I have also emphasized the deliberative role of reasons. In many domains, at least with some stretching, pluralist forms of consequentialism can aspire to mimic many of the features of the balancing explanations provided by reasons. Instead of balancing reasons, they simply appeal to positive and negative values of different kinds. But the deliberative role is distinctive of reasons. Reasons can be acted on. The fact that reasons can be acted on makes them particularly apt for accounting for *well* properties like moral worth, doxastic justification—and knowledge.

And as I argued in Chapter 10, appealing to reasons in the account of well properties requires us to understand the underlying *right* properties in terms of the balance of reasons. The reasons that you must act on in order to count as not just acting rightly, but acting well, can't be just whatever helps to explain why that action is right. If they were, then the Well Principle would recursively overgeneralize, creating *well* properties corresponding to acting well *well*, and so on. So the reasons appealed to by the Well Principle are not just any old things that explain why something is right, but the reasons that figure in the *balancing* explanation of why it is right. The Kantian Theory of knowledge in Chapter 11 made good on this insight.

This gives us a second, even more important argument for the centrality of reasons in normative explanations. Whereas I've called Ross's argument the classical argument, because it is the traditional, most obvious, motivation to believe that reasons play a central explanatory role in much normative theory, this second argument is properly dubbed the *fundamental* argument. The fundamental argument is fundamental to understanding the centrality of reasons, because it draws on both the explanatory and deliberative roles of reasons.

Finally, we have seen throughout the book that reasons are instrumental in helping us understand why an explanation *rationalizes*. Pure externalist theories in epistemology such as process reliabilism and pure counterfactual theories of knowledge try to explain why beliefs are justified. But they have seemed to most of their critics to leave something out—something, intuitively, about the perspective of the agent. Strong internalist theories have tried to articulate what pure externalist theories have left out. They have said, for example, that you must be in a position to access whether your beliefs are justified, or whether you have a propositional justification for some belief. But this condition is arguably too strong. If it is the only diagnosis of where pure forms of externalism go wrong, then maybe they do not go wrong at all.

I have been suggesting an alternative diagnosis of where pure forms of externalism go wrong. They don't go wrong because they appeal to explanatory materials that fall outside the scope of what agents are aware of or even have potential access to. Where they go wrong, is in offering attempted explanations that explain without rationalizing. Rationalizing explanations appeal to *reasons*, and not just causes. So what we need are explanatory accounts that explain why some things are reasons, and then explain the right reasons in order for a balancing reasons explanation to get the right prediction about what is rational, correct, or justified. Ordinary thinkers do not need to know about reasons, much less about the explanation of what is a reason or why. So, strong forms of internalism are all mistaken. But they *do* need to *have* reasons—and that is what pure forms of externalism typically leave out.

There are many questions that I have not pursued in this book. I have not, for example, made any claims about the ontology of reasons. I have noted that we can attribute both objective and subjective reasons by citing propositions, but although this is compatible with the view I took in Schroeder (2007) that both objective and subjective reasons are propositions, it is also compatible with many other views about their nature—including that objective and subjective reasons have different ontologies, and that, as claimed by Howard (2019), their natures are not exhausted by the propositions by which we can cite them. I don't claim that these further questions are independent of those that I have considered here, but avoiding them has allowed me to paint with a broader brush, in order to make the big picture as clear as I am able.

I have also made no claims in this book about the relative priority of the objective and subjective reason relations. Both objective and subjective reasons are act-oriented factors that compete in the determination of normative properties and can be acted on (believed for, etc.). So they both satisfy my central criteria for being *reasons*. That is enough for my purposes. Yet it is surely no coincidence that in general, the same cases in which we can cite a subjective reason by mentioning what someone believes, we can cite the same proposition as an objective reason, if it is true—and conversely. So, objective and subjective reasons are surely closely related. A deeper look at what comes first in explanatory normative theory would therefore aspire to tell us something about which of objective or subjective reasons grounds and explains the other, or whether they are two manifestations of some third, common core.[1]

Strikingly, especially given the title of the book, I have barely even discussed the priority relationship between reasons and goodness or value. Neither of the central arguments for the centrality of reasons in explanatory normative theory—the classical argument or the fundamental argument—are direct arguments that the reason relation has either explanatory or analytic priority among *all* normative properties and relations. They simply give us the argumentative bones for more specific arguments that the reason relation has explanatory and analytic priority over *specific* other normative properties and relations. The classical argument gives us the bones to generate such an argument wherever there is a normative property whose behavior is complex and not subject to easy generalizations, but can be predicted instead as the balance of competing factors. And the fundamental argument gives us the bones to generate such an argument for each any pair of corresponding right/well properties. Since I haven't considered whether there is a kind of well property corresponding to something being good, I haven't given any insight into whether the fundamental argument will help us to settle the priority of reasons and the good.

These are all topics which, though important for an ultimate defense of the priority of reasons, would have taken us far too far aside. Nor have I covered every topic even among those treated in the book at the level of detail that it deserves, or fully addressed even the most obvious things that others will want to say about them. Instead, I have focused on what I think I have to add to what others have said. In most places I have merely touched on arguments that I have developed at greater length elsewhere, or else the book would have gotten much too far out of hand. And in some places I have focused on new arguments that complement but don't replace arguments that I have given elsewhere.

Nevertheless, my hope is that by bringing these topics together, even if in less fully developed forms, it is possible to gain a much better perspective on the scope of their consequences. If reasons can do this much work, and this interesting of work, even in the relatively hostile territory of epistemology, then maybe—just maybe—reasons really do come First.

---

[1] The issues at stake in evaluating the priority of objective and subjective reasons are complex. See, for example, Schroeder (2018a).

To φ or not to φ   © 2020 Tanya Kostochka

References

Ackerman, Terrence (1974). "Defeasibility Modified." *Philosophical Studies* 26(5–6): 431–5.

Adler, Jonathan (2002). *Belief's Own Ethics*. Cambridge, MA: MIT Press.

Alston, William (1985). "Concepts of Epistemic Justification." *Monist* 68(1): 57–89.

Alvarez, Maria (2018). "Reasons for Action, Acting for Reasons, and Rationality." *Synthese* 195(8): 3293–310.

Annis, David (1973). "Knowledge and Defeasibility." *Philosophical Studies* 24(3): 199–203.

Aristotle (2012). *Nicomachean Ethics*. Trans. Robert Bartlett and Susan Collins. Chicago, IL: University of Chicago Press.

Armstrong, David (1973). *Belief, Truth, and Knowledge*. Cambridge: Cambridge University Press.

Arpaly, Nomy (2002a). "Moral Worth." *Journal of Philosophy* 99(5): 223–45.

Arpaly, Nomy (2002b). *Unprincipled Virtue: An Inquiry into Moral Agency*. Oxford: Oxford University Press.

Arpaly, Nomy, and Timothy Schroeder (2014). *In Praise of Desire*. New York: Oxford University Press.

Asarnow, Samuel (2016). "Rational Internalism." *Ethics* 127(1): 147–78.

Asarnow, Samuel (2017). "The Reasoning View and Defeasible Practical Reasoning." *Philosophy and Phenomenological Research* 95(3): 614–36.

Ayer, A.J. (1956). *The Problem of Knowledge*. London: MacMillan.

Barker, John A. (1976). "What You Don't Know Won't Hurt You?" *American Philosophical Quarterly* 13(4): 303–8.

Basu, Rima (2018). *Beliefs That Wrong*. Los Angeles, CA: University of Southern California Press.

Basu, Rima (2019). "The Wrongs of Racist Beliefs." *Philosophical Studies* 176: 2497-515.

Basu, Rima, and Mark Schroeder (2019). "Doxastic Wrongs." In Bryan Kim and Matthew McGrath, eds., *Pragmatic Encroachment in Epistemology*. New York: Routledge, 181–205.

Bennett, Jonathan (1990). "Why is Belief Involuntary?" *Analysis* 50: 93.

Benton, Matthew A. (2018). "Pragmatic Encroachment and Theistic Knowledge." In Matthew A. Benton, John Hawthorne, and Dani Rabinowitz, eds., *Knowledge: Belief, and God: New Insights in Religious Epistemology*. Oxford: Oxford University Press, 267–87.

Berker, Selim (2013). "Epistemic Teleology and the Separateness of Propositions." *Philosophical Review* 122(3): 337–93.

Bero, Stephen (2017). *Responsibility and the Emotional Structure of Relationships*. PhD Dissertation, University of Southern California, Los Angeles.

Block, Ned (2008). "Phenomenal and Access Consciousness." *Proceedings of the Aristotelian Society* 108: 289–317.

Block, Ned (2011). "Perceptual Consciousness Overflows Access Consciousness." *Trends in Cognitive Sciences* 15(12): 567–75.

Bonjour, Laurence (1985). *The Structure of Empirical Knowledge*. Cambridge, MA: Harvard University Press.

Bonjour, Laurence (1996). *In Defense of Pure Reason*. Cambridge: Cambridge University Press.

Bradford, Gwen (2013). "The Value of Achievements." *Pacific Philosophical Quarterly* 94 (2): 204–24.

Bradford, Gwen (2015). *Achievement*. Oxford: Oxford University Press.

Bratman, Michael (1987). *Intention, Plans, and Practical Reason*. Stanford, CA: Center for the Study of Language and Information (CSLI).

Brentano, Franz (1889). *The Origin of Our Knowledge of Right and Wrong*. Oxford: Routledge.

Brewer, Bill (2002). *Perception and Reason*. Oxford: Oxford University Press.

Brewer, Talbot (2006). "Three Dogmas of Desire." In Timothy Chappell, ed., *Values and Virtues: Aristotelianism in Contemporary Ethics*. Oxford: Oxford University Press, 253–85.

Brewer, Talbot (2009). *The Retrieval of Ethics*. New York: Oxford University Press.

Brogaard, Berit (2011). "Are There Unconscious Perceptual Processes?" *Consciousness and Cognition* 20: 449–63.

Broome, John (2004). "Reasons." In R. Jay Wallace, Philip Pettit, Samuel Scheffler, and Michael Smith, eds., *Reason and Value: Themes from the Moral Philosophy of Joseph Raz*. Oxford: Oxford University Press, 204–28.

Broome, John (2013). *Rationality through Reasoning*. Oxford: Wiley Blackwell.

Brown, Jessica (2008a). "Subject-Sensitive Invariantism and the Knowledge Norm for Practical Reasoning." *Noûs* 42(2): 167–89.

Brown, Jessica (2008b). "Knowledge and Practical Reason." *Philosophy Compass* 3(6): 1135–52.

Brown, Jessica (2013). "Impurism, Practical Reasoning, and the Threshold Problem." *Noûs* 47(1): 179–92.

Brown, Jessica (2018). "Pragmatic Approaches to Belief." In Conor McHugh, Jonathan Way, and Daniel Whiting, eds., *Normativity: Epistemic and Practical*. Oxford: Oxford University Press, 26–46.

Brunero, John (2009). "Reasons and Evidence One Ought." *Ethics* 119(3): 538–45.

Burge, Tyler (1993). "Content Preservation." *Philosophical Review* 102(4): 457–88.

Burge, Tyler (1997). "Interlocution, Perception, and Memory." *Philosophical Studies* 86(1): 21–47.

Burge, Tyler (2010). *Origins of Objectivity*. Oxford: Oxford University Press.

Byrne, Alex (2014). "Perception and Evidence." *Philosophical Studies* 170(1): 101–13.

Carlson, Erik (1995). *Consequentialism Reconsidered*. New York: Springer.

Carnap, Rudolf (1928). *Der Logische Aufbau der Welt*. Leipzig: Felix Meiner Verlag.

Chalmers, David (1996). *The Conscious Mind*. Oxford: Oxford University Press.

Chignell, Andrew (2007a). "Belief in Kant." *Philosophical Review* 116(3): 323–60.

Chignell, Andrew (2007b). "Kant's Concepts of Justification." *Noûs* 41(1): 33–63.

Chisholm, Roderick (1966). *Theory of Knowledge*. Englewood Cliffs, NJ: Prentice Hall.

Christensen, David (2010). "Higher-Order Evidence." *Philosophy and Phenomenological Research* 81(1): 185–215.

Clark, Michael (1963). "Knowledge and Grounds: A Comment on Mr. Gettier's Paper." *Analysis* 24(2): 46-8.

Clarke, Samuel (1738). *Sermons on Several Subjects*. Ed. John Clarke. London: John and Paul Knapton. Available at https://play.google.com/store/books/details?id=xGlZAAAAYAAJ& rdid=book-xGlZAAAAYAAJ&rdot=1.

Cohen, Stewart (1984). "Justification and Truth." *Philosophical Studies* 46(3): 279–95.

Cohen, Stewart (2002). "Basic Knowledge and the Problem of Easy Knowledge." *Philosophy and Phenomenological Research* 65: 309–29.

Cohen, Stewart (2010). "Bootstrapping, Defeasible Reasoning, and A Priori Justification." *Philosophical Perspectives* 24: 141–58.

Cohen, Stewart (2012). "Does Practical Rationality Constrain Epistemic Rationality?" *Philosophy and Phenomenological Research* 85(2): 447–55.

Cohen, Stewart (2016). "Theorizing about the Epistemic." *Inquiry: An Interdisciplinary Journal of Philosophy* 59(7–8): 839–57.

Cohen, Stewart (unpublished]). Paper presented at Central Division meeting of the APA, February 2014.

Cohen, Stewart, and Juan Comesaña (2013a). "Williamson on Gettier Cases and Epistemic Logic." *Inquiry* 56(1): 15–29.

Cohen, Stewart, and Juan Comesaña (2013b). "Williamson on Gettier Cases in Epistemic Logic and the Knowledge Norm for Rational Belief: A Reply to a Reply to a Reply." *Inquiry* 56(4): 400–15.

Comesaña, Juan, and Matthew McGrath (2014). "Having False Reasons." In Clayton Littlejohn and John Turri, eds., *Epistemic Norms*. Oxford: Oxford University Press, 59–79.

Comesaña, Juan, and Matthew McGrath (2015). "Perceptual Reasons." *Philosophical Studies* 173(4): 991–1006.

Conee, Earl (1980). "Propositional Justification." *Philosophical Studies* 38(1): 65–8.

Conee, Earl, and Richard Feldman (2004). *Evidentialism*. Oxford: Oxford University Press.

Constant, Benjamin (1797). *Des Reactions Politiques*.

Cozzo, Cesare (2011). "Is Knowledge the Most General Factive Stative Attitude?" In Carlo Celluci, Emiliano Ippoliti, and Emily Grosholtz, eds., *Logic and Language*. Cambridge: Cambridge University Press, 84–8.

Crabill, Joshua (2015). *Describing Authority*. PhD Dissertation, University of Southern California, Los Angeles.

Dallmann, Justin (2014). "A Normatively Adequate Credal Reductivism." *Synthese* 191(10): 2301–13.

Dallmann, Justin (2016). *Belief as Credal Plan*. PhD Dissertation, University of Southern California, Los Angeles.

Dallmann, Justin (2017). "When Obstinacy is a (Better) Cognitive Policy." *Philosophers' Imprint* 17(24): 1–17.

Dancy, Jonathan (2000). *Practical Reality*. Oxford: Oxford University Press.

Dancy, Jonathan (2004). *Ethics Without Principles*. Oxford: Oxford University Press.

Danielson, Sven, and Jonas Olson (2007). "Brentano and the Buck-Passers." *Mind* 116(3): 511–22.

D'Arms, Justin, and Daniel Jacobson (2000a). "Sentiment and Value." *Ethics* 110(4): 722–48.

D'Arms, Justin, and Daniel Jacobson (2000b). "The Moralistic Fallacy." *Philosophy and Phenomenological Research* 61(1): 65–90.

Darwall, Stephen (2006). *The Second-Person Standpoint: Morality, Respect, and Accountability*. Cambridge, MA: Harvard University Press.

Davidson, Donald (1963). "Actions, Reasons, and Causes." *The Journal of Philosophy* 60(23): 685–700.

DeRose, Keith (1992). "Contextualism and Knowledge Attributions." *Philosophy and Phenomenological Research* 52(4): 913–29.

Dreier, James (1993). "The Structure of Normative Theories." *Monist* 76(1): 22–40.

Dreier, James (2011). "In Defense of Consequentializing." *Oxford Studies in Normative Ethics* 1. Oxford: Oxford University Press.

Dretske, Fred (1971). "Conclusive Reasons." *Australasian Journal of Philosophy* 49(1): 1–22.

Dretske, Fred (1981). *Knowledge and the Flow of Information.* Cambridge, MA: MIT Press.

Driver, Julia (1999). "Modesty and Ignorance." *Ethics* 109(4): 827–34.

Easwaran, Kenny (2016). "Dr. Truthlove, Or How I Learned to Stop Worrying and Love Bayesian Probabilities." *Noûs* 50(4): 816–53.

Engelhardt, Tristram (1975). "Defining Death: A Philosophical Problem for Medicine and Law." *American Review of Respiratory Disease* 112(5): 587–90.

Ewing, A.C. (1948). *The Definition of Good.* London: Routledge and Kegan Paul.

Fantl, Jeremy, and Matthew McGrath (2002). "Evidence, Pragmatics, and Justification." *Philosophical Review* 111(1): 67–94.

Fantl, Jeremy, and Matthew McGrath (2010). *Knowledge in an Uncertain World.* Oxford: Oxford University Press.

Fantl, Jeremy, and Matthew McGrath (2019). "Clarifying Pragmatic Encroachment: A Reply to Charity Anderson and John Hawthorne on Knowledge, Practical Adequacy, and Stakes." *Oxford Studies in Epistemology* 6: 258–66.

Faraci, David (2020). "We Have No Reason To Think There Are No Reasons for Affective Attitudes." *Mind* 129(1): 225–34.

Farkas, Katalin (2015). "Belief May Not Be a Necessary Condition for Knowledge." *Erkenntnis* 80(1): 185–200.

Feldman, Richard (1988). "Having Evidence." Reprinted in Conee and Feldman (2004), 219–41.

Feldman, Richard (2002). *Epistemology.* Upper Saddle River, NJ: Prentice Hall.

Finlay, Stephen (2014). *A Confusion of Tongues.* New York: Oxford University Press.

Firth, Roderick (1978). "Are Epistemic Concepts Reducible to Ethical Concepts?" In Alvin Goldman and Jaegwon Kim, eds., *Values and Morals.* Dordrecht: Kluwer, 215–29.

Fletcher, Guy (2013). "A Millian Objection to Reasons as Evidence." *Utilitas* 25(3): 417–20.

Fogal, Daniel (2016). "Reasons, Reason, and Context." In Errol Lord and Barry Maguire, eds., *Weighing Reasons.* Oxford: Oxford University Press, 74–103.

Foley, Richard (1993). *The Theory of Epistemic Rationality.* Cambridge, MA: Harvard University Press.

French, Craig (2012). "Does Propositional Seeing Entail Propositional Knowledge?" *Theoria* 78: 115–27.

French, Craig (2013). "Perceptual Experience and Seeing that *p.*" *Synthese* 190: 1735–51.

Fricker, Elizabeth (2009). "Is Knowing a State of Mind? The Case Against." In Patrick Greenough and Duncan Prichard, eds., *Williamson on Knowledge.* Oxford: Oxford University Press, 31–59.

Ganson, Dorit (2008). "Evidentialism and Pragmatic Constraints on Outright Belief." *Philosophical Studies* 139(3): 441–58.

Gendler, Tamar (2011). "On the Epistemic Costs of Implicit Bias." *Philosophical Studies* 156 (1): 33–63.

Gert, Joshua (2008). "Putting Particularism in Its Place." *Pacific Philosophical Quarterly* 89 (3): 312–24.

Gettier, Edmund (1963). "Is Justified True Belief Knowledge?" *Analysis* 23(6): 121–3.

Gibbard, Allan (2003). *Thinking How to Live.* Cambridge, MA: Harvard University Press.

Goldman, Alvin (1967). "A Causal Theory of Knowing." *The Journal of Philosophy* 64(12): 357–72.

Goldman, Alvin (1976). "Discrimination and Perceptual Knowledge." *Journal of Philosophy* 73: 771–91.

Goldman, Alvin (1979). "What is Justified Belief?" In George Pappas, ed., *Justification and Knowledge*. Boston: D. Reidel, 1–25.

Goldman, Alvin (1988). *Epistemology and Cognition*. Cambridge, MA: Harvard University Press.

Greco, John (2003). "Knowledge as Credit for True Belief." In Michael DePaul and Linda Zagzebski, eds., *Intellectual Virtue: Perspectives from Ethics and Epistemology*. Oxford: Oxford University Press, 111-34.

Greco, John (2010). *Achieving Knowledge: A Virtue-Theoretic Account of Epistemic Normativity*. Cambridge: Cambridge University Press.

Greenspan, Patricia (2005). "Asymmetrical Practical Reason." In Maria Reicher and Johan Marek, eds., *Experience and Analysis: Papers of the 27th International Wittgenstein Symposium*. Kirchberg am Wechsel: Austrian Ludwig Wittgenstein Society, 387–94.

Gregory, Alex (2016). "Normative Reasons as Good Bases." *Philosophical Studies* 173(9): 2291–310.

Grice, H.P. (2001). *Aspects of Reason*. Oxford: Oxford University Press.

Gross, Steven, and Jonathan Flombaum (2017). "Does Perceptual Consciousness Overflow Cognitive Access? The Challenge from Probabilistic, Hierarchical Processes." *Mind and Language* 35(3): 377–89.

Grzankowski, Alex (2015). "Not All Attitudes Are Propositional." *European Journal of Philosophy* 23(3): 374–91.

Grzankowski, Alex (2016). "Attitudes Towards Objects." *Noûs* 50(2): 314–28.

Harman, Gilbert (1986). *Change in View*. Cambridge, MA: MIT Press.

Harman, Gilbert (2002). "Practical Aspects of Theoretical Reasoning." In Al Mele and Piers Rawling, eds., *The Oxford Handbook to Rationality*. Oxford: Oxford University Press, 45–56.

Harman, Gilbert, and Brett Sherman (2004). "Knowledge, Assumptions, Lotteries." *Philosophical Issues* 14 (Epistemology): 492–500.

Harman, Gilbert, and Brett Sherman (2011). "Knowledge and Assumptions." *Philosophical Studies* 156(1): 131–40.

Hatcher, Michael (2017). *A Deontological Explanation of Accessibilism*. PhD Dissertation, University of Southern California, Los Angeles.

Hawthorne, John (2004). *Knowledge and Lotteries*. Oxford: Oxford University Press.

Hawthorne, John, and Ofra Magidor (2018). *Reflections on the Ideology of Reasons*. In Daniel Star, ed., *The Oxford Handbook to Reasons and Normativity*. Oxford: Oxford University Press.

Hawthorne, John, and Jason Stanley (2009). "Knowledge and Action." *The Journal of Philosophy* 105(10): 571–90.

Hazlett, Allan (2010). "The Myth of Factive Verbs." *Philosophy and Phenomenological Research* 80(3): 497–522.

Hazlett, Allan (2012). "Factive Presupposition and the Truth Condition on Knowledge." *Acta Analytica* 27(4): 461–78.

Hazlett, Allan (unpublished). "False Knowledge." Unpublished paper.

Henning, Tim (2014). "Normative Reasons Contextualism." *Philosophy and Phenomenological Research* 88(3): 593–624.

Hershowitz, Scott (2011). "The Role of Authority." *Philosophers' Imprint* 11(7). Availabe at: www.philosophersimprint.org/011007/, accessed Nov 24, 2020.

Hieronymi, Pamela (2005). "The Wrong Kind of Reason." *Journal of Philosophy* 102(9): 437–57.

Hieronymi, Pamela (2006). "Controlling Attitudes." *Pacific Philosophical Quarterly* 87(1): 45–74.

Hieronymi, Pamela (2013). "The Use of Reasons in Thought (and the Use of Earmarks in Arguments)." *Ethics* 124(1): 114–27.

Hills, Alison (2009). "Moral Testimony and Moral Epistemology." *Ethics* 120(1): 94–127.

Holton, Richard (2014). "Intention as a Model for Belief." In Manuel Vargas and Gideon Yaffe, eds., *Rational and Social Agency: Essays on the Philosophy of Michael Bratman.* Oxford: Oxford University Press, 12–37.

Hornsby, Jennifer (2008). "A Disjunctive Account of Acting for Reasons." In Adrian Haddock and Fiona McPherson, eds., *Disjunctivism: Action, Perception, and Knowledge.* Oxford: Oxford University Press, 244–61.

Horty, John (2007a). "Reasons as Defaults." *Philosophers' Imprint* 7(3). Available at: www.philosophersimprint.org/007003/, accessed Nov 24, 2020.

Horty, John (2007b). "Defaults with Priorities." *Journal of Philosophical Logic* 36: 367–413.

Horty, John (2012). *Reasons as Defaults.* Oxford: Oxford University Press.

Horty, John (2014). "Deontic Modals: Why Abandon the Classical Semantics?" *Pacific Philosophical Quarterly* (special issue on deontic modality, ed. Stephen Finlay and Mark Schroeder) 95: 424–60.

Howard, Nathan (2019). *The Dual Aspects of Normative Reasons.* PhD Dissertation, University of Southern California, Los Angeles.

Howard, Nathan (forthcoming). "Primary Reasons as Normative Reasons." Forthcoming in *The Journal of Philosophy.*

Howard, Nathan (ms). "Getting it." Manuscript, University of Southern California, Los Angeles.

Hubbs, Graham (2013). "How Reasons Bear on Intentions." *Ethics* 124(1): 84–100.

Huemer, Michael (2001). *Skepticism and the Veil of Perception.* Lanham, MD: Rowman and Littlefield.

Huemer, Michael (2006). "Phenomenal Conservativism and the Internalist Intuition." *American Philosophical Quarterly* 43(1): 147–58.

Huemer, Michael (2007). "Compassionate Phenomenal Conservatism." *Philosophy and Phenomenological Research* 74(1): 30–55.

Hughes, Nick (2014). "Is Knowledge the Ability to φ for the Reason that P?" *Episteme* 11(4): 457–62.

Hurka, Thomas (2001). *Virtue, Vice, and Value.* Oxford: Oxford University Press.

Hurka, Thomas (2003). "Moore in the Middle." *Ethics* 113(4): 599–628.

Hurka, Thomas (2015). *British Ethical Theorists from Sidgwick to Ewing.* Oxford: Oxford University Press.

Hurka, Thomas, and Daniel Elstein (2009). "From Thick to Thin: Two Moral Reduction Plans." *Canadian Journal of Philosophy* 39(4): 515–35.

Hursthouse, Rosalind (1999). *On Virtue Ethics.* Oxford: Oxford University Press.

Hyman, John (1999). "How Knowledge Works." *Philosophical Quarterly* 49(197): 433–51.

Hyman, John (2014). "The Most General Factive Stative Attitude." *Analysis* 74(4): 561–5.

S.M. Ishtiaque, K.R. Salhotra, and R.V.M. Gowdra (2003). "Friction Spinning." *Textile Progress* 33(2): 1-68.

Jackson, Elizabeth (2019). "How Belief-Credence Dualism Explains Away Pragmatic Encroachment." *The Philosophical Quarterly* 69(4): 511–33.

Jeffrey, Richard (2002). *Subjective Probability: The Real Thing.* Princeton, NJ: Princeton University Press.

Johnsen, Bredo (1974). "Knowledge." *Philosophical Studies* 25(4): 273–82.

Johnson King, Zoë (2020). "Accidentally Doing the Right Thing." *Philosophy and Phenomenological Research* 100(1): 186–206.

Kant, Immanuel (1798). "On a Supposed Right to Lie from Philanthropic Concern."

Kant, Immanuel (1999). *Critique of Pure Reason*. Trans. Paul Guyer and Allan Wood. Cambridge: Cambridge University Press.

Kant, Immanuel (2002). *Groundwork for the Metaphysics of Morals*. Trans. Arnulf Zweig, Ed. Arnulf Zweig and Thomas E. Hill, Jr. Oxford: Oxford University Press.

Karttunen, Lauri (1973). "Presuppositions of Compound Sentences." *Linguistic Inquiry* 4 (2): 169–93.

Kavka, Gregory (1983). "The Toxin Puzzle." *Analysis* 43(1): 33–6.

Kearns, Stephen, and Daniel Star (2008). "Reasons: Explanations or Evidence?" *Ethics* 119 (1): 31–56.

Kearns, Stephen, and Daniel Star (2009). "Reasons as Evidence." *Oxford Studies in Metaethics* 4: 215–42.

Keller, Simon (2004a). "Friendship and Belief." *Philosophical Papers* 33(3): 329–51.

Keller, Simon (2004b). "Welfare and the Achievement of Goals." *Philosophical Studies* 121 (1): 27–41.

Keller, Simon (2009). "Welfare as Success." *Noûs* 43(4): 656–83.

Kelly, Thomas (2002). "The Rationality of Belief and Some Other Propositional Attitudes." *Philosophical Studies* 90(1): 163–96.

Kiesewetter, Benjamin (2016). 'You Ought to φ only if You May Believe that You Ought to φ." *Philosophical Quarterly* 66(265): 760–82.

Klein, Peter (1971). "A Proposed Definition of Propositional Knowledge." *Journal of Philosophy* 68(16): 471–82.

Kornblith, Hilary (2015). "The Role of Reasons in Epistemology." *Episteme* 12(2): 225–39.

Korsgaard, Christine (1986). "Skepticism about Practical Reason." *The Journal of Philosophy* 83(1): 5–25.

Kruglanski, Arie (2004). *The Psychology of Closed Mindedness*. New York: Psychology Press.

Kvanvig, Jonathan (2003). *The Value of Knowledge and the Pursuit of Understanding*. Cambridge: Cambridge University Press.

Kyburg, Henry (1961). *Probability and the Logic of Rational Belief*. Middletown, CT: Wesleyan University Press.

Lackey, Jennifer (2007). "Why We Don't Deserve Credit for Everything We Know." *Synthese* 158(3): 345–61.

Lackey, Jennifer (2010). "Acting on Knowledge." *Philosophical Perspectives* 24(1): 361–82.

Lasonen-Aarnio (2010). "Unreasonable Knowledge." *Philosophical Perspectives* 24: 1–21.

Lasonen-Aarnio (2014). "Higher-Order Evidence and the Limits of Defeat." *Philosophy and Phenomenological Research* 88(2): 314–45.

Lehrer, Keith (1965). "Knowledge, Truth, and Evidence." *Analysis* 25(5): 168–75.

Lehrer, Keith (1970). "The Fourth Condition of Knowledge: A Defense." *Review of Metaphysics* 24(1): 122–8.

Lehrer, Keith (1974). *Knowledge*. Oxford: Clarendon Press.

Lehrer, Keith, and Thomas Paxson (1969). "Knowledge: Undefeated Justified True Belief." *Journal of Philosophy* 66: 225–37.

Levy, Stephen (1977). "Defeasibility Theories of Knowledge." *Canadian Journal of Philosophy* 7(1): 115–23.

Lewis, C.I. (1946). *An Analysis of Knowledge and Valuation*. La Salle, IL: Open Court.

Lewis, David (1980). "Veridical Hallucination and Prosthetic Vision." *Australasian Journal of Philosophy* 58(3): 239–49.

Lin, Hanti (2013). "Foundations of Everyday Practical Reasoning." *Journal of Philosophical Logic* 42(6): 831–62.

Littlejohn, Clayton (2012). *Justification and the Truth-Connection*. Oxford: Oxford University Press.

Locke, Dustin (2015). "Knowledge, Explanation, and Motivating Reasons." *American Philosophical Quarterly* 52(3): 215–32.

Logue, Heather (2013). "Visual Experience of Natural Kind Properties: Is There Any Fact of the Matter?" *Philosophical Studies* 162(1): 1–12.

Lord, Errol (2010). "Having Reasons and the Factoring Account." *Philosophical Studies* 149 (3): 283–96.

Lord, Errol (2018). *The Importance of Being Rational*. Oxford: Oxford University Press.

Louise, Jennie (2004). "Relativity of Value and the Consequentialist Umbrella." *Philosophical Quarterly* 54(4): 518–36.

McDowell, John (1994). *Mind and World*. Cambridge, MA: Harvard University Press.

McDowell, John (1995). "Knowledge and the Internal." *Philosophy and Phenomenological Research* 55(5): 877–93.

McDowell, John (2006). "The Disjunctive Conception of Experience as Material for a Transcendental Argument." *Teorema: Revista Internacional de Filosofía* 25(1): 19–33.

McDowell, John (2008). "Avoiding the Myth of the Given." In Jakob Lindgaard, ed., *Experience, Norm, and Nature*. Oxford: Wiley-Blackwell, 1–14.

MacFarlane, John (2005). "Knowledge Laundering: Testimony and Sensitive Invariantism." *Analysis* 65(2): 132–8.

McGrath, Matthew (2007). "Memory and Epistemic Conservatism." *Synthese* 157(1): 1–24.

McGrath, Matthew (2017). "Knowing What Things Look Like." *The Philosophical Review* 126(1): 1–41.

McGrath, Matthew (2018a). "Looks and Perceptual Justification." *Philosophy and Phenomenological Research* 96(1): 110–33.

McGrath, Matthew (2018b). "Pragmatic Encroachment: Its Problems are Your Problems!" In Conor McHugh, Jonathan Way, and Daniel Whiting, eds., *Normativity: Epistemic and Practical*. Oxford: Oxford University Press, 162-78.

McGrath, Sarah (2011). "Skepticism about Moral Expertise as a Puzzle for Moral Realism." *Journal of Philosophy* 108(3): 111–37.

McHugh, Conor, and Jonathan Way (2016). "Fittingness First." *Ethics* 126(3): 575–606.

McNaughton, David, and Piers Rawling (2010). "The Making/Evidential Reason Distinction." *Analysis* 71(1): 100–2.

Maguire, Barry (2018). "There Are No Reasons for Affective Attitudes." *Mind* 127(3): 779 805.

Markovits, Julia (2010). "Acting for the Right Reasons." *Philosophical Review* 119(2): 201–42.

Markovits, Julia (2012). "Saints, Heroes, Sages, and Villains." *Philosophical Studies* 158(2): 289–311.

Marmor, Andrei (2011). "An Institutional Conception of Authority." *Philosophy and Public Affairs* 39(3): 238–61.

Marušic, Berislav (2012). "Belief and Difficult Action." *Philosophers' Imprint* 12(18): 1–30.

Marušic, Berislav (2015). *Evidence and Agency: Norms of Belief for Promising and Resolving*. Oxford: Oxford University Press.

Mehta, Neil (2016). "Knowledge and Knowledge and Other Norms for Assertion, Action, and Belief: A Teleological Account." *Philosophy and Phenomenological Research* 93(3): 681–705.

Mill, John Stuart. (1861). *Utilitarianism*. Indianapolis, IN: Hackett.

Milona, Michael, and Mark Schroeder (2019). "Desiring under the Proper Guise." *Oxford Studies in Metaethics* 14: 121–43.

Mitova, Veli (2015). "Truthy Psychologism about Evidence." *Philosophical Studies* 172(4): 1105–26.

Molyneux, Bernard (2007). "Primeness, Internalism, and Explanatory Generality." *Philosophical Studies* 135(2): 255-77.

Moore, G.E. (1903). *Principia Ethica*. Cambridge: Cambridge University Press.

Nagel, Jennifer (2008). "Knowledge Ascriptions and the Psychological Consequences of Changing Stakes." *Australasian Journal of Philosophy* 86(2): 279–94.

Nagel, Thomas (1970). *The Possibility of Altruism*. Princeton, NJ: Princeton University Press.

Nair, Shyam (2014). "A Fault Line in Ethical Theory." *Philosophical Perspectives* 28(1): 173–200.

Nair, Shyam (2016). "How do Reasons Accrue?" In Errol Lord and Barry Maguire, eds., *Weighing Reasons*. Oxford: Oxford University Press: 56–73.

Nair, Shyam, and John Horty (2018). "The Logic of Reasons." In Daniel Star, ed., *The Oxford Handbook to Reasons and Normativity*. Oxford: Oxford University Press, 67–84.

Nelkin, Dana (2000). "The Lottery Paradox, Knowledge, and Rationality." *The Philosophical Review* 109(3): 373–409.

Nelson, Mark (2010). "We Have No Positive Epistemic Duties." *Mind* 119(1): 83–102.

Nolfi, Kate (2015). "Which Mental States are Rationally Evaluable, and Why?" *Philosophical Issues* 25(1): 41–63.

Nozick, Robert (1974). *Anarchy, State, and Utopia*. Cambridge, MA: Harvard University Press.

Nozick, Robert (1981). *Philosophical Explanations*. Cambridge, MA: Harvard University Press.

Oddie, Graham, and Peter Milne (1991). "Act and Value." *Theoria* 57(1–2): 42–76.

Olin, Doris (1976). "Knowledge and Defeasible Justification." *Philosophical Studies* 30(2): 129–36.

Olson, Jonas (2004). "Buck-Passing and the Wrong Kind of Reasons." *The Philosophical Quarterly* 54(3): 295–300.

Owens, David (2000). *Reason without Freedom*. New York: Routledge.

Parfit, Derek (1997). "Equality and Priority." *Ratio* 10(3): 202–21.

Parfit, Derek (2001). "Reasons and Rationality." In Dan Egonson, Jonas Josefson, Björn Petterson, and Toni Rønnow-Rasmussen, eds., *Exploring Practical Philosophy: From Action to Values*. Aldershot: Ashgate, 17–39.

Parfit, Derek (2011). *On What Matters*, vol. 1. Oxford: Oxford University Press.

Perl, Caleb (2020). "Presuppositions, Attitudes, and Why They Matter." *Australasian Journal of Philosophy* 98(2): 363–81.

Piller, Christian (2001). "Normative Practical Reasoning." *Proceedings of the Aristotelian Society*, Suppl. Vol. 25: 195–216.

Piller, Christian (2006). "Content-Related and Attitude-Related Reasons for Preferences." *Philosophy* Suppl. Vol. 59: 155–81.

Pink, Thomas (1996). *The Psychology of Freedom*. Cambridge: Cambridge University Press.

Podgorksi, Abelard (2016a). "Dynamic Conservatism." *Ergo* 3: 349-76.

Podgorksi, Abelard (2016b). "Dynamic Permissivism." *Philosophical Studies* 173(7): 1923–39.

Pollock, John, and Joseph Cruz (1999). *Contemporary Theories of Knowledge,* 2nd ed. New York: Rowman and Littlefield.

Portmore, Douglas (2005). "Combining Teleological Ethics with Evaluator Relativism: A Promising Result." *Pacific Philosophical Quarterly* 86(1): 95–113.

Portmore, Douglas (2011). *Commonsense Consequentialism: Wherein Morality Meets Rationality.* Oxford: Oxford University Press.

Prinz, Jesse (2013). "Siegel's Get Rich Quick Scheme." *Philosophical Studies* 163(3): 827–35.

Pritchard, Duncan (2012). *Epistemological Disjunctivism.* Oxford: Oxford University Press.

Pritchard, Duncan, Alan Millar, and Adrian Haddock (2010). *The Nature and Value of Knowledge.* Oxford: Oxford University Press.

Pryor, James (2000). "The Skeptic and the Dogmatist." *Noûs* 34(4): 517–49.

Pryor, James (2005a). "What's so Bad About Living in the Matrix?" In Christopher Grau, ed., *Philosophers Explore the Matrix.* Oxford: Oxford University Press, 40–61.

Pryor, James (2005b). "Is there Non-Inferential Justification?" In Matthias Steup and Ernest Sosa, eds., *Contemporary Debates in Epistemology.* Oxford: Blackwell.

Pryor, James (2007). "Reasons and That-Clauses." *Philosophical Issues* 17: 217–44.

Rabinowicz, Wlodek, and Toni Rønnow-Rasmussen (2004). "The Strike of the Demon: On Fitting Pro-Attitudes and Value." *Ethics* 114: 391–423.

Radford, Colin (1966). "Knowledge: By Examples." *Analysis* 27(1): 1–11.

Railton, Peter (1984). "Alienation, Consequentialism, and the Demands of Morality." *Philosophy and Public Affairs* 13(2): 134–71.

Reed, Baron (2012). "Resisting Encroachment." *Philosophy and Phenomenological Research* 85(2): 465–72.

Reed, Baron (2018). "Practical Interests and Reasons for Belief." In Conor McHugh, Jonathan Way, and Daniel Whiting, eds., *Normativity: Epistemic and Practical.* Oxford: Oxford University Press, 200–20.

Regan, B.C., Julliot, C., Simmen, B., Viénot, F., Charles-Dominique, P., and Mollon, J.D. (2001). "Fruits, Foliage, and the Evolution of Primate Colour Vision." *Philosophical Transaction of the Royal Society of London B* 356: 229–83.

Reiter, Raymond (1980). "A Logic for Default Reasoning." *Artificial Intelligence* 13(1): 81–122.

Ross, Jacob, and Mark Schroeder (2014). "Belief, Credence, and Pragmatic Encroachment." *Philosophy and Phenomenological Research* 88(2): 259–88.

Ross, W.D. (1930). *The Right and the Good.* Cambridge: Cambridge University Press.

Russell, Bertrand (1914). *Our Knowledge of the External World.* London: George Allen and Unwin.

Ryan, Sharon (1996). "The Epistemic Virtues of Consistency." *Synthese* 109(1): 121–41.

Scanlon, T.M. (1998). *What We Owe to Each Other.* Cambridge, MA: Harvard University Press.

Scanlon, T.M. (2003). "Metaphysics and Morals." *Proceedings and Addresses of the American Philosophical Association* 77(2): 7–22.

Scheffler, Samuel (1982). *The Rejection of Consequentialism.* Oxford: Oxford University Press.

Schellenberg, Susanna (2013). "Experience and Evidence." *Mind* 122(3): 699–747.

Schellenberg, Susanna (2014). "The Epistemic Force of Perceptual Experience." *Philosophical Studies* 170(1): 87–100.

Schoenfield, Miriam (2015). "Bridging Rationality and Accuracy." *Journal of Philosophy* 112(12): 633–57.

Schroeder, Mark (2007). *Slaves of the Passions.* Oxford: Oxford University Press.

Schroeder, Mark (2008). "Having Reasons." *Philosophical Studies* 139(1): 57–71.

Schroeder, Mark (2010). "Value and the Right Kind of Reasons." *Oxford Studies in Metaethics* 5: 25–55.

Schroeder, Mark (2011a). "What Does it Take to 'Have' a Reason?" In Andrew Reisner and Asbjørn Steglich-Peterson, eds., *Reasons for Belief*. Cambridge: Cambridge University Press, 201-22.

Schroeder, Mark (2011b). "Holism, Weight, and Undercutting." *Noûs* 45(2): 328-44.

Schroeder, Mark (2012a). "Stakes, Withholding, and Pragmatic Encroachment on Knowledge." *Philosophical Studies* 160(2): 265-86.

Schroeder, Mark (2012b). "The Ubiquity of State-Given Reasons." *Ethics* 122(3): 457-88.

Schroeder, Mark (2013). "State-Given Reasons: Prevalent, if Not Ubiquitous." *Ethics* 124 (1): 128-40.

Schroeder, Mark (2014). *Explaining the Reasons We Share: Explanation and Expression in Ethics*, vol. 1. Oxford: Oxford University Press.

Schroeder, Mark (2015a). *Expressing Our Attitudes: Explanation and Expression in Ethics*, vol. 2. Oxford: Oxford University Press.

Schroeder, Mark (2015b). "Knowledge is Belief for Sufficient (Objective and Subjective) Reasons." *Oxford Studies in Epistemology* 5: 226-52.

Schroeder, Mark (2015c). "In Defense of the Kantian Account of Knowledge: Reply to Whiting." *Logos and Episteme* 6(3): 371-82.

Schroeder, Mark (2015d). "What Makes Reasons Sufficient?" *American Philosophical Quarterly* 52(2): 159-70.

Schroeder, Mark (2016). "Knowledge Based on Seeing." *Logos and Episteme* 7(1): 101-7.

Schroeder, Mark (2018a). "Getting Perspective on Objective Reasons." *Ethics* 128(2): 289-319.

Schroeder, Mark (2018b). "The Unity of Reasons." In Daniel Star, ed., *The Oxford Handbook to Reasons and Rationality*. Oxford: Oxford University Press, 877-95.

Schroeder, Mark (2018c). "Rational Stability under Pragmatic Encroachment." *Episteme* 15 (3): 297-312.

Schroeder, Mark (2018d). "When Beliefs Wrong." *Philosophical Topics* 46(1): 115-27.

Schroeder, Mark (2019). "Why You'll Regret Not Reading This Paper." *Royal Institute of Philosophy Supplements* 85: 135-86.

Schroeder, Mark (forthcoming). "The Fundamental Reason for Reasons Fundamentalism." *Philosophical Studies*.

Schroeder, Mark (ms). "Rationality in Retrospect." Paper manuscript. Provisionally forthcoming in *Oxford Studies in Metaethics*.

Searle, John (1983). *Intentionality*. Oxford: Oxford University Press.

Sen, Amartya (1983). "Evaluator Relativity and Consequential Evaluation." *Philosophy and Public Affairs* 12(1): 113-32.

Setiya, Kieran (2014). "What is a Reason to Act?" *Philosophical Studies* 167(2): 221-35.

Shah, Nishi (2002). "Clearing Space for Doxastic Voluntarism." *The Monist* 85(3): 436-45.

Shah, Nishi (2006). "A New Argument for Evidentialism." *Philosophical Quarterly* 56: 481-98.

Shah, Nishi, and Matthew Silverstein (2013). "Reasoning in Stages." *Ethics* 124(1): 101-13.

Shanklin, Robert (2011). *On Good and "Good"*. PhD Dissertation, University of Southern California, Los Angeles. Available at: http://digitallibrary.usc.edu/cdm/ref/collection/p15799coll127/id/632791, accessed Nov 24, 2020.

Shope, Robert (1978). "The Conditional Fallacy in Contemporary Philosophy." *Journal of Philosophy* 75(8): 397-413.

Shope, Robert (1983). *The Analysis of Knowing*. Princeton, NJ: Princeton University Press.

Sidgwick, Henry (1907). *The Methods of Ethics,* 7th ed. Indianapolis, IN: Hackett.

Siegel, Susanna (2006). "Which Properties are Represented in Perception?" In Tamar Gendler and John Hawthorne, eds., *Perceptual Experience*. Oxford: Oxford University Press: 481–503.

Siegel, Susanna (2010). *The Contents of Visual Experience*. Oxford: Oxford University Press.

Siegel, Susanna (2012). "Cognitive Penetrability and Perceptual Justification." *Noûs* 46(2): 201–22.

Siegel, Susanna (2013). "The Epistemic Impact of the Etiology of Experience." *Philosophical Studies* 162(3): 697–722.

Silins, Nico (2007). "Basic Justification and the Moorean Response to the Skeptic." *Oxford Studies in Epistemology* 2: 108–40.

Silman, Jeremy (2007). *Silman's Complete Endgame Course: From Beginner to Master*. Los Angeles, CA: Siles Press.

Silverstein, Matthew (2016). "Reducing Reasons." *Journal of Ethics and Social Philosophy* 10 (1): 1–22.

Silverstein, Matthew (2017). "Ethics and Practical Reasoning." *Ethics* 127(2): 353–82.

Sinclair, Neil (2016). "On the Connection between Normative Reasons and the Possibility of Acting for those Reasons." *Ethical Theory and Moral Practice* 19(5): 1211–23.

Skorupski, John (2007). "Buck-Passing About Goodness." In Rønnow-Rasmussen, Petersson, Jesefsson, and Egonsson, eds., *Hommage à Wlodek: Philosophical Papers Dedicated to Wlodek Rabinowicz*. www.fil.lu.se/hommageawlodek.

Skorupski, John (2010). *The Domain of Reasons*. Oxford: Oxford University Press.

Sliwa, Paulina (2012). "In Defense of Moral Testimony." *Philosophical Studies* 158(2): 175–95.

Sliwa, Paulina (2016). "Moral Worth and Moral Knowledge." *Philosophy and Phenomenological Research* 93(2): 393–418.

Smith, Martin (forthcoming). "Four Arguments for Denying that Lottery Beliefs are Justified." In I. Douven, ed., *Knowledge and Rational Belief: Essays on the Lottery Paradox*. Cambridge: Cambridge University Press.

Smith, Michael (1994). *The Moral Problem*. Oxford: Basil Blackwell.

Smith, Michael (2003). "Neutral and Relative Value After Moore." *Ethics* 113(4): 576–98.

Smithies, Declan (2011). "Attention is Rational Access-Consciousness." In Christopher Mole, Declan Smithies, and Wayne Wu, eds., *Attention: Philosophical and Psychological Essays*. Oxford: Oxford University Press, 247–73.

Smithies, Declan (2018). "Reasons and Perception." In Daniel Star, ed., *The Oxford Handbook to Reasons and Normativity*. Oxford: Oxford University Press, 631–61.

Snedegar, Justin (2013). "Reason Claims and Contrastivism about Reasons." *Philosophical Studies* 166: 231–42.

Snedegar, Justin (2014). "Contrastive Reasons and Promotion." *Ethics* 125(1): 39–63.

Snedegar, Justin (2016). "Reasons, Ought, and Requirements." *Oxford Studies in Metaethics* 11: 155–81.

Snedegar, Justin (2017). *Contrastive Reasons*. Oxford: Oxford University Press.

Sosa, Ernest (1964). "The Analysis of 'Knowledge that *P*'." *Analysis* 25(1): 1–8.

Sosa, Ernest (1970). "Two Conceptions of Knowledge." *Journal of Philosophy* 67(3): 59–66.

Sosa, Ernest (2009). *Reflective Knowledge: Apt Belief and Reflective Knowledge*, vol. 2. Oxford: Oxford University Press.

Sosa, Ernest (2011). *Knowing Full Well*. Princeton, NJ: Princeton University Press.

Sosa, Ernest, and Kurt Sylvan (2018). "The Place of Reasons in Epistemology." In Daniel Star, ed., *The Oxford Handbook to Reasons and Rationality*. Oxford: Oxford University Press, 555–74.

Staffel, Julia (2019). "How Do Beliefs Simplify Reasoning?" *Noûs* 53(4): 937–62.

Stalnaker, Robert (1984). *Inquiry*. Cambridge, MA: MIT Press.

Stalnaker, Robert (2008). *Our Knowledge of the Internal World*. Oxford: Oxford University Press.

Stanley, Jason (2005). *Knowledge and Practical Interests*. Oxford: Oxford University Press.

Star, Daniel (2011). "Two Levels of Moral Thinking." *Oxford Studies in Normative Ethics* 1: 75–96.

Steup, Matthias (1992). "Memory." In Jonathan Dancy and Ernest Sosa, eds., *A Companion to Epistemology*. Oxford: Basil Blackwell, 276-8.

Stratton-Lake, Philip (2000). *Kant, Duty, and Moral Worth*. New York: Routledge.

Stratton-Lake, Philip (2005). "How to Deal with Evil Demons: Comment on Rabinowicz and Rønnow-Rasmussen." *Ethics* 115 (4): 778–98.

Stroud, Sarah (2006). "Epistemic Partiality in Friendship." *Ethics* 116(3): 498–524.

Suikkanen, Jussi (2011). "Consequentialism, Constraints, and Good-Relative-To: A Reply to Mark Schroeder." *Journal of Ethics and Social Philosophy* 3(1): 1–8.

Swain, Marshall (1974). "Epistemic Defeasibility." *American Philosophical Quarterly* 11(1): 15–25.

Swain, Marshall (1979). "Justification and the Basis of Belief." In George Pappas, ed., *Justification and Knowledge*. Dordrecht: D. Reidel Publishing, 25-50.

Sylvan, Kurt (2015). "What Apparent Reasons Appear to Be." *Philosophical Studies* 172(3): 587–606.

Sylvan, Kurt, and Errol Lord (unpublished). "Believing for Normative Reasons: Prime, Not Composite." Unpublished paper.

Tappolet, Christine (2013). "Evaluative vs. Deontic Concepts." *The International Encyclopedia of Ethics* 1791-9.

Thagard, Paul (2006). "Desires are Not Propositional Attitudes." *Dialogue* 45(1): 151-6.

Turri, John (2009). "The Ontology of Epistemic Reasons." *Noûs* 43(3): 490–512.

Turri, John (2010a). "Does Perceiving Entail Knowing?" *Theoria* 76(3): 197–206.

Turri, John (2010b). "On the Relationship between Propositional and Doxastic Justification." *Philosophy and Phenomenological Research* 80(2): 312–26.

Unger, Peter (1975). *Ignorance: The Case for Skepticism*. Oxford: Oxford University Press.

van Fraassen, Bas (1984). "Belief and the Will". *Journal of Philosophy* 81(5): 235–56.

Väyrynen, Pekka (2013). *The Lewd, the Rude, and the Nasty: A Study of Thick Concepts in Ethics*. Oxford: Oxford University Press.

Villanueva, Eduardo (2012). *Constraining Assertion: An Account of Context-Sensitivity*. PhD Dissertation, University of Southern California, Los Angeles. Available at http://digitallibrary.usc.edu/cdm/ref/collection/p15799coll3/id/26882, accessed Nov 24 2020.

Vogel, Jonathan (2000). "Reliabilism Leveled." *Journal of Philosophy* 97: 602–23.

Vogelstein, Eric (2012). "Subjective Reasons." *Ethical Theory and Moral Practice* 15(2): 239–57.

von Kriegstein, Hasko (2014). *Shaping the World in One's Image: An Essay on the Nature and Value of Achievements*. PhD Dissertation, University of Toronto, Ontario.

Walton, Douglas (1979). *On Defining Death: An Analytic Study of the Concept of Death in Philosophy and Medical Ethics*. Montreal: McGill-Queen's University Press.

Way, Jonathan (2012). "Transmission and the Wrong Kind of Reason." *Ethics* 122(3): 489–515.

Way, Jonathan (2017). "Reasons as Premises of Good Reasoning." *Pacific Philosophical Quarterly* 98(2): 251–70.

Weatherson, Brian (2005). "Can We Do Without Pragmatic Encroachment?" *Philosophical Perspectives* 19(1): 417–43.

Weaver, Brian, and Kevin Scharp (2019). *Semantics for Reasons.* Oxford: Oxford University Press.

Wedgwood, Ralph (2007). "Conditionalization, Reflection, and Self-Knowledge." *Philosophical Studies* 135(2): 179–97.

Wedgwood, Ralph (2009). "Intrinsic Values and Reasons for Action." *Philosophical Issues* 19: 342–63.

Wedgwood, Ralph (2012). "Outright Belief." *Dialectica* 66(3): 309–29.

Wedgwood, Ralph (2013). "A Priori Bootstrapping." In Albert Casullo and Joshua Thurow, eds., *The A Priori in Philosophy.* Oxford: Oxford University Press, 226–46.

Weisberg, Jonathan (2007). "Conditionalization, Reflection, and Self-Knowledge." *Philosophical Studies* 135(2): 179-97.

Weisberg, Jonathan (2020). "Belief in Psyontology." *Philosophers' Imprint* 20(11): 1–27.

White, Roger (2006). "Problems for Dogmatism." *Philosophical Studies* 131(3): 525–57.

Whiting, Daniel (2014). "Keep Things in Perspective." *Journal of Ethics and Social Philosophy* 8(1): 1–22.

Whiting, Daniel (2015). "Knowledge is *Not* Belief for Sufficient (Objective and Subjective) Reason." *Logos and Episteme* 6(2): 237–43.

Wiland, Eric (2003). "Psychologism, Practical Reason, and the Possibility of Error." *Philosophical Quarterly* 53(2): 68–78.

Williams, Bernard (1973a). "Deciding to Believe." In his *Problems of the Self.* Cambridge: Cambridge University Press, 148.

Williams, Bernard (1973b). "A Critique of Utilitarianism." In J.J.C. Smart and Bernard Williams, eds., *Utilitarianism: For and Against.* Cambridge: Cambridge University Press, 75–155.

Williams, Bernard (1981). "Internal and External Reasons." In his *Moral Luck.* Cambridge: Cambridge University Press.

Williamson, Timothy (2000). *Knowledge and Its Limits.* Oxford: Oxford University Press.

Williamson, Timothy (2007). "On Being Justified in One's Head." In Mark Timmons, John Greco, and Al Mele, eds., *Rationality and the Good.* Oxford: Oxford University Press, 106–22.

Williamson, Timothy (2011). "Improbable Knowing." In Trent Dougherty, ed., *Evidentialism and Its Discontents.* Oxford: Oxford University Press, 39–52.

Williamson, Timothy (2013). "Response to Cohen, Comesaña, Goodman, Nagel, and Weatherson on Gettier Cases in Epistemic Logic." *Inquiry* 56(1): 77–96.

Wodak, Daniel (2019). "An Objectivist's Guide to Subjective Reasons." *Res Philosophica* 96 (2): 229–44.

Worsnip, Alex (2018). "The Conflict of Evidence and Coherence." *Philosophy and Phenomenological Research* 96(1): 3–44.

Wright, Crispin (2004). "On Epistemic Entitlement." *Proceedings of the Aristotelian Society,* suppl. vol. 78: 167–245.

Wright, Crispin (2009). "The Perils of Dogmatism." In Susana Nuccetelli and Gary Seay, eds., *Themes from G.E. Moore: New Essays in Epistemology.* Oxford: Oxford University Press, 25–48.

Young, P.T. (1928). "Localization with Acoustical Transposition of the Ears." *Journal of Experimental Psychology* 11(6): 399–429.

Zagzebski, Linda (1994). "The Inescapability of Gettier Problems." *Philosophical Quarterly* 44(2): 65–73.

Zagzebski, Linda (1996). *Virtues of the Mind: An Inquiry into the Nature of Virtue and the Ethical Foundations of Knowledge.* Cambridge: Cambridge University Press.

Index

For the benefit of digital users, table entries that span two pages (e.g., 52–53) may, on occasion, appear on only one of those pages.

Acceptance 168
Adler, Jonathan 5
Admiration 46–7, 146–9, 156–8
Agent-Relative Teleology 32–4
Analytic Priority 4, 18–19, 27, 39–40
Anxiety 157
Apology 185–6
Apparent Factive Attitude View 73–5, 101–2,
    107–11, 201–2, 244–50
Appearance Condition 111–16
Arbitrary Closure 132–3, 135–6
Aristotle 206–7, 211, 248
Armstrong, David 58, 246–7
Avada Kedavra 134
Ayer, A.J. 8

Banks 132, 139, 194–5
Basu, Rima 184–5, 191–2
Bayesianism, Subjective 10, 163–4
Beethoven 156
Belief
  as Binary 163, 252
  Differences from Action 9
Blame 46
Blindsight 112
Bratman, Michael 173
Bridges 168–9
Bonjour, Laurence 56
Bootstrapping 99, 118–20
Bradley, *see* Dancing
Broome, John 39
Burglar 232–4

Caesar, Julius 131–2
Caroline 97–8
Charybdis' Revenge 65
Clarke, Samuel 24–5
Classical Argument, *see* Reasons First, Classical
    Motivation For
Cleanup Package 224–5
Cohen, Stewart 196
Coherentism 56
Comesaña, Juan 61–2, 107

Common Factor Arguments 209–11
Concepts
  Normative Concepts 4
Conclusive Reasons 10
Conditional Fallacy 237–8, 247
Conditionalization 161–2
Consciousness
  Access 113
  Phenomenal 112
Consequentialism 29
Contempt 46
Contrastivism 42
Control, Problem of 188–9
Coordination Problem 189–91
Core Hypothesis 9, 51, 75–6, 86–7, 116, 127,
    141–2, 181, 201, 203, 213, 215, 240,
    244–5
Correctness 220, 226
Costs of Error 139
Credal Eliminativism 163–4
Credal Reductivism 163–4
Credence 161–3, 170, 179
Cudworth, Ralph 187

Daily Nous 187
Dallman, Justin 147–66, 168, 174, 183, 251
Dancing 79–80
Dancy, Jonathan 25, 35
Death 8n.9
Decision Theory 161
Default Reliance Account 168–70, 172–3, 175,
    177, 182
Defaults 94
Defeasibility Analyses of Knowledge 237
Defeat
  Objective 103, 108–9, 229–30, 249–50
  of Perceptual Reasons 101–7
  of Perceptual Modalities, *see* Perceptual
    Modalities
  Subjective 90–1, 103–4, 108–10, 229–31,
    249–50
Defeater Dialectic 236–7, 240, 247
Deliberation 134–40

Deliberative Role of Reasons 204–6, 225–6, 252
Directed Wrongs 186
Disjunctivism 62–71, 101–2, 116–17, 121, 202, 246–7, 249
Dogmatism 56–8, 117
Doxastic Wrongs 183–8
Dualism 164–6
Dutch Books 178–9

Egalitarianism 5
Egoism 28, 33
Endgame Theory 212–13
Endoxastic Method 248
Epistemic Obligations 190
Epistemology
  As a Normative Discipline 6–7, 127
  Hostility to Reasons First 17–21, 51
Ethics of Belief 183–4
Evidence
  About external world 53–4
  Assumptions About 11–12
  Availability of 138–9
  Basing on 12
  Competition of 12
  Objective vs. Subjective 12
  Phenomenal 104–5
  Possession of 12
  Preponderance 132
  Quantity 131–2
  as Right-Kind Reason 160
  Undercutting 32–3
  World-implicating, see Reasons, Basic Perceptual
Evidence As Reasons 16–17, 23, 244
Evidentialism 5, 118
Experience, see Perceptual Experience
Explanatory Priority 4, 18–19, 27
Externalism 58–60, 65
Externalist In 58, 75, 118, 246–7

Factive Attitude View 61–2, 101, 105–6, 108, 110
Factive Content View 60–2, 72, 101, 105–6, 108, 110
Factivity of Subjective Reasons 77–9, 86, 88, 99, 202
Factoring Account 79–81
Fake Barns 103–7, 122, 229–30, 249
Fantl, Jeremy 176–8, 250–1
Fear 46, 146–7, 157, 217
Feldman, Richard 18
Fitting Attitudes 46–7
Fogal, Daniel 41, 69–70

Franklin, John Hope 186–7, 193–4, 196–7
French, Craig 89–90
Friendship 180, 186, 196
Fundamental Argument, see Reasons First, Fundamental Motivation For

Games 208, 211–13, 245
Ganson, Dorit 178
Gendler, Tamar 186–7, 189, 197
Gettier, Edmund 234, 242
Gin and Tonic 69, 77–8, 82–3, 85–6, 225–6
Good
  As Outcome-Oriented 30
  and Reasons 254–5
  For 32–3
  In Consequentialism 29
Good-case boostrapping 67–9
Grabit, Tom and Tim 236–7
Greco, John 59
Gregory, Alex 205

Harman, Gilbert 56, 129, 141–2
Harmony 191–3
Hatcher, Michael 113
Having Reasons 79–80
Hawthorne, John 116, 176–7, 250–1
Hieronymi, Pamela 135, 155–8
Horty, John F. 24–5, 92–9
House of Cards 43–4
Howard, Nathan 35, 253
Hubbs, Graham 135
Hurka, Tom 31–2
Hursthouse, Rosalind 211, 213

Inertia, Rational 133, 136, 173–5
Intention 146–7, 151–4, 156, 158
Internalism 68, 70–1

Johnson King, Zoë 217
Justification
  Normativity of 7
  Propositional vs. Doxastic 37, 208, 211, 214–15
  and Subjective Reasons 87

Kant, Immanuel 24n.3, 36, 187, 206–7, 211, 213, 215–16
Kantian Account 203, 227–9, 231–2, 237–9, 241, 245–52
Kavka, Gregory 151–2, 179
Kearns, Stephen 13–16
Keller, Simon 186, 189, 191–2
Kiesewetter, Benjamin 38
Klein, Peter 235–8, 240–1

Knowledge
    and Credence 179
    Defeasibility of 103, 231
    Disjunctivist treatment of 66, 117
    and Doxastic Wrongs 190
    and Epistemic Reasons 145–7
    Explanatory Role of 232–4
    as Matching 228–31
    and Moral Worth 216, 220
    Normativity of 7–8, 211, 245
    and Reasons 203–4
    and Subjective Reasons 81–2, 87–8
    as The Most General Factive Stative
        Attitude 88–92
    as a Well Property 208, 221–3, 227–8,
        241–2
Knowledge-Action Principles 176–8, 194
Korsgaard, Christine 204–5
Kruglanski, Arie 173
Kvanvig, Jonathan 242–3

Lehrer, Keith 56, 236
Lewis, David 114
Lockeanism 163–4
Looks 121–2
Lord, Errol 68–9
Lotteries 130–1, 137–8
Luck 207, 216

Magidor, Ofra 116
Markovits, Julia 13, 227
Marušic, Berislav 187–8, 191–2, 197
McDowell, John 61–2, 65, 107, 117
McGrath, Matthew 61–2, 107, 121–2, 176–8,
    250–1
Mediating Beliefs 55–7
Methodology 10–11, 42–3, 115, 176, 181, 215,
    242–3, 245–6, 248, 255
Millar, Alan 61–2
Milne, Peter 31
Monotonicity 96
Moral Worth 215–18
Mozart, Wolfgang Amadeus 46–7
My Cousin Vinny 186, 196

Near Ties, Problem of 129–30, 140–3
Nelson, Mark 190
New Evil Demon Problem 64–5
New New Evil Demon Problem 68–9
Newtonian Mechanics 168–9
Non-Factive Content View 72–5, 101, 106–7
Normativity
    Contentful vs. Relevance 7–8
    Definition 5–6

Object-Given/State-Given Theory 150–4
Oddie, Graham 31
Owens, David 135

Parfit, Derek 5, 151, 191
Particularism 25, 239–40
Pascal, Blaise 128
Pascalian Considerations 128, 144–5, 148–9,
    151–2, 154
Paxson, Thomas 236
Penicillin 160–1, 196
Perceptual Experience 53–4, 89–90, 104
Perceptual Modalities 110–11, 115–16
Phil 133, 136
Photo-sharing technology 3
Podgorski, Abelard 136
Poker 36
Position to Know 91
Pragmatic Credal Reductivism 163–4, 178
Pragmatic Encroachment 132, 166, 175–6,
    230, 250
Pragmatic Intellectualism 127–8, 167–8, 175–83,
    188–92, 197, 201, 234–5, 245–7, 250–1
Preferences 161
Presupposition 83–4, 86
Prima Facie Duties 25–7
Primeness 228–9
Priors 118
Pritchard, Duncan 61–2
Probability 131
Pseudo-Conditionalization 170

Quitting Smoking 187–8, 197

Rationalism 56
Rationality
    Of basic perceptual belief 66
Reasons
    Acting for 13, 34–9, 47, 68–9, 148–9, 154,
        203–6, 224–6
    Against 142–3, 145–6, 160, 175, 182,
        202–3, 244
    As Act-Oriented 29, 34, 46–7, 147–9, 154,
        203–4
    Basic Perceptual
        Non-Factive 25, 99
        Phenomenal 55
        World-Implicating 25, 60–1, 67, 71–2,
          75, 103
    Basing on, see Reasons, Acting For
    Competition of 13, 23, 25–7, 34, 46, 147, 149,
        203–4
    Countervailing 13
    Epistemic 20, 128, 144–7

Reasons (*cont.*)
  Explanatory 43–4
  Motivating 43, 84–6
  Object-Given 150
  Objective/Subjective Distinction 13, 25–6,
    42–3, 77–8, 201, 226, 253–4
  Ontology of 41, 52–3, 69, 82
  Phenomenology of 3–4, 23–4
  Possessing 7, 13, 108
  State-Given 150, 158–9
  Subjective 75–84, 117, 248
  Sufficiency of 128
  Undercutting 13
  Wrong Kind, *see* Wrong Kind of Reasons
    Problem
Reasons As Evidence 13–16
Reasons First
  Classical Motivation for 23–6, 40, 143–4,
    202–4
  Definition 5
  Fundamental Motivation for 40, 209, 218–23,
    251–5
  Orthodoxy of 11
Reed, Baron 178–81
Reflection 179
Reflexivity 97
Reiter, Raymond 94
Remembering 92
Report-Based Arguments 81–6
Right Reasons Accounts 218–19, 224–9
Right/Well pairs 207–9, 224, 252
Ronnie, *see* Dancing
Ross, W.D. 25, 251–2
Russell, Bertrand 234

Safety 233
Scanlon, T.M. 42
Searle, John 113–14
Seeing that 88–92, 107–8
Self-Presenting 113–14
Self Worth 187, 197
Sensory Modalities, *see* Perceptual Modalities
Setiya, Kieran 205
Shah, Nishi 135, 189
Sherman, Brett 56
Shope, Robert 238–9
Sidgwick, Henry 24–5, 27–9
Silverstein, Matthew 135, 205
Single-Tier Pragmatic Encroachment 179
Skepticism 54–5
Slaves of the Passions 35, 37–8
Sliwa, Paulina 216–18, 220

Smith, Michael 34–5, 216
Smithies, Declan 113
Snedegar, Justin 42
Socrates 131–2
Sosa, Ernest 221–2
Spilled wine 185–6
Staffel, Julia 170
Stakes 132, 160, 179–80, 189, 195–6, 230
Stalnaker, Robert 159–61
Stanley, Jason 176–7, 179, 230–1, 250–1
Star, Daniel 13–16
Steup, Matthias 91
Stroud, Sarah 186, 189, 191–2
Sufficiency, Problem of
  and the Classical Motivation for Reasons
    First 240–1
  Explained 19–21
  How to Answer 127–8, 144, 181–2
Surprise Party 37–8, 205

Toxin Puzzle 151–2, 179
Turri, John 89–90, 211, 213
Tweety 94
Two-Stage Strategy 134–41

Umbrellas 170–2
Unjustified Belief, Problem of
  Connection to Problem of How Perception
    Provides Reasons 76, 86–92
  Explained 17–19
  How to Answer 51–2, 99–100, 127
Utilitarianism 28
Utilities 161

Value 45–7
Van Fraassen, Bas 179
Veridical Hallucination 107–8, 114

Way, Jonathan 205
Weatherson, Brian 178
Wedding Planning 158
Wedgwood, Ralph 31–2, 170
Well Principle 214–16, 219–21, 223, 252
Will 133, 136
Williams, Bernard 77–8, 188, 204–5
Williamson, Timothy 18, 61, 70–1, 78–9, 88–92,
    131, 228–9, 231–4, 239, 242–3
Wright, Crispin 56
Wrong Kind of Reasons Problem 20, 146–55, 245

Zagzebski, Linda 238–9
Zombies 112

Printed and bound by CPI Group (UK) Ltd, Croydon, CR0 4YY